TROPICAL AFRICA

VOLUME TWO

SOCIETY AND POLITY

GEORGE H. T. KIMBLE, presently Chairman of the Department of Geography, Indiana University and formerly Director of the American Geographical Society, made three extended trips to Africa to gather facts and gain firsthand impressions for this study. He enlisted a team of experts to prepare working papers on specialized subjects and drew upon these in drafting his text. He was a naval officer in World War II and is the author of several books and numerous magazine articles.

TWENTIETH CENTURY FUND

PARTICIPANTS IN THE STUDY

CONSULTANTS: Sir Philip Mitchell, G.C.M.G., *Chief Consultant;* Stanley G. Browne, M.D., B. J. Garnier, J. H. G. Lebon, J. Gus Liebenow, Leo Silberman.

CONTRIBUTORS OF WORKING PAPERS: David E. Apter, Nancy Gouinlock Berg, Kenneth Bradley, George W. Carpenter, R. J. Harrison Church, James S. Coleman, L. Gray Cowan, Frank Debenham, Hubert Deschamps, Walter Deshler, St. Clair and Elizabeth Drake, Eugene P. Dvorin, F. Grévisse, Alfred and Grace G. Harris, George R. Horner, D. Hobart Houghton, Sir Bernard A. Keen, Hibberd V. B. Kline, Jr., Gaston Leduc, Jacques Lefebvre, Jacques J. Maquet, Jacques M. May, M.D., Peveril Meigs, Paul Mercier, N. C. Mitchel, Eduardo C. Mondlane, William Dawson Moreland, Jr., W. B. Morgan, Thomas G. Murdock, Margaret Nairn, B. S. Platt, R. M. Prothero, Tor Fr. Rasmussen, Rebecca Reyher, Kurt Roselius, Cecil W. Scott, Ruth C. Sloan, Helmer Smeds, Hugh Tracey, Glenn T. Trewartha, Kimani Waiyaki, A. T. de B. Wilmot, Alvin D. Zalinger, Wilbur Zelinsky.

MAPS: Robert C. Kingsbury, *Cartographic Editor;* Patricia R. Kingsbury and Jean Paul Tremblay, *Cartographers.*

PHOTOGRAPHS: Omar Marcus, *Photographer;* Anita Ventura, *Picture Editor.*

TROPICAL
AFRICA

VOLUME TWO

SOCIETY

AND POLITY

GEORGE H. T. KIMBLE

ABRIDGED EDITION
WITH PHOTOGRAPHS, MAPS AND CHARTS

ANCHOR BOOKS
DOUBLEDAY & COMPANY, INC.
GARDEN CITY, NEW YORK

Tropical Africa was originally published by The Twentieth Century Fund in 1960. The Anchor Books edition is published by arrangement with The Twentieth Century Fund.

Anchor Books edition: 1962

The following firms in Germany generously presented the study's photographer with photographic equipment: Albert Schacht G.m.b.H., Optical Equipment, Ulm, Donau; Multiblitz, Mannesmann Electronic Equipment, Porz-Westhoven, Cologne; Agfacolor, AGFA A.G., Leverkusen.

FOREWORD

To embark upon a major study of tropical Africa seemed to the Trustees of the Fund a challenging undertaking when it was first considered. The years during which this book has been written have certainly not made the task any easier, or any less important.

These years have seen swift and profound changes in the political structure of tropical Africa. The flood of independent nations beginning in the fall of 1958 has advanced by a schedule which foreshortened history and radically compressed time itself. To keep up with such a situation means, necessarily, to go below the surface. That is what the author has aimed to do, projecting the basic conditions which set the framework within which change occurs.

The Twentieth Century Fund considers itself fortunate in having secured George H. T. Kimble, now of Indiana University, as director of the study. A geographer by profession, Dr. Kimble interprets geography to involve not merely physical facts but the whole mysterious relationship between man and the environment of which he is a part. A scholar, Dr. Kimble does not assume that scholarship precludes good writing. The number of people who helped in gathering and weighing the information is indicated by the Acknowledgments; yet the whole massive body of fact has been shaped by the mind of one man and bears the unmistakable imprint of his style.

It is a particular pleasure to record here the help provided the project at a critical stage by President Herman B Wells of Indiana University. He cooperated with the Fund in making possible Dr. Kimble's freedom to complete the work, though it meant postponing teaching and administrative services which the University was anxious to draw upon. As a result the large undertaking has been brought to conclusion in the happiest of circumstances.

For Americans to know what they should do about the problem of African development is important. But it is important, first of all, that they know the full facts about Africa itself. The danger, from the point of view of a sound policy and approach, is that the complete ignorance which formerly prevailed should be replaced by incomplete knowledge. The issues in this part of the world are of an importance which calls for the fullest possible understanding.

The Fund hopes that this study will make a contribution to knowledge about Africa—the startling kind of knowledge which may let Americans see what is really there and not merely what their imagination and unanalyzed assumptions have told them is there.

August Heckscher
DIRECTOR, THE TWENTIETH CENTURY FUND

41 East 70th Street, New York
August 1960

ACKNOWLEDGMENTS

No book is entirely the author's own, and probably few books are less so than this one. It might even be contended that the main reason for having a single name on the title page is that somebody had to take responsibility for the mistakes! Certainly, to have listed all those who had a hand in this book would have set the printer a ticklish problem, and heaven knows he has had his share of problems. From start (all too long ago) to finish (if, indeed, such a theme is ever finished), *Tropical Africa* has been nourished by many minds and groomed by many more.

The idea for the book came from Evans Clark, before his retirement as Executive Director of the Twentieth Century Fund. The material for it was derived in large measure from the working papers of the forty-six contributors listed opposite the title page. Material was also provided, along with much excellent criticism, by those—likewise listed opposite the title page—who served as consultants, and by those who did the map-making and photography. No less substantial was the help, administrative and editorial, supplied by colleagues in the Fund. Individually smaller but indispensable contributions were made by persons (on a conservative count, more than a thousand) in Africa, Europe and the United States who uncomplainingly endured the author's questioning, and greatly facilitated his field work and that of his associates. The study's photographer, in particular, received courtesies and help from innumerable sources on his travels in Africa. The author owes hardly less to people he never met—newspapermen, novelists, Africanists and others whose insights into what has been happening in tropical Africa during the time of its travail have been a constant source of illumination. To all of these he tenders his sincere thanks.

Inevitably, an author senses a deeper indebtedness to some than to others. Special thanks are due to Sir Philip Mitchell, who read and reported on each working paper, on the draft of each chapter and on several hundred galleys, and who was at once an uncompromising critic, a wise counselor and an elegant host. Similar thanks are due to Dr. Herman B Wells, President of Indiana University, for providing office space and granting released time during the later stages of the study; to Robert Lemaignen and Emmanuel Mayolle for their sustained interest and memorable Gallic hospitality; and to August Heckscher, Director of the Twentieth Century Fund, for his energetic support and encouragement. Also gratefully acknowledged is the invaluable assistance of Paul M. Henry, Ian Hess, Phyllis M. Horwitz, Lilly Kay (Lesin), André Némo, Esther I. Persson, Anne C. de Nanteuil, Anna Rapaport (Paul), Hugo Fosco, Ian B. Thompson, Roger Vaurs and Richard E. Webb. Most of all, the author wishes to pay tribute to his editor, Elizabeth Blackert, Assistant to the Director of the Fund. Her understanding of what a book should be is matched only by her ability to delude an author into thinking he can write that kind of book, and to make any book better than it would otherwise have been. Her exertions to this end will long be remembered with appreciation—and awe.

George H. T. Kimble

Solsberry, Indiana

CONTENTS

VOLUME TWO

SOCIETY AND POLITY

TABLES

ILLUSTRATIONS

TROPICAL AFRICA

Main Railroads

0   500
miles

RELIEF AND
MAIN
RAILROADS

St. Louis
Dakar
Conakry
Freetown
Monrovia
FOUTA
DJALLON
Kayes
Bamako
Kankan
Timbuktu
Niger
Ouagadougou
Kumasi
Abidjan
Accra
Lomé
Cotonou
Lagos
Benin City
Ibadan
Kano
SAHARA
DESERT.

GULF OF
GUINEA
Douala
Libreville
Yaoundé
Ft. Lamy
Pointe Noire
Matadi
Léopoldville
Luanda
Lobito
Mocâmedes
Brazzaville
Bangui
Congo
CONGO
BASIN
Kindu
Stanleyville
Nile
Khartoum
El Obeid
Port
Sudan
Asmara
Addis Ababa
Djibouti
Kampala
Elisabethville
Lusaka
KALAHARI
DESERT
Bulawayo
Salisbury
Beira
Lourenço
Marques
INDIAN OCEAN
Mombasa
Zanzibar
Dar-es-Salaam
Mtwara
Lumbo
Mogadishu
Tuléar
Tamatave
Tananarive

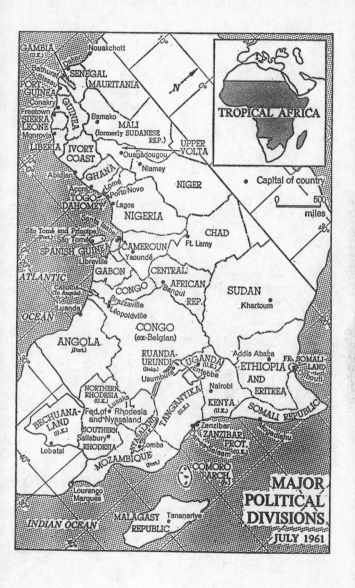

GAMBIA (U.K.)
Nouakchott
Bathurst
PORT. GUINEA
Bissau
Conakry
SENEGAL
Dakar
MAURITANIA
SIERRA LEONE
Freetown
GUINEA
Monrovia
LIBERIA
Bamako
MALI (formerly SUDANESE REP.)
IVORY COAST
Abidjan
GHANA
Ouagadougou
UPPER VOLTA
Niamey
NIGER
Accra
Lomé
Porto Novo
TOGO
DAHOMEY
Lagos
NIGERIA
CHAD
Ft. Lamy
CAMEROUN
Fernando Po
São Tomé and Principe (Port.)
São Tomé
SPANISH GUINEA
Libreville
Yaoundé
GABON
CENTRAL AFRICAN REP.
Bangui
SUDAN
Khartoum
CONGO
Brazzaville
Léopoldville
CABINDA (To Angola)
Luanda
ATLANTIC OCEAN
ANGOLA (Port.)
CONGO (ex-Belgian)
RUANDA-URUNDI (Belg.)
Usumbura
UGANDA (U.K.)
Entebbe
Addis Ababa
ETHIOPIA AND ERITREA
FR. SOMALI-LAND
Djibouti
Nairobi
KENYA (U.K.)
SOMALI REPUBLIC
NORTHERN RHODESIA (U.K.)
Lusaka
TANGANYIKA (U.K.)
Zanzibar
ZANZIBAR PROT.
Dar es Salaam (U.K.)
Mogadishu
BECHUANA-LAND (U.K.)
Fed. of Rhodesia and Nyasaland
Salisbury
SOUTHERN RHODESIA
NYASALAND (U.K.)
Zomba
Lobatsi
MOZAMBIQUE (Port.)
COMORO ARCH. (Fr.)
Lourenço Marques
INDIAN OCEAN
MALAGASY REPUBLIC
Tananarive

TROPICAL AFRICA

• Capital of country

0   500
miles

N

MAJOR POLITICAL DIVISIONS

JULY 1961

INTRODUCTION

When David Livingstone "discovered" tropical Africa a century or so ago, most Americans were too busy discovering their own country to pay much heed to his despatches. Of those who went there in his footsteps, few came back. Those who did had no great opinion of the place. It was a white man's grave, and, what with its slave raiding, its tribal warfare, its hungry seasons and its climate of fear, no health resort for the African either. There were, seemingly, no prairies to plow; no uniform stands of timber to cut; and no minerals worth talking about. Nobody had anything to sell or any great need to buy. It was, they said, little more than a Stone Age museum; and no American was then greatly interested in the Stone Age. Accordingly, it was ignored as far as possible.

Today we couldn't ignore tropical Africa if we wanted to, and for at least three reasons. First, because it is no longer ignorant of us. Fifth graders in the schools of Nigeria know as much about America as most American school children know about Canada. Decisions reached last week on Capitol Hill are being discussed this week in the hills of Kenya. The ripples made by our "Little Rocks" have a way of penetrating overnight into the backwaters of the Nile and Congo.

Second, because the rest of the world has no intention of ignoring tropical Africa, or any part of it. In the past two years, a score of European and Asian suitors have gone to Guinea laden with gifts and good words, seeking to sell its leaders the keys to their kingdom. And what is true of Guinea is true of every other independent territory.

Third, because its peoples plainly do not intend to be ignored. The Nkrumahs, Tourés and Mboyas of tropical Africa are among the most articulate of men and among the most successful in making themselves heard, whether in the United Nations, the Afro-Asian conferences or elsewhere. And throughout Europe, North America and, increasingly, Asia, students from almost every part of the region are busy proclaiming that the kingdom of Africa is at hand.

We owe it to ourselves, therefore, to learn more about what is happening in tropical Africa—to its land and its people, to their livelihood, society and polity. We may not like all we learn, but *not* to learn is to live in a darkness more dangerous than any Africa ever knew. For that matter, we owe it to the Africans: after all, more than 18 million of us are related to them. It's high time we began behaving like relations.

What is the land of tropical Africa? Areally, it is that part of the mainland and those offshore islands lying between the Sahara and the Limpopo River—the region, roughly, between the Tropics of Cancer and Capricorn. Environmentally, it is a mosaic. Large parts of it conform to the Hollywood stereotypes of dank, gloomy forest where bread and boots go moldy in a night, and baked, shimmering veld where shade is precious and water the greatest wealth. But parts of it are neither very African nor very tropical. Some look and are like the hills of Idaho and Wyoming, where a man can see a hundred and fifty miles and be glad of a blanket on the bed almost any night in the year. Others are as bare as the Painted Desert and every bit as beautiful. The region presents as many different types of landscape as do all the fifty states. And the environmental variety goes deeper. Differences arising from sunshine and soil, height and slope, moisture and drainage are compounded by differences in the distribution of cultivable and edible plants, noxious insects and useful animals, malleable metal and clay, workable wood and reed, and harnessable power. The land is more than mineral, vegetable and animal; for most of its indigenous inhabitants it is the begetter of the unborn, the upholder of the living, the custodian of the dead; it is, in fact, "mother earth."

The people are as various as the land. They consist, on the most conservative basis of reckoning, of not less than 600 groups—African,[1] European and Asian—that do enough things differently from their neighbors to be recognizably different. Most of these 600 groups talk differently from their neighbors. Many of them have different ways of raising food and family, of settling disputes, of dealing with illnesses and emergencies, and even of burying the dead.

Superimposed on these cultural differences, but in no sense obliterating them, are the differences resulting from the "opening up" of Africa by European powers in the nineteenth and early twentieth centuries. Largely as a result of this, the people of tropical Africa today live under 40 different managements, none of which is entirely of their own devising, or entirely of their wanting. It is true that more than half of the 40 are now self-managing,[2] but in none of them do the political boundaries coincide with cultural boundaries, and in no case are all the included people well pleased with the arrangements. Not infrequently the political boundaries have the effect of separating tribal kin and allies, and joining enemies.

The rest of the 40 still (July 1961) owe varying degrees of allegiance to their European founders. Two of them—(Belgian) Ruanda-Urundi and (British) Tanganyika—are administered as United Nations Trust Territories.[3] Four (Portuguese Guinea, São Tomé and Príncipe Islands, Angola and Mozambique) are administered as "overseas provinces" of Portugal. One (Spanish Guinea) is administered as a colony of Spain. Four (Bechuanaland, Northern Rhodesia, Nyasaland and Uganda) are British protectorates. Two (Gambia and Kenya) have the status of British "colony and protectorate."

[1] An "African," in the customary sense of the term, is a person whose forebears were domiciled in Africa before the coming of the European and Asian. The term is so used throughout this study except where otherwise indicated.

[2] As of July 1961, these were: Cameroun, Chad, Congo (former French Middle Congo), Congo (former Belgian Congo), Central African Republic, Dahomey, Ethiopia and Eritrea, Gabon, Ghana, Guinea, Liberia, Malagasy Republic, Mali (former French Sudan), Mauritania, Niger, Nigeria, Senegal, Sierra Leone, Somalia, Sudan, Togo and Upper Volta.

[3] Both are due to become autonomous in the near future: Tanganyika in December 1961; Ruanda-Urundi in 1962.

One (Zanzibar, including Pemba) has the status of British-protected sultanate. And one (Southern Rhodesia) is a self-governing British colony.[4] One (French Somaliland) is administered as part of overseas France.

The most populous of the 40, Nigeria, has over 37 million inhabitants, or twice as many as New York State and more than half as many again as the next most populous territory, Ethiopia (including Eritrea). The least populous territory, São Tomé and Príncipe, has about 62,000 inhabitants; this is less than one eighth the population of the Nigerian city of Ibadan.

All told, the 40 territories have a population of probably not less than 175 million[5] and occupy an area well over twice the size of the United States. They constitute the largest understudied and underdeveloped area in the world and, in the opinion of many, the most underrated.

*   *   *

In the first edition of this book the record was brought up to the end of 1959 or early 1960, within the limits of the data then available; the territorial names used were those current when the book went to press in the summer of 1960. In this abridged edition for Anchor Books, the same cutoff dates have been used, but the frontispiece maps give the names and political status of the 40 territories as of July 1961. See Selected Territorial Data at the back of the book for the latest statistical information obtainable at that time.

[4] The federating of the two Rhodesias and Nyasaland in 1953, to form the Federation of Rhodesia and Nyasaland, while it added yet another management, did not alter the existing constitutional relationships.

[5] Derived from the United Nations *Demographic Yearbook,* 1959 edition.

CHAPTER 1

SOCIAL CHANGE

Tropical Africa is more than a fabric of physical and economic threads—of lands and livelihoods. It is a mosaic of peoples, cultures and beliefs. Within its borders live Bantu and Bushman, Semite and Hamite, European and Asian and Colored. Its market places and mines echo with the confusion of a hundred tongues. Its governments employ republican and monarchist, tribalist and nationalist, neutralist and Communist. Its schools and colleges teach animist and Christian, Hindu and Mohammedan. Its homes shelter prince and commoner, the learned and the unlettered, the very rich and the wretchedly poor.

But it is a mosaic with a difference. Some of the "pieces" in it are anything but fixed and durable, being given to changing both their shape and position; and there are some that have been unable to withstand the disintegrating influence of time, and the wear and tear of alien forces.

Measured by the inflated standards of our age, the changes wrought in the fabric of a primitive society are generally small. Over a period of a hundred years they would be unlikely to involve anything more than, say, the refinement of a tree-felling technique, the development of a better firing clay, the discovery of a speedier pain killer, or the acceptance of a new code of sexual conduct for unmarried youths. But the will to change is almost always there, and so, almost always, is the capacity to change with changes in the pressures that bear upon the society.

These pressures are both external and internal. They can be generated as readily by somebody else's greed as by one's own hunger. They can be built up as effectively by periodic visitations of locusts as by outbreaks of sleeping sickness. Conquest by a powerful neighbor has often been as good a way to infiltrate a new cultural trait as competition among one's own kin for the possession of a prized piece of land.

What George R. Horner, a contributor to this study, has written about the Bulu (see pp. 37–46) is of wide applicability. "Change was the norm, the expected." There was "a constant intrusion of elements" from other African cultures and a competitive pattern of life that led to frequent shifts of fortune and material wealth. This perhaps was just as well; at least it helped to cushion the shock of that greatest of all intrusions, the white man's conquest and colonization of the region.

But no African-made cushion was proof against the shock of a thousand shellbursts. It required more than a tradition of gradual change to prepare the Stone Age rain forest dweller for the arrival overnight of the Iron Age, the Air Age and the Electronic Age, and the social furnishings that went with them. The qualities needed to cope with a decline in tribal fortunes, with the recovery of a stolen herd of cattle, with the loss by fire of one's belongings, are of a very different order from those needed to cope with an invasion from an outside world as foreign in its resources, skills and ideas as the world of Flash Gordon from that of mankind. It is one thing for equals or near-equals living in the same world to exchange ideas and habits on the basis of a leisurely observation of their social efficacy in given situations. It is a very different thing for societies as unequal in power, speed of evolution, and sophistication as those of the Stone Age and the Electronic Age to do so. There were no engines, no assembly lines, no housing developments, no central government, no hospitals, no Christianity, no police forces in the African's world.

Then again, whereas social change among equals or near-equals is more a matter of option than compulsion (most African reformers have tended to run out of zeal rather quickly), between people as unevenly matched as African tribesman and European townsman, the acceptance of change by the weaker party becomes virtually essential to his survival. The man who does not work in a European-run community does not find it easy to marry; for where will he secure the bride wealth if not in the European's house, mine or factory? The group that does not raise cash crops cannot raise the taxes that are needed to run the local government that is needed to maintain a safe water supply, serviceable roads, schools and clinics. And the tribe that does not renounce its grosser malpractices—cannibalism, sorcery, the raiding of its neighbors, and the like—can scarcely hope to convince its rulers of its readiness to graduate into the world of free men.

As the association between the two worlds lengthens, the causes of social change become more numerous, complex and subtle. No longer is it simply, or even mainly, a matter of change by necessity—the necessity of earning more money to buy more goods to employ more people to raise more revenue to finance more schemes. At least four other important factors are at work.

There is the initiative of government and private agencies in providing better homes and services—frequently out of non-African money. Much of the Colonial Development and Welfare money, raised by the British government from its tax-payers, has been used for such purposes, to the evident social gain of rural groups in British West and East Africa, Northern Rhodesia and Nyasaland. The Fonds du Bien-Être Indigène and the Fonds du Roi in the Belgian Congo and FERDES (Fonds d'Equipement Rural et de Développement Econo-mique et Social) in French Africa have served similar ends. So have the individually smaller but cumulatively large social undertakings of the mining companies of Northern Rhodesia, the Belgian Congo and elsewhere.

Closely related is the idealism of those who see in Christi-anity the answer to all that is base and debasing in indigenous African cultures. It is an idealism that has come to be shared as much by Africans as by non-Africans and is almost certainly the greatest single force for social change in tropical Africa. Christianity has no monopoly of social idealism, it is true, but it takes a strong breed of idealism to flourish in the African climate, and not even its harshest critics are disposed to doubt that Christianity is such a breed.

Following hard on the heels of these comes incentive, much

of it the progeny of initiative and idealism. The government builds a house—one with plumbing and electricity, privacy and security—a better house than the African has ever known. The missionary—evangelist, educator, counselor and "living witness"—shows how a man and his family may lead a fuller life in that house. An incentive is thereby born—one that has already spurred miners and factory workers in a hundred plants to exchange the tribe-centered, custom-hallowed society of the bush for the still fluid multitribal and often multiracial associations of the town. An industrial corporation—the Rhodesian Selection Trust, to name only one of many which have taken the initiative in such matters—builds a social center for its African workers. A European, Africa-born welfare worker of high ideals and uncommon sense is appointed to run it. But soon it is the Africans who are doing most of the running of its soccer and gymnastic teams, its dance band, glee club and stage group. Properly handled, the African finds it difficult not to respond to the incentives of competitive enterprise and good companionship.

Some incentives are of poorer parentage, alas. More than a little of the social change to be observed in tropical Africa today appears to stem from a desire to keep up with the Joneses, African and non-African, in their failings as well as their virtues. Conspicuous consumption of alcoholic beverages is no longer confined to the well-to-do Europeans. Nominal Christianity, long good enough for many Europeans, is now good enough for many African converts. European indifference to the feelings and rights of others has contributed to many an African's failure to keep the second half of the Decalogue. On the side of virtue, let it be said that the incentive to "keep up" appears to be in no small way responsible for the desire of many Africans to give their children, girls and boys alike, the best education that money can buy—in Europe or North America if need be—and their womenfolk the kind of consideration commonly given by Europeans to theirs.

A no less important factor making for social change is the emergence of money as the symbol of wealth and its by-products, power and prestige. The times have certainly changed.

In the old days personal wealth was in a form that set a very severe limit to selfishness. A chief might own a hundred times as many cows as a peasant, and his lands might be a hundred times more extensive. . . . But all [the] outward signs of his wealth and power were communal. In one sense all [his] wives and retainers were his chattels, but it was also true that they were his dependants. Inevitably wealth meant responsibility and its benefits had to be shared. Very little of it could be used for private indulgence. You can't put your cattle in your pocket, but you can put your cash there—and when your pockets are full of it you can put all the rest in the bank. Money made possible for the first time an irresponsible wealth . . .[1]

In a land lacking the tradition of chivalry (African folk tales are more often tales of cunning than of rescue and sacrifice), and producing no St. Francis of Assisi, no Florence Nightingale and no Albert Schweitzer, it may prove difficult to stop "the root of all evil" from undermining the social structure. Already, there are evidences that it is weakening it. To name only a few: the "dash," or commission, demanded for almost any service rendered, from the awarding of a multi-million-dollar road contract to the giving of a bedpan in a hospital ward; the propping up of ailing enterprises, personal and corporate, with improperly acquired funds; the unethical use of hospital supplies and other species of white man's magic (which may be one reason why even *"le grand docteur"* of Lambaréné always carries his keys with him); and the reluctance of many African college graduates to take jobs that do not pay well, or promise to pay well very soon. Maybe none of these things greatly matters, as some of the new intelligentsia contend; maybe the foundations of African

[1] The Reverend John V. Taylor of the Church Missionary Society in Uganda, in a lecture (September 1955) given at the Ecumenical Institute, Bossey, Switzerland.

society are too strong to be undermined by a little selfishness and a little corruption. But if they are, they must surely be very strong—stronger than any that have gone before, whether in ancient Greece or medieval Ghana.

Fortunately, there is a brighter side to the picture. Though tropical Africa has yet produced no Schweitzer, Nightingale or Saint, it has produced an Aggrey (one of the founding fathers of Achimota College in Ghana), a Waruhiu (the Kikuyu chief of Kiambu, Kenya, martyred by the Mau Mau for his Christian faith) and a Prester John. It has also produced many young men and women—as almost any government and mission schoolteacher can testify—who are putting service to their people above personal advantage, and righteousness before the applause of the crowd. Perhaps African folk tales a thousand years hence will even include a cycle on the Twentieth Century Knights of the Round Table.

Magnitude of change. The most advertised characteristic of African social change is its magnitude. Students of the social sciences are constantly telling us that there is scarcely a tribe or a family in the whole of tropical Africa that lives today as it did a generation ago, or a field of investigation that does not repay a periodical going over for the evidences of change it discloses. Some of these evidences are discussed in the companion volume on *Land and Livelihood:* the breakdown of old food taboos; the rise of new trades, towns and means of transport, and the new physical and economic mobility that results from it; the modification of indigenous cropping practices, and of the land tenure systems that went with them; the less general but significant modification of such indigenous practices as the keeping of cattle for currency, and pastoral nomadism; the increasing importance of women in commercial life; and the development of new forms of association, such as the cooperative society.

But the scope of the change is much wider than this. Consider the African's home, for instance. While most homes continue to be fashioned of traditional materials in the traditional way and pattern, increasing numbers, even in remote villages, are being built in the style of the simple European home. Single-story dwellings with two or three rooms, they are made of brick or cement slab, galvanized iron, plaster, planed or pressed wood, equipped with some plumbing and perhaps electric light, and furnished with beds, chairs, a kitchen table and dresser, curtains and linoleum. In the better-class African homes, in such towns as Léopoldville, Accra and Dakar, it is not unusual to find a kitchen range, an ice-box, a shelf of books, and a radio or a portable phonograph with powers of endurance equaled only by the nerves of those who listen to it. Even in the bush it is exceptional to come upon a home that does not have some untraditional feature—an iron bedstead, pages from an American news magazine used as wallpaper, or castoff gasoline cans used to brew native beer.

Consider, too, the personal and family life of the African. True, the impress of the past upon it is still plainly seen in most groups—in such diverse "culture traits" as lineage systems, age groups or sets, fertility rituals and rituals relating to puberty, marriage and the other great epochs of life, prayer to one's ancestors, hair styles, and the decoration of clay pots and dugout canoes. But its outlines are becoming blurred, at some points to the extent of being hardly recognizable. The clothes an African wears are, with rare exceptions, no longer those of his own making or design. At least part of the food he eats is likely to have been raised by hands other than his or his family's; and some of his most highly prized panaceas are likely to be pills and potions no witch doctor ever thought of. Instead of having two or more wives, he may have but one. The work he does for at least part of the time is of a kind for which there is no tribal precedent; frequently it needs to be done away from home and in company with men of other tribes.

It follows that for part of his time a man is *dépaysé* if not detribalized, footloose if not fancy-free, and able to forget his status role—often with results as damaging to his health and integrity as to the cohesion of his family. As for his wife, the chances are that she works harder than if she were in a polygynous household because there are fewer hands to help her; that she has little in common with her husband since his concerns are no longer solely those of the local clan; and still less in common with her children, who, most likely, spend part of their early years pursuing the white man's learning, of which she has no more than an inkling.

Of course, not all wives stay at home these days. Numbers of them go along with their husbands, living at or near their place of work. In Léopoldville alone there are quarters for more than 40,000 married couples, and many of them have been occupied by the same tenants for years on end. For the women, as for the men, the move to a town or a mining compound means more than a change of place. It means new ties and relationships, and difficulty in making them because of linguistic and sociological differences; new ways of doing things, such as drawing water from taps, washing the baby with soap, and disposing of human waste in a flush toilet. Often it means no way of doing things that have always been done by women, such as growing the family's food and running initiation schools and other kinds of secret organizations. Inability to do these things can result in a considerable loss of prestige.

The changes in home and family have been accompanied by changes of similar magnitude in the community. The kind of society desired by most modern African governments calls for cooperation on a bigger scale and in more ways than were needed in the days of tribal autonomy. The administering of public programs, such as the building of roads, bridges and dams, the securing of watersheds against erosion, and the control of mosquitoes, locusts and other pests, calls for cooperation by large intertribal groups rather than small clans. So does the raising of money to finance such programs. So also does the organization of peasant cash crop economies capable of competing, as they must, with the highly capitalized and well-run economies of older lands. What is true of these largely nonpolitical concerns is true of political ones. Democracy may begin at home—in the grassroots of the family, clan and tribe—but it needs the winds and rains of a wider domain to make it strong. In these days especially, democratic governments need all the good men they can find to come to the aid of the party, and no one tribe has enough of them.

All of this helps to explain the coming into existence in recent years of the local district council and treasury, the voluntary self-help association, the mass literacy and adult education movement, the cooperative society, the political party, and both regional and federal forms of government.

Speed of change. A no less striking characteristic of African social change, in the opinion of many, is the speed with which it has come about. Certainly it is not difficult to find supporting evidence. Thus, it is still less than a hundred years since David Livingstone witnessed (1871) the massacre by slavers of 300 to 400 market people—mostly women—on the banks of the Lualaba River. It is less than seventy years since the British came upon the last evidence of wholesale human sacrifice in Nigeria (1897 in Benin City). It is less than sixty years since the last slave caravan was intercepted (1903) in what is now the Federation of Rhodesia and Nyasaland. And there are Africans still living in that territory who clearly remember seeing the man who fathered the Federation, Cecil John Rhodes.

There is scarcely a theme of African life on which some rapid changes have not been rung. An instance may be cited from education. A few miles outside Nairobi there is a boarding school—the Alliance High School—for 200 African boys, drawn from all parts of Kenya. In eleven years down to 1955, only one boy had failed to graduate, and the next year he passed the graduating examination—which was the same as that sat for by thousands of the brighter products of British schools. Nearly half the graduates, averaging fifty a year, received the equivalent of a straight A. In such matters as athletic, musical and theatrical ability, industry, courtesy and courage, nearly all of them, in the opinion of the headmaster, would have stood comparison with their European counterparts. But what is perhaps most significant from our stand-

point is the fact that nearly all of them were only one generation removed from total illiteracy. Until they went to this
school they knew practically nothing of the meaning of
money. Few of them came from homes where either books
or newspapers were regularly read, or where there was any
intelligent conversation beyond that necessary for the conduct
of domestic affairs. And this school, though a leader in its
field, is by no means untypical of what has been happening
elsewhere, in almost every territory. To cite another instance:
down to the early 1940s there was only one institution in the
whole of tropical Africa where students could do work of university caliber, namely, Fourah Bay College, at Freetown,
Sierra Leone. Today more than a dozen such institutions exist
in almost as many territories.

Similarly impressive statistics can be gleaned in the field of
health and health services. Whereas at the turn of the century less than half of all west African children are believed to
have lived to their first birthday, today the ratio is nearer
seven out of ten, and in some areas (e.g., Lagos, Nigeria)
more than nine out of ten. And whereas in the first five years
of the present century the number of people killed by sleeping sickness in Uganda was of the order of 100,000, in the
first five years after mid-century it was almost certainly less
than 100. Several other territories can point to equally dra-
matic declines in a wide range of diseases.

In the field of government administration there have likewise been changes as conspicuous for their speed as for their
size. It goes without saying that at the beginning of the present century there were no ballot boxes, no political parties,
and, beyond Liberia and Ethiopia, no autonomous governments. No Africans held posts in any colonial administration,
and very few in any civil service above the rank of clerk.
And there was as yet no serious talk of partnership, let alone
self-government. Today (1959) five territories are autonomous; twenty more are in process of becoming autonomous.
In the region as a whole there are not less than 40 million
qualified electors. In almost every territory the Africanizing
process in the civil service, business, industry and the pro-

fessions is proceeding about as fast as the supply of "Europeanized" Africans will allow. Many of the leaders thrown up by these rising political tides would scarcely be recognized by their own fathers. Some of them would have difficulty in recognizing themselves as they were ten or twenty years ago, so great is the change wrought in them by the changes around them.

What is frequently as striking as the speed of social change is its acceleration. In the 1920s and 1930s the speed of change in education, social welfare and government was barely more than a trot, even on the fastest African courses; it was fast only by comparison with the customary tempo of African life. Since World War II, on the same courses, it has become a gallop that gives the spectators almost as much to think about as the riders, and keeps the backers in a state of nerves. And more horses are getting into the field all the time.

Statistics of change, like those of horse racing, are apt to obey the law of diminishing returns. But, since it is impossible to measure acceleration without them, one or two more must be cited. For our first example we take the growth of what the Belgians call the *population extra-coutumière*, the population living outside the tribal area. At the beginning of the century not a single Congolese African, it may be safely said, resided outside his tribal area. Not only would he have been scared to, but he would have had no way of making an honest living outside. As late as the outbreak of World War II fewer than a million Congolese were living extra-tribally. By 1951, however, 2 million, and by 1959 more than 3 million—approximately 25 per cent of the total African population in the Belgian Congo—were living away from their tribes.

For a second illustration we go to Uganda, and to an expression of change that is perhaps as much economic as social, namely, the growth of the cooperative movement. The figures speak for themselves: the number of cooperative societies (exclusive of producers' marketing unions) increased from 118 in 1947 to 1,423 in 1957; membership surged from 7,447 to 136,172 between the same years; and working capital grew more than fivefold, from less than £20,000 to more than £100,000.[2]

But one must not get the impression that everyone—African, Asian and European alike—is happy about the changes taking place, or that everyone has been greatly changed by them. On the contrary; if there are two things as certain as the magnitude and speed of the changes taking place in the social life of tropical Africa, they are the patchiness of the change and the superficial look of much of it.

Uneven incidence. Some areas show far fewer evidences of social change than others. Put a traveler down among the tribal peoples of the great escarpment country of Ethiopia and he might think that he was back in the sixteenth century with Pedro de Covilham and his Portuguese colleagues who wrote of them. If he should see these people coming toward him with garlands of flowers round their necks and playing pan pipes, he might feel even more at home reading a book of Greek mythology. A traveler would also have no difficulty in finding "stubborn unlaid ghosts" in such out-of-the-way places as the southern shore of Lake Rudolf in northern Kenya, where the El Molo tribe, one of the smallest in Africa, seemingly prefers extinction to change; in the Kalahari Desert, where the Bushman still uses the cupid's bow in his love-making ritual and often manages still to live without any of the white man's aids; and in the Lobi country deep in the interior of the Ivory Coast, where the custom that sons murder either their fathers or mothers to prove their manhood is still honored when the authorities aren't looking.

Nor would a traveler need to go as far as this from "civilization" to find the past. He could find it on the airfield at Malakal in Sudan, if by chance a Dinka had chosen to graze his herd around its margins; for a Dinka continues to make few concessions to the Western view of propriety and none where clothing is concerned. He could find it in the Aberdare

[2] *Cooperative Information Bulletin for the British Commonwealth,* various issues (published by the Cooperative Union Ltd., Manchester, England).

Mountains of Kenya, within sight of Nairobi on a good day; for it is here that the Mau Mau had their hide-outs and conjured up the witches of a pagan past. He could see whole panoramas of the past from the windows of a train running through the Middle Belt of Nigeria or the back country of Angola.

On the other hand, put a traveler down in Léopoldville's western suburb of Kalina and no amount of familiarity with Stanley's travels would enable him to identify it as the place where the explorer persuaded some 400 Congolese chiefs to sign treaties of friendship. For almost everything about Kalina except the climate is a cultural import. Its houses and apartments are built in the style favored in Palm Beach and Miami. Its streets are well paved and lined with shade trees—as few indigenous village roads are. Its shops are stocked with high-quality products of European and North American factories. Its restaurants feature the finest in imported foods. Its places of worship and its schools are of Belgian design and Palestinian inspiration.

Or put the traveler down in Kampala, Uganda, near the Kabaka's Enclosure, with a copy of John Hanning Speke's *Journal of the Discovery of the Source of the Nile,* and about the only things to strike him as familiar would be the fence of "tall yellow reeds of the common Uganda tiger grass" around the palace, the regal hauteur of the womenfolk about its gates, and the very general liking for a potent native beer known as *pombe.* As to the rest—the four-storied Bulange (the parliament building of the Kabaka's government) equipped with electricity and a public address system; the hilltop cathedrals, Protestant and Catholic; Makerere College with its many-styled halls of learning and leisure rampant on a field of green, its English-speaking student body drawn from eighty tribal backgrounds and living in the manner hallowed by centuries of British academic convention; and, not less important, the business quarter, where Europeans, Asians and Africans match wares and wits, stir the poor man's imagination with pictures of plumbing and flatter the rich man's pride with talk of the latest in fashions for himself and his wife—all this and much more is out of Speke's world.

The same could be said of any of a hundred other cities. And not of cities only; there are countrysides in which the traveler of earlier days would be hard put to it to find his social bearings.

In much of the Kikuyu country of Kenya, for instance, dispersed settlement has given place to nucleated settlement. This "villagization" program, originally intended as a security device against Mau Mau terrorists, has proved so widely acceptable that a whole new way of African life is being built around it. To reduce the walking time to and from the characteristically scattered bits of farm land (which was increased for most farmers as a result of the program), the Kenya government has been pushing through a parallel program of land consolidation by exchange. Hundreds of square miles of Kikuyuland have already been divided into compact small holdings to which owners have a clear title and on which they can more readily apply the principles of good husbandry and so make more money to support, among other things, the greatly improved services now being made available to the villagers. Each of the larger villages has a health clinic, a clean and reliable water supply, a school, a recreation center and a church. The shops are much better than those found in the bush, where the turnover is slow and consequently the range of offerings small. In most villages babies—formerly back-loaded almost everywhere—can be left at day nurseries in charge of trained sitters while their mothers are at work in the fields. Many villages have facilities to train women in hygiene, housekeeping and—greatest innovation of all!—ball playing. For the men the "villagization" program means change, too: more scope for the leaders among them to show their quality, and more reason for the led to see that the quality is good; closer touch with the outside world by means of radio, newssheets, pep talks, and the comings and goings of neighbors; firmer discipline, but more distractions; more problems, but higher hopes.

Many other rural communities provide equally notable evidences of change. Some, like those of the Gezira in Sudan and the upper Niger valley in the Sudanese Republic (formerly French Sudan), virtually owe their existence to the white man's initiative. Frequently the only things the people attracted to such developments have in common are their tiredness, poverty, wretchedness and yearning to be free. The welding of such people into cohesive groups inevitably calls for social improvisation. Other communities have undergone an economic metamorphosis—in the case of the Kipsigis of Kenya, from nomadic pastoralists to sedentary farmers. No community can make such a break, involving its internal and external relationships, without rewriting parts of its social testament. Then there are many communities, mostly small, that have embraced Christianity as a living faith. In them, the New Testament has become the guide to both belief and conduct. And any community that takes the New Testament for its guide quickly finds itself in the midst of social change of the most radical kind.

Superficiality. When we have said all this, however, the fact remains that we have been talking only about "minorities," and that among these much of the evident change has a superficial, or "topped-up," look about it. As for the "majorities," in most cases they continue to think of themselves as belonging to the old social order. To most of the cattle-keeping Masai, for instance, the world of classroom, clinic, lathe, legislative assembly and Christian church is still as foreign as the world of their crop-raising neighbors, the Kikuyu and Chagga. They want to have as little to do with either as possible, and as a rule they have their wish. So, too, the pygmies of the Congo basin forest. From time to time they may do some light work for the local *commandant,* but they show little desire to live like him, or to trade the seclusion of their hutments for the exposure of his housing projects. Nor is this point of view held only by herders and hunters. Tens of thousands of cultivators find that the newcomers' homes, offices, workshops, mines and plantations where they sometimes work as laborers are new jungles—sources of food and excitement, but also of fear and trouble, frequently coming to them in the guise of sickness. As soon as they can conveniently do so, they go back home, taking with them such symbols of their prowess as they have managed to come by. They have been in the new world, but they are not of it; to all appearances, they are not much interested in becoming part of it.

But what of those who have come to think of themselves, or to be thought of, as changed men, and as being the product of the white man's world as much as of their own? Of these, it is arguable that many—perhaps a majority—are still commuters, citified Westerners one week, bush Africans the next, their permanent address and roots being still deep in the country. They may live as Europeans do, work as they do and worship as they do, but after a while the European mantle slips from their shoulders and they are children of the African earth again—until they weary of the role or are forced to abandon it temporarily. Many miners, machine shop workers, clerks and artisans "commute" in this fashion; many doctors, lawyers, teachers and other professional men find it easy and pleasant to do the same, though not, it would seem, without impairment of their skills.

And what of those who have done with the bush, who never leave the world of the European? They may be lost to the tribe, but rarely are they lost to the world of the tribe and rarely do they seek to be. Peter Abrahams, himself an Africa-born negro, makes this point very clearly in his *A Wreath for Udomo*. Set in a west African territory called Pluralia, and reading in places like an eye-witness account of social change in the Gold Coast of the early 1950s, the story is largely framed around the "dual personality" of a promising young politician, Mhendi, who could never forget that there were two Pluralias. He was torn between two worlds, "that of the cities and the white men and that of the countryside and the old tribal ways. And though I had been to school in the cities and had gone to Europe, I was still a son of the tribe.

They couldn't think of me as anything but a son of the tribe. I couldn't outrage my old father's great dreams."[3]

Meanwhile it seems that plenty of Africans are less fastidious, taking what they fancy from the foreigner and also keeping what they fancy of their own, much as children do when faced with a supply of new toys which they have not space to stow. And as with children, the things they fancy frequently provide the student with a wonderful field for sociological and psychological inquiry. More important, they frequently provide the advocate of early political autonomy with a shock. For no man is greatly changed by acts of parliament, by grant of license to teach or to practice law, by adoption of another man's dress, or even by the rite of baptism into another man's religion. How he is changed "in depth"—in his thinking and feeling, his values and judgments—is beyond our competence to tell; but of one thing we can be sure: time is a factor in the process. In most of tropical Africa, there apparently hasn't yet been enough time.

THREE CASE STUDIES

To catch the real meaning of social change, one must see it at work in whole communities. Of the many communities that might be studied with advantage, three have been chosen, partly because they have been investigated at great length and partly because they typify three of the most general situations in tropical Africa today.

A RAIN FOREST GROUP

The indigenous inhabitants of the section of the equatorial rain forest which lies in and adjacent to the French Cameroons belong to a number of negroid groups distinguishable more by the languages and dialects they speak—more than a hundred in number—than by the way they live. The following account of these people is derived from a paper written

[3] *Op. cit.*, Alfred A. Knopf, New York, 1956, p. 22.

for our study by George R. Horner. Horner believes that, with the exception of the coastal fishing groups, they all belong to the same culture group, since they have all had the same kind of economic and social organization, and much the same general views about the nature of the world in which they live and their place in it. They also traditionally followed the same livelihoods—hunting (for small game as a rule) and the cultivating by the usual bush-fallowing methods of such subsistence crops as yam, manioc and banana. They formerly did little trading, as their surpluses were few and unreliable; and they seldom went far from home, partly because of fear[4] and partly because of linguistic difficulties. Among the more important of these groups are the Fang and the Bulu.[5]

During the past fifty to seventy-five years these forest dwellers, like all other colonized peoples, have come to accept the fact of interference. They have become accustomed to the exactions (mostly small) of the *commandant*, the ministrations (mostly welcome) of the mission teacher, pastor and doctor, and the pushing and shoving of the entrepreneur (mostly unavoidable). Many have become accustomed to living in towns, without which the white man—or so it seems to them—can do nothing well. Chief among such towns are Douala, Yaoundé and Kribi in the French Cameroons; Bata in Spanish Guinea; Bangui in the Central African Republic (the onetime French province of Ubangi-Shari); and Libreville and Port Gentil in Gabon. Those—still by far the great majority—who continue to live in the forests have become accustomed to the idea of growing cash crops. Cocoa, coffee, tobacco, peanuts, bananas and palm kernels enable them to pay their taxes and to be in the market for a limited range of goods.

[4] Even today there are men in some of the deeper forests who refuse to go anywhere unless accompanied by at least two blood brothers, each armed with lance and cutlass.

[5] It would apparently be wrong to speak of these people as "tribes." Each of them can say "my family" or "my clan," but none of them has a word for "my tribe." When a Bulu wants to refer to all the Bulu people he is forced to use the word "race," wrong though it is ethnically.

To what extent has the social order of these rain forest peoples been changed by these changes in their economy? In externals, at least, it has been greatly changed. To start with some of the most obvious and agreeable changes: Slavery has disappeared and along with it the practice of burying slaves alive (sometimes wives, too) in the graves of their masters. Cannibalism has also disappeared, assuming one can discount the stories that still, from time to time, come out of the deep forests of killings made for the sheer pleasure of eating human flesh. Most of the secret societies that used to terrorize everyone have been snuffed out. There has also been a satisfactory decline in the status and activity of the sorcerer.

Coming to more prosaic matters, there have been changes in the stratification of society, in its family institutions and relationships, and the day-by-day doings of its members.

In pre-European times there were no chiefs, either hereditary or elected. Each village was run by a group of older men belonging to the clan family. Though no one man had greater power than any other, because of the prestige attaching to wealth the word of the richest man usually commanded greater attention than that of the not so rich; the rich man was, in fact, an uncrowned king—the headman of the group.

Today this old one-level society (the head man of it was never more than the first among equals) is slowly being replaced by a three-level society, founded on Western criteria of schooling and civilization, instead of on the African criteria of wealth and prestige. Horner characterizes the three levels as follows: (1) the elite class, composed of government officials, rich and educated planters and store owners, directors of schools, pastors, priests, etc.; (2) the *évolué* class, consisting of lesser school and government *fonctionnaires*, clerks in commercial employ, small planters, carpenters, masons, truck drivers, domestic workers ("boys"), specialists in ivory and ebony handicrafts, tailors, and educated women; (3) the great mass of uneducated, illiterate or pre-literate villagers—all those living where there are no schools, or where schools have been started too recently to have produced a literate class.

This is not a classification that means anything to more than a few Africans. As Horner says, "Only a small percentage of the elite class, those who have given up their culture for Western culture, would recognize these social divisions." The rest have not yet begun to think of themselves as belonging to a society in which there are superiors and inferiors, privileged and unprivileged, in which favor is to the *évolué* and riches to the elite.

Most people, nevertheless, have begun to see that they belong to a society that does not stop where the village stops. The ties that bind them to their ethnic kin in other clans and villages may be loose, and articulated poorly if at all, but the awareness of the ties is there. Nowadays language is no longer the barrier to understanding it was, since almost every man, if not yet every woman, has a smattering of French. Insecurity is no longer the barrier to travel it was, for a man may go the length of the land without fear of being attacked or maltreated. Many, indeed, have gone beyond the length of the land—and to North Africa and Europe as part of the Free French army that played so large a role in the liberation of Occupied France—and in doing so have discovered how little of the world they know who only know the rain forest. The postwar awards of citizenship, voting rights, representation in the French National Assembly, and scholarships for bright students served to enlarge the intellectual borders still further. Some of the rain foresters are today more conscious of country than of tribe or group; and a few are world-conscious—to the extent of seeking, and winning, U. N. recognition of their political hopes.

A number of changes have come about as a result of sending children to the white man's school. If they go to a day school, they are away from home from early morning to late afternoon. If they go to a central, or boarding, school, they may be away from home for months on end. In either case they are no longer free to work in their parents' fields or to go hunting or fishing except during vacations; and they are no longer able to spend large amounts of time, if any, in the "bush schools"—the initiation societies of their age groups.

Whether they go to day or boarding school, the disciplinary role of the parent is diminished. Most teachers assume the role of father. In doing so they oblige children to work for them, in both house and garden, and to submit to their jurisdiction in all social matters. Frequently this spells punishment far more harsh than any the child will have known at home.

The schools, particularly the central schools, are responsible for other, more disturbing changes. Away from their home communities, boys and girls find it easy to break the traditional rules governing sexual conduct. They find it equally hard to obey the white man's rules, with the result that neither the old nor a new code of behavior has real meaning for them. This has not been without effect on the system of marriage and divorce.

As in most other parts of tropical Africa, marriage was traditionally thought of in the rain forest as a community matter. Its primary function was to ensure the survival of the two families concerned, and so of the community of which they formed part. Accordingly, a marriage had to be arranged, and the terms of the contract agreed upon, not only by the two contracting parties but by all the elders of the village, or villages, from which the parties came. Bride wealth formed an important part of the contract. Characteristically the securities transferred took the form of two or more bundles of iron bars (each bundle containing twenty pieces), ivory, sheep, cloth and a dog.

Today marriage means different things to different people. To many young men and women it means little more than elopement and a clandestine home in the bush. To many others it means a quick civil ceremony performed, with or without the families' and elders' consent, by the nearest available government official. To baptized Christians it means vows performed in a church or chapel, often followed at a discreet interval by a traditional pagan ceremony in the woman's village.

In the first case, no payments or securities are required; and it is probable that none are available, since the commonest reason given for the "bush marriage" is the inability of the man to find the cash or goods demanded of him by the woman's people. In the second case, it is unusual for payments or securities to be required, for it is an un-African form of marriage to begin with, and one that is not generally approved of by the families of the contracting parties. In the third case, the practice regarding payments or securities varies widely. Some parents, Christian and pagan, require that certain specified gifts be made by the man; but others do not. On the whole the churches, Protestant and Catholic, discourage the practice, both because it is un-Christian and because the amount of cash or goods demanded in these days makes "legitimate" marriage increasingly difficult for most young men. And the demands are high. Writing in the mid-1950s, Horner reported that even in the bush they would commonly include a phonograph, a suit for the bride's father, a sheep (worth the equivalent of about $12), a saw (worth about $50) and $300 in cash—more (up to $500) for a well-educated girl. To come by such wealth takes most young men more years of hard work than they are willing to wait.

Along with the consequent increase of unrecognized marriages has gone an increase in divorce. In the old days divorce was rare. A man could divorce a woman for one of three reasons only: sterility, adultery and refusal to cook. A woman could not divorce her husband legally for any reason, though she could leave him if he were too cruel or would not eat the food she prepared for him. Nowadays a man can demand a divorce on any of four grounds: adultery, crime, prolonged absence from the home, and plain bad conduct. A woman now can also demand a divorce, on any of four grounds: beatings, venereal disease, "continual infamous condemnation," and, in the case of a polygynous household, failure to treat her on an equality with the other wives. For this easing of divorce, both church and state must, it seems, be held responsible; the church by insisting that a polygynist could not become a member in good standing until all but one of his wives were divorced, and the state by increasing the number of grounds on which divorce could be obtained and by insisting that marriage needed neither the blessing of the church nor the approval of village families—that it was a matter which could be ended as it was begun, by consent solely of the parties concerned.

There have also been changes in the way the rain forest dwellers dress, feed and house themselves. Today it would be hard to find a young Bulu man or woman who does not aspire to be able to dress—though not necessarily to be dressed all the time—in the style of the European. So strong is this aspiration in many minds that the question of the suitability of a given fashion for local use scarcely arises. If close-fitting slacks for women are the mode in Paris, then they become the mode in Douala, notwithstanding the notable difference in the figure of the average Parisian and the average Doualan. If white buckskin shoes are in style on the paved promenades of the Riviera, they are likely to be fashionable in the unpaved, muddy tracks of the bush—on the heads, if not the feet, of their owners.

It is difficult, of course, for the man or woman who wants to be able to look like a European not to want to be able to live like one. More and more are seeking to do it—to the extent, at any rate, of having chairs to sit on, beds to lie on, bicycles to ride, and metal on the roof, linoleum on the floor, windows in the walls, canned goods in the cupboards and "canned" noise everywhere. Some Bulu town houses are far better appointed than some town houses in metropolitan France.

There is, then, no minimizing the changes that have taken place, and still are taking place, in the culture of the rain forest peoples. At the same time, the cultural climate and the "soil" of the rain forest—the sources of strength and inspiration of the forest dwellers—appear to have changed very little; the lopping, pruning, trimming, clearing, and planting up with exotic growths that have been going on have altered little more than its looks.

At heart, Horner contends, the man of the rain forest is still unrepentantly African. As supporting evidence he cites, among other things, the increasing incidence in recent years of polygyny. In a society as poor in things as the old rain forest society, wealth must be measured by other criteria. One of the most widely accepted of such criteria, both in and out of the rain forest, has long been the number of wives and children a man has. A man with one wife was considered poor, for two reasons. First, women, as wives, were the only ones he could normally get to work for him in his gardens; men and boys shun manual work, while girls marry and leave home almost as soon as they are capable of doing a day's work. Second, death rates being what they were, a man could not expect one woman to raise enough children to assure him of a succession. Consequently almost every rain forest man desired to have more than one wife. Frequently he would be abetted in his desire by his wife, who looked forward to having less work and more prestige in a polygynous household. For a while it looked as though the strictures of the Christian church would strangle sentiment for the old pagan creed, but this has not proved to be the case. As the incomes of the rain forest peoples have increased, thanks to the demand for their cash crops and their services in commerce, industry and government, so has the number of those willing to give up membership in the Christian church for the privilege of living in the manner of their forefathers.

Other lines of evidence pointing in the same direction are the fact that most rain forest people, Christian and pagan, still strongly approve of the traditional way of arranging a marriage and of stabilizing it with the help of payments or securities, and the fact that most of them show no desire whatever to cut themselves loose from their homes. As Horner puts it, "Though many young men and women leave home these days, hardly any of them leave home psychologically." Away from home they may dress and talk and eat like Europeans, but at home they are not *like* anybody; they are themselves. There they will frequently discard not only the speech, dress and living style of the European, but also his way of thinking and his skills.[6]

[6] Horner tells of a trained medical assistant who, on returning to the bush after working in a modern hospital, gave up using

As a further line of evidence—in Horner's view, the most important line of all—we may cite the fact that the highest good and chief end of the ordinary rain forest man remains what it has ever been: wealth and status. Only the methods used to reach this end have changed, and these not always greatly. Thus, whereas a man interested in winning status or keeping it was expected to divide up the bag of a hunting expedition according to a long-established "division of wealth" procedure among a group that included his wife, his close friend, his village brothers, his parents and parents-in-law, nowadays he is expected to follow much the same procedure with the earnings of his crops. Upon receipt of cash for his crop, he is expected to give his wife any sum she asks; to give his close friend usually the equivalent of twenty kilograms of cocoa; to give something to any village brother who asks for it; to help a village son raise his marriage money; to send gifts to his parents and parents-in-law; and to give aid to any stranger who asks it.

Again, whereas in the old days a man sent gifts to a village brother in the hope of receiving richer gifts and of raising his prestige with his neighbors and relatives in the process, now he is quite likely to send gifts to the nearest white man—who, by the sender's standards, is almost always rich in goods, influence and power. Or, again, whereas in the past a boy would spend time in the bush school being initiated into the secrets of his people's greatness and learning how to become as great as they, today he is likely to spend much more time in the white man's school being initiated into the secrets of the white man's greatness; for, increasingly, "white" and "wealth" are thought of as two sides of the same coin. The fact that much of the white man's education is unrelated

---

Western medicines in favor of native ones. When asked why, he replied that the white man's medicine did not always work for Africans. "He would never have said this while working at the hospital, that is, while he was a 'European'; but now, at home, he was once more an African and solved his conflict of identification by becoming a member of the group and once more—at least for six months—following the established customs and mores of his culture."

to the needs of bush life does not seem to matter greatly. Indeed, where an "Africanized" curriculum, complete with instruction in local geography and folklore and the care of the locally grown cash crops, is offered as an alternative to the standard curriculum, the student is commonly encouraged by his people to choose the latter, on the grounds either that it is a stronger kind of magic or that to study like a white man is, in time, to have his wealth and status.

It is perhaps not too much of an exaggeration to say that almost the only things the ordinary rain forest man wants as yet of the white man are his "power tools" and symbols: the ability to read, write and calculate (many men argue that this is the basic tool, and that now they have it, they are "as good as the white man"), the ability to make and maintain machinery, travel fast, grow fine crops, print money ("you are rich because you print all the money," is a complaint that is often heard) and, when it serves his social purpose, to eat, live and dress like a white man. In so far as the white man is willing to put him in the way of these tools and symbols, the ordinary rain forest man is happy enough to court his company; but once the willingness ceases to be apparent, the courtship flags.

As for the other things the white man has been offering him—politics, citizenship, nationhood, the Code Napoléon, sectarianism, class distinctions—the rain forester remains for the most part unconvinced of their relevance to his social good, let alone of their intrinsic goodness.

When asked by Horner if he thought the white man had brought "good" to the African, a Bulu replied: "We Bulu will not know if you have brought good until fifty years after you have gone." Not that every Bulu, any more than every Briton or Brahmin, is above finding uses for things that his descendants half a century from now will decide were really very bad for him!

A HILL PEOPLE

The country of the Teita (singular: Mteita) of the Coast Province of Kenya, whose life is the subject of a case history prepared for this study by Alfred and Grace G. Harris, differs from that of the Bulu and Fang in several respects. For one thing, it is much smaller, consisting merely of a group of three hills. These hills, lying about a hundred miles northwest of Mombasa, are a far cry from the typical Cameroonian rain forests. They are higher (up to 7,000 feet in elevation), rougher, cooler and, for the better part of the year, drier. They also have a more lived-in look, most of their native vegetation having long since been destroyed. Not being able to expand outward because of the aridity of the surrounding plains, the cultivators dwelling at the base of the hills had to expand inward and upward, toward the head of every little valley with a supply of water and a cover of soil. At the present time, the hills carry a population of over 60,000, representing a density of roughly 175 to the square mile, or about ten times the density of the Cameroonian rain forest—and this notwithstanding the greater difficulties they present to the inhabitants. For, by any criterion, it is difficult country, by turns wooing and whipping, drowning and desiccating, scorching and chilling. Nature may have spread her tables in the wilderness of the rain forest, but not in the Teita Hills.

However, the difficulties appear to have kept the Teita on their toes and given them a sizable capacity for improvisation and resilience—for rolling with the punches, and returning them. These hillsmen early learned that the price of harvest was watchfulness, hard work and willingness to raise almost anything. Maize (the staple for about half the year), yams, sugar cane (mainly for beer), bananas, sweet potatoes, beans, peas, cucurbits and other vegetables, all found a place in their diet. So, too, did chickens. And every man tried to keep a few cows and goats—though more for their money than their food value. The Teita also learned that there were times when all the watchfulness, hard work and willingness in the

world could not win an adequate harvest and when they had
to look elsewhere than to the hills for help. They may live on
an island, but they have long known that it is not entire of
itself. Indeed, the Harrises contend that the Teita, unlike the
Cameroonian rain foresters, have always been part of a wider
economy. This included not only their Bantu neighbors but
also the half-Hamitic Masai, and Arabs from the coast whose
caravan routes passed by their hills.

Europeans—travelers, explorers, missionaries, road builders,
traders and administrators—have been coming and going
among the Teita for well over a hundred years. Today the
Teita are caught in a widening net of economic, social and
political relationships.

To find the money for the taxes and school fees he must
pay and the commodities he feels the need of but cannot
make with his own hands, the Mteita must have something
to sell. To have a surplus of goods, such as cattle or crops,
he must have either more land or better yields, or both, than
he has been in the habit of having. To get the land he must
either reacquire tribal land that has been alienated for the
building of missions and schools, the running of demonstration plots and similar purposes or get hold of some new, non-
tribal land in the surrounding plains and valleys. In both
cases, he finds himself dealing with agencies whose offices are
a long way off—in Mombasa and Nairobi, perhaps in London.
To get the yields means learning new techniques (frequently
developed in other parts of the colony or in other territories),
following practices that are, in many instances, as foreign as
their exponents, and, perhaps, spending time away from his
hills seeing how other people tackle the problem. And when
he has the surplus the chances are that he will not be able to
sell it unless it is of a kind and quality to attract outside
buyers; in a small area like the Teita Hills most farmers are
producing surpluses of the same things and therefore are not
in the market for their neighbors' produce. The customers
for his surplus chillies and other vegetables are more likely
to be at the coast than in Voi and Mwatate, the chief local

trading centers; his ability to market his coffee is more likely to be governed by demand in the United Kingdom than in the neighboring provinces of Kenya.

If he has little or no good land—and in these days many lack adequate amounts of such land—he must seek to sell his services. The chances are that this will also mean going "outside," for while the hills can generally provide him with work, the "outside" can generally provide him with better-paid work. The nearest large labor market is Mombasa. Nowadays the Teita go there in increasing numbers to search for work or on business. At the last census almost 50 per cent (1,776) of the total (3,654) number of employed adult Teita males were located in Mombasa and another 25 per cent (898) were working outside the Teita district in other parts of Kenya.[7]

The economic net has widened in another sense. The range of employment open to the Teita is nowadays much greater than it was in precolonial times. Not that it was ever as small as in the Cameroonian rain forests, with their traditionally small scope for animal husbandry, trading and porterage. Today Teita men work in railway shops, sisal estates, government departments, business offices and cooperatives; and as tinkers, tailors and teachers. Increasing numbers of them are doing jobs that rank as semiskilled and skilled.

As in the Cameroons, the enlarging process has been at work, yeastlike, in almost every compartment of life, with marked effect on its looks and "consistency."

Take, for instance, the look of the Teita house and its inhabitants as the Harrises describe them: "Material objects of European provenance, and a few European practices, are to be found or observed in any household, pagan or Christian, schooled or unschooled. Virtually everyone wears some form

[7] It should not, however, be inferred that approximately 75 per cent of the adult males were away from the Teita Hills at the time of the census. At least 75 per cent were actually living in the Teita district, presumably self-employed, unemployed or just "between jobs."

of European clothing, and most households possess such things as enamel plates, cups, bowls, wooden chairs, and perhaps a table or two. Tea drinking is universal." The higher the education or the higher the income, the more evident is the "Europeanization." The home of the well-educated man is almost always rectangular or L-shaped, in contrast to the traditional circular house, and occasionally has more than three rooms.

The roof is often made of galvanized iron or, failing that, of petrol tins which have been flattened out. The walls, if they are of mud, are ordinarily smoothed and white, or color-washed both inside and out. China tea sets, knives and forks, replace or are added to enamel plates and mugs and spoons. Often, in such a household, the wife has also gone to school for some time; and the furnishings bear witness to this in crocheted or embroidered cotton tablecloths and bedspreads. The household head will have forsaken khaki shorts and shirts for a suit, sometimes accompanied by a stiff-collared shirt, or for slacks and a jacket or blazer; he seldom goes barefoot any more. Among the most recent and least frequently seen material changes are the provision of extra clothing for the children, and of really modish clothes for the wife . . .

For many a wife modishness does not stop with the clothes she wears. In the past the Teita wife ran her home with little or no help other than what she might get from her small children, or from the other wives if there were any. Today it is not unusual for her to have a hired boy or girl to help with the heavy work. Whereas formerly she was expected to be—and often had to be—a universal provider, now she is as likely to be complimented on the quality of the corned beef bought in the village store as on the excellence of her home-grown chillies or chickens. While making more use of the resources of the village store each year, she is not neglecting those of her garden. If she has had some schooling, the chances are she will be making better use of them, and serving better meals. Also if she has been to school, she is likely to have new ideas about the care and feeding of her children. In some Teita homes infants are now fed protective foods based on scientific formulas, and given the additional protection of rubber sheets and mosquito nets. Older children and adults are likely to be protected by patent medicines.

Formerly the paths of the wife and the husband seldom crossed during the daytime, but now it is not uncommon to see the two eating together at table, and by no means unknown for them to display companionability publicly. It is in this realm of personal and family relationships that some of the most striking changes have taken place. As in the Cameroonian rain forest, most of them have come in the wake of the Christian missions. Thanks largely to the close control of the school system by the missions during the past half century, the wake is a strong one. Generally, the teachers are themselves missionaries or converts of missionaries, and regard their mission as something more than an educational one. Being concerned with the whole of life, and having judged Teita life to be almost wholly unserviceable for Christian ends, they feel that the Teita must be "separated" from it, freed from conformance with tribal ways and loosened from the bonds of old superstitions. "Freedom from the old pressures, both external and psychological, is supposed to go hand in hand with greater conformance to the principles of Christian morality and true acceptance of the Christian faith. Not only pagan ritual practices, but many domestic customs and leisure-time activities have been viewed as wrong, or at least as obstructing the path to enlightenment and faith. Very little of the old culture, apart from folk tales or riddles and handicrafts, has escaped either criticism by the missions, or efforts in the schools to substitute Europeanized forms."

Many Teita have already been separated from their old ways. They have abandoned polygyny. They no longer practice clitoridectomy or other *rites de passage.* They no longer consort with witch doctors, rain makers and other diviners, or keep charms and shrines, or make ritual sacrifice. They no longer condone drunkenness and similar excesses. On the positive side, many of them have accepted the Christian view of equality "before the Lord" of man and woman, of the brotherhood of man, and of the need for higher standards of righteousness, compassion and even cleanliness in daily living.[8]

Such changes are nothing short of revolutionary, whether they are recorded in the Teita Hills or in Beverly Hills. For most people they are too revolutionary, with the result that where there was once agreement, there is now division. Fathers are divided against their sons, mothers against their daughters, daughters-in-law against their mothers-in-law. Increasingly, families are being split along generational lines as the children of non-Christian and unschooled parents reject the tribal beliefs and customs. Many of the children who attend school are eventually baptized and confirmed in one of the Christian churches. "Sometimes this differentiation causes little friction while the children still live at home; and . . . when they marry they simply set up households which differ in greater or lesser degree from their parents', depending on how Europeanized they have become, and how firmly devoted to a church. Occasionally there is acute disruption of family relations when young men and women adopt a contemptuous attitude toward their parents on the grounds that they lack education, or adhere to the old religion, or both."

Even where the commitment to the Christian faith is little more than nominal, the degree of external change has often been quite large. In the mission schools a student is exposed daily to Christian teaching and example. Such prolonged exposure could hardly fail to cover the sensitized film of his mind with unpagan—if not orthodox Christian—images. It is probably no exaggeration to say that nine out of every ten Teita who have been through a mission school are rebels against some aspect or other of their society and converts to

---

[8] "For various reasons, cleanliness takes on much importance, and carries a high emotional charge," the Harrises observe. "The women of [Christian] households undertake all the extra sweepings, washings and so on that their meager resources of implements, soap and water will bear."

some aspect or other of Christian society. And among the un-rebellious tenth there are those who seem to feel that a little external change does no great harm so long as it simplifies the business of "getting on." For in the Teita Hills, as else-where, "getting on," whether as an employee of the govern-ment, a mission or a business, is often as much a matter of being a conformist as a man of character.

Before the coming of the British the Teita governed them-selves in the manner of the Cameroonian rain forest people. Upon occasion, men from all parts of the hills demonstrated their tribal solidarity by joining together under one leader to raid other tribes. But there were no chiefs and no large ad-ministrative units. Members of a village were expected to keep the peace under the direction of the most senior and most dominating man or men. Such "elders" ruled largely by dint of their moral authority and status, and the supernatural sanctions at their disposal. Save under exceptional circum-stances, they had no means of backing up their decisions with force, and needed none. Differences of opinion between elders were resolved either by referring them to the public at large or by administering an ordeal-oath. Peace between villages was maintained by blood-brotherhood pacts to which elders drawn from all parts of the tribal area were party. Besides simplifying cattle transactions and the trading of medicines and other goods, these pacts provided a kind of political unity in the absence of a formal government.

Today the Teita are part of a colony-wide administrative system which they neither devised nor direct. The system has its central offices in Nairobi, its provincial office in Mom-basa, its district office in Voi and subdistrict offices in the Teita Hills. In most of these, executive power is in the hands of Europeans, few of whom have had an opportunity of get-ting to know much about the Teita at first hand. Three agen-cies of this system bring members of the tribe directly into the business of governing it. These are the African (formerly Native) Authorities, the African District Council and the African Courts (formerly Native Tribunals). However, by

the Harrises' account these three organs of government neither
represent indigenous institutions nor make use of them to any
great extent.

The *African Authorities* are the British counterpart of the
Teita system of government by village elder. The tribal area
is divided into administrative districts called locations, which
are in turn divided into sublocations. Each location is put in
charge of a headman (by courtesy, chief), who has under
him a number of subheadmen (by courtesy, headmen), each
of whom is in charge of a sublocation and has one or more
village elders to assist him. Both chiefs and headmen are appointed by the central government and paid a salary. Their
major responsibilities are to maintain order; to organize the
collection of the poll tax and local rates; to arrest offenders;
to settle by arbitration (provided no fees are charged) petty
disputes arising within their area; to see that the rules governing the cutting of timber, the burning of bush and the
making, selling and drinking of beer are observed; to keep
the local roads in repair; to enforce anti-erosion measures
wherever the administration considers them necessary; and to
carry out the resolutions and by-laws of the African District
Council.

The *African District Council* is a local government body,
partly elected and partly nominated, composed of representatives from each of the locations, and normally presided over
by the District Commissioner. As a rule it meets only a few
times a year. It is authorized to pass resolutions on many
matters. These resolutions, once they have been approved by
the Governor of the colony, become by-laws which it is the
duty of the African Authorities to administer. Among the
matters covered are the imposition of local taxes and licenses,
land rights and responsibilities, the annual budget for maternity and ambulance services, dispensaries, primary and
adult education, agricultural services, and the salaries of those
employed by the council and by the African Authorities and
African Courts.

The *African Courts* come nearest, of the three bodies, to
being an indigenous institution. The Harrises report that

"they have jurisdiction over Africans only, are staffed entirely by Teita, and in general are subject to much less supervision than many other activities in which Europeans and Teita are associated." Most of their work has to do with the trying of offenses, both criminal and civil, against "native law and custom." Each court has a President, a Vice President, and a panel of six judges, appointed by the District Commissioner. It may impose sentences involving short-term imprisonment or fines in cash or kind. In the absence of an African Appeals Court, appeals go to the District Commissioner and from him to the Provincial Commissioner. Some idea of the importance of the system may be gleaned from the fact that in a recent year more than 1,000 cases were heard in the two Teita district courts.

In addition to these courts, there are large numbers of smaller courts, one to every sublocation. These are the Beni Mwana Councils.[9] Their field is likewise native law and custom, but their work consists mainly in arbitration, admonition and the setting of compensation. They handle several times as many cases in a year as do the African Courts, and they are very popular—even, it seems, with many of the offenders. After all, they were sired by the Teita; they may have been groomed by the British to increase their efficiency, but they belong to the tribe. In an age when country-bred stock is seldom regarded by its trainers as worth the price of its keep, the Teita have every reason for satisfaction with their Beni Mwana Councils.

Not that this is the only foal from their stable to survive. "Below the level of the Beni Mwana Councils, the old form of arbitration still goes on in the villages under the guidance of elders. A great number of disputes and offenses against custom are dealt with much as they have always been, and a whole host of matters never reach the sublocation or location councils, or the tribunals [i.e., African Courts]. For example, the Teita, unlike some other African peoples, do not like to have ordinary bride wealth discussions come before anyone besides

---

[9] *Beni mwana* is an idiomatic phrase meaning "indigenous (or local) inhabitants."

those concerned, and only a very small fraction of such cases ever go beyond village discussions."

The fact is that behind the changing visage of Teita government lies an almost unchanging disposition. What was right and wrong, good and bad, safe and dangerous for the Teita of fifty years and more ago is just about as right and as wrong, as good and as bad, as safe and as dangerous today. This is illustrated by the selection of men to occupy the posts of chief and headmen. District commissioners have naturally placed emphasis on the personal qualities and attainments which *they* consider desirable—efficiency, vigor, initiative, a progressive outlook and a better-than-average education. As a result the posts generally go to professing Christians, young men at that. But the Teita are inclined to use a rather different yardstick of competence. They may concede that it is a useful thing for a chief or headman to be literate, to have a working knowledge of English, and some experience of government service. But they will be most unlikely to concede that it is a useful thing for him to have spent much time away from home, as in this event he will almost certainly have lost touch with his people and their ways. Further, as they see it, the utility of knowing European ways is less in being able to copy them than in knowing what Europeans are likely to do in given circumstances.

The Teita also have different ideas from the Europeans about the importance of age. "By the standards of the old way of life as it continues today, a man in his twenties, thirties, or even his forties, is 'just a child.' . . . The education which young men often have is unquestionably valued by the Teita for its usefulness in dealing with the modern situation. But schools are far from being regarded as conferring the wisdom which, in the Teita view, is one of the requisites for the legitimate exercise of authority . . . Attempts on the part of a young man to exercise the 'leadership' and forcefulness valued by Europeans become, in this light, the effrontery of a youngster who must be put in his place."

The pagan Teita, who still constitute about three fourths of the population, do not share the British government's customary esteem of the Christian, either. Christian chiefs, in their view, are no better than young chiefs. Because they are Christians they cannot acquire their own shrines and so pass into the ranks of ritually validated elders; and their wealth cannot bring them much prestige since it has not been ritually validated, nor can it be used by them for the blood-brother pacts so important among elders. Without ritual knowledge and perquisites, a chief remains a man without wisdom, a "little child," even though he be old and well schooled.

Thus, on more than one flank of the Teita Hills, "the articulate, audible voice of the past" continues to be heard. In point of fact there is scarcely a spot where the voice is not heard, and respected. And, as the Harrises show, Christians pay almost as much heed to it as pagans. Christian church elders tend to share the traditional pagan attitudes toward youth, and to feel that they themselves occupy among Christians the same position as elders do among pagans, with the same rights to the exercise of authority in daily life as they have in church matters. This feeling is inclined to make them, like the pagan elders, uncooperative toward a young chief, whether Christian or pagan. Some Christian chiefs feel their lack of prestige keenly enough to take a second wife, trying thereby to enhance their status in pagan eyes by acquiring one of the frequent accompaniments of traditional elderhood. Most Teita Christians still seem to feel that it is both decent and right for their daughters to undergo some sort of initiation ceremony on reaching the age of puberty. Many of them also remain convinced of the uses of the old medicines, of divination and, in extreme cases, of sorcery. Almost all of them continue to support the institution of bride wealth. So far as the style of daily life is concerned, many Christian households differ hardly at all from non-Christian households.

If the voice of the past can beguile the Christian, we need not be surprised if it continues to bewitch the pagan. The Harrises leave us in no doubt that it does. Among other things, they point out that there has been very little detribalization of the Teita. A man may spend years of his working life

in Mombasa, but he seldom spends more than a few months
there at a stretch, and by the time he has a son old enough
to go out to work the chances are that he will settle back
in the hills for good. Again, while there is unquestionably a
growing tendency to balk at the obligation to contribute to the
support of parents, sisters and younger brothers, the young
man who refuses to help his family remains subject to strin-
gent sanctions and strong disapproval. Much the same can be
said of the young man who aspires to be wealthy. "Accumulation of important goods—originally almost exclusively cattle,
but today a variety of other things as well—is a prerogative
of old men. It is considered unseemly for younger men to have
large numbers of cattle, and few do. Nor do many young men
dare to acquire houses roofed with corrugated iron, or maize
grinders, even when they can afford them. These also have
become symbols of a man's place in the community . . .
[This] means that young men tend to buy consumable goods
of a narrowly restricted type, such as colorful clothing, and
even in this instance older men resent the display as unbe-
coming . . ."

The path of the economic or social climber is rough, for
the Teita are nothing if not egalitarian. Even their old men
who had a "right" to be rich could be only so rich; to be
more than "so rich" was to incur the serious displeasure of
the village. Today this displeasure can be incurred by a man
who makes money in a shop or plies a skilled craft. "In general," the Harrises remark, "using special knowledge to gain
a better living is viewed as the exercise of an unfair advantage over others." It is this same ingrained egalitarianism
that keeps chiefs and headmen from appearing "better than
other people," and spending a good deal of time and money
entertaining guests from whom they stand to gain nothing
directly.

Largely because there has been little detribalization, there
has been little change in the dimensions of a man's thought
or his loyalties. A man may be appointed chief over a location, but "the farther away [he] goes from his own village,
the more likely people are to contend that there is no reason

for obeying him since 'he is a man of such-and-such a place, and why should we have anything to do with him, as he is not our man?'" More or less the same applies to the African who tries to interest the Teita in any colony-wide movement, whether it is a political association, a trade union or a welfare society. If he comes from "outside" he will be regarded as an upstart who, without the wisdom of the elders, is taking too much upon himself. Accordingly he will be either ignored or disbelieved by the large majority of his hearers. If he comes from within the tribe, he will be respected only so long as he does not assume the posture of leadership. This, in the nature of the case, he is almost bound to do, sooner or later.

It is clear that here, as in the Cameroonian rain forest, we have a society in which forces making for change are opposed by forces making for stability, both forces being, up to now, sufficiently well balanced not to endanger the society's foundations. As the Harrises put it, "Christian and non-Christian, schooled and unschooled, Europeanized and traditional, are members of a single community." Needless to say, such forces give rise to friction, and where there is friction there is heat. The "progressives" often lose patience with the "conservatives," who, they seem to feel, lower the prestige of the tribe in the eyes of outsiders and reflect unfavorably on themselves. The conservatives sometimes accuse the progressives of being custom breakers and seekers after strange gods. At the same time few of the progressives are custom breakers and "idolaters" enough to accept the notion of complete Europeanization, and few of the conservatives are sufficiently single-minded not to see merit in some of the material changes for which the Europeans have been responsible. Most of the Teita people, progressives and conservatives alike, would probably settle for the best of both worlds.

All the time their ideas of what is best are so divergent, they might do worse than bear in mind the words of George Horner's Bulu friend quoted earlier in this chapter. The only trouble is that fifty years is a very long time to wait, especially if you are a progressive.

A CITY POPULATION

To savor fully the taste of social change, from its sickening worst to its astringent best, one must go to the town. For the town is the biggest distillery of social change.

With the exception of the "native" towns of west Africa, such as Timbuktu, Kano and Benin, a few "Arab" towns along the eastern coast, such as Zanzibar and Bagamoyo, and one or two Portuguese ports like Luanda and Mozambique, there were no towns in tropical Africa before the present century. Now there are hundreds. The town therefore represents a new milieu for almost all of those who live in it, one to which the traditional sociological criteria of "normalcy" do not apply. It is neither clan nor country, neither hallowed ground nor fruitful earth. It neither feeds a man's children nor lodges his ancestors. It is an uncharted wilderness, for which tribal man lacks both guiding star and measuring rod. European man made the town, and made it for European ends—which, as has been shown, were not African ends.

While every one of these towns could provide grist for a case study of social change, not many of them have as yet been through the sociologist's riddle. Of those that have, few if any have been sieved and sifted as carefully as Stanleyville, capital of the Orientale Province of the Belgian Congo. From 1952 to 1954 Stanleyville was under almost continuous scrutiny by a three-member team of the International African Institute, working in collaboration and under contract with UNESCO. The team consisted of an anthropologist, Pierre Clément; a statistical sociologist, V. P. Pons; and a psychologist, Nelly Xydias. The account that follows is based very largely on the team's findings as published by UNESCO in its *Social Implications of Industrialization and Urbanization in Africa South of the Sahara*.[10] A report made for this study

[10] By Nelly Xydias (prepared under the auspices of UNESCO by the International African Institute, London), UNESCO, Tensions and Technology Series, Paris, 1956.

by Jacques J. Maquet on the drift to the towns has also been drawn upon.

Stanleyville is situated at the upper limit of navigation of the middle Congo, roughly a thousand miles above Léopold-ville, at the foot of the rapids known as Stanley Falls. When H. M. Stanley saw the locality in 1877 it was nothing but a fishing village backed by seemingly endless, uninhabited and untamable bush. Today Stanleyville is a center of trade, transport (rail, road and river), administration and industry. Of its approximately 75,000 inhabitants, more than 70,000 are Africans. More than 80 per cent of the Africans live in the three separate quarters, known as Belge I, Belge II and Brussels, which very roughly form the apexes of a triangle in the middle of which lies the European town. Almost all of the rest live in a large *arabisé,* or Moslemized, village a half mile or so from the European town, and in the railway workers' camp beside the station.

What sort of people are these Africans? What did they do for a living before they went to Stanleyville? And where did they come from? Approximately two thirds of them were born in the bush. At the time of the UNESCO study nearly half of them had been in Stanleyville less than five years; only slightly more than one sixth had been there more than twenty years. Although there is bush and bush, for all practical purposes this means that most of the inhabitants of Stanleyville were raised in the world of village, clan and tribe, a world strong in local loyalties, weak in central authority. It also means that they were raised in a world of self-sufficiency (or semi-self-sufficiency since the coming of the Belgian administration), of simple living, and of scant opportunity for acquiring wealth and power.

Of the 66 different tribal groups making up the population, not one was represented by more than 6,000 people at the time of the survey, and only five by more than 2,000. Fifty were represented by groups of less than 500. While the great majority of these tribes had their homes within 200 to 300 miles of Stanleyville, not less than 15 per cent of the persons surveyed by the team came from outside the Orientale

Province, some from as far as Katanga, Kasai and Ruanda-Urundi, upward of 750 miles away.

What sort of people are they becoming? What are they doing, and how are they living in Stanleyville?

Most of them are getting some education. At the time of the survey more than half of the adult males had had at least one year of general schooling, and nearly four fifths of the boys between the ages of 6 and 15 were attending school. Even one third of the girls between those ages were attending school. But not many of them were as yet getting much education. "Only a minute proportion leave school equipped for the new life awaiting them," according to the UNESCO report. "The majority have not been trained for any particular trade and have no idea how to fit into a changing economy." Only 15 to 20 boys were being graduated each year from the Stanleyville technical school, out of a total working population of approximately 20,000. Not many Stanleyville Africans as yet see the need for much education. After putting a boy through five or six years of primary schooling the parents like to think that he has a claim to a white-collar job, if only that of a junior clerk. A girl after two or three years of primary schooling—if she gets as much as that—is generally thought to be wasting her time—and she probably is, in the context of the life her parents led when they were young.

Largely because of this limited schooling, most of those who are gainfully employed do work for which very little previous education or experience is required. They are laborers, night watchmen, messengers, and helpers to truck drivers, mechanics, masons and the like. Exact figures are unavailable, but the ratio of unskilled to total workers is perhaps four to five. The remaining 20 per cent of the labor force is made up of skilled and semiskilled wage earners (chauffeurs, mechanics, cobblers, masons, carpenters, painters, cooks, houseboys), white-collar employees (clerks, schoolteachers, medical orderlies, managers of European-owned shops serving Africans), and self-employed persons (shopkeepers, dealers in palm wine and beer, cultivators and so on).

What education can do—and does—for the worker is clearly
shown in Table 1. As more schooling becomes available—or

Table 1

PERCENTAGE DISTRIBUTION OF ADULT AFRICAN
MALES (16 PLUS) BY OCCUPATIONAL CATEGORY AND
LEVEL OF EDUCATION, STANLEYVILLE, BELGIAN
CONGO, MID-1950S

OCCUPATIONAL CATEGORY	YEARS OF GENERAL SCHOOLING				NUMBER
	0	1–3	4–6	6+	
Total	49.5	20.9	23.0	6.5	1,894
Unskilled wage earners	64.7	21.2	12.3	1.8	694
Skilled and semiskilled wage earners	43.4	25.2	28.8	2.6	812
White-collar employees	7.9	7.8	42.6	41.7	176
Self-employed	73.3	12.4	10.7	3.6	88
Not gainfully employed	48.2	17.0	25.9	8.9	124

Source: Jacques J. Maquet, quoting the preliminary report of
the UNESCO–International African Institute research team.

as some schooling becomes available to more people—the occupational status of the African may be expected to improve.
Indeed, it is already doing so. Thus, whereas 46.1 per cent
of the "first-generation" workers—those who began life in the
bush—were engaged in unskilled work at the time of the survey, only 27.7 per cent of the "second-generation" workers
were so engaged. The corresponding figures for those engaged
in skilled and semiskilled work were 46.3 and 53.5 per cent;
and for those in white-collar work, 7.6 and 18.8 per cent.
Where there has been an improvement in occupational status,
it is reflected in the worker's way of life: in the growing
amount of luxury spending being done (on such things as
radios, phonographs, tobacco and beer); in the unwillingness
of increasing numbers of white-collar workers to let their
wives live like bush women; and in the formation of workers'
councils and occupational unions—though it must be added

that it is European more often than African interest that so far has kept most of these alive.

Most of the Africans living in Stanleyville are still poorly off. The UNESCO investigators found the earnings of the majority "insufficient to enable [them] to feed well and live decently in an urban center." At the time of the survey most of the unskilled workers were getting less than 850 francs (approximately $17) a month, and most of the white-collar workers less than 1,750 francs ($35).[11] Many workers supplement their wages by income from family "side lines," covering everything from hawking fish caught in the Congo to hairdressing and laundering. On the other hand, it is only fair to say that many salaried workers were making more than 7,000 francs (approximately $140); that every worker was entitled to free dispensary and hospital treatment, and to receive from his employer the amount of the food ration and one quarter of his wage whenever he was certified sick. Further, every worker was insured by his employer against industrial accidents and occupational disease.

With the increasing attractiveness of urban employment, many Africans are coming to think of the city as a place where a man may make a permanent home, raise a family, form new associations, and fashion a new kind of community. Evidences of this line of thinking abound. The occupational ambitions of African school children show it clearly. Whereas 21 per cent of the primary school boys questioned on the subject expressed a desire to become mechanics of various sorts, 24 per cent a desire to become clerks and 30 per cent carpenters, only 6 per cent wanted to become farmers. Whereas 9 per cent of the secondary school boys questioned expressed a desire to become either doctors or medical assistants, 24 per cent teachers and 59 per cent clerks, only 2 per cent wanted to do manual work. Only 15 per cent of the primary school boys stated that they wanted to follow

[11] By way of comparison, the average monthly pay and allowances of the European civil servant (never overpaid!) was 37,500 francs, or approximately $750.

the work of their fathers (or brothers); as for the secondary
school boys, not even one per cent of them wanted to do as
their fathers did. The preferences expressed by girls attending primary school were even more "uncustomary." Thirty-
three per cent of those questioned wanted to become seam-
stresses, 21 per cent embroideresses, 21 per cent teachers, 10
per cent either nurses or midwives, 2 per cent nuns, while
13 per cent wanted nothing more than to go on with their
studies.

Equally far removed from tribal life were the preferences
expressed by educated grownups when questioned about their
choice of friends and about the kind of community they would
like to live in if they could choose freely. Already it is clear
that common interest is for many educated people at least as
strong a tie as "brotherhood" or kinship. Thus, 69 per cent of
the clerks questioned had a teacher, mechanic or clerk for
one or more of their three best friends. Only 35 per cent of
the drivers questioned had friends, one or more, in these occupational categories, and only 27 per cent of the unskilled
laborers questioned had such friends. Though the answers
given to the "kind of community" question were harder to
analyze statistically, they were on the whole "untribal" answers. "People can be of the same tribe, but have very different situations in life. Tribe is not enough." "You feel freer
when the tribes are mixed." "One must take into account
education, occupation, the home, the private life, decency,
wealth." Sentiments like these were expressed by *évolué* Africans often enough to constitute something of a trend.

The phenomenon of the voluntary association is also indicative. The African, ever a lover of tribal group activities,
ritualistic and recreational, secret or otherwise, is busying himself increasingly in the work of groups designed to fill the
empty hours—and the emptiness—of his new town life. He
has organized voluntary associations for almost everything
from "helping the dead" and getting more pay for the living
to promoting true religion and comradeship. In some of these
causes the women are as active as the men. A few associations
are open to both men and women—tribal apostasy if there

ever was! Some are single autonomous groups; others, like the Brotherhood of Congolese Veterans, form an integral part of large organizations. Almost all make a feature of mutual aid, and increasing numbers of them are interested in broadening the basis of membership and in fostering the moral and intellectual progress of the members along the still rough paths of their new social domain. And as the basis of membership of a given association broadens, the range of its interests ceases to be parochial, bound by tribal and regional attitudes of mind. Instead, as the UNESCO study notes, it becomes concerned with "the gradual integration of the various subgroups (ethnic, religious, professional . . .) of the urban centers' advanced community into a society as a whole."

At the same time, most of the Africans of Stanleyville still have more than half a foot in the bush. They may be urbanized, civilized and Christianized (or Moslemized, as many are), but very few of them are completely detribalized. There may have been some weakening of hereditary bonds and authority, but most of the traditional institutions of bush society, such as the kinship system, *rites de passage*, bride wealth, age sets and brotherhoods, retain their vigor. Few if any town families have renounced the customary bush practice of accommodating those of their kin, brotherhood and acquaintance to whom they are beholden. As in the bush, when "brothers" settle down on a man's compound, while waiting to find work or on the occasion of a visit, they are put up free. And as in the bush, the visit may last for the remainder of a lifetime. Even in *évolué* households, tribal values die hard. Thus, while many educated men try to get their wives to play the part of an equal—by sharing in the conversation of the table or by developing some outside interests—few have succeeded, and many say they have given up trying.

Most town dwellers, first and second generation alike, periodically go back to the bush, either for the pleasure of it or to honor tribal obligations. A large proportion of them belong to associations open only to persons of their own tribal or ethnic group. In such associations what counts is not so much a man's education, economic status or ability to speak French, as his knowledge of tribal custom and language, and the qualities of leadership prized by the tribe.

The durability of the old tribal bond is nowhere seen to better advantage than in marriage forms and procedures. A random sample study covering 77 case histories of marriage disclosed the following facts: (1) More than two thirds had married within the tribe. (2) Nearly nine tenths of the marriages were of the customary sort, binding not only the individuals but also the families or groups of relations; only about 11 per cent of them involved a religious (Christian or Moslem) ceremony. (3) Payments in cash or kind were made in all but one case, and in the case of more than one third (35.1 per cent), payment was made either partly or wholly in kind. (4) More than one fourth of the marriages had been arranged by members of the family. (5) More than half of the married persons questioned admitted to having been divorced one or more times—a ratio not substantially smaller, it would seem, than that prevailing in the bush. The grounds for divorce were, for the most part, the customary ones: loss of desire, desertion, refusal to live as man and wife, barrenness, neglect of household duties, quarreling, "in-law" troubles, habitual adultery and so on.

Even in regard to marriage, nevertheless, the old order has been coming in for its share of battery and assault. Increasing numbers of marriages break up because the parties concerned are drawn from different tribal backgrounds and fail to make the necessary adjustments. Increasing numbers of men resort to concubinage because of the exorbitant marriage money demanded of them. Increasingly, also, urban marriage is coming to be a matter for decision by the principals only, not by parents and clans.

But this is not to say that the old order, whether in marriage, home, village or community, whether in Stanleyville, the Teita Hills or the Cameroonian rain forest, is done for. If its days are numbered, nobody is telling—not even the sociologists.

THE TREND

Those who have spent any time studying them know that weather maps are always changing, and that the changes do not always agree with the predictions. Indeed, the weather seems to have an infinite capacity for confounding the experts. To study the phenomena of social change is not infrequently to come to the same opinion about man. He, too, is an inveterate innovator, and confounder. Even while we are measuring his mores, he is altering them, and the direction in which he alters them is not always the direction in which the sociologist is led to believe he will alter them. What follows should therefore be viewed more as an interpolation than an extrapolation—as an index of what has been happening rather than a prospectus of what is to come.

Increasing differentiation. There has been a notable differentiation between African and African. The primeval African was made in the image of the group, and the group was constantly on the lookout for imperfect images; it had no time for deviations. But the group mold is no longer what it was. Indeed, there is no longer a single mold. Instead there are many molds, each the work of different hands, incorporating different designs of what a man should be and how he should live. The look-alike African may not yet have gone, but he is no longer in production. His place is being taken by the distinguishable African: the miner and merchant; shop clerk and houseboy; politician and preacher; the Christian and the pagan; the schooled and the unschooled; the *évolué* and the elder; the progressive and the conservative.

Some groups, it is true, are working with more molds than others, and with molds of more radical design. But in every group new molds are being fashioned and new differentiations being achieved. Here and there the differentiating process has reached the point where a man now feels a closer kinship to men of other groups than to those of his own group. Many *évolués* in the French Community think of themselves as

Frenchmen rather than as Bulu or Bangi; outwardly at least, they live like Frenchmen. Some of the Stanleyville *évolués* would much prefer to live alongside Europeans than their own *non-évolué* kinsmen. Even among the Teita the Harrises came upon one man who contended, with vehemence, that he was nothing if not British. Each of the "new" countries now has people who are so far removed from the tribal mold as to think of themselves as men of Ghana and Nigeria rather than as men of Ashanti and Yoruba. Every territory has converts to Christianity who assume that because Europeans (or Americans) brought them their salvation, Europeanization is part of the price of it. Every territory, also, has many more who while not repudiating their cultural heritage are sufficiently far removed from it as to think of themselves—in the words of another Mteita—as "men of half-and-half."

These differentiations do not stop at the group level. They cut deep into villages and households, often separating generations more widely than tribal groups were separated in the precolonial era. Such differentiations spell divisions, and all too often divisions spell estrangement. Already there are places where the estrangement between African and African is as conspicuous as the estrangement between African and non-African. Wherever such estrangement is found it represents a gangrenous infection of an already deep social wound. Some of its manifestations are as tragic as they are shortsighted. There are Christians for whom all pagans are dirty and barbarous; pagans for whom all Christians are government "yes men" and traitors. There are students who treat their "boys" with disdain and thoughtlessness, the like of which is seldom seen in non-African households; illiterates who see in the wealth and status of their well-educated kinsmen only an opportunity to live an easier life than they have ever known. There are husbands who abandon their wives and families because they cannot talk their language or share their interests; wives and families who make no attempt to learn the man's language or share his interests. There are farmers who, by following the white man's advice, become wealthier than their neighbors—only to have their cattle stolen and their storehuts and houses burned down. And there are some who are willing to kill in order to keep a man from dishonoring his ancestors.

Not all differentiations lead to estrangement. Some lead to emulation. Ask a group of school children to draw a man or a woman and the chances are that, even if they are bush children, they will draw a European figure, complete with hat, umbrella and cigarette and, in the case of a woman, high-heeled shoes. Give a man who has just learned to read the run of a bookshop and the books he will first ask for are those that tell him "How To"—how to do everything from becoming a mechanic, an accountant or a medical assistant to winning friends and influencing people the way his political leaders do.

But the course of the emulator is not easy. Frequently the man who aspires to run it has no idea how long it is or how difficult, let alone how much is expected of him over and above the piece of parchment, the passport, the suit of clothes or the bank balance that symbolizes for him his successful completion of it. Frequently, too, he has little idea how small are his chances of being able to exploit the status he has emulated and acquired, either because of his unwillingness to put expediency before principle and pride before honor or because of somebody else's prejudice, conceit or fear.

Increasing selectivity. There is a growing disinclination by the educated African to believe that Europe, or the West, has the final answer to his social problems. It is not that he is unaware of his indebtedness to Western missions, medicine, engineering, welfare and administration. He knows—none better —that without these he would still be groping his way through a roadless, hospital-less, unproductive, ungoverned and ungovernable jungle. Nor is it that he wants "to go it alone" from now on, fortified with the white man's technology but unwilling to take his advice. On the contrary, he knows—again none better—that there simply are not enough of his kind to do all the complicated things that must be done if his now useful lands are not to be given back to the jungle. However, he is no longer entirely content to conduct his affairs according to the white man's prescription.

The following are straws of evidence. First, the appeal of what the sociologist calls syncretistic movements. In the realm of religion alone there are said to be over a thousand sects in the southern part of Africa, from the Rhodesias to the Cape, most of them nominally Christian but almost all of them incorporating, in varying amounts, pagan ritual and belief. Second, and related, the appearance of such overtly anti-white movements as Watu wa Mungu (People of God) and Mau Mau in Kenya and Kimbanguism and Kitawala in the Belgian Congo. Third, the reluctance of many well-educated Africans to abandon belief in witchcraft, sorcery, divination, and the importance of keeping in with one's ancestors, and in magic generally when sitting for an examination. (Camara Laye, the author of *The Dark Child*, apparently set as much store by the magic liquid given to him by his teacher as by the quality of the instruction he had received.) Fourth, the difficulty of getting Africans to believe that Western ways of dealing with civil and criminal offenses are either as expeditious or as acceptable to the offender as tribal ways. Fifth, the rather poor showing to date of the higher Western virtues in the conduct of business. When asked by Elspeth Huxley what he thought would happen after the Europeans withdrew, a prominent African replied that the climate of his continent was not too favorable to the spirit of puritanism. "It needs a cold winter . . . You never find it in the sunny countries—Spain, Italy, South America . . . It may be that we shall revert to more human standards."[12] Sixth, and perhaps most significant of all, the continuing strength of indigenous forms of self-expression in music, dancing, singing and the plastic arts, notwithstanding the appeal of Western forms of art and entertainment.

No doubt it takes more than a handful of straws to thatch a theory, but two or three are usually enough to tell which way a wind is blowing—at least which way it is blowing *from*.

[12] Elspeth Huxley, "Two Revolutions That Are Changing Africa," *New York Times Magazine*, May 19, 1957.

And since even meteorologists name the wind for the quarter from which it comes—never the one to which it appears to be going—perhaps we who study the winds that sweep across the face of society should exercise similar caution. The strongest "prevailing" winds fail from time to time; and today's trends have a habit of being tomorrow's retractions.

CHAPTER 2

THE ASSAULT ON IGNORANCE

Nobody can travel in tropical Africa without soon being made aware of the importance attached by the African to learning. Ask a hundred literate men what they consider to be the greatest need of their people, and ninety will unhesitatingly reply "education." Ask a hundred schoolboys what they want to be and at least one fourth of them are likely to reply, "Either an education officer or a schoolteacher." In education the African politician sees the key to better government; the African businessman, the key to greater output and higher consumption; the African welfare worker, the key to happier, healthier living.

Nor is this zeal to educate and be educated confined to the lettered. The enthusiasm of the unlettered is frequently just as great. On a wet morning it is not unusual in some places to see a crowd of children waiting hopefully outside a village school on the off-chance that the teacher will allow them to occupy the seats of those who have been kept away by the rain. On any evening in almost any African town, grown men and women may be seen studying reading primers by the light of a candle or a street lamp. Even in the deepest bush, where none can read or write, it is not uncommon to find communities that have either gone so far as to build their own school with the help of donated labor and materials—sometimes before they knew where the teacher was coming from —or managed to underwrite the cost of sending some of their brightest youngsters to a distant mission school.

This is not to say that all Africa is hungering for the white man's learning. Many people have had as yet no chance to savor it; they are still subject to all the sanctions, constraints and limitations of their indigenous culture. For some it has lost the savor it once had, if for them it ever held more than a passing appeal. "Africans educated in Europe—very able men at that—frequently 'go native' on returning home, for Western culture is at best a thin veneer." The words were spoken by a high government official in Mozambique, but the phenomenon is by no means confined to that territory. Many are sincerely afraid of the white man's learning. These see it only as a destroyer of their social solidarity, as an *agent provocateur* sent to spread confusion of tongues, disaffection and self-contempt. They admire its "magic"—its medicines, machines, illustrated magazines and so on; but they deplore its meanness—its barely concealed scorn for their customs and laws, its impatience with their beliefs, values and patterns of behavior, and its insensitivity to their standards of beauty in natural forms, art and language. They suspect, if indeed they do not know, that because they are unlettered, they are in the European's eyes unlearned and therefore the target of his educational enthusiasm; and that the longer they are exposed to that enthusiasm, the greater the risk of losing their cultural identity—a prospect that no man can view with equanimity.

But whether there is hunger for the white man's learning or not, there is everywhere a realization of the importance of the learning process in fitting a people for the responsibilities of life. There may have been few schools in Africa, as we know schools, until the missionaries arrived; there may have been fewer books and alphabets until more recently still; but if education be defined as the whole process by which one generation transmits its culture to the next, then there has been no lack of education in Africa. On the contrary, Africans have shown themselves second to none in the punctilious pursuit of this end. They neglected no phase of life—economic, ethical, sexual, artistic, familial—and they deemed no discipline too harsh or sacrifice too great to ensure the safekeeping of their cultural heritage. In content and method African schooling may have had little or nothing in common with its European counterpart, but it provided a matrix in which the latter could develop and a mental atmosphere in which it could thrive. Part of the success which has attended the endeavors of the Western educator in Africa during the past one hundred years or so arises from the tradition of tribal instruction which he found and the esteem in which men versed in the lore of their peoples were characteristically held. A part of the commonly observed resistance to modern ideas and methods is an expression of that same esteem.

EDUCATIONAL AGENCIES

To look for the beginnings of formal education in Africa we must go back much further than a hundred years. As early as the eleventh century the Mohammedans had established schools, where children were taught to read and write Arabic and to repeat verses from the Koran, at many important sub-Saharan caravan centers. There were similar schools, at about the same epoch, at the Arab ports of call along the east coast from Mogadishu to Sofala. The interest of the West in the educational needs and potential of the African likewise goes back a long way, certainly to the thirteenth century. In his *Blanquerna* (1283), Raymond Lull, the Catalan mystic, tells of a mission which the Pope of his day sent to the lands of the Sahara, and which "by the grace of God" led to the conversion of "the Saracen King, and a great number of people."[1]

It was, however, many decades before the West did anything more than skirt the edges of the African's mind. When, in the nineteenth century, it did at length come to grips with the challenge of "heathen darkness," it was the churches which took the initiative. Frequently their men—doctors, teachers, translators and priests—bored into the interior before any other men; frequently they worked without the assurance of civil support or protection. It is they, and the women who went with them, who, ever since that time, have held the initiative; who have reduced hundreds of African languages to writing (over 400 already); who have provided most of the vernacular literature, and not only Bibles and Testaments either; who have developed most of the mass-ed-

[1] *Blanquerna*, A. Peers' edition, p. 356.

ucation techniques and been behind most of the literacy campaigns. It was they who built most of the early hospitals and trained most of the African laboratory technicians and nurses. It is they who still man most of the schools.

Governments and missions. Until recent years the role of metropolitan and territorial governments in the field of education was, understandably, no more than modest. Prior to World War II the budgets of almost all of the territories were small. By the time law and order had been enforced, roads built and repaired, endemic diseases kept in check, and postal and telegraph services established, not much money was left for education. Notwithstanding, some of the colonial governments had begun to accept partial responsibility for the planning, direction and coordination of education in their territories well before 1939. In doing so they were guided by two things. First, by the realization that the results of the well-intentioned but often amateurish and sometimes bigoted work of the missionary were uneven, and, as one government memorandum of the time worded it, "not . . . altogether satisfactory." Second, by a growing conviction that the success or failure of their civilizing mission turned upon the quality of the education the indigenous peoples received—upon their grasp of the goals, their willingness to cooperate in winning them, and their ability to do the things required of them—and that they were more likely to get the desired education if the control of it was not left entirely in the hands of people who were answerable only to their consciences, or their sponsoring societies.

With the general principle of government support of primary and, to a lesser extent, secondary education, most mission societies have long agreed. They had little to lose by agreeing, except the sense of independence (and this was often more imagined than real in view of the chronic difficulty many of them have had in raising their budgets), since almost all governments view the educational work of the missions as indispensable. On the other hand, they had much to gain by agreeing, for agreement meant better buildings and equipment, greater administrative efficiency, higher scholastic standing and, not least, better-qualified teachers. All the same, some missions have hesitated to accept financial help, lest they become identified with the state. And some of those that show no such hesitation are beginning to find that as the role of the government increases so does the volume of paper work and the amount of attention given to secular studies, with consequent curtailment of their evangelistic and pastoral activities.

Whatever happens in the future, one thing is certain: government schools have come to stay, in Africa as elsewhere in the world. The missions do not command the funds that are necessary to provide the African with the trade schools, demonstration shops, experimental farms, colleges and universities he expects, and needs if he is to assume the leadership of his own people. If they did, they would not be able to fill the posts from within their own ranks. As it is, many mission schools are indifferently staffed, and the flow of new recruits is quite inadequate. Yet the need for teachers who have something more to share with the African than a knowledge of things, theories and techniques was never more widely affirmed, by administrator, student and missionary alike. There would certainly be deep regret in many council chambers were the missions compelled or persuaded to relax their educational effort. Kenneth Bradley, himself an "African" veteran with more than twenty years' administrative service, expresses, in a paper prepared for this study, a common conviction when he says that "the greatest contribution which the West has made and will continue to make to Africa is Christianity . . . [for] all education for citizenship must, if democracy is to be true and lasting, be firmly based on sound religion. Our fathers who . . . left education to the missions because in those days their embryo governments were very poor, builded better than they knew."

Bradley does not speak for all, needless to say. There are many, mostly Westerners, who have no use for the mission school, or what it stands for. In their view it is the nursery of discontents that cannot be appeased; it teaches ideas of equality and brotherhood that have no place in the African's world and no justification in theirs; it tends to confuse dogma with truth, and to teach Christianity with the same authority as physics and arithmetic. There are many, mostly Africans, who see in the mission school the destroyer of "traditional sanctions which previously ensured good behavior"; the "instrument of imperialism" (all the more so since most of the schools have come to be subsidized by the "imperial" governments), and in its expatriate teachers the paid agents of a religion that sets "a man at variance against his father, . . . the daughter against her mother and the daughter-in-law against her mother-in-law." Both groups would like to see the schools taken away from the missions. Some, it seems, would like to see them taken away from the government.

Private secular schools. So far private schools have not had much of an inning in Africa. Most of those that exist serve the privileged few who can afford to pay the high fees and who do not care to, or cannot, send their children to either the mission- or government-run schools. A few, however, serve a very different purpose, one that most missions and governments find difficulty in viewing with pleasure. These are the nativistic, and syncretistic, schools that have as their aim the preservation of as much of the old customs, laws and beliefs as is necessary to satisfy the African's self-esteem and to ensure his survival, as an African, in an increasingly un-African world.

Until the Mau Mau emergency of 1952 several dozen such schools were operating in Kenya alone. The most notable and numerous of these schools, the Kikuyu Independent Schools, came into existence as a result of the unwillingness of many Kikuyu Christians to discontinue, as required by their mission church, the custom of clitoridectomy. Since this was regarded "as a vital part of Kikuyu religion and social practice"—to quote Kimani Waiyaki, a Kikuyu and the author of a paper prepared especially for this study—"the elderly Kikuyu converts interpreted the church's attack on the custom as a condemnation of the whole Kikuyu social order." They therefore

revolted against the "foreign" church and established one of
their own which legalized polygamy and the drinking of alcoholic beverages (both of which were proscribed by the missions in question) along with clitoridectomy. And they decided, Waiyaki says, that the best way in which "the gap
between Christianity and Kikuyu tribal life could be bridged
was by taking only those things from Christianity that could
enhance Kikuyu culture" and teaching them in schools of their
own. The schools they were able to build and operate with
their meager funds were poor, even by the poorest of mission
school standards, but they were the Kikuyu's own. The teachers were Kikuyu; the curriculum was Kikuyu-designed; its objective was to foster Kikuyu solidarity. The popularity of these
schools, it is claimed by Waiyaki, was due to the fact that
"they aimed at developing Africans who are proud of their
culture and . . . who want to be free."

Such movements have occurred elsewhere. Wherever Africans suspect that the European is, as Waiyaki puts it, out to
"produce Africans who are ashamed of being Africans," they
do not lack for followers. As more and more Africans in the
dependent countries become able to articulate their hopes for
their people and their fears of continuing subjection to the
white man's educational philosophies, interest in the independent type of school is sure to increase. It is unlikely to
have the same appeal to those Africans who can foresee the
day of self-government. Among these and among those who
are already self-governing, private schools of the European
type have more chance of finding favor. Already many well-
to-do Africans send their older children to such schools in
Europe and elsewhere.

Also falling in the "private" category—in the sense that admission to them is restricted—are the schools maintained by
some of the larger corporations. Corporations like the Union
Minière du Haut-Katanga and the Société des Mines d'Or
de Kilo-Moto (both of the Belgian Congo) have consistently
held that education was part of their business; that they could
not hope to build up an efficient work force unless they had
the means of training it; and that they would be most un-

likely to recruit the children of their workers unless they could provide school facilities at least equal to the best available in the larger towns. This they have done, with profit to themselves in higher output and smaller turnover, and to their employees in a better, longer and fuller life than most of their fellow countrymen enjoy.

SOME OF THE PROBLEMS

Educational advance is beset, always and everywhere, with difficulties. If anything, tropical Africa has rather more than its share of difficulties and a greater capacity for slowing down the rate of educational advance than most places. Indeed, there can be few parts of the world where small difficulties develop into large problems with such ease and resist solution so obstinately. The problems are of many kinds and show no particular preference for people or place. Most of them, however, fall into four categories: environmental, social, financial and philosophical.

Environmental. Tropical Africa does not suffer the intruder gladly, whether he comes armed with axe, bulldozer, blueprint or Bible. If he is not careful, and knowledgeable, he may find that he has misjudged the pleasure of the land and its inhabitants. The educator may find that the site of a bush school has to be selected with due regard not only for soil drainage, ease of access and availability of building material, but also for the wishes of the local headman and his favorite fetisher, and the habits of mosquitoes and larger fauna. He may find that one of the most stubborn entries in his school accounts is one he had never thought of before going to Africa: dilapidation of fabric, building and supplies due to torrential rainstorm, mildew, moth and termite. If his planning of the school calendar does not accord with the calendar of the farmers around him, he will find that his pupils vanish when the first rains fall and the planting season begins. A washout on the road has prevented many a tutor from reaching his weekly adult education class.

More serious is the debilitating effect, aggravated by the intestinal diseases from which most Africans suffer, of the high humidities and monotonously high temperatures of the rainy season. Habituated though many of Africa's indigenous peoples are to heat and moisture, they are palpably discomfited by them, as, of course, is the European. Statistical evidence of the loss of intellectual drive resulting from exposure to such conditions is harder to come by than evidence of the slowing down of manual processes, but clerks, ministers, teachers and students are wont to speak with a common voice on the subject, whether they live in Nigeria, the Belgian Congo or Sudan. The following extract from a letter written in the Belgian Congo to the author is only too typical: "I am finding that I need all the rest I can get now. [The writer was a strapping twenty-seven at the time.] Three years in the wet and warm climate of the equatorial forest seem to sap one's energy thoroughly, and I shall be quite ready for my turn for furlough next April. Not that I am not fit, for, apart from a couple of attacks of bacillary dysentery and a malarial fever, I have kept very well; but the chronic fatigue which assails particularly the medical staff who fail to practise what they preach in the matter of regular rest at night is becoming a reality to me just now." Other manifestations of impaired mental efficiency are the so-called "west coast memory" that Africans and Europeans of that section frequently cite in extenuation of their verbal lapses, and the common confession of expatriate teachers in west African colleges that their best research work is done while on furlough in Europe.

It is not only the equatorial lowlands that make life difficult for the educator. The highlands are an unaccommodating environment, too. Although they are not afflicted with prolonged periods of oppressive heat or perpetually high humidities, the wide diurnal range of temperature, coupled with the rarefaction of the atmosphere and the associated intensity of actinic rays, puts a strain on the system.

Social. Educational problems having their origin in the African's way of life—in his attitudes toward land and kin, his valuation of leisure, comfort and commodities, and his regard for the world of spirits—are at once the most numerous and the most serious. The administrator finds them wherever he goes, and among all sorts of men. Rather than disappear when people have learned to read and write, they may become more acute.

The problem of educating an African girl is one that Rebecca Reyher discusses at length in her working paper. In the first place, there is the problem of getting the girl inside a school. Outside the towns, most parents contend that all a girl needs to know of such matters as cleanliness, good manners, industry in the house and field, sex, morality and family living, they or the initiation schools are capable of teaching her. They are also likely to say that the things she might learn in a white man's school could bring them and her future husband no profit, if indeed they might not make her less docile and effective in the performance of her wifely duties. If the parents are willing to enroll the girl—as more and more are, especially in the towns—they will still need to be persuaded of the advantages of keeping her in school after she has reached the age of puberty. Since a marriageable daughter is quite likely to be one of their chief "capital assets," it is asking much of them to deny themselves such advantage as an early marriage contract may confer.

If the parents are willing to allow their daughter to complete both primary and secondary school courses and go on to college, other problems arise. What shall she be taught, and for what shall she be trained? For a profession? Unquestionably the need for women trained in teaching, nursing, medicine and so on is great; the facilities exist, and the compensations are considerable. But in many parts of tropical Africa the one respectable profession is still marriage; and the earlier the marriage, the more respectable. Where this holds, a girl who enters a profession and remains unmarried soon gains a reputation for easy virtue. In some tribes, such as the Sukuma of Tanganyika, where girls are allowed much sexual liberty before marriage and where even having an illegitimate child is not considered unseemly, this may not cause anxiety or prejudice the chances of a good marriage later. But in other tribes, such as the Sumbwa, where virginity at marriage is highly prized, the entry of a girl into a profession tells badly against her, as does any kind of advanced training, academic or otherwise. As a result girls are still scarce on most college campuses. Makerere College, at Kampala, Uganda, graduated its first Kenya woman student (an Mteita) only in June 1958.

A solution to this problem is not easy to find. It is nonetheless necessary if the security of the African home is not to be imperiled. At the present time, for every thousand well-educated men in tropical Africa there are less than ten well-educated women. Most of the educated men must therefore marry women with whom they have nothing in common, save perhaps the desire for children. The embarrassment of the educated Westernized man married to an illiterate woman who still follows her African folkways is matched only by the woman's inability to sense his pride and share his thoughts. There are those who believe that the illiteracy of the Kikuyu women is partly responsible for the evils of Mau Mau. If the women, with the innate conservatism common to their sex, had been able to share in the discussion of the troubles that lay upon the land, they would have been able, it is contended, to curb the more violent and unreasonable political aspirations of their menfolk. Certainly they would not have been the first wives to counsel moderation, or the first to keep their husbands from going to war.

No less an educational problem is posed by the African's regard for taboo, juju and the like, and the Westerner's determination to eradicate it along with all other evidences of ignorance and superstition. One can teach children, or adults, the food value of an egg, but it is hard to persuade people to eat eggs when they have been brought up to believe that they make a man impotent and a woman barren. One can show that two well-favored cows yield more milk than any ten scrawny and diseased animals, but it is hard to persuade the owner of the ten to switch from herding to dairy farming. Any teacher can explain, and most students can be made to understand, the principles of combustion, but few students seem to know how to apply the teacher's reasoning when it comes to finding out why a particular combustion engine doesn't work. The common approach to machines is still essentially magical.

In their desire to root out ignorance and superstition, many educators have overlooked the good that flourishes along with the bad, to the African's deep resentment and their own bedevilment. Kimani Waiyaki speaks for many of his generation, and not only in Kenya, when he says that the disparagement of African culture has been "one of the fundamental weaknesses of educational practice" there and that the resulting mental havoc is all the more serious because the Kenya African is coming to regard education "as the panacea of all his ills." Europeans generally have taken a poor view of indigenous African education. They have made very little attempt to discriminate between the forms which that education takes and the aims behind it, which are often not so very different from their own. As Elizabeth Hoyt says in a magazine article,[2] "They have seen the outer framework, which they did not like, rather than the urge to self-development which is there also." They have been quick to point out the defects of the social organization which the African has established for himself, but slow to give him the credit, Miss Hoyt adds, for "trying to organise something for himself and others which fits the situation as *he sees it*," often at considerable sacrifice of his time and resources.

The Kikuyu Independent Schools are a case in point. Not the least of their intended functions was the preservation of the good in Kikuyu culture and the bridging of the gap between the Kikuyu and Western worlds. Unfortunately, most Europeans were unable to see any good in the movement. They condemned it as pedagogically unsound, as nativistic, exploitative, and, when the Mau Mau trouble arose, as subversive. There was substance in all these accusations; but there might have been less had the Europeans, at the outset,

[2] "The Spender's Choice," *Corona*, September 1954.

helped to combine the advantages of Western education with Kikuyu tradition.

Similar situations arise wherever people with a mission go to people with a need; and the more palpable the need, the greater the temptation to write prescriptions. In tropical Africa the educational need is so obvious and compelling that it calls for extraordinary humility and perception in the "missionary" not to assume that the things worth preserving in the indigenous system are so small a part of the whole that no great harm can be done, and much time can be saved, by not attempting to preserve any of it. It is much the same as when an African prefers to destroy a rat-infested house rather than spend time hunting for the rats, the main difference being that the African succeeds in harming nobody, not even the rats.

However, we can be of good courage. There is mounting evidence, Miss Hoyt assures us, that the educator, along with his professional colleagues in sociology, anthropology and the missions, is learning to discern "the difference between the constructive and generous action of a people seeking self-expression and the mistakes which in their ignorance they may easily make, and the perversion of their action by the unscrupulous." He, with his colleagues, is beginning to understand that the willingness of a people "to sacrifice so much for such causes is proof of their idealism, and [that] it is the obligation of policy-makers to see that the creative core of such idealism is preserved and fostered."

Financial. Almost all countries have trouble raising money for education; those of tropical Africa certainly have. The needs of the place are so many and per capita incomes so low that governments have tended rather naturally to give priority to enterprises promising early returns. Casting bread upon the waters of ignorance is not usually numbered among such enterprises; the returns come only after many days—indeed, years. Yet the cost of ignorance is such that no territory concerned with the long-range good of its peoples can afford to bear it. For just as knowledge is power, ignorance is weakness; and weakness is poverty—poverty of ideas, skills and ambition, if not of resources.

In these days there is little that a poor country can do, unaided, to redeem its life from ignorance. The kind of knowledge poor countries need most—applied knowledge—must be imported. This costs money, and in tropical Africa money goes very little further than it does elsewhere in the world. Judged by the criterion of hourly rates African labor is cheap, but most employers prefer to measure it by other criteria. They are more interested in such things as hourly output, turnover, care and maintenance of equipment. By these criteria the labor showing is not so good. Although many of the materials used in the construction and equipment of schools can often be obtained locally at small cost, almost all laboratory supplies, books, writing materials and instruments have to be brought in from great distances. So, too, have most of the senior grades of secondary school and college teachers. Because of this, almost every secondary school and college must make provision in its budget for periodic furloughs with all expenses paid, and for early pensioning of some members of its faculty. Those teachers who do not have to be "imported" have, in many instances, to be trained abroad, which likewise costs money. There must also be provision, in many parts of Africa, for the rapid depreciation of buildings and supplies.

How to snap the crippling chain of ignorance-weakness-poverty-ignorance has long been one of the most disconcerting questions to confront African administrators. It is still not resolved; but at least all governments are agreed upon the necessity of resolving it. Almost without exception, they are now spending far more money on education than they were doing at the end of the war. In some countries expenditures on education have come to constitute the largest single item in the territorial budget. In Nigeria the three regions (Eastern, Western and Northern) each spent about one third of their ordinary budgets on education in 1956–1957; and they have spent approximately one fifth of their capital budgets for the 1955–1960 period on educational projects. In Liberia, long the most illiterate of African countries, between one tenth and one fifth of the budget is currently earmarked for "public instruction." This is not to say that any one government is spending enough to break the chain, let alone exorcise the evil spirits that dance upon it. The revenue of Tanganyika in 1957–1958 amounted to some $65 million, or less than $8 per capita; of the eight dollars less than two were available for educational purposes.

To increase the national income of such countries to the point where universal primary schooling, to say nothing of secondary schooling, becomes a feasible goal is obviously going to be difficult, if not impossible, unless it is bolstered from outside sources. Thanks to the development funds made available by the metropolitan countries and the growing conviction that the best, and perhaps the only, way to win the uncommitted African over to the democratic camp is to educate him fully and fast, this is, in fact, happening. The postwar grants made by the Belgians, British and French for primary and higher education have been generous by any standard. In the view of people on the spot, some of them were too generous and made too soon. As evidence they point to the needless elegance, as they see it, of the new university colleges and the difficulties they are having in filling them with students of good caliber. The ability of countries like Ethiopia and Liberia to find money has been less conspicuous. They have no rich relatives; however, since World War II they have been receiving considerable sums for educational purposes from United States government agencies. And some of the colonial territories (notably the British and Belgian) have had windfalls from such American agencies as the Carnegie Corporation of New York, the Ford Foundation and the Rockefeller Foundation.

Sooner or later, adventitious aid of this sort is bound to come to an end. Neither the metropolitan countries nor American agencies can be expected to subsidize African education indefinitely, and it is clear that they have no intention of doing so. Their function is essentially that of pump primers. They hope, by injecting enough education of the right kind, to stimulate a flow of trained men and women sufficient to transform the countries of their concern from their present poor and underdeveloped state into countries that are not only viable economically but autonomous culturally and socially, if not in every case politically.

Realizing that the day of ready money would, sooner or later, end, both the benefactors and beneficiaries have been giving thought to the question of cutting education costs. Thus, the basic education campaigns which UNESCO and other agencies have been conducting rely as far as possible (which, alas, does not always amount to very much) on the enthusiasm of the newly literate and his readiness to pass on freely what he has learned. The Laubach technique of teaching illiterates likewise requires few paid instructors, little equipment and less organization.[3] Even many of the regular grade schools are contriving to keep costs very low by employing teachers with no more than six or seven years' education, and curtailing the curriculum to reading (from a couple of books or so), writing (on slates and in sand) and a little blackboard arithmetic. At the secondary, technical and college levels cost cutting is much more difficult. To be worthy of its name, higher education must be in the hands of highly qualified teachers—teachers, that is, who have had a long and expensive education. It must provide the student with facilities for conference and debate, for laboratory, library and field work, and for extracurricular activity. But it is hard to confer without privacy or to act without "props," and quite impossible to browse without books or to experiment without equipment. Moreover, the certificates and diplomas which are among the most highly prized dividends of such an education must be of international currency. No African would long be content with a medical diploma that gave him professional standing only among his own people—and why should he be?

[3] Basically, the "each one teach one" technique developed by Dr. Frank C. Laubach consists in finding a symbol for each sound in a language, and learning to visualize, by means of readily identifiable pictures, key syllables and words formed by such sounds.

For all these reasons higher education is costly and its rate of expansion slow.

While the European administrators are generally resigned to this, many of the Africans are not. They demand universal primary education; technical and professional training facilities for all who can profit by them; and vocational and non-vocational courses for every willing adult. And they want all of it in a hurry. Consequently, they are inclined to belittle the difficulties and dangers of accelerating the rate of educational progress; to believe that a third-rate teacher is better than no teacher; and to argue that it is preferable to crowd a thousand children into a school intended for five hundred and give them half a schooling than to give half of them no schooling at all. In a still largely illiterate world, it is hard not to sympathize with them. Yet it is impossible to agree with them, for in our immensely complex world there are few more dangerous persons than the undereducated—those who have acquired the jargon of education but little skill in the exercise of it, who are bloated with knowledge but barren of wisdom.

Where dilution of educational standards is being countenanced, as it is in some territories, it is already causing concern to members of the African elite as well as to Europeans. Because money is short, salaries are low. Frequently they are too low to attract and hold the more intelligent and better-educated person, who finds no difficulty in getting bigger money, often for less work, in industry, commerce or the civil service. For the same reason, the supply of textbooks and materials is often quite inadequate. It is by no means unknown for students to prepare for an examination by first copying out whole sections of the set textbook, simply because there are too few books to go around. In Nigeria the Reverend James H. Robinson of New York came upon a student who had prepared himself for his examination in the New Testament by first writing out in longhand all four Gospels and the Acts of the Apostles.[4]

[4] *New York Times*, June 30, 1954.

It is entirely possible that, as his standards of living advance, the African's ability to contribute more largely to the education of his children will increase. To judge from his past performance in finding school fees, his willingness to go on doing so can hardly be in doubt. Whether he will be allowed to do so is another matter. Throughout most of the developed world free primary and secondary, if not as yet college, education is regarded as a child's birthright. The peoples of the underdeveloped African world can hardly be expected to settle for less without a struggle. On the social and economic level there is likewise much to be said for free education. At present the local boy who makes good at school or college with the help of his family's savings, including perhaps those of his aunts and uncles, cousins and grandparents, is likely to find himself paying off his indebtedness for years thereafter. No sooner does he start to earn his living than the erstwhile beneficiary becomes the benefactor. Some of his relatives may even move in on him indefinitely. Small wonder that many school and college graduates ask their employers to post them as far away as possible from their families. On the other hand, it must be conceded that many Africans have difficulty in believing that something worth having can be got for nothing. One of the commonest complaints voiced by administrators is that "the African is slow to learn the value of a free service"; once education is free, they contend, he will cease to esteem it as highly as he now does. "This," says Kenneth Bradley in the paper already referred to, "is one of those psychological factors which are so important in Africa and which give rise to so much ignorant criticism elsewhere."

Very likely, many years will pass before the economy of tropical Africa as a whole is robust enough to support the heavy cost of universal free education. If by then there are still any dependent territories, the chances are that they will get it first, because independence has a nasty habit of taking the wind out of a nation's financial sails.

Philosophical. By now it will be apparent that there is hardly an educational problem in tropical Africa that does not force one to consider the question of ends. The environments and cultures of Africa are different from those of Europe and North America; they make radically different demands upon the people and elicit very different responses from them. No educator can possibly ignore these demands and responses. But what shall he do about them? Shall he adapt his curriculum to fit them? Or shall he endeavor to change them, Westernizing the African's land, life and livelihood alike? What shall he do about religion? Shall he try to winnow the good from the bad in African belief and practice, or shall he assume that nothing of either is worth the winnowing? What shall he do about the African's political aspirations? Shall he educate for self-government, for association or for servitude? If there is insufficient money to do all that he would like for the African, what kind of schools shall he run with the money he has? And so on, *ad infinitum*.

Philosophical questions of this kind are more easily asked than answered. Some of them have not yet been answered; others have been answered differently by different administrations; and there may be some that will simply have to be lived with. But at least we can begin to discern the directions in which answers to some of the questions are being sought.

THE EDUCATION OF THE SCHOOL-AGED

While there is wide agreement among the rulers and the ruled that education is the African's greatest need, there is no such agreement on the extent of the need, the manner of meeting it or the means for doing so. The differences of viewpoint arise from several causes. Some of them are geographical in origin. Thus, it is the climate more than any other single factor that accounts for the absence of a "white-settler" population in most of west Africa, and its presence in east and central Africa. In the former the question of multiracial schooling has never arisen and probably never will; in the latter it has become more important with the passage of time until today it is, in the opinion of some, the dominant policy issue. Then again, it is much easier to establish a good school system in a relatively well endowed, accessible and populous little country like Ghana than it is in a relatively poor, mountainous, unevenly peopled and large country like Ethiopia. Other differences are political in origin. The Portuguese, having no intention of handing over their provinces to the African, are less concerned to provide him with higher education on the metropolitan level (though, truth to tell, they already have a number of very fine high schools in Mozambique and Angola) than they are to provide him with first-class primary and trade schools, by means of which they can turn him into a highly skilled artisan. The French, on the other hand, have felt obliged, within the limits of their resources, to provide the African with schools not unlike those in France. There are religious differences, too. Thus, the presence of Mohammedan emirates in northern Nigeria led Lord Lugard in his original treaty with them to agree not to disturb the established religion by introducing Christian missions and mission schools. In central and southern Nigeria, which in Lugard's day was more pagan than Christian and more Christian than Mohammedan, the British did not feel themselves to be under any such obligation; as a result, there are today in the south many mission schools in which Mohammedans sit alongside Christians and pagans, even during the periods of religious instruction.

The French Community. The aim of French educational policy down to 1958 was very simple—namely, to make worthy French citizens of all the inhabitants of the French possessions south of the Sahara. To achieve this aim, the government argued that it must provide schooling in French, along the general lines of the metropolitan curriculum, and for everybody. To implement such an ambitious policy posed an enormous problem. The area administered—consisting of French West Africa, French Equatorial Africa, French Somaliland, Madagascar and the Trusteeship Territories of Togoland and French Cameroons—was more than fifteen times as large as metropolitan France. Its total population was approximately 33 million, or about 70 per cent as large as that of the mother country. Now that almost all the component parts of these territories are either autonomous members of the French Community or independent, some changes in their educational systems may be expected, but what those changes will be it is too early to say.

The people within this vast domain are widely scattered, much given to wandering and, for the most part, have not been greatly interested in French citizenship. With few exceptions they are too poor to support a heavy tax load. The languages and dialects are many. In what was French West Africa there are approximately a hundred, none of which is spoken or understood by a sufficient number of people to justify an attempt to make it the *lingua franca*. All of them are poor in the kinds of words and concepts with which the modern educator is concerned. Large sectors, moreover, are unattractive climatically, unpromising economically and all but inaccessible. It takes an uncommonly dedicated teacher to stand the cultural and physical isolation of the more primitive areas. While there are such teachers, the supply has never been equal to the demand, for few educated Africans, it seems, are willing to submit for long to such discipline.

Consequently, the French have found it impossible to provide in tropical Africa education on the scale on which it is available in France. Even today, there are still many disconcerting blanks on the primary school map, and with few exceptions only the bigger towns offer post-primary educational facilities. (See Table 2.) In 1957, in the whole of French *Afrique noire,* some 1.2 million children, out of 5 million of school age, were enrolled in European public or private schools. Of these, only about 5 per cent were enrolled in post-primary schools. In French Equatorial Africa out of a total enrollment of approximately 176,000 in 1957, only some 8,000 students were attending secondary or technical schools. In French West Africa the corresponding figures were 380,-000 and 20,000; in Madagascar, 332,000 and 19,000. Down to 1958 the only institution in the whole area offering academic and technical training at the university level was the

Table 2

FRENCH TROPICAL AFRICA: NUMBER OF PUBLIC AND
PRIVATE EDUCATIONAL INSTITUTIONS, JANUARY 1, 1957

TERRITORY	TOTAL	PRIMARY	TECHNICAL	SECONDARY	HIGHER
Total	9,263	8,454	460	342	7
Fr. West Africa	2,546	2,339	128	75	4
Fr. Equatorial Africa	1,254	1,126	93	35	0
(Fr.) Cameroons	2,504	2,370	68	66	0
(Fr.) Togo	478	465	6	7	0
Malagasy Rep. (Madagascar)	2,481	2,154	165	159	3

Source: *African Affairs* (French Embassy, Service de Presse et
d'Information, New York), May 1958, pp. 8–9.

University of Dakar. But even these figures represent a remarkable advance on those of the early postwar period.

The French might have had more schools and more children enrolled in them if they had cared less about quality.
But they have consistently striven to maintain metropolitan
standards, particularly at the post-primary levels. And not
without success, for it is claimed that neither the African nor
the European students attending high schools in the overseas
territories find it difficult as a rule to "make the grade" when
they switch to similar schools, or go on to college work, in
France. Certainly, few concessions are made to the color of a
man's skin or to his cultural background. To become a university student, a teacher or a doctor, an African must have
all the paper qualifications a Parisian would have. He is also
expected to have much the same grasp of the French language as the Parisian.

Almost the only kind of concession the French have been
willing to make is to the African's physical setting. As far
back as 1920, Albert Sarraut, Minister for Colonies, advised
his governors and governors-general that "while it is unques-

tionably necessary to have an élite, selected strictly on the basis of their proven capacities [and given every] access to the higher spheres of learning and [opportunity for] the complete development of personality, it is also important to bear in mind from the very first the economic utility of education for the masses, and efforts should be directed toward insuring above all a full development of primary, technical and vocational education."[5] The desirability of teaching the African how to live better has been stressed from time to time in later declarations of policy. It finds its expression today in the increasing attention that is being paid in primary and technical school curricula to husbandry, health and hygiene, and to indigenous arts and crafts.

By proceeding in this way the French held it would be possible "to avoid a disequilibrium which would be fatal to society and to the indigenous family," and to ensure "the formation of an indigenous élite which will be called upon to fill an increasing number of jobs in commerce, industry and administration."[6]

To serve this conception of its educational responsibility, the French government developed various types of schools. At the primary level, the "standard model" has been the six-grade school, the leading functions of which are to make the student literate and to equip him, according to its location, for life in the bush or in the town. A good many "substandard" schools still offer only a two-to-three-year curriculum.

At the post-primary level, there are technical and vocational schools, secondary schools, higher technical schools, teacher-training schools, and the University of Dakar.

The technical and vocational schools offer courses varying in length from three to six years. These courses are designed "to give young Africans greater familiarity with modern developments and techniques in agriculture, industry and com-

[5] Circular by Minister for Colonies, Albert Sarraut, to the Governors-General and Governors of the Colonies, October 10, 1920.

[6] United Nations, *Non-Self-Governing Territories: Summaries and Analyses of Information Transmitted to the Secretary-General during 1949*, New York, 1950, p. 172.

merce."[7] Satisfactory completion of the three-year course wins a "certificate of professional aptitude"; of the longer courses, a teaching diploma.

The secondary schools offer a three-year course (roughly equivalent to the first three years of high school in the American system) leading to a certificate (*Brevet d'Etudes du Premier Cycle*), and a further three-year course leading to the *Baccalauréat*, which is generally reckoned to put the student on a par academically with a junior at the average American university. The principal aim of these courses has been to provide a cadre of men and women capable of assuming responsibility for the efficient running of the public services of the communities in which they live.

The higher technical schools offer work at approximately the freshman and sophomore levels, in a wide variety of subjects including surveying, electronics, the repair and maintenance of machinery, roads and other public works, and agriculture. Graduating students are awarded the *Baccalauréat Technique*. To handle the rapid postwar expansion of primary education and the demand for more teachers, the government established, often with very considerable assistance from the missions, normal schools in various parts of its African dependencies, and introduced "continuation programs" in many of its secondary schools.

The University of Dakar also had its origins in the postwar surge of educational interest. Starting, in 1950, as the Institute of Higher Studies with modest facilities and a very small enrollment, it now has more than a thousand students enrolled in three faculties (science, liberal arts, and law and economics) and the National School of Medicine and Pharmacy. Its campus, on the western shore of the peninsula on which Dakar stands, is destined to rank as one of the most spectacular, for site and plant, and one of the most salubrious in the whole of Africa. Its academic standards already bear comparison with those prevailing in metropolitan France. Al-

[7] *African Affairs* (French Embassy, Service de Presse et d'Information, New York), May 1958, p. 8.

though the doors of the university are open to all qualified students, its curricula are designed primarily to serve "the aspirations and needs of the African peoples."

While government schools have been the norm, mission and other private schools have enjoyed equal rights, so long as they maintained the approved academic standards, conducted their work in French, and were staffed by teachers holding metropolitan certificates. Until quite recently many missions preferred to use the local vernacular, or vernaculars, and so were disqualified from doing formal educational work. However, the majority of mission societies are coming to see that a well-run school enjoying official recognition is a good thing to have on any mission station, especially in these days when the African's main reason for consorting with white men is frequently to learn their "magic" in order to qualify himself for "European" jobs. It is fair to say that the French government has generally been of much the same mind.

Portuguese territories. The educational policy of the Portuguese is more modest than that of the French and rather differently conceived. Unlike the French, the Portuguese are in no hurry to make citizens, though they leave the way open to those who wish to become citizens and can measure up to the set requirements. Consequently, they do not feel under the same obligation to duplicate in Africa all the educational facilities provided in the homeland; nor have they attempted to do so. They also differ from the French in regarding instruction in religion as forming an integral part of their teaching responsibility. Marcelo Caetano, in his book *Colonizing Traditions, Principles and Methods of the Portuguese,* speaks for the Portuguese government when he says: "On the principal that political unity is founded on a moral unity . . . Portuguese colonization has attached great importance to the religious factor in civilizing natives."[8] And because Catholicism is the official religion of the country, the government has, from the beginning, insisted that the responsibility for "civilizing

[8] Agencia Geral do Ultramar, Lisbon, 1951, p. 44.

natives" be vested in the Catholic missions operating in its African territories. The diffusion of Catholicism is regarded as being of such importance as to warrant government protection of all Catholic missions, no matter what their national affiliation. Since 1935 the position of Catholic-controlled schools has been fortified by a decree restricting educational subsidies to such schools.

In the matter of language medium, the Portuguese share the French government's preference for the mother tongue. Indeed, they go further than the French. Because of the great diversity of ethnic groups and languages, they contend that their goal of "cultural assimilation" can be reached only when there is a common tongue, and that tongue Portuguese. It would seem that to the Portuguese administrator the native languages are part of the barbarism he is seeking to overcome.

In line with their narrower conception of African needs, the Portuguese have limited the scope of their elementary school offerings to Christian morals, reading, writing, arithmetic and vocational training in such fields as farming, carpentry and needlework. By so doing, they affirm that they will effect "a preliminary penetration of Portuguese culture" without turning the Africans "from their tribal life or from their traditional way of living."[9]

It might be supposed from this that the Portuguese government had no use for non-Catholic schools, but this is not the case. It "broadly [welcomes] missions of all Christian confessions," according to Caetano, and though the warmth of the welcome has frequently been questioned by Protestant missionaries, the fact is that, until recently, in some parts of Angola more children were attending Protestant mission schools than Catholic, and the educational standard of those schools was higher than that of the Catholic schools. To this many government officials in Angola have readily testified. In Mozambique Protestant schools have had to work under greater difficulties, and since 1935 the majority of them have been closed. In addition to their financial handicap, the Prot-

[9] *Ibid.,* p. 45.

estant schools labor under the necessity of having to permit all those of their students who wish to enter the teaching profession or to go into government service, or even to continue their studies at a higher level elsewhere, to take an examination in Catholic doctrine as well as in secular subjects. However, "the syllabus for teachers is sufficiently broad to permit Christian and ethical teaching in the classroom to be fairly general in character; and the complaints from Protestants are less sharp than one might expect."[10]

Primary education is free to all Africans residing within three kilometers (roughly two miles) of a school, but it is still not available to more than a minority. In 1957, in the whole of Angola, out of an estimated school-age population of more than a million, only 80,000 children were enrolled in primary schools. In all of Mozambique, out of an estimated school-age population of 1.5 million, approximately 360,000 children were attending primary schools. In Portuguese Guinea, with a school-age population of not less than 150,000, the number of enrolled students was about 11,000. To get to these schools, many children were walking more than three kilometers. But more schools are being built, at a faster rate now than ever before, and it is hoped that in the course of the next decade the theoretical compulsion upon Africans to send children between the ages of 7 and 12 to school can be transformed into a practical possibility.

Wherever feasible, the Portuguese provide separate elementary schools for European children and the children of Europeanized or "assimilated" Africans. The basis of segregation is cultural rather than racial. The curriculum calls for four years of instruction in the case of European children or children of Europeanized Africans. African children who have not learned Portuguese at home may begin the curriculum only after two years of preparatory work.

Post-primary education is even less developed, and is generally available only in the big towns. In the whole of Angola

10 M. Searle Bates and others, *Survey of the Training of the Ministry in Africa,* Part II, International Missionary Council, London and New York, 1954, p. 27.

in 1957 fewer than 13,000 students were enrolled in secondary, technical and normal schools. In Mozambique about 10,-
000 were enrolled; in Portuguese Guinea and São Tomé
and Príncipe, about 600. Significantly, in the light of Portuguese policy, most of these students were attending technical
schools. In Portuguese Africa as a whole some 15,000 students, or over 60 per cent of the total number of post-primary
students, were attending technical schools; not more than
8,500, or 35 per cent, were attending secondary schools; only
820, or less than 4 per cent, normal schools. Significantly, too,
most of the technical schools were simple affairs, offering instruction in such artisan subjects as carpentry and shoemak-
ing. The normal schools were concerned mainly with training
Africans to run small bush schools.

But those attending the secondary schools were clearly regarded as a class apart, for they enjoyed facilities comparable
to those found in any progressive American community. The
liceus at Luanda in Angola and Lourenço Marques in Mozambique would be an adornment to most such communities,
and their students would have little difficulty in standing their
ground against any comparable American group.

Although the criterion of entrance into the *liceus* is solely
merit, the ratio of African to European students is still low,
much lower than it has been in the French areas. In line with
its policy of cultural assimilation, the government requires that
the curriculum in all high schools, and the standards of
achievement, be identical with those demanded of similar
schools in Portugal. Those African students who have qualified for entry into the *liceus* sit side by side with, and take
the same examinations as, the children of high-ranking Portuguese officials. The full seven-year secondary school curriculum is divided into three parts, lasting two, three and two
years respectively; but not all secondary school pupils complete all three parts. Such post-secondary education as students, European and African, may wish to pursue, or may be
permitted to pursue, can be had only by going to Portugal
or the Union of South Africa. Down to 1959 there were no
plans for establishing, in any of Portugal's African territories,

institutions comparable to the colleges of university rank in Ghana, Nigeria, Sudan and elsewhere.

Belgian territories. The Belgians predicated their African educational policy on two assumptions. First, that it is better to have 90 per cent of the population capable of understanding what the government is trying to do for them and competent to help the government in doing it than to have 10 per cent of the population so full of learning that it spends its time telling the government what to do. Second, that all education is the better for being in the hands of men of faith. From the beginning, the policy of the government was to favor mission schools. By the Concordat of 1906 which Léopold II concluded with the Vatican, the Catholic missions were given virtual control of the African's education and were provided with government subsidies. Protestant missions were also allowed to run schools, but it was not until the mid-1920s that they became eligible for government grants. At the present time (1959) subsidies, adjusted to work done in various phases of general education, are given to such schools and teachers, Protestant and Catholic alike, as meet government standards. Only about half the schools have met these standards.

In addition to subsidizing mission and other private schools, the government has operated, since 1954, a number of schools of its own. Not the least of the functions of these schools is to keep the non-government schools wide awake and so bring about "an improvement in the general quality of education for the [Africans]."[11] Several schools are also operated by the big commercial and industrial companies and mining corporations.

Thanks to the joint efforts of government, churches and corporations, the educational provision for the African is impressive. In 1957 there were approximately 30,000 schools (28,500 of them primary) and 46,000 teachers (40,000 of them African) in the Belgian Congo and Ruanda-Urundi. In

[11] A. Buisseret, the then Minister of Colonies in the Belgian government, in the *New York Times*, January 4, 1955.

the same year more than 1.64 million students were enrolled
in primary and pre-primary schools, and more than 50,000
in post-primary schools of one kind or another. All together,
between one third and two fifths of the school-age children
of the Congo were receiving some formal European education.
At the rate at which schools were then being provided and
teachers being trained, almost the entire school-age population, girl and boy alike, was expected either to be in primary
school or to have had some such schooling by the early 1960s.
Post-primary facilities were expected to be available then for
those living in the more accessible areas and capable of profit-
ing by them. By 1970 the government hoped to be able to
offer "the best elements" in the population academic and
technical training that would allow them to get to the top of
the educational pyramid without ever having been separated
from their native environment. Some students have already
got to the top, for since 1954 there has been a private university—Lovanium—at Kimwenza near Léopoldville, and since
1956 a state university with headquarters at Elisabethville
and branches in other Congo and Ruanda-Urundi cities. At
the beginning of the 1958–1959 session Lovanium had 236
students (most of them Africans) and the state university
171 (most of them Europeans).

While the properly qualified African student is not prevented from going abroad to further his academic interests, as
a general rule the Belgians have preferred that he did not.
The African student educated abroad has tended to become,
in their view, "a stranger and a pilgrim"—a stranger to his
own people and a pilgrim to unpatriotic places.

The school system has been kept flexible, and its organizers
have not hesitated to alter it whenever their resources allowed
or circumstances dictated. At the present time the system
calls for a two-year pre-primary (nursery) course followed
by a primary course which can be completed in four years
but may be spread over five or six years. Wherever possible,
the better students are encouraged at the end of their second
primary year to embark on a further four-year course designed to prepare them for work at the secondary school

level. Students who are unable or unwilling to consider doing six years of secondary schooling may, on completing the standard four-year primary course, enroll either for teacher-training courses ranging in duration from two to four years, or for courses of comparable length that will qualify them for clerical positions in business or government.

The secondary schools are of two types, modern and classical. As their name suggests, the classical schools stress languages, literature, history and philosophy. In making this type of school available to African as well as Belgian students, the government sought to demonstrate that it was "not reserving for [Belgian] children alone the monopoly of a high intellectual training"[12] and, as a consequence, the professions to which it gives *entrée*. The so-called modern schools provide three years of well-rounded education, and three years of specialization in administration and commerce, surveying, general science or teacher-training.

To those not interested in getting white-collar jobs (there are some), the Belgians have offered the attractions of artisanship. In recent years they have opened many well-equipped and well-staffed technical schools and workshops, with courses ranging in length from two to four years, in which students can learn to become furniture makers, masons, motor mechanics, lathe workers, workshop supervisors, plant foremen and, at a higher level, medical assistants (*infirmiers*) and dispensers. In 1957 more than 22,000 students were enrolled in some 650 such schools and workshops.

In order to be able to proceed to one of the two universities, students must either have completed successfully the full six-year secondary school program or have made good any deficiencies in their school record by attending classes in the "pre-university" section of the university. At the university level itself work is offered in all the traditional fields and in some that are still almost virgin. By 1958 Lovanium was already offering courses in African philology and sociology,

[12] Pierre Wigny, *A Ten Year Plan for the Economic and Social Development of the Belgian Congo,* Belgian Government Information Center, New York, 1951, p. 29.

tribal law, African history, art and literature, and the economy of underdeveloped countries, as well as in tropical medicine, hygiene and agriculture and more conventional subjects.

As in the French territories, government-subsidized education is free at every level. In those pre-primary and primary schools which serve African communities the medium of instruction is normally the dominant language of the district, French being merely one of the subjects taught. At most post-primary schools, instruction is given in French. Flemish, which has been the other official language of the Belgian Congo, has the rank of second modern European language in most high schools.

Unlike the French and Portuguese governments, the Belgian government has not prescribed what language shall be used in schools which it has not supported or officially recognized. All the same, it has made increasing effort to secure the adoption of French as the *lingua franca* of its school system. Neither Swahili, which was introduced by the Arab slave traders, nor any of the vernaculars, it is argued, "meets the requirements of the elite who seek to be initiated into the things of the mind . . . [and to have opened] to them a wider gateway to civilization."[13]

Progress toward parity of educational facilities for boys and girls has been slow for several reasons, not the least important of them being the inertia of the unschooled, both male and female. However, the tempo is quickening as funds become available for girls' education, and the practical advantages of efficiently run homes, rational child care and emancipation become more widely appreciated. Since the war the Belgians have introduced several "woman-oriented" programs into their school system. At the primary level there are now home economics courses (*études ménagères*). At the post-primary level vocational courses are offered in such subjects as teaching, midwifery and dressmaking, and more general courses covering the theory and practice of homecraft. A measure of the progress made by the Belgians in this postwar

[13] *Ibid.*, pp. 29–30.

period is provided by the following figures: in 1948 less than 5 per cent of the African children attending school were girls; in 1958 the percentage was more than 20.

Commonwealth territories. Habitually shy of statements of policy, the British have no special fancy for educational policies which leave nothing to the imagination. For long, they left questions of policy in the hands of the local authorities. The *raison d'être* of their educational endeavor is clear, at least. In the words of W. E. F. Ward, the main business of education, as they see it, is "to take boys and girls and develop them as human beings to the highest possibility that they have: to train them to make the best use of their gifts." He adds: "Our job as educators, whether Europeans or Africans, is to get the schools and colleges and universities into good order: to provide more trained teachers, to develop institutes of education and professional associations of teachers, to develop African local education authorities, and, of course, to provide more education as well as better education. If self-government and partnership are to work in Africa, the educational problems have to be solved. Once you begin education, you cannot stop it; you must go all the way."[14]

From 1925 onward the British government periodically issued memoranda dealing with the education of the African, but it was never the government's intention that the principles set down therein should be interpreted uniformly; nor could they be. The territorial differences in racial composition (e.g., between the largely monoracial west African territories and the multiracial east and central African territories), religious affiliations (e.g., between the Mohammedan Northern Region and the Christianized Eastern and Western Regions of Nigeria), economic development (e.g., between comparatively advanced Uganda and comparatively backward Tanganyika), and inclination (e.g., between the Kikuyu, who eagerly embraced the chance of schooling, and the Masai, who didn't) ruled out any such possibility.

[14] *The Listener,* July 9, 1953, p. 54.

Nevertheless, these memoranda leave no doubt about the kind of education the British government believes the African should have, or the problem of giving it to him. What it has been trying to do is to provide primary school facilities for all children; secondary or technical training for the cream of the primary scholars; and university training for the cream of the secondary and technical school graduates. Its purpose in so doing has been to give enough Africans enough instruction in the art of civilized living to enable them sooner or later to "run their own show" and to do it successfully. Or, as a Colonial Office Memorandum of February 1954 put it rather more formally: "[African education] must develop qualities of citizenship and the capacity for self-government; it must provide training in all the various skills and techniques which a self-governing nation needs; and it must give its peoples an understanding not only of the potentialities of their own country, but of the essentials of Western culture."

All of this is more easily said than done, of course. The building of "pyramids" in Africa has always been a slow and costly process. But progress has been substantial, at all three levels of the pyramid, in all the Commonwealth territories, especially since the war. Literacy may still be as low as 10 per cent in many out-of-the-way places, but in most of the larger towns at least 50 per cent of the African children now attend primary school, and in some (notably Lagos, Nairobi, Salisbury, Dar-es-Salaam) the percentage is as high as 75. Within the next ten years or so several governments expect to be able to provide free primary education for their entire school-age populations. Among these are the governments of Nigeria and Ghana. The educational ten-year plan embarked on in Nigeria in 1946 had as its main objective the provision of junior primary education within a generation for all Nigerian children of school age. This plan was later superseded by the even more ambitious 1955–1960 development plans of the federal and regional governments, which have devoted a large proportion of their development moneys to "crash" programs of educational expansion. As a result of these, school enrollments went up in the Western Region by two thirds of a million between 1954 and 1956, and in the Eastern Region by three quarters of a million to 1,330,000. In Ghana, the Minister of Education was able to report in 1957 that "throughout the length and breadth of southern Ghana and Ashanti, primary school facilities are available for the great majority of children of school age. In 1951 there were just over 1,000 primary schools; in 1957 the number has risen to over 3,000, and the period of tremendous expansion in primary education is over."[15] This in a country where the rate of expansion of educational facilities down to the mid-1930s was so slow that it would have taken six hundred years to achieve universal primary education!

The development of secondary schools has been much slower. Such schools, to serve their function—which, in the eyes of the student, is to enable him to obtain on graduating a certificate from one of the senior British universities that will be his password to "white-collar" service—must be well equipped, well staffed, commodious (most schools have to reckon on having boarders as well as day scholars and many are for boarders exclusively), and must maintain educational standards comparable to those found in British schools of the same kind. Then again, until the recent expansion of primary education, the number of primary school graduates who were either able or willing to attend secondary schools and complete the arduous five-to-six-year curriculum was small. Many of those who were willing did not pass the highly competitive entrance examinations, and many of those who did, found it difficult to pay the tuition and, where they applied, the boarding fees.

Consequently, it is not surprising that up to the early 1950s, the percentage of primary school graduates who went on to do secondary school work was nowhere higher than about two, and in some territories less than one. Such figures, it has long been recognized, are too low for the good of any territory moving toward self-government, to say nothing of territories already self-governing. Accordingly, large sums of

[15] *Ghana Today*, July 10, 1957.

money have been spent in the past decade on the building of new schools and the training of new African teachers. Between 1951 and 1958 the number of secondary schools in Ghana increased from 13 to approximately 60, and the number of secondary school students from less than 3,000 to more than 12,000. Over the same period the number of teacher-training colleges increased from 20 to 34, and the number of trainees from less than 2,000 to more than 4,000.

In Commonwealth tropical Africa as a whole the number of secondary schools more than doubled (to over 600) in the first postwar decade, and the number of students more than trebled (to over 75,000). By the end of 1960 the number of such schools is expected to exceed 1,000 and the number of students to be well over 150,000. By the mid-1960s, therefore, the number of secondary school graduates coming onto the labor market in such territories as Ghana, the Western Region of Nigeria and Uganda will bear comparison with the number in some comparably sized American states. There will still be many primary school graduates who are unable to get a secondary education, but there should be enough to ensure that the foreseeable needs of government, commerce and industry for white-collar African employees can be met in most territories.

The reasons that may be advanced for the slow progress of secondary education apply even more strongly to college and university education. It is at once the costliest and most demanding of all scholastic enterprises. It is also, from the standpoint of priorities, the least urgent. For many years the number of Africans capable of taking advantage of such education was so small that governments and mission boards found it much cheaper to send those who did measure up to the required standards to foreign universities than to attempt to provide local facilities. Those colleges that did offer post-secondary courses of instruction, for example Achimota College in Ghana, were habitually hard-pressed for funds and faculty. But no government that announces its intention of preparing its wards for self-government can deny them the right to a university education, costly and demanding as it may prove to be, and no elite that has begun to ponder the implications of autonomy can be expected long to forego the prestige, the authority and the convenience that comes from having its own university. Among the "new" nations the university is apt to be as much a symbol of national spirit as it is of intellectual maturity.

Shortly after the conclusion of World War II, the British government, acting on the recommendations of two wartime commissions, voted funds for the setting up of four African university colleges. Two of these were located in west Africa (at Achimota, Ghana, and at Ibadan, Nigeria),[16] one in east Africa (at Kampala, Uganda) and one in Sudan (at Khartoum). What Dr. Kenneth Mellanby, the first principal of the University College, Ibadan, said in his opening address on April 22, 1948 about the purpose of the Nigerian college may fairly be said to represent the government's intention for all four: "The University College is being established with the primary object of producing a university which will be a center of learning and culture and which will make the maximum contribution to all aspects of the development of the country. The standards of the University College must be equal to those of the best universities of any country, but the college must also have an African bias, and while not neglecting any branch of learning must concentrate on subjects of special interest and importance to Africa."

Each of the four colleges has already done much to justify these high hopes. There has been no trimming of academic standards. The University of London, with which each college has enjoyed a "special relationship," and for whose degrees the students of three of the four still (1959) work, has never been known to temper the wind to the shorn lamb, white or black. There has been very little frittering of effort or opportunity; such expansion as there has been of the initial programs has occurred usually after the needed funds have been

[16] At Freetown, Sierra Leone, Fourah Bay College was already offering courses of college caliber and capable of earning bachelor degrees in the University of Durham, England. In 1960 it was granted the status of university college.

assured, and has been related closely to the realities of African land and life. There has been no trimming of material standards, either. "Only the best is good enough for Africa" is written large across the blueprints of chemistry laboratories, cafeterias, chapels—and candelabras. When the British leave Africa they will at least be able to say: "If you seek a monument, look around." Whether the African student will be as much impressed by what he sees as his British tutors, it is too early to say.

Meanwhile, the idea of bringing higher education within the reach of all qualified students, of whatever race or creed, is spreading throughout Commonwealth Africa. In 1957 at Salisbury, Southern Rhodesia, a fifth university college, the University College of Rhodesia and Nyasaland, opened its doors to 68 full-time students—European, African and Asian.[17] Plans have been made for a second university college in Nigeria (in the Eastern Region) and for two more in British East Africa (at Nairobi in Kenya and Morogoro in Tanganyika). Since the war, too, several technical colleges and other centers of higher education have been established. Outstanding among these are the Nigerian College of Arts, Science and Technology (which has campuses at Zaria, Ibadan and Enugu and confines itself largely to professional education), the Kumasi College of Technology in Ghana, and the Royal Technical College at Nairobi, Kenya.

Until a few years ago, the keystone of the whole educational system was the missionary. As in the Belgian, Portuguese and French territories, the missionary provided the bush African with almost his only opportunity of observing the white man at close quarters. It was he who, in the absence of the overworked administrator, was called upon to settle petty disputes; who dispensed medical "magic"; who was ready to hunt meat in time of hunger, and to dig wells in time of drought; who was able to build a bridge, or pole a ferry across a stream, make bricks and repair tools; and who

[17] In March 1959 the number of full-time students had increased to 169.

built the schools and ran them. Though the missionary facto-
tum is disappearing, the influence of the missionary teacher
continues to be strong. Most of the primary and secondary
schools are still staffed and administered by the missions, and,
fortunately for the recruiters, a high percentage of the faculty
members of government colleges are "mission-minded."[18]

If, in recent years, the British government has assumed
greater and greater responsibility for African education, the
reason is not dissatisfaction with the work of the mission societies, but rather the desire to strengthen it and extend it,
especially in the predominantly Moslem areas, to which Christian missions have been denied access. Yet it is hard not to
believe that the heyday of the mission school is past, especially in those territories which are nearing the end of their
colonial tutelage and about to become masters in their own
house. It is harder still to see how the educational goal of
all the Commonwealth African administrations can be reached
unless responsibility for the financing, directing and supervising of all types of education is vested in government bodies
created for the purpose. Alone, the missions cannot be sure
of either the necessary funds or the personnel, and because of
their confessional differences they cannot be expected to
speak with one voice on matters of curriculum, teacher-training or pedagogic method. Nor are they likely to submit
readily to dictation from secular authorities in such matters.
Even so, it is likely to be many years before the mission
school disappears from the scene, if it ever does. Already
some Commonwealth governments are beginning to find that
what makes a good school is not the amount of the equipment or the size of the budget, but the quality, ethical as
much as intellectual, of its staff members and their sense of
vocation—qualities that tend to find their strongest roots in
religious faith.

[18] In conversation one principal confessed that he could see no
professional reason why a physicist or chemist should take a post
in his college, which could never begin to compete with British
universities or industrial corporations, either in intellectual stimulus
or opportunities for research.

Spanish territories. The fact that the Spanish government does not make a habit of publicizing its colonial administration has led many people to infer that there is little to tell that any government would wish to tell. But in the field of education such an inference would seem to be unwarranted. Thus, in Spanish Guinea[19] in 1957, out of an estimated school-age population of approximately 65,000, not less than 21,000 were in primary school, over 200 in technical school and nearly 200 in secondary school. Such figures compare well with those of several much larger non-self-governing territories, including Bechuanaland, British Somaliland and Somalia, and, on a proportional reckoning, they outrank those of most other tropical African territories, non-self-governing or otherwise.

The educational systems for the children of European stock and for those of African stock are, in the phrase once so familiar to Americans, separate and unequal. The objectives of African education are stated to be the improvement of the African's living conditions and the inculcation of Spanish virtues, patriotism and culture to the degree that this is possible without making him a rootless person.

In line with these objectives, the African is offered training of three types. The first, or pre-primary, type is concerned, in the main, with practical, manual matters, and is conducted largely by African "auxiliaries." The second, or primary, type offers the student the alternatives of training for "the activities of the country in general" or preparation for the "higher school," where he will receive the third type of training, namely, for auxiliary service in such fields as public health, public works, business and teaching. In addition, there are schools which offer instruction in clerical, agricultural and domestic work. So far little thought appears to have been given to the subject of higher education, possibly because it would almost certainly lead to Europeanization, and so to rootlessness.

[19] Comprising Rio Muni, or continental Guinea, the nearby islands of Corisco, Great and Little Elobey, and the islands of Fernando Po and Annobón in the Bight of Benin.

The education of the sizable European population of Spanish Guinea follows in all essentials the metropolitan pattern. The responsibility of providing education for Africans and Europeans is shared by the government and the missions; but only Catholic missions are eligible for grants and subsidies.

Liberia. For the first eighty years or so of its history, the Liberian Republic had the unenviable distinction of being the most illiterate sovereign state in the world. Even some of the presidents had difficulty with their reading and writing. The only education to be had was provided by the few undernourished Christian missions, the Koranic schools, which did little more than teach the children of the northern Moslemized tribes to recite the Koran in Arabic, and the initiation schools.

With the setting up in the present century of a Department of Public Instruction, the government took formal cognizance of the subject. In 1912 a law providing for compulsory elementary schooling was enacted. A general education code was promulgated in 1937, and amended in 1942 and 1944. But as there was little or no money in the national exchequer for the building of schools and the training and payment of teachers, the children of Liberia had very little more schooling than before. In 1920, Ruth Sloan notes in a paper prepared for this study, the government appropriation for education was $2,000, not all of which was actually spent. As recently as 1946 the government spent only $154,000, or nearly $50,000 less than the missions. Until the end of World War II, only 3 per cent or so of the school-age population was actually attending school, and 80 per cent of the educational work was being done by Christian missions.

Throughout this period most of those attending school were children of Americo-Liberian stock. The Afro-Liberians of the hinterland were regarded by the Americo-Liberians for the most part as being intellectually inferior. All instruction was given in English, the official language of the country. The curriculum was similar to that in general use in the United States, where most of the missions had their headquarters.

Very little of it was free. With rare exceptions the elementary schools were poorly staffed and supervised, inadequately financed and shockingly short of equipment, textbooks and other supplies. There were no secondary schools worthy of the name, and such colleges as there were (for instance, Liberia College, the College of West Africa, and Cuttington College and Divinity School) found it necessary to give most of their attention to what was euphemistically called "preparatory" work—in other words, basic education.

Since about 1946 the educational picture has brightened considerably. Each year has seen more and more effort directed to preparing the peoples of the country, Afro- as well as Americo-Liberian, for life in a Christian democratic society. Fortunately, the large American corporations operating in Liberia, such as the Firestone Plantations Company and the Liberia Mining Company, have been able to provide President Tubman's government with a larger operating budget just when it was needed to give teeth to this intention. By the late 1950s the budget of the Department of Public Instruction was roughly $2 million, several hundred times what it was in 1920. It was still an inadequate budget, amounting, at the most, to about $5 per school-age child, but it was being put to good use.

In the first postwar decade the number of children attending elementary school more than quadrupled, increasing from about 10,000 to over 40,000. The teacher-training program was strengthened by the opening of the William V. S. Tubman School of Teacher Training and several demonstration schools where apprentice teachers could gain valuable practical experience, and also by the setting up in different parts of the country of training institutes conducted under the auspices of the International Cooperation Administration of the United States. During the same period the College of West Africa, Liberia College and the Booker Washington Institute, along with some smaller centers of learning, were reconstituted by Act of the Legislature (February 15, 1951) into the University of Liberia. Following a visit in 1948 by Dr. Frank C. Laubach, literacy programs conducted in both the vernacular and English were begun among the neglected Afro-Liberians and those of the Americo-Liberians who were still unlettered. Plans were also made to place at least one elementary school in every town or tribal community.

Even so, at the present rate of expansion, it will be many years before Liberia can match the educational performance of, say, Ghana or Nigeria. In 1957 the number of children enrolled in primary schools was still less than 15 per cent of the estimated school-age population, and not more than 10,-000 of those enrolled were expected to go beyond the third grade. In the same year the number of primary school teachers was still less than 8 per cent of the number (approximately 25,000) needed to make it possible to enforce Liberia's compulsory education law; and of these teachers, only about one in six had more than a sixth-grade education.

The position regarding post-primary education was still more depressing. In 1958 the total enrollment in the 24 secondary and technical schools was about 2,600; and in the three institutions of higher education (including the University of Liberia at Monrovia[20]), less than 500. The levels of performance required in most of these institutions are low, both by the better American standards and by those of neighboring west African countries.

Ethiopia (including Eritrea). In education, as in many other respects, Ethiopia does not fit into the stock African mold. It is, in fact, unique among the territories of tropical Africa. When the Portuguese reached the country at the end of the fifteenth century, they found themselves among people who could read and write; who knew the rudiments of astronomy, music and mathematics; who ran seminaries and schools, and filled libraries with their parchments. True, the number of people who did any of these things was small, but so, for that matter, was the number who did in Europe; else-

---

[20] Now (1960) in process of being moved to Paynesville. By 1962 the country is expected to have two more universities, one a Catholic university and the other the gift of a group of American businessmen.

where in tropical Africa there were none who did these things. Three hundred years later, Protestant and Catholic missionaries entering the country found children reading the Psalter and other sacred books in Ge'ez (the liturgical language of the Ethiopian Orthodox Church), writing in Amharic and doing exercises in arithmetic. They also saw—what their fifteenth-century predecessors had not seen, for the Moslem conquest did not take place until the sixteenth century—*imams* teaching the children of the faithful to recite verses from the Koran, and to read and write in Arabic. At the same time, it did not take the missionaries long to realize that the majority of the people were completely illiterate and that many of the "literate" were no better off than the Ethiopian eunuch of the New Testament story who did not understand what he was reading.

It was not until 1908 that the government of Ethiopia, under the Emperor Menelik II, seems to have sensed the inadequacy of the education provided by the Orthodox and Moslem schools (and, to a lesser extent, by the Western missions) for the responsibilities which the children of the ruling class were being called upon increasingly to assume. Though several government schools were established in the years that followed, fewer than a thousand boys and girls—including the hundred or so who were studying abroad—were receiving anything in the nature of a modern education when the Italians invaded the country in 1935. The Italians, who made little effort to conceal their contempt for the ruling classes, closed the government schools and, along with them, most of the non-Catholic mission schools. In their place they established a number of primary schools designed to make good working-class Fascists out of the pupils. Only among the Moslems, whose protector Mussolini declared himself to be, were higher studies allowed. Throughout the Italian occupation, the great mass of the population remained illiterate.

With the defeat of the Italian army in 1941 and the return of Emperor Haile Selassie I, a new education era began. Schools long disused were reopened. Those damaged were repaired. New ones were built as quickly as labor and materials could be found. By 1945 eight new primary schools had been built in the provinces. In addition, several post-primary schools, designed for technical, teacher-training and secondary work (including the fine Haile Selassie Secondary School in Addis Ababa), were already in operation.

The educational policy of the Ethiopian government was set down at some length about the same time (August 1944). Its major provisions are as follows:

1. Universal elementary education, for both boys and girls (hitherto neglected if not ignored), with a curriculum that prepares the child for life in a land where there are few short-cuts to ease and affluence, and whose great need is for better artisans, cultivators and cattlemen. The government insists that, along with academic studies, opportunity for education through handicraft and other practical activities should be made available to every child.

2. The expansion of secondary, technical and university facilities, subject to the country's financial limitations, which, of course, are very considerable and likely to remain so for many years to come.

3. Mass education of unschooled adults to spread literacy, promote better hygiene and encourage community activities, including recreation.

4. The use of Amharic, the official language of the country, as the principal medium of instruction in the lower grades of the state schools, and of English and Amharic in the upper grades and in the secondary schools. (Amharic remains the sole medium of instruction in the schools administered by the Orthodox Church, and Arabic in the Koranic schools.)

5. The employment of well-qualified foreigners at all teaching levels, but especially in secondary schools and colleges, until such time as enough Ethiopians are qualified to take over this work.

6. Closer and more effective association of the Orthodox Church and Christian missions in the country's educational program.

This is an ambitious policy, though not more ambitious than it needs to be if Ethiopia is to overtake the twentieth century before it is gone. For the fact is that until the Italian invasion Ethiopia was more medieval than modern; indeed, it *was* medieval. If Haile Selassie's exile in England served no other purpose, it afforded him ample opportunity of learning the uses of universal education, technical no less than academic, for girls as well as boys, for both the laboring and the governing classes. It also enabled him to see something of the resilience and stamina, in time of stress, of people who are well aware of what they are fighting for, who are kept informed of the ebb and flow of their fortunes through press, radio and personal encounter with their leaders, and who are united by common traditions, faith and language. Almost none of these conditions existed in Ethiopia. Those who were educated lived for the most part withdrawn from their fellows, in church, monastery and mosque. The languages of the country numbered more than fifty, of which only three were written and not one was understood by more than half the population. There was practically no intercourse between the people of one language and another, and consequently no sense of community, let alone common loyalty. Many tribal chieftains kept their own armies in the manner of feudal lords and went to war with almost the regularity of the monsoon. Most of those who did the fighting had no idea what they were fighting about or for, and very little share in the spoils.

However, the Emperor is not a man to be easily dismayed. Having set the educational goal, he proceeded to busy himself in its pursuit, guiding every program, visiting every school and college in the land (in the manner of an inspector oftentimes), and being in almost everything but name the country's Minister of Education. It was at his insistence that in the early postwar years the annual appropriation for education became the largest in the government budget, and has since been running between 15 and 20 per cent of the total.

Notwithstanding, the appropriation still does not come to $10 million U. S. This is not much in a country that is thought by many to have around 4 million children, that stands in the direst need of schools, books and supplies of all kinds, and that has, for the time being, to lean heavily in the running of its schools on expatriate help. Of necessity, therefore, the tempo of educational progress remains slow.

In 1958 there were in the whole of Ethiopia's 395,000 square miles fewer than 450 government primary schools, a bare score of post-primary schools, and one university. The enrollment in the primary schools was roughly 150,000; in the post-primary schools, less than 5,000; in teacher-training colleges, less than 1,000; in the university, less than 400 full-time students. There were fewer than 4,000 government-employed teachers and administrators, of whom about one tenth were foreigners. The 10,000-odd schools administered by the Ethiopian Church, Islam and various private agencies (such as the European and American missions) claimed almost 300,000 students; but it is questionable whether the work done in most of the "Ethiopian" and Koranic schools spells progress.

But progress there is, and wherever the visitor journeys he sees evidences of it. Here it takes the form of new professional training schools, such as the Air Force Cadet Training Center, the Public Health College and Training Center, the School of Building Technology, the Ethiopian College of Engineering, the Harar Teacher Training School, the Agricultural Technical School, and the Imperial Ethiopian College of Agricultural and Mechanical Arts (sponsored and partly financed by the International Cooperation Administration of the United States). There it comes in humbler guise: a crowd of barely literate youngsters looking at a window display of English reading matter, a group of young farmers watching a demonstration of cattle-dipping, an adult evening class discussing West-East diplomacy, village gossips listening to a radio program in the local coffee shop. Elsewhere it is more in evidence as an attitude than an accomplishment, as among the students of the Haile Selassie Secondary School, who are receiving as fine an education from as competent a faculty as could be found in any state in the Union and who seem to sense it; or in the offices of ICA consultants, who are tackling gallon-sized problems with pint-sized resources and extemporizing solutions which more timid spirits might regard as risky, and teaching the Ethiopians to do the same.

In the long run, of course, it is the attitude of a people toward its problems that matters most. The present attitude of the government and people of Ethiopia offers strong grounds for believing that the country's educational problems will be solved, and in the twentieth century.

Somalia. Until the late 1940s there was no such thing as an educational policy in Somalia, and next to no education of a modern kind. Before and during the fascist Italian occupation, little or no thought was given to the educational needs of the indigenous population. Almost the only educational agencies were the Koranic schools for the children of the faithful, and the Catholic missions, whose work was done mainly among the immigrant Italians. The British administration, which lasted from 1941 to 1950, was, to all intents, an interregnum during which the authorities were reluctant to go much beyond the "care and maintenance" requirements of international law. By the time the British handed back the territory to the now democratized Italian government (acting as administering authority for the United Nations Trusteeship Council), fewer than 7,500 Somali children, out of an estimated school-age population of 350,000, were getting any formal education.

Early in the 1950s the Italians, working closely with the indigenous leaders of the country, set themselves the threefold task of creating a Somali teaching corps adequate in numbers and training; increasing the number of children going to school and ensuring regular attendance; and developing vocational and higher education. A measure of the progress they have made with these tasks may be gathered from enrollment figures for the 1957–1958 session. The number of Somalis enrolled in government primary and pre-primary schools in that session was approximately 31,500 (around 14,000 children, the rest adults). The number enrolled in government secondary schools—of which there were only two for Somalis in the country, both of them in Mogadishu—was

246. Of these, only 57 were enrolled at the "senior high" level, and only about four out of every five of those enrolled were in regular attendance. Another dozen or so Somalis were enrolled in secondary schools designed primarily for Italians and other Europeans. Vocational schools of various kinds (technical, teacher-training, commercial, agricultural, veterinary, domestic science and fisheries) had about 80 students on their registers. Of these, only 33 were in the teacher-training school, though 98 had been so enrolled in the previous session.

Higher education in 1958 was available only at the School of Islamic Discipline and the Higher Institute of Law and Economics, both in Mogadishu. At the former, which has a broad curriculum covering many "non-Islamic" studies, there were 270 students; at the latter, which is principally interested in producing a cadre of administrators, executives and teachers, there were about the same number of students.

The official languages of instruction are Italian and Arabic. Italian is generally employed in the teaching of civil subjects, Arabic in the teaching of religious subjects.

Besides the government schools, mention should be made of those run by private agencies. Chief among them are those of the Somali Youth League (with Somali directors), the National Model Schools (started by groups of civic-minded Somalis in various parts of the country and staffed, for the most part, by teachers provided by the government of the United Arab Republic), the Italian schools (for the children of Italian administrators and business people and, for that reason, patterned closely on the metropolitan model) and the Koranic schools (of which, the United Nations Advisory Council on the territory has reported, there are several "in each of the large towns of every region and district and . . . at least one . . . in every village").

As in most other parts of the Mohammedan world, it is the boys who get most of what education is going. In the 1957–1958 session the number of Somali girls enrolled in primary schools, government and non-government, was approximately 3,000 and the number of women 1,800. The number of girls and women doing post-primary school work is, in the words of the above-quoted report, "negligible." Some 40 were enrolled in the territory's one domestic science school, 15 in its secondary schools, and one in the Higher Institute of Law and Economics. No women were in training as teachers.

Besides all the problems that customarily confront the non-self-governing territory, Somalia has two which are peculiarly her own. The first of these is the fact that "the Somali language has not yet been reduced to a written form which is either widely accepted or acceptable . . . The problem posed has thus far proved to be almost insoluble."[21] Technically the problem is no worse than that tackled successfully by linguistic experts in almost every other African territory; indeed, a written form of the language, called Osmania after its originator, already exists. What has made it "almost insoluble" is the unwillingness of the Somali people to agree among themselves on what they want. Some want Somali with the Osmania alphabet, some want Somali with a Latin alphabet, but most people favor, for religious reasons, the use of the Arabic alphabet. Until the problem is solved, Somali students must continue to be educated in tongues that are not their own and in lore that does nothing to feed their self-esteem. This, to rate it no worse, is an unpromising basis for national cohesion.

Almost as intractable is the problem posed by the nomadic habit of life followed by most of the population. Somalia is goat and camel country. To keep their estimated 10 million goats and 5 million camels alive in a land of fugitive rains and largely seasonal streams, the Somali herders must be mobile. They must be willing to strike camp at any time and to do it, if need be, fifty times a year in as many different districts. In recent years the Italians, aided by the U. S. government, had drilled many sweet-water wells which have made some of the journeys unnecessary; but so far the herders have shown no sign of wanting to settle down. Until they do, they have no more chance of getting a formal education

[21] Lawrence S. Finkelstein, "Somaliland under Italian Administration: A Case Study in United Nations Trusteeship," Woodrow Wilson Foundation, New York, 1955, pp. 17–18.

than the wandering gypsy. A few fleet-footed teams, jointly sponsored by the government and UNESCO, have been put into the field, but even these, it seems, have had difficulty in keeping up with the nomads.

Sudan. When, in 1898, General Kitchener entered Khartoum at the head of his Anglo-Egyptian force and so completed the reconquest of Sudan, there were only two schools in the country other than those teaching the Koran. These two were for boys and had an enrollment of about 300.

As in all other tropical African territories, the development of educational facilities was for long hindered by shortages of funds and qualified teachers. It was also hindered somewhat by lack of agreement, at the policy level, on what was educationally good for the Sudanese people. Where there was agreement, it tended in the early days to follow the thinking of Lord Cromer, who, in 1902, announced his government's aim as being to impart "such a knowledge of reading, writing and arithmetic to a certain number of young men as will enable them to occupy with advantage the subordinate places in the administration of the country." In the circumstances it is not surprising that in 1910 only 39 elementary (or primary) schools and 6 intermediate (or middle) schools —most of them in the towns—had been opened, or that the total enrollment was little more than 3,000. In Khartoum, Gordon Memorial College, founded in 1902 on an endowment raised largely by Kitchener, was taking some young Sudanese beyond the three R's into the realms of engineering, accounting, law, business and pedagogy.

While the second and third decades of the century saw an increase in the number of both schools and scholars, it was not until the 1930s that anything much was done either to satisfy the needs of the rural areas or to provide an adequate supply of teachers and other professionals. As the result of a special inquiry, the government then put into operation in northern Sudan an ambitious scheme which included the establishment of a university college, expansion of secondary and technical education, and teacher-training facilities. Thanks largely to this scheme, the country found itself much better prepared to meet the responsibilities of independence than any of its nationalist leaders had supposed possible ten years before. On January 1, 1956, when Sudan became an independent state, there were over 1,100 government schools, with a total enrollment of nearly 100,000. Of these schools, roughly 1,000 were primary and pre-primary schools (200 of them for girls); 40 were intermediate, or middle, schools (6 of them for girls); 8 were secondary schools (one for girls); 11 were teacher-training colleges (4 for girls); and one was the coeducational University College (formerly the Gordon Memorial College). Approximately 650 non-government schools were in existence, with an enrollment of well over 50,000. Most of these schools were in the southern (so-called pagan) part of the country and were mission-run.

Since 1956 there has been further expansion of the country's educational system. There are now (1959) approximately 2,000 schools and 300,000 students. Secondary education of high quality is available at some 20 government and non-government schools. Technical education is provided by a number of intermediate industrial schools and the Khartoum Technical Institute. There are also several night schools, at which both academic and vocational subjects are taught. The University College, formerly affiliated to the University of London, is now an autonomous, degree-granting institution, called the University of Khartoum, with faculties of arts, science, agriculture, engineering, veterinary science, medicine and law, and with an enrollment of approximately 1,000. Not the least important area of expansion has been female education. In the same year well over 40,000 girls were in regular attendance at elementary, secondary and vocational schools (notably teaching and nursing), or more than twice the number in 1950.

Much remains to be done, especially for the southerners, whom the Anglo-Egyptian administration left largely to the missions and whom the Arabic-speaking, Islamic northerners have tended to despise for their uncouth, unclothed and unaccommodating ways. However, in April 1957 the central government took over responsibility for all primary education in the country. It is now in process of bringing the schools owned by the missions under its supervision, and of adding considerably to the number of primary schools in the southern provinces of Bahr-el-Ghazal, Equatoria and Upper Nile. It has also required all post-primary schools in the non-Arabic areas to teach Arabic.

THE EDUCATION OF THE ADULT

There can be no spectators of the African assault on ignorance. For ignorance is not a localized infection to be dealt with by a small educational first-aid team; nor is it a passing affliction to be speeded on its way by the ministrations of a few certified teachers. Rather is it a malignant disease—a cancer—that can be extirpated only when every thinking person in the land is aware of its presence and consequences.

Important as is the role of the school-aged in this assault, it is probably not more important than—if as important as—that of the adult. It is the adult who suffers most from the consequences of ignorance. It is he who sees his wife die in childbirth because he knows nothing of asepsis; who gets cheated in a business transaction because he cannot count or calculate; who misses the point of a technician's advice because he cannot follow him in his tongue; who "loses" his children because, being schooled, they live in a different world from his. It is the adult—man or woman—who is the arbiter of the child's education; who decides how long the child shall remain at school and, in many cases, whether the child shall have any schooling at all. It is the adult who, in the absence of enough qualified younger persons, must take up many of the responsibilities of government which are being off-loaded by the administering authorities. In short, it is the adult who is most aware of the consequences of ignorance, and so of the need to enlist in the forces marshalled against it.

All over tropical Africa there are adults who, during the past ten to twenty years, have enlisted in these forces. Their numbers vary from territory to territory; there are many more in, say, Ghana than in the Belgian Congo, and more in the Belgian Congo than in Ethiopia or Angola. There are wide differences, too, in the motives behind their enlistment. For many the motive is primarily economic—to increase the market value of one's labor or crops. For some the motive is primarily social—to learn how to appreciate Western art, literature and music, or merely how to be at home in Western society. For some the motive is political—to find out how the machinery of modern government works; how laws are made, amended and administered; how the United Nations Trusteeship Council functions and how to get invited to its hearings. And for many, perhaps most, the motive is a compound of all three, being, above everything else, the desire to "understand the forces of change, and to see that these changes are taking them in the direction they want to go."[22]

The quality and scope of the education offered at the adult level vary widely. Some of it is outstanding, and highly spoken of even by those who feared at the outset that too much was being offered too soon by educators too advanced in their views. Much of it would scarcely be thought of as education by those for whom education is now more a technology than an art. Some of it is as devoid of technical apparatus as it is of art; but it is probably no worse on that account, since it draws its strength from the opened eyes, the quickened ears and the guided hands of those who, until yesterday, were themselves ignorant and unaware.

Taking the adult field as a whole, it is possible to distinguish three main educational needs: (1) the need of those adults who want to supplement their formal schooling by taking courses in non-vocational subjects that interest them; (2) the need of those, likewise literate, who want to improve themselves by undertaking vocational training; (3) the need of those—the large majority in all but a very few territories—who are still illiterate or nearly so. Some territories are making

[22] David and Helen Kimble, *Adult Education in a Changing Africa: A Report on the Inter-African Seminar held in the Gold Coast from December 10 to 23, 1954*, International Federation of Workers' Educational Associations, London, 1955, p. 7.

stronger, and more successful, efforts to serve these needs than others; but not all territories see the need, or have the resources, to pay equal attention to all three. Some have so far paid little attention to any.

General education. Without question, the need of the first group is being served best in those territories which have colleges doing extension work, or, as it is widely spoken of in English-speaking Africa, extramural work. These institutions carry high prestige with the educated African, and are able to offer him a wide choice of subjects having relevance to his life and times. In a country such as Ghana, these subjects are as likely to include cabinet government as English composition, international affairs as economic geography, and comparative constitutions as raw materials and their uses. But they are subjects which, for their adequate presentation, call not only for highly qualified teachers but also for the use of a good library and, in some cases, for audio-visual aids and equipment. They are also subjects which lend themselves to extended debate, conference and written work; subjects, too, which can best be studied in an environment free of intellectual constraint and philosophical prejudice. For these reasons, they are best handled by high-caliber colleges and, within such colleges, by departments or institutes set up for the purpose.

Such departments or institutes now exist in all the university colleges of Commonwealth tropical Africa and in more than one corresponding institution in French and Belgian Africa. A few excerpts from a recent annual report of the Institute (formerly Department) of Extra-Mural Studies of the University College of Ghana will serve to indicate something of the scope of the work being undertaken by them:

In the bigger towns, it has been possible to break down classes into introductory and advanced groups, and to offer a wider range of specialist subjects, as numbers increased. In Accra, twenty-seven different classes were offered throughout the session, with Economics and English each being taught at four different levels, and French at three. . . .

[Each] course is conducted by a graduate tutor, who meets students weekly for a period of 1½ to 2 hours; lectures are followed by guided group discussion, and supplemented by students' own reading and written work. A detailed syllabus, with a list of recommended books, is distributed to each member as a guide to study, and a box of about thirty books is provided on long loan from the Institute's own library . . .

The extra-mural library now possesses a total of approximately 10,000 books. [During the 1954–1955 session nearly 150 book boxes, containing over 4,200 books, were issued on long loan] . . .

One hundred and twenty part-time tutors [including 21 of the College's own graduates and sixteen internal members of the University College] were employed during the year . . . Others were recruited by the Institute from a variety of occupations, and all were appointed on the basis of their qualifications and competence to conduct classes, irrespective of their political views.

The institute conducted 159 extramural classes or short courses of lectures in the 1954–1955 session. It also organized 5 residential courses, 13 weekend conferences and a great number of one-day schools and public lectures. In addition, the extramural students, through their voluntary independent national organization, the People's Educational Association, ran five conferences of their own.

These courses and conferences lead to no degrees, not even certificates of attendance. The only doors they open are those of the mind. For all that—perhaps because of it—they are always well attended. During 1954–1955 the number of "effective students" enrolled in the institute's long courses (twenty lectures or so) was nearly 2,300; another 300 were enrolled in the short courses. The people who attended these courses were recruited from almost every rank and calling. Those attending the fifteen-week course on the British Constitution in the small, fairly typical, Northern Region town of Bawku consisted of 11 teachers, 2 headmasters, 2 cooperative officers, and one of each of the following: treasury officer, postmaster, health inspector, member of the Legislative Assembly of the then Gold Coast, clerk of local council, clerk, local council officer and works foreman. In almost every course students with university degrees and students with little or no formal education at all worked side by side.

Vocational training. The needs of literate adults who are interested in vocational training are being served—where they are being served, which is by no means everywhere—through the medium of continuation schools provided by either government or private agencies. Among the schools falling into this category, none surpass and few equal Jeanes School at Kiambu, near Nairobi, Kenya.

Named for Anna T. Jeanes, the Philadelphia philanthropist who did so much to raise the standard of teaching of negroes in the American South, this school was at first (1926) concerned primarily with rural development. Since 1949, when it was taken over by the Kenya government, it has become "an institution to support community development in Kenya by means of adult education," as a school circular states. At the present time, the work of the school, as described in the same circular, is divided into three distinct sections: "first, the preparation of young adult Africans for work in various government departments or with African District Councils; secondly, help given to older members of the community who are already established as farmers, shopkeepers, civil servants, etc., and who come to Jeanes School in order to obtain not only a better knowledge of their own particular job, but also a wider knowledge of the affairs of the country; and thirdly, women's work."

One of the most important courses offered to students in the first category is that designed to turn out community development assistants. Students for the course, which lasts anywhere up to a year, are recruited from the lower echelons of local and central government and from business organizations.

While in residence, they receive instruction in such diverse fields as labor relations, village management, and the running of adult literacy classes and recreational clubs.

Other courses are designed to train health inspectors and health assistants, probation assistants, cooperative assistants and inspectors, rehabilitation officers, farmers, traders and shopkeepers, bakers, librarians and choral singers (the last in an effort to revive the better forms of traditional African music). Courses in Swahili are given for European civil servants, and courses are offered in such non-vocational, but highly practical, subjects as citizenship.

Most of the training in what is called the women's work section is done in a homecrafts department, which has its own headmistress. Here some 80 to 100 women a year are instructed in child care, health and hygiene, needlework, cooking, laundry, agriculture, and in the running of literacy campaigns. On leaving the course, these women undertake to set up women's clubs in their home areas; there, under guidance, they can pass on the knowledge they have acquired during their training. These Progress of Women's Clubs, as they are called, already have well over 50,000 members in Kenya.

The fact that people in many other progressive parts of tropical Africa are pressing their governments to build schools of the Jeanes type, and are succeeding in getting such schools built, is as much proof of the widely felt need for vocational training of adults as it is of the conviction that such schools can go a long way toward satisfying it.

To satisfy the need completely would, of course, be quite beyond the reach of governments having difficulty—as all are —in meeting the demand for primary education of the school-aged. Fortunately, the governments of several territories have been able to lean heavily on the training arm of commercial and industrial companies. As was pointed out earlier, such companies were among the first organizations to see the need for schooling, both for the children of their employees and the employees themselves; and some of them have had outstanding training programs for many years. Among these are the Union Minière du Haut-Katanga (Belgian Congo), the United Africa Company (Commonwealth West Africa), and the East African Railways and Harbours (British East Africa).

To the adolescent brought up in its schools and wishing to work in its installations, the Union Minière offers the alternatives of attending apprentice school (which will train him to do either technical or administrative work) and on-the-job training. To the regular African employee who wants to qualify for a better position, it offers night-school courses in such academic subjects as mathematics and French, and in such skilled trades as cabinetry, metal working, draftsmanship and electronics. The company also operates on-the-job training for its European employees. According to a company statement, this is designed to give them basic principles for the education of the African and "to establish good working relations between Europeans and Africans."

In line with its long-followed policy of Africanization, the United Africa Company offers its employees a wide range of educational opportunities. In each of the larger towns where it does business, it makes provision for the in-service training of clerks, typists, machine operators and so on. A company booklet reports: "In Kano and Freetown young employees attend small clerical schools for short periods daily under the experienced eye of a full-time teacher. In Kingsway Stores, Lagos, staff attend courses on salesmanship. The Manager in charge of the Nigerian Kingsway Shops organization gives lectures to salesmen when he visits their branches, and these lectures are linked with follow-up postal courses leading to promotion examinations."

The company also runs four separate schools for indentured apprentices and for those who already rank as skilled artisans. One of these, at Burutu, on the delta of the Niger River, specializes in the training of apprentices (over a hundred at a time) in marine engineering and allied trades. Two others, at Lagos and Accra, specialize in motor repair and maintenance. The fourth, at Sapele (near Burutu), provides training for technicians employed in the company's timber operations. All four offer refresher courses for members of the company's staff. Elsewhere training courses are arranged for laboratory assistants, coopers and typewriter mechanics, while each year the company sends one or two students to the Government School of Pharmacy in Yaba outside Lagos. Recently arrangements have been made for the training of a number of Africans as engineers, deck officers or pursers on Palm Line ships.

In addition to this specialist training, the United Africa Company has an agreement with one of the large British correspondence schools which enables employees to take, at much reduced fees, courses of practical value to them in their careers. It also makes a regular practice of sending its ablest African shop managers to the United Kingdom for study, and exchange-of-duty tours.

The Kenya and Uganda Railway and Harbours (now incorporated into the East African Railways and Harbours) opened its first training school in 1919. Confined in the early years to telegraphy, the curriculum of the school later came to include such subjects as the running of railway stations, the handling of passenger and freight traffic, and the driving of locomotives. Today, in a block of modern buildings, costing over $1.25 million, E.A.R. and H. provides residential training facilities for several hundred young Africans, Asians and Europeans interested in making a career of railroading. The training covers every phase of activity—operational, commercial and engineering. For boys of average scholastic attainment (those with the equivalent roughly of a grade school education), the company offers a five-year indentured apprenticeship to various trades. Those who complete their apprenticeship satisfactorily are engaged as artisans in the railway workshops, or as tracers in the drawing office. For boys with more schooling, the company offers apprenticeships leading to higher grades of employment, including charge-hand and foreman. A measure of the popularity—prestige, one might say—of these apprenticeships is seen in the fact that in 1957 no fewer than 15,000 people applied for the training school's 200 vacancies.

Literacy training. The basic need of the third group of adults, the illiterates or near-illiterates, is obviously the ability to read and write, preferably in a language which is widely understood and for which there are some printed materials. While reliable statistics of illiteracy are scarce, it is pretty safe to say that in tropical Africa as a whole eight out of every ten adults are still unable to meet the criterion of literacy suggested by UNESCO: "[to] read with understanding and write a short simple statement on . . . everyday life." There are considerable regional differences in the rate. Thus, it is certainly lower—down to less than 50 per cent—among the people of Buganda in southern Uganda than it is among the people of Karamoja in northeastern Uganda. In Uganda as a whole it is probably much lower than it is in, say, the Central African Republic, Liberia and Somalia. Whatever the figures are, they are not as high in most territories as they were twenty, even ten, years ago. In Ghana they may well be less than half what they were ten years ago.

As in the other fields of adult education, credit for the advances being made belongs to many agencies. In some territories, Ghana and Uganda among them, most of it belongs to the government, working through its community development or social welfare agencies. In two or three, including Somalia and Liberia, much of it belongs to UNESCO; and in almost all territories, some of the credit belongs to the missions. But whether the agencies are public or private, their funds large or small, their methods modern or primitive, the results are the same: the intellectually blind receive their sight, the economically lame begin to walk, and the politically poor have the gospel of nationalism preached unto them. And thanks to the techniques developed in the past generation by Laubach and others, it does not take the willing adults long to start seeing and walking—or, for that matter, long for the preachers to arrive.

Not all adults are willing to be made literate. Many teachers find the process of educating the illiterate in the values of education slow and hard. After a generation of effort, the Firestone Plantations Company in Liberia reported that the ratio of literate to illiterate employees was still less than one in ten. Many who are willing learners to begin with do not stay willing very long. In a recent annual report, the Department of Community Development in Uganda had to confess that interest in literacy seemed to be on the wane among the Ganda—usually regarded as the most progressive people in the country. Regrettable as this is, it is perhaps not surprising. Since literacy is commonly held to be a species of white man's magic, should it not be discarded when it fails to make its possessor either as rich or as powerful as the white man? But if the newly literate man is willing to take disillusionment, he can hardly be expected to take the dearth of reading matter in his stride. In far too many written African languages, the only reading matter available to the new literate consists of portions of the Bible, religious tracts and badly printed newspapers.

Important as the ability to read and write is, it is not indispensable to an adult's better understanding of his life and times. As extramural tutors have found, many illiterate adults are quite capable of discussing their economic and social problems intelligently, and are willing to do so regularly week by week. The African countryside shows many evidences that they are quite capable of solving some of them, too. Many of the community welfare schemes—the well digging, the mosquito spraying, the school building and the mass inoculating —are being carried out by illiterate people. Many other illiterates have learned to perform highly skilled jobs in workshop, factory and mine.

All the same, so long as men and women remain unable to enlarge their experience through reading and develop their powers of self-expression in writing, they are unlikely to perceive the full penalty of their ignorance, let alone discover the means of removing it.

THE MASS COMMUNICATIONS MEDIA

Of all the weapons in the educator's armory, none have wider appeal than the mass communications media. In tropical Africa the chief of these weapons are the press, the radio and motion pictures. (As of the end of 1959 there was no television anywhere in tropical Africa. The Federal Government of Nigeria hoped to have a station going by October 1960, in time for its independence celebrations. There were also plans for commercial television in several other territories, including Kenya and the Federation of Rhodesia and Nyasaland.)

The reasons for their appeal are obvious. In the first place, as the name implies, they are media for the masses, and it is to the masses that the administrator, the preacher, the politician and, increasingly, the advertiser seek to "get across." Second, they are the media that deliver the largest audiences per unit of cost—a major consideration in all poor countries. Third, they reach the people where they are—in their homes, market places and villages; even motion pictures may be sent to the people in this age of mobility. Fourth, in a part of the world where conversation is still an art and the "bush telegraph" still a highly efficient form of telecommunication, the reach of these media exceeds their grasp; indeed, the second-hand audiences are frequently the largest.

To measure the precise impact of these media is impossible. For one thing, in many areas the poll taker is likely to be told what the person being polled thinks he would like to be told. For another, impact is as much a matter of imponderable depth as of measurable length and breadth, of stored memories as of shared reaction, and of past experience as of present circumstance. But impact there most certainly is. To this every educated African and every government and mission agency can testify. What is more, it is growing in every territory, for as the siren songs of editor, announcer and producer become louder, the audiences' addiction to them becomes stronger.

THE PRESS

The first to enter the "mass" field, the press has known all the excitements of pioneering and all of its frustrations. It has also been guilty of most of the excesses of pioneers. At the same time, when given the right environment, it has shown a capacity for growth in intellectual stature and for gumption in the handling of controversy. Although newspapers have been published in tropical Africa for many years, it is only in the past generation that they have become an important educational force. Even now, though, there are many areas which, because of illiteracy, poverty, or lack of distribution facilities, or all three, have no newspapers. According to the 1957 and 1959 *Statistical Yearbooks* of the United Nations, nine territories had only one newspaper each in the latest year for which information was available, and the combined circulation of these nine was only a little over 46,000, more than one third of which was accounted for by a single paper.

For convenience, the newspapers can be divided into two groups: those serving African needs, and those serving either European or Asian needs. Where the press serves a bi-racial or multiracial constituency it is generally because only one paper is available, or because one paper is superior to another in news coverage and so forth.

The African press. The region with the most influential African press is Commonwealth West Africa (Gambia, Sierra Leone, Ghana and Nigeria). It was here—in Sierra Leone in the early nineteenth century—that the first tropical African newspaper was printed, and it is here that most tropical African newspapers run today for the benefit of Africans are published. More than 50 newspapers of differing frequency of appearance are now published in Commonwealth West Africa. In Nigeria alone there are about 30, and in Ghana a dozen or more. Of the total, not more than about six use vernacular languages; the rest use English. By Western standards their aggregate circulation is small, amounting to perhaps 400,000. The readership, though, is large. Probably nowhere else in the world do newspapers get read so often, so completely, and over so long a period. But this and their "Africanness" are about all they have in common. The circulation of individual papers varies enormously, as does their technical and journalistic competence; there is no average.

At their best, they can stand comparison with those of almost any medium-sized American town, for they are competently printed, well illustrated and thoughtfully edited. They are no less interested in promoting the health and welfare of their readers (women included) than they are in presenting the news of the community, country and wider world; they are as keen to applaud economic gain as they are to condemn political trickery and malfeasance. But there are few such papers. Until 1947, when a London newspaper (the *Daily Mirror*) became interested in the region and formed the West African Press, there were almost none at all. Today, this group alone runs three highly successful daily papers—the *Daily Graphic* (Ghana), the *Daily Times* (Nigeria) and the *Daily Mail* (Sierra Leone)—with a combined weekday circulation of approximately 150,000 and a Sunday circulation of some 100,000.

The great majority of the newspapers, however, are inadequately staffed, indifferently written and edited, and poorly printed on presses of antique design. With a circulation numbered in hundreds rather than thousands, the editor frequently finds himself doubling as reporter when he is not reading proof or pushing sales. His lot has been feelingly described by Abiodun Aloba, a Nigerian editor.

> The Lagos editor who is master of all trades, interviews everybody who cares to call because they all insist on seeing him, rushes through every provincial news item, runs after the half-illiterate compositors below and sweats through four editorials to go to print on time . . . [If] this Lagos editor were editing a provincial [newspaper] his fate

would still be worse. There will probably be no telephone to check the story of an accident occurring only a couple of miles from his office. . . .

As for the reporters who do the field work, their fate is to get a "fair" idea of what has happened, rush to the office on their flat and sometimes shoeless feet, and write anything to help them escape the fury of their tired editor; for the editor is not in good temper, the sun is already on the decline and the third leader [editorial] has not gone down . . .

Now, what about the manuscripts that have just come in at 2 p.m. because the train came in late yesterday? The first is a "Press Release" from the Public Relations Department. It contains no scoop, it has been passed to a couple of dozen other newspapers in the country, and those in the capital have already published it . . . The second manuscript in the pile is plain libel. The third is an obvious fabrication, the fourth a mixture of unintelligible Latin mixed up with worse French but meant, for all that, to read as English; the fifth has been sent in by a village vicar begging the editor to announce a harvest thanksgiving which unfortunately took place last Sunday.

So we go on.[23]

The wonder is that they do go on, for it is unremitting toil and poorly paid at that. Few "small-town" editors earn more than a bus driver; most of the reporters earn considerably less. But such is the hunger for news and such is the prestige enjoyed by both reader and editor in a world where the majority of people are still unlettered, that most of the papers do manage to carry on. And there is no doubt that newspapers have been influential in molding public opinion, especially political opinion. Many of these papers began as the mouthpiece of politicians in search of a party. To those who formed the party, what mattered was not the quality of the newspaper or the writing, but the justice (as they saw it) of

[23] Quoted in *The Press in Africa*, edited by Helen Kitchen, Ruth Sloan Associates, Inc., Washington, D. C., 1956, pp. ii–iii.

the cause it stood for and the eloquence of those who proclaimed it. More than anything else, perhaps, it was the constant plugging by the little African-run papers of the case for self-government that hastened the end of colonialism in Commonwealth West Africa. (Judging by the speed with which it ended in Ghana, it is probable that some of the British readers of these newspapers had their opinions molded by them, too.)

The political influence of the larger, European-owned papers addressed to Africans has also been considerable. However, for the most part, this influence has been exerted in favor of the constituted authority of the country, and so has been in the nature of a counterweight to the prevailing political forces. This means that these newspapers have been spectators of political evolution rather than active participants in it. At times this has annoyed the African politician as much as it has disturbed the government. But they have generally tried to give their readers both sides of the problem of political change; and in a world of astigmatic readers, there is always room for editors with 20:20 vision.

For all its shortcomings, the African press of Commonwealth West Africa is still a long way ahead of the African press in other sections. Large sections do not yet have an African press, whether run by Africans or for Africans. Among these are Mozambique, Angola and Portuguese Guinea, and the Spanish colonies of Fernando Po and Rio Muni. Elsewhere it is at best a rather weak press.

In some areas the press is weak because there is not a large enough concentration of literate people to support the costs of even a small paper; and so long as distribution is a problem, the incidence of potential readers per square mile is likely to be a more critical factor than their incidence per 1,000 population. At the present time, few territories, or parts of territories, can begin to compete with Ghana and the Eastern and Western Regions of Nigeria in this respect. One of the few that comes close to doing so is Uganda. In 1954 it was estimated that "About 70,000 of [Uganda's] five million inhabitants buy a paper at least once a week, and [that] the number of readers must be five times that number. In addition, some 75,000 government newssheets are distributed gratis weekly."[24] Today the readership may be half as high again, but the difficulties of distribution are such that not less than nine out of every ten readers live within fifty miles of Kampala where most of the papers are published—which is to say that not less than nine out of every ten readers live in Buganda, the most progressive province in the protectorate.

The political power of this press is already considerable. A large part of the opposition to the British government (and to its chief representative, Sir Andrew Cohen, the then Governor) during the 1953–1954 Kabaka crisis[25] almost certainly emanated from the local vernacular press. It is also arguable that "the Uganda National Congress has grown up around its press, rather than around a solid membership."[26] Unlike the African press of Ghana and Nigeria, which does most of its publishing in English, the Uganda press works mainly with Swahili, the *lingua franca* of east Africa, and Luganda, the language of the Ganda.

Other regions which have been able to reckon on a comparatively high incidence of African readers are southern Kenya (especially in and near the large towns and in Kikuyu country), northern Tanganyika (especially the Meru-Kilimanjaro-Dar-es-Salaam area), the Copperbelt of Northern Rhodesia, the urbanized districts of Southern Rhodesia, and the Katanga and metropolitan areas of the Belgian Congo. In each of these regions there is a growing African press. But in each region it is beset by weakness of one kind or another. In some regions the weakness is primarily economic—lack of cash for anything but essentials, or things considered to be essentials. Even in districts where the average pay is high by African standards, newspaper circulation is noticeably cyclical, most

[24] "An African Press Survey: 3—East and Central Africa," *New Commonwealth*, August 19, 1954, p. 171.

[25] This crisis arose over the refusal in 1953 of Mutesa II, the Kabaka (King) of Buganda, to abide by decisions taken by the British government, a refusal that led to his temporary deportation to England.

[26] *Loc. cit.*

of the newspaper buying being done within a week or so of payday. (This applies also in Commonwealth West Africa.) In some regions the weakness, until recently, has been more political than economic. This was especially true of Belgian and French territories, the governments of which were in the habit of keeping close watch on the content of papers intended for African consumption, and of censoring anything that would put their administration in a poor light or make for unrest. The same has been true of the Kenya government, which, at the time of the Mau Mau troubles of 1952, found it necessary to suppress some 40 vernacular newspapers (most of them Kikuyu), and for a while thereafter forbade the circulation of all mimeographed vernacular newssheets.

Frequently the control, whether by way of censorship or suppression, is exercised behind the reader's back rather than overtly. Lacking the funds to subscribe to any of the large news agencies, most African newspapers have to rely heavily on what the government information services choose to give them. While most governments give generously, they give selectively; and the principles governing their selection of news are usually different from those that would be applied by African editors. What is bread to the one is often a stone—if not a serpent—to the other. Then again, it is not only governments that exercise censorship, overt or otherwise. Many European-run African papers are equally inclined to put all incoming items of news through the fine screen of "public interest."

This brings us to another weakness, as it is widely judged to be, namely, the extent to which the African press is controlled by non-Africans. Many African papers are government-run as well as government-controlled. Many others are owned either by missions or by mining and other industrial corporations. Many more are in the hands of publishing firms owned and directed by Europeans. European control may be of small consequence in countries like Ghana and Nigeria, where there are competing African-owned and -operated presses and where, anyway, the government would make short work of any directorate that was found guilty of indulging in un-

African activity. But it is different in a country like Southern Rhodesia, where the African press is dominated by a single European company, African Newspapers Co., Ltd. Granted that the Europeans who own this company—the Paver brothers—offer the literate African of Southern Rhodesia good-quality English and vernacular newspapers (weekly, bi-weekly and monthly); that they use African editors, reporters and photographers, and run their presses with African help; and that the ordinary reader—to judge by the correspondence columns—is well satisfied with the product. The fact remains, however, that the policy of these papers is set by Europeans who, while not afraid to criticize the government (as they did on the Federation issue), share its conviction that the African is still unready for true, interracial partnership and self-government. In these immoderate times, the holders of middle-of-the-road policies are almost everywhere finding the going hard. Like middle-of-the-road drivers, they incur the displeasure not only of those seeking to overtake them but also of those headed in the other direction. In Southern Rhodesia there are plenty of each, since hardly anybody wants to stay where he is.

It is easy to diagnose the ills of the African press; they are there for every African and European to see. It is the cure for them that poses the problem. In the case of the African-run press, it will no doubt require large and frequent injections of capital. Such capital will not be easy to come by. Few outside investors would be impressed by the look of the average African press, its management or its product; and most local investors have other ideas about what to do with their capital. Some governments might be willing to supply it, but it is unlikely that many editors would care to be tied to the attendant strings. Most of the capital will have to be self-generated.

Already advertising plays an important role in some newspapers. In Commonwealth West Africa, for instance, it accounts for 25 to 50 per cent of the space in the larger papers and an even higher proportion in some of the smaller ones.

And the outlay on advertising is growing as manufacturers of consumer goods discover that advertising creates sales for branded products and the big trading and industrial companies begin to see the value of "public relations" advertising. Perhaps it is not too much to hope that, by stimulating the African appetite for manufactured goods, advertising will come to provide the much needed incentive to higher productivity and living standards. As these rise, so will the output, and the profits, of the press.

All of this will take time, and its twin, patience. Patience will also be needed in other matters—not least, as Abiodun Aloba observes, "patience to wait until telephone exchanges do not keep you waiting for hours to get in touch with your sources of news, and telegrams do not have to go by 30 m.p.h. trains."

Quite as important as capital and patience is the question of training. Prior to 1959, the only way an aspiring journalist could get training was by apprenticing himself to a local newspaper, and most papers had neither the facilities nor the skills to take him very far. For formal training he had to go to either Europe or America, where, not infrequently it seems, he became more interested in the propagandist than the educational value of news. There have been some notable exceptions, such as Lawrence Vambe of Southern Rhodesia, E. M. K. Mulira of Uganda, and Abiodun Aloba himself, but their number is small. All the same, the need for formal training in journalism is coming to be recognized. The first tropical African school of journalism opened its doors in Accra, Ghana, in 1959. Others are in the planning stage.

With training, it is not too much to hope that there will emerge a stronger sense of public stewardship, compounded of awareness of the power inherent in the printed word, restraint in the uses made of it, and tolerance for the uses made of it by others. Certainly such a sense will not come by wealth or waiting; if it is to come at all, it must come through the insights born of intellectual discipline and honesty.

As for the African newspapers controlled by Europeans, their weakness—as also their strength—derives from the colonial matrix in which they were reared. Invaluable as they have been in providing the African with good-class reading material of all kinds, and desirable as their continued existence in many areas would seem to be, they must be counted a poor risk almost everywhere, since almost everywhere the colonial matrix is disintegrating. The fact that these newspapers are, for the most part, run, edited and supported by Africans is of small consequence to most African patriots beside the fact that they are not controlled by Africans. To the patriot, foreign control is not something to be cured; it is something to be eradicated.

The European press. Wherever Europeans go, the press is sure to follow. In tropical Africa, it has generally followed close behind. Salisbury, Southern Rhodesia, has had a newspaper (the *Rhodesia Herald*) since 1891; Bulawayo in the same colony has had one (now called the *Chronicle*) since 1894. Kampala, Uganda, and Mombasa, Kenya, had newspapers before World War I; Nairobi has had a daily newspaper (the *East African Standard*) since 1914. Elisabethville, Belgian Congo, has had one (*L'Essor du Congo*) since 1928; and Dakar, Senegal, one (*Paris-Dakar*) since 1935. Today there are few towns that do not have a paper or journal addressed primarily to a European readership. Nor is this surprising. In almost every town the European element consists largely of well-educated people with money to spend, time on their hands, and a self-imposed obligation to have opinions on what is going on around them. Today, too, many Europeans, expatriates and settlers alike, also feel an obligation to know the opinions others have of them.

Like the African press, the European is far from uniform in quality. This, too, need not surprise us. The constituency served by some of the papers is very small, partly because of their isolation from other European centers and partly because there is only a limited local demand for this kind of paper. Many papers have a circulation of less than 5,000. One or two in the Belgian Congo have a circulation of not more than 1,000. Without subsidies, such papers barely manage to keep going. They do so largely by dint of using local news, government handouts, and as much advertising matter and as little paid help as possible. Moreover, some of the European —as some of the African—papers are less concerned with news than with propaganda. This is especially true of some of the "settler" papers published in the Belgian Congo, Kenya and the Federation of Rhodesia and Nyasaland. In more than one instance, the propaganda has been sufficiently seditious, or racist, to bring government action against the publishers.

Thanks as much to their advertising as to their circulation revenues, the larger papers—such as *Le Courrier d'Afrique* of Léopoldville, *Paris-Dakar,* the Bulawayo *Chronicle,* the Salisbury *Rhodesia Herald,* the Nairobi *East African Standard* and the Salisbury *Sunday Mail*—have considerably bigger budgets to work with. They can afford to subscribe to news agencies, to keep a switchboard going, and to pay their employees a decent wage. But even the 50,000 circulation of the *Sunday Mail*—the largest in the region—is small by European standards, and too small to give its readers more than an inkling of what is going on beyond the range of the territorial telephone and telegraph system. Nor does it buy much in the way of journalistic skill, overseas field staff, or photoengraving work.

As a result, most of the news and comment contained in the European papers is focused on the local scene, its alarms and excursions, its passions and pains. It is uncommon to find a paper in which the works of the world command more linage than those of the flesh and the devil. It is likewise uncommon to find a paper that is free to plot its own editorial course and change it at will. In some cases this lack of freedom is a result of outside control. Thus, six of the largest papers in the Federation—the *Rhodesia Herald,* the *Sunday Mail,* the *Chronicle,* the *Sunday News* (Bulawayo) and the *Northern News* (Ndola)—are published by a company (the Rhodesian Printing and Publishing Co.) that is a subsidiary of a newspaper group having its headquarters in the Union of South Africa and anxious, on that account, not to give offense to either the Union or the Federation governments, with both of which it feels it has to curry favor. In other cases it stems from the conviction, which many publishers have, that since they are Europeans in lands predominantly non-European, they ought to support the constituted European authority in their midst. In the case of many smaller papers, it is an automatic consequence of the fact that, like many African papers, they exist to promote the political ideas of their founders.

But there are "free" papers, and their following is growing. Among them the *Central African Examiner* of Salisbury has been outstanding. Calling itself a "fortnightly journal for thinking people," from its inception in 1957 it has maintained an independent attitude toward the questions, political, industrial, social and racial, that have come under its scrutiny. While claiming to have no axes to grind, it has kept plenty in stock and has not been afraid to wield them when occasion demanded—and in the Federation of the past few years there have been plenty of occasions. On some of these it was the Europeans rather than the Africans who had to watch out for the wielder. The circulation has been small (less than 5,000), but probably no paper published in tropical Africa has had a more influential or widespread readership. Other journals that have displayed considerable independence of viewpoint and have been addressed to "thinking people" are the *Kenya Weekly News, La Presse du Cameroun, La Côte d'Ivoire* and *Pourquoi Pas?* (Léopoldville).

Since World War II, the European press in most territories has found an increasing sale for its publications among educated Africans. This, of course, must not be taken to mean that it has been making "converts" of them. In most cases it merely means that the African's hunger for news, and for reading matter of all kinds, is not adequately met in the papers which are published for his benefit. In a good many cases, however, it also means that he is coming to see the necessity of looking at both sides of the questions that confront him and his rulers. The results of his doing this have sometimes surprised him as much as the European. Perhaps one reason why the French still have as many friends as they do in tropical Africa is that their newspapers have seldom shown any inclination to coddle the reader, let alone corral him.

Another significant postwar development has been the growth in circulation of newspapers and periodicals published in Europe. Primarily this increase is a reflection of the development, and speeding up, of air transport that now makes it possible to buy *Figaro* in Douala the day of publication, and to have the London *Times* delivered in Salisbury the day after publication. To some extent, though, it reflects the desire for a better news service than is provided by the local papers. Up to now, most of the subscribers to these journals have been Europeans, but the number of African subscribers to papers like *Figaro* and the *Times* and to periodicals like the international edition of *Time* is steadily growing. The attitude of these publications toward the African is sympathetic, their reports are generally reliable, and, in these days of fast fame, there's always the chance that he who reads may run into his own name.

In British East Africa, notably in Kenya and Zanzibar, there is an Asian press of considerable size and influence. Among the more widely circulated of the papers published in Kenya under Asian auspices are the *Kenya Daily Mail*, the *Observer*, the *Colonial Times*, the *Daily Chronicle*, and the *Goan Voice*. The first two appear in two editions, Gujerati and English; the last three in English only. Their total circulation is probably of the order of 25,000. Most of the Zanzibar papers are small weeklies, but at least one of them, the *Samachar*, claims to have "a wide and extensive circulation throughout East and South Africa, Rhodesias, Madagascar, India, Pakistan and West Africa . . . [and to be] recognized by all influential advertisers as the best medium for advertising in East Africa . . . among the rich and middle classes."[27]

While these papers are oriented toward Asian (including Arabic) needs and interests, some of them are read approvingly by Africans. This is particularly true of those (the *Daily*

[27] Quoted by St. Clair and Elizabeth Drake in a paper prepared for this study.

Chronicle for instance) which lean toward the left and so find themselves opposing the government—as, of course, do the Africans—most of the time.

Broadcasting in tropical Africa began in the early 1930s as a service to the European population. Rather naturally, therefore, Kenya, Mozambique, Angola, Southern Rhodesia and the Belgian Congo were among the first territories to be served by local transmitters. The first programs directed to the African population began a few years later. However, until the outbreak of World War II, most of them relied on rebroadcast and rediffusion of overseas programs rather than on direct transmission. As St. Clair and Elizabeth Drake put it, they were "wired rather than wireless programs."

Down to 1939 only 7 tropical African territories possessed transmitting facilities. At the war's end 15 had such facilities. In the case of 2 of the 15—French Equatorial Africa and the Belgian Congo—these facilities were used primarily for short-wave overseas broadcasts in the interest of the Free French and Belgian war efforts.

With the possible exception of the Portuguese territories, where broadcasting is in the hands of "radio clubs" run by and for Europeans, most of the postwar effort in this field has been directed to the task of reaching the indigenous peoples. The spoken word continues to carry a far greater appeal for them than the printed word, even where the latter is understood. It has, needless to say, been a task of ample proportions.

To begin with, the average African household is still far too poor to be interested in buying a radio set. Even in Nigeria, which has one of the highest income levels in tropical Africa, the price of a good battery-run set—the only kind that is any use away from the larger towns—represents approximately two to three months' take-home pay of the average worker. Then, there is the difficulty of providing servicing, including battery-recharging facilities. In most rural areas they simply do not exist; and few towns can boast of a reliable radio repairman. There is also the question of transmission. Most of the territories are large and call for powerful transmitters. But not even the most powerful transmitters can silence the static which fills the tropical air during the rainy season. Programs that come through "loud and clear" tend to be the exception. A further difficulty arises from the absence in most territories of a single, widely understood language. To reach its radio audience, the Nigerian Broadcasting Corporation uses no fewer than 13 languages, a fact that adds greatly to its operating costs. Another circumstance that tends to push up operating costs is the scarcity of qualified Africans to fill the senior technical and administrative positions. European labor, while efficient, is expensive, especially in the non-settler regions.

Perhaps the biggest difficulty of all is the raising of revenue. The usual European device of raising it by license fees is subject to serious limitations. The number of sets is still almost everywhere small. Even in Nigeria, which is credited with having the most, there are probably not more than 250,-000 at the outside—a considerable increase, to be sure, from the 73,000 reported in 1958. In territories like Togo and Somalia the number is nearer 3,000. Besides, few African owners of radios are in a position to pay more than a nominal license fee. Even if they were, most of the territories are so large and their populations so scattered that the cost of collecting such fees is likely to be almost as great as the revenue obtained from them. Furthermore, evasion is easy. In 1958 the Nigerian Broadcasting Corporation obtained about £4,000 from license fees; at 10 shillings a license this represented about 8,000 radios, or approximately the number being sold each month.

What of commercial advertising as a source of revenue? So far most of the corporations have shied away from using it. Among their reasons for doing so is the fact that they do not wish to lose control of the programs to people whose aims are likely to be very different from their own. Some corporations also feel, as one director recently put it in conversation, that "with business and politics being so closely mated in most of the newly independent countries, they would soon find themselves in the pay of politicians if they once attempted to go in for sponsored programs." But the pressures for such programs are almost everywhere growing. Already there are "commercial" stations in Mozambique, Southern Rhodesia and Liberia.

Up to now, therefore, almost all of the money for broadcasting has had to come from government sources, either from current income or from capital funds made available for the purpose through such agencies as the British Colonial Development and Welfare grants. A very few stations derive their funds from private sources only. One of the most important of these is the high-powered station (ELWA) owned and operated by the Sudan Interior Mission in Liberia.

The difficulties notwithstanding, radio broadcasting is making strides in most parts of tropical Africa. At the end of the 1950s the region had over 80 transmitters, as against fewer than 10 in 1939. It also had a rapidly growing number of relay stations. Some territories (Nigeria, for instance) now have enough relay stations and transmitters to give radio coverage to every inhabitant able to pay for it. Judging by the growth in the number of receiving sets, a large number of Africans are able to pay for it. The total number of sets has grown since 1939 from 50,000 (at the most) to 550,000 (at the least). Every year sees a lowering of the price and an improvement in the design of the models put onto the African market. The "Saucepan Special" (so called because of its housing) developed by the British for use in the bush sells in most places for less than $20 and, short of being used as a saucepan, gives good service.

Increased facilities have resulted in greatly increased services. Whereas twenty years ago few stations were on the air for more than an hour or so a day, now many stations keep going more than 8 hours a day.

Nor has the growth been merely numerical. The intellectual growth of radio broadcasting has been, if anything, more impressive. Entertainment, it is true, continues to be an important ingredient of almost all programs. But most stations now see their job as threefold—to inform and instruct no less than to entertain. The actual "air" time given to the pursuit of the first two objectives seldom, if ever, exceeds that given to the third, but the amount of planning (to say nothing of money) that goes into this pursuit leaves no doubt as to the importance attached to it. What the Federal [Rhodesian] Broadcasting Corporation has said of its Lusaka programs could be said of many other services catering primarily to Africans: "As a whole, the Lusaka programmes can be considered . . . as programmes for the education of adults." Where most of the adults are country dwellers, illiterate and otherwise backward, the emphasis tends to be put, as in the Lusaka programs, on instructing—how to grow bigger crops, get a clean water supply, conduct an anti-malaria spraying campaign, cook manioc and like it, and so on. Where most of the adults are either town dwellers or school graduates, or both, more emphasis is generally put on informing—about everything from the running of the government and the threat of communism in underdeveloped territories to the evils of prostitution, alcoholism and polygamy.

Many stations also offer "straight" educational programs. Depending on the type of constituency served by the stations, their programs range from elementary reading to economics, world geography and musical appreciation. Although often designed for use in schools, these courses seldom fail to draw an audience of adults. If the interested adult has no set of his own, he is likely to seek out the nearest community or coffee shop set. Today in most territories there are literate adults whose only "formal" schooling was obtained, by proxy, in this fashion. Such is the appeal of the educational type of program, both formal and informal, that some stations are now devoting 25 per cent or more of their time to it. In a recent year, the Central African Broadcasting Station at Lusaka devoted about 10 per cent of its time to news, about 10 per cent to talks, and another 10 per cent or so to quizzes and similar features.

A great deal of attention has also been given since the war to the entertainment side of radio, which, in Africa as elsewhere, is what most people spend most of their listening time looking for. Of necessity, in view of their small operating budgets, most stations continue to rely heavily on recorded music. But the range of musical taste catered for by the average station is now wide, embracing everything from African traditional to European classical and American modern. Some stations, responding to listener demand—as they have quickly learned to do in the areas of overlapping coverage— now find themselves putting out almost as much non-African as African music. And the quality is generally good, for here, too, the African is showing himself to be a discriminating listener, ready at the drop of a disk to tell the announcer what he thinks of him, and to take his place if need be. In fact, most stations serving a largely African audience now use African announcers, in some cases even for their European-language broadcasts. When given half a chance, the African has also shown himself capable of becoming a highly accomplished radio artist, whether singer, instrumentalist or actor. Not only the African man, either. Many stations use almost as much female as male talent. Stations in Ghana, Nigeria and the former French dependencies have been doing so for several years.

But the progress, great as it is, has been far from uniform in either direction or degree. Thus, while the Belgians, French and British have all made impressive strides in getting their dependent peoples radio-minded, they have not all stridden down the same path. The Belgians have, for the most part, taken the view that the needs of the people are best served by providing community listening facilities in the rural areas and rediffusion systems in the larger centers, and that the needs of the government are best served by speaking to the people in their own vernaculars and in the official languages of the country. While sharing the Belgian preference for community listening, the French have taken the view that since the one "mass" language is the language of government, it is cheaper, and in the long run most effective, to use this as the vehicle of communication. The British, on the other hand, have preferred, wherever possible, to speak to the people in their own tongues in their own homes over their own sets. (For this reason, assessments of the comparative "reach" of the radio programs based on the number of receiving sets per 1,000 population in the various territories need to be treated with caution.)

Then again, there are very considerable territorial differences in the kinds of programs offered to the African and in the proportion of radio time given to each. Not all of the territories give as much attention as, say, Northern Rhodesia, Ghana, Nigeria and the Belgian Congo to educational matters. Some, like British East Africa and Southern Rhodesia, still seem to feel that the primary function of radio is to entertain. There are stations that still devote more than 90 per cent of their time to such features as "Music While You Work," "Dancing Time," "Town and Country Songs," "Marching Songs," "Folk Songs" and "War Dances." In some parts there are also considerable intraterritorial differences. This is particularly true of those territories which have large regional concentrations of Moslems. In Nigeria, for example, the amount of time devoted to readings from the Koran and other religious items over the Kano station, which serves the Northern Region, is very much greater than the amount given to religious programs of all kinds over the Lagos station, which serves the predominantly non-Moslem south. Then, too, most Moslem areas are still nervous of novelty—of anything that might sow the seeds of disaffection among the faithful. These areas, consequently, have so far tended to lag behind the Christianized areas in their use of radio's informing and instructing services.

There are some territories in which progress of any sort or in any direction has been slow. The Portuguese and Spanish territories, for instance, continue to offer the African listener almost nothing except European programs. The Somalilands and Bechuanaland offer little of anything to anybody. But for ELWA, Liberia would have little to offer its people, either —and since ELWA is mission-operated, most of its offerings are of a religious character.

However, we must not judge the role being played by radio in tropical Africa solely on the basis of territorial facilities.

For radio is footloose and free for the receiving. Unlike the press and motion pictures, its products are not subject to border control; frequently they can be "delivered" to homes 3,000 miles or more away as easily as to those 300 miles or 30. Once a Copperbelt miner has the price of a receiving set, it is scarcely more difficult for him to tune in to Brazzaville, Cairo, Moscow or Monrovia than to his own local station. Though there are no means of telling how many listeners, in the Copperbelt or elsewhere, such stations have, it is certain they have some. It is also beyond question that the number will increase as the African's awareness of his position and potential increases. But what of it? The following snatch of conversation with a Nigerian radio official, reported by St. Clair Drake, suggests that what some find frightening, others find challenging:

"If sets are placed in hands of the ordinary people, won't they listen to Brazzaville and Monrovia instead of to Lagos?"

"What would be wrong with that?"

"You might end up with an elaborate broadcasting system and no regular listeners."

"Well, it's up to us to deliver a program that will hold their attention. What is democracy for, if it doesn't mean the right of people to listen to any station they want to?"

Unfortunately, there is still too little sign in many territories that the radio people are capable of delivering such programs —or, for that matter, that the listeners are interested in democracy.

MOTION PICTURES

In most parts of tropical Africa the educational impact of motion pictures on the African has so far been weak to the point of being impalpable. True, almost every town has at least one commercial movie house; and the larger towns have several. But it is not every movie house that is allowed to admit

Africans, nor is it every African who has the price of admission. Anyway, most of the films shown are the standard, full-length—and fully aged—productions of Hollywood and Ealing; and those who show them are no more interested in the film as a weapon with which to do battle against ignorance than most movie companies are interested in producing documentaries. If such films have any "educational" impact at all, it is the unfortunate one of representing most Americans as knaves and most Europeans as fools. For the American films are strong for fighting between fast-talking, tobacco-spitting, gun-packing cowboys and savage, monosyllabic Indians who have decamped with their overstuffed, underdressed, scheming women. And many of the European films are concerned with messy domestic situations the solution to which every African in the audience sees after the first five minutes and thereafter makes little attempt to keep to himself—situations, furthermore, that no self-respecting African would have got himself into in the first place.

The problem of exploiting the educational value of the film is, of course, formidable. To begin with, there are the usual "African" difficulties: lack of funds—for making good documentaries and the mobile units needed to show them; lack of technicians—capable of handling the projection equipment and maintaining it in serviceable shape; and lack of agreement on what is needed most—and how to go about supplying it on a shoestring budget. But there are frequently other difficulties. Among these is the difficulty of forecasting audience reaction to a given type of film. In some of the unsophisticated parts of Africa what was straight "documentary" to the producer turns out to be straight comedy to the audience. Many films dealing with such indispensable matters as cattle dipping and inoculation, bush clearance, conservation and road building have failed for no other reason than that they had Europeans doing some of the demonstrating—and who had ever seen real Europeans using their hands for anything but eating and such like? Again, most African audiences still find it difficult to suppress their interest when watching a film of any kind. Each sequence brings forth a swarm of questions, the answers to which fly like fireflies and do about as much to lighten the questioner's darkness. Meanwhile, the film has moved several sequences nearer its end, and the real point of it may have been lost.

But if the problems are great, so is the promise. Where government film units have been active, as in Ghana, the caliber of their work has been generally high, and in some instances quite outstanding. Films such as "Bamiri Village," which dealt with the building of a community center in a small Ashanti village, "Amenu's Child," which was designed to encourage better nutrition, and "The Gold Coast Votes," which recorded the general elections held in that country in 1954, can take their place with the best documentaries of any land.

Here again not all the territories have yet seen the promise. Among those that have, in addition to Ghana, are Nigeria, Kenya, the Rhodesias, the Belgian Congo and the onetime French-administered territories. Most of the rest have either done little or left the field to other agencies, such as the United Nations, and public-spirited corporations like the Firestone Plantations Company of Liberia. The large commercial film companies continue to concentrate almost all of their interest on the seven-foot Tusi, the four-foot pygmy, and the even tireder game.

The real drama of today's Africa lies elsewhere, in the war on ignorance and its twin progeny, poverty and sickness—a war rich in hope, excitement and prowess, and fought by people who are no strangers to tears, sweat or blood, including their own. It is the kind of war to which Hollywood could do ample justice. To film it might not be to make a fortune; but it would certainly be to make friends, and in these days even Hollywood needs friends.

CHAPTER 3

THE ASSAULT ON SICKNESS

In the African social drama sickness has a strong claim to being the archvillain. It is bad enough that a man should be ignorant, for this cuts him off from the commerce of other men's minds. It is perhaps worse that a man should be poor, for this condemns him to a life of stint and scheming, in which there is no time for dreams and no respite from weariness. But what surely is worst is that a man should be unwell, for this prevents his doing anything much about either his poverty or his ignorance.

In tropical Africa most men, women and children are habitually unwell. Many are unwell from the day of their birth to the day of their death. Many are more than unwell; they are sick of diseases, such as sleeping sickness, that are incapacitating; or of diseases that are debilitating, such as malaria and bilharziasis; or of diseases, such as bronchopneumonia and tuberculosis, that are distressing. Most of the sick are sick of more than one disease. It is nothing unusual for a person admitted to a leprosarium to be suffering from malaria, sleeping sickness, tertiary yaws, river-blindness and worm infections as well as leprosy. Left to their own devices, most of the sick have no prospect of ever being not sick. The pharmacopoeia of the medicine man is an awesome assortment of herbs, entrails, charms and incantations. Its cures say more for the fortitude of the patient than for the skill of the practitioner.

Nor is it only a matter of the African suffering from diseases. It is also a matter of his living in a physical, social and psychological environment and on a diet that make it hard for him to keep well even when he is not actually ill. The assault on sickness, therefore, calls not only for tactical warfare against specific diseases and localized foci of disease, but also for a strategy aimed at removing the predisposing causes of both disease and ill-health. It calls for prevention no less than cures.

MEDICAL FACILITIES

Although there were doctors and nurses in tropical Africa before the end of the nineteenth century, most of them doubled as explorers, surveyors or evangelists. Almost all they were able to do was to dispense a few simple "household" remedies and hope that the people who took them would follow the directions. Notwithstanding the many moving pleas made by men like David Livingstone, years went by before either public or private agencies did much to bring the consolations of modern medicine within reach of the ordinary African. As recently as 1930, Nigeria—one of the better-served colonial territories—still had less than 1,500 hospital beds for its then roughly 20 million people.

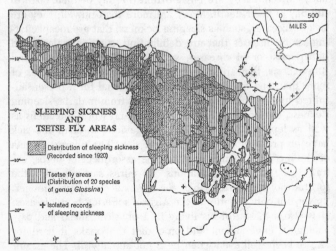

SLEEPING SICKNESS
AND
TSETSE FLY AREAS

Distribution of sleeping sickness
(Recorded since 1920)

Tsetse fly areas
(Distribution of 20 species
of genus Glossina)

+ Isolated records
of sleeping sickness

Today, in the whole of tropical Africa, there are approximately 7,500 doctors and 125,000 hospital beds. By Western standards, these are still very modest figures—a doctor to about every 22,000 persons and a bed to about every 1,300.[1] Large parts of tropical Africa do not have a doctor to 100,000 persons or a bed to 10,000. In 1957 Ethiopia was reported as having one doctor for every 164,800 inhabitants;[2] the number of hospital beds was not known, but it was probably less than one for every 20,000. Some territories do much better, of course—better in a few instances than many "older" countries. In 1956 the doctor-to-population ratio was approximately 1:3,660 in Southern Rhodesia and 1:8,800 in Kenya. In the same year the ratio of hospital beds to population in the Belgian Congo was approximately 1:400, or more than sixteen times higher than in India and more than four times higher than in Mexico.

In almost every African country, no matter where it stands in comparison with its neighbors, there is an acute awareness of the need for more doctors and more hospitals. In most, this awareness is being matched by action worthy of the need. Name almost any large city from Dakar to Addis Ababa or from Khartoum to Lourenço Marques, and you will find either that its largest, most up-to-date and often most handsome building is a hospital or that it has plans for such a building. Few American towns of comparable size can compete with Dakar, Kumasi, Ibadan, Luanda, Léopoldville or Brazzaville when it comes to hospitals. Or name any university or university college, and it is safe to say that no faculty has a higher priority with its treasury than the medical faculty, where it exists. And where none exists, it is equally safe to say that the establishment of one capable of standing comparison, in the quality of its equipment, instructors, research workers and students, with those of North America and Europe is one of the authorities' chief preoccupations. In the past few years, medical faculties have been established at Dakar, Ibadan, Kampala (Makerere College), Khartoum, Elisabethville and Léopoldville (Lovanium University). Others are to be established at Accra, Salisbury and Addis Ababa. When all

[1] The corresponding figures for the United States are about 1 to 750 and 1 to 100.
[2] *New York Times*, December 3, 1957.

of them are in operation, they will be able to turn out between 500 and 1,000 fully qualified doctors annually. The 1958 enrollment in the medical schools was less than 400.

But there is much more to the tactical assault on sickness than the provision of doctors and hospitals. If, to pursue our military analogy, the doctors are the officers and the hospitals the base repair and maintenance centers, the medical auxiliaries are the no less necessary "other ranks," and the clinics, dispensaries and mobile units the indispensable field casualty stations.

In all of tropical Africa there are between 10,000 and 12,500 midwives and pharmacists and perhaps as many dispensers and nurses, most of them African. While some of these are attached to base hospitals, more are field workers who carry the fight right into the enemy's camp, to places seldom if ever visited by doctors, and to people who have never seen a hospital. It is impossible to weigh in a statistical balance the worth of the medical services rendered by these people, for each statistic is a sufferer, and who can measure the suffering caused by a single disease, or the relief from it that can come from a shot in the arm, a course of antibiotics, or even a bottle of antiseptic? But none who have seen the "other ranks" at work can doubt that, without them, the assault on sickness would have faltered badly. With the best will in the world the 594 doctors working in the Belgian Congo in 1953 could not have handled alone more than a small fraction of the 3,054,-324 hospital outpatients, the 443,582 in-patients, the 15,112,-363 rural dispensary cases, the 6,197,486 Africans examined for endemic disease by mobile teams, the 2,607,543 who were vaccinated against smallpox, or the 413,494 women who received prenatal or postnatal treatment. What is true of the Belgian Congo is true, in kind if not in the same degree, of almost all the tropical African territories.

This is not to say that the army of auxiliaries is everywhere large enough to contain the enemy, let alone prevail against him. But at least it is growing everywhere—in places quite impressively, as the following two reports indicate.

The first comes from Kenya:

During 1955 the following number of [African] students qualified: Hospital Assistants (male) 13; Laboratory Assistants 5; Assistant Radiographers 1; Grade II Dressers (male) 1; Grade II Dressers (female) 5; Kenya Registered Nurses 2.

The total number of students at the Medical Training School [in Nairobi] at the end of 1955 was 254, composed as follows:—Hospital Assistants Attending Promotion Course 6; Hospital Assistant Trainees (male) 144; Hospital Assistant Trainees (female) 11; Compounder Trainees 14; Laboratory Assistant Trainees 12; Kenya Registered Nurse Trainees 14; Grade II Dresser Trainees (male) 27; Grade II Dresser Trainees (female) 26.[3]

The second comes from Sudan, in the days when it was still the Anglo-Egyptian Sudan:

Nurses' Training Schools. Ten schools were recognized [during the year 1953–1954] for the "in-service" training of nurses covering the full period of three years. A further nine schools were recognized as capable of undertaking the shortened training course of one year.[4]

The auxiliary army is growing in versatility as well as in numbers. The following report comes from Uganda, but the progress it speaks of can be paralleled in a dozen territories:

Auxiliary medical staff are trained at departmental training schools for work in Government units. These schools, which are being increased in size and number, provide training for medical assistants, nursing orderlies, nurses, midwives, dispensers, laboratory assistants, assistant radiographers, assistant health inspectors and hygiene orderlies

[3] *Medical Department: Annual Report, 1955*, Government Printer, Nairobi, 1956, p. 6. At the end of 1958 the corresponding number of students in training was 349.

[4] *Report of the Medical Services, Ministry of Health, Sudan Government, for the Year 1953–1954*, Khartoum, 1954, p. 35.

. . . Training is carried out in Kampala, where the Queen Elizabeth Nurses' Hostel at Mulago Hospital provides modern accommodation for 350 nurses, midwives and student nurses and midwives. There are other training schools at Masaka, Jinja, Mbale and Lira, and a midwives' training school will shortly be opened at Gulu. An assistant medical storekeepers' hostel is to be started at Entebbe, where a course of instruction will be given at the Central Medical Store.[5]

Although increase in skill often lags behind increase in the number of skills, many medical auxiliaries have acquired outstanding ability. In some instances their skill exceeds that of their tutors, it would seem. At any rate, one European leprosy specialist working in the Belgian Congo has an *infirmier* (himself a former patient) who, he claims, is "the finest leprosy diagnostician" he knows.

As the strength, numerical and professional, of the assault force increases, so does the need for physical facilities. This need, too, is slowly being met in most territories. Since World War II there has been a sharp increase in the number of rural dispensaries and clinics, hospital out-stations, mobile vaccination and inoculation units, maternity centers and so on. Some administrations have, in fact, given a higher priority to the provision of such facilities than to the provision of hospital beds, on the ground that the best way—socially, financially, medically, epidemiologically—to press home the fight against almost any disease is to attack it before it has had time to do much damage. To do this effectively may necessitate a "smoking-out" campaign, since, in some areas, Africans are still reluctant to undergo hospital treatment except as a last resort. For that matter, in some areas Africans are still unwilling to present themselves even for a medical examination. However, with perseverance, abetted by flattery, material inducements and mild pressure, these inhibitions are almost everywhere being overcome. For example, at the Kabou clinic

[5] *Colonial Office Report on Uganda for the Year 1954*, H.M.S.O., London, 1955, p. 84.

in Togo, soap and sugar are given to every woman who comes for prenatal consultations; and the local chiefs are requested to round up pregnant women for such consultations. If the child is delivered at the clinic the mother is sometimes given a dress for it. Even the United Nations Visiting Mission of the Trusteeship Council, which is not often heard to champion colonial practices, conceded that this was "a very good system in order to attract sick people to attend hospitals and dispensaries."

In some areas it is no longer a matter of finding inducements, but of finding facilities for those seeking treatment. This is particularly true of those areas, such as the Belgian Congo, where the assault on smallpox, sleeping sickness and other greatly feared diseases has been pressed with vigor. The assault may have been mounted only on bicycles and led only by African auxiliaries, but once the success stories began to get around by "bush telegraph" few dispensaries and mobile units had much difficulty in attracting custom. And success there certainly has been; for it is thanks largely to the work of these agencies that malaria and plague, as well as smallpox and sleeping sickness, are now under control in the Belgian Congo, and that most of the cases in that territory of leprosy, yaws and river-blindness have been diagnosed and treated. Where difficulty sometimes arises is in restraining patients from living on the dispensary doorstep until they are cured or, too often, in persuading them to stay when they become disenchanted and want to go back to their own "dispensers."

Besides the agencies that operate domestically, there are a number that work on an international front. Of these the World Health Organization of the United Nations is the foremost. The following extracts from the "African Region" part of the 1958 report of the Director-General of WHO indicate the type of forces being thrown into the assault by this organization, and the strategy it is pursuing.

In dealing with the health problems of the Region [covering all of Africa south of the Sahara, except Ethiopia, Somalia and Sudan], the advantages of inter-country programmes have been always emphasized, since they make it possible to plan more effective and economical projects. . . .

An important procedure in the work of the Regional Office [in Brazzaville] has been the many visits paid by members of the office staff to countries and territories in the Region, particularly to those that have asked WHO for assistance with their health programmes. During those visits information was collected about the health conditions of the area, discussions were held with the health authorities on their proposed programmes, help was given in preparing plans for operations, and the progress of programmes already launched was discussed on the spot with the responsible officers.

Probably the most practical means of reinforcing and developing the existing health services is the instruction and training of competent personnel of all grades to staff these services, and a high priority was therefore given to assisting teaching and training programmes. In the regional fellowships programme, the number of fellowships awarded (128) was nearly double the number in the previous year. About sixty per cent. of those fellowships were related to the organization of public health services and about thirty-five per cent. to the control of communicable diseases, in particular of malaria and tuberculosis. Medical officers, engineers, nurses and auxiliary personnel have benefited from the fellowships programme. Governments are giving increasing attention to the training of health services staff in protection against atomic radiation, and a number of fellowships were awarded for this purpose.

Fellowships or grants were provided for attendance at courses or seminars, such as the social paediatrics course at Dakar . . ., the mental health seminar, held in Brazzaville . . . the training course on brucellosis [undulant fevers] at Elisabethville . . . [and] the course on the ophthalmological aspects of onchocerciasis, at Bamako . . .

The assistance to countries and territories in the Region has been largely given to the organization, expansion and co-ordination of work on communicable diseases . . .

Considerable progress has been made in the study of the technical difficulties and special problems of breaking the transmission of malaria in several parts of Africa. . . . One of the advisory teams, provided to assist countries in assessing the progress of their schemes for malaria control, continued its work . . . and similar teams are being set up to make surveys and prepare sound plans of operation for the areas in which schemes of malaria eradication are already in prospect . . . The great majority of malaria control projects in the Region have been assisted by UNICEF.

The African Regional Office has been giving similar support to projects for the control of bilharziasis, leprosy, tuberculosis, river-blindness, smallpox and yaws, the improvement of maternal and child health, the raising of nutritional and sanitary standards, and the training of nurses and rural health workers. At the end of 1958 the list of projects being directed (either

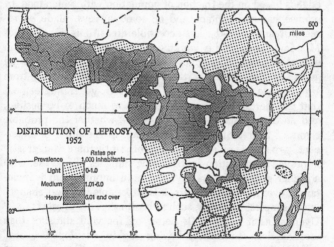

DISTRIBUTION OF LEPROSY, 1952

Prevalence	Rates per 1,000 Inhabitants
Light	0-1.0
Medium	1.01-6.0
Heavy	6.01 and over

by WHO alone or in conjunction with other international agencies) from this office was more than one hundred items long. Another twenty or so projects were being directed in Ethiopia, Sudan and Somalia from the Eastern Mediterranean Regional Office in Alexandria.

To measure the strength of the forces engaged in the assault presents no great difficulty, since all medical agencies keep records of personnel, equipment and supplies. To measure the progress made by them is much more of a problem because of the many "unknowns." Nobody knows exactly how much disease there was when the assault began. There was plenty, to be sure, but in no area was the precise incidence or the morbidity of a given disease known. Nobody knows the size of the population at that time, or anything concerning its mortality. For that matter, nobody knows the exact size of the population today, as census material is still lacking in some areas. Adequate vital statistics are likewise lacking; the majority of the territories still have no comprehensive system of registration, and those that do lack the means of implementing it. Then, too, many pathological phenomena are still unobserved; if observed, they are not always reported; and if reported, they are not infrequently diagnosed wrongly. Our knowledge is based on the fraction of population with which modern science has had contact, and on some surveys, made by research teams, into the less accessible areas. It is, Dr. Jacques M. May asserts in his working paper, little better than "an educated guess." Sometimes it is no more than a half-educated guess, as the writers of the following report, coming from Uganda, are frank to admit: "There is . . . general agreement that the mortality figures available leave much to be desired, and no data exists on which to decide whether the probable errors of figures quoted in reports are of the order of 2 percent, 5 percent, or even 10 percent. Until there is a greatly improved organization for collecting statistics of real use, with a higher degree of accuracy, and until improvement is maintained over a period of years, it is impossible to assess changes in the simplest variables, such as birth rates, death rates . . ."[6] Uganda, as it happens, is better off for vital statistics than most African territories, having highly developed central and local governments and a network of dispensaries and district hospitals.

[6] *A Development Plan for Uganda and the 1948 Revision of the Plan*, Entebbe, 1949, p. 46.

But progress there has been, as any elderly African will testify. Indeed, there is probably no better assurance of medical progress than the fact that the number of elderly Africans is increasing.

EVIDENCE OF GAINS

How mortality rates have been changing in several territories may be traced in Table 3. Imperfect, approximate and

Table 3

MORTALITY RATES OF SELECTED TERRITORIES,
1950 AND 1957

(*Number of Deaths, Excluding Stillbirths, per 1,000
Population*)

TERRITORY	1950	1957
Angola[a]	6.3	6.8
Gambia: Bathurst only	n.a.	16.0
Ghana (Gold Coast)[a,b]	19.9[c]	n.a.
Malagasy Rep. (Madagascar)[a]	17.6	12.6[d]
Mozambique[a]	6.1	4.9
Nigeria: Lagos only	n.a.	14.2
Nyasaland[a,e]	13.6	n.a.
São Tomé & Príncipe[a]	27.3	22.7[f]
Spanish Guinea[a,e,g]	8.5	8.2
Zanzibar & Pemba[a]	15.6	8.4

Source: United Nations, *Demographic Yearbooks* for 1956, 1957 and 1958.

[a] Data are affected by irregularities in registration or incomplete coverage.

[b] Data are for compulsory registration areas only, comprising about one tenth of total population.

[c] Not computed by the Statistical Office of the United Nations.

[d] 1956.

[e] Data are based on year of registration rather than year of occurrence.

[f] 1955.

[g] Data exclude deaths of infants dying before registration of birth.

n.a.: not available

partial as these figures are, there is little doubt that they indicate a downward trend. At the same time, it is impossible, on the basis of such material, to come to any definite conclusions as to the degree of decline, or to compare the figures of one territory with those of another.

The accompanying infant mortality table hints at a similar downward trend. While there is reason to believe that this trend is a real one, the given level of the figures is very questionable and comparison from territory to territory is impossible. The level is questionable because, where small sample surveys of infant mortality have been made, the rates are generally higher than those found in the official handbooks. And territorial comparison is impossible because no two sets of figures are derived in the same way. The Gambia figures in Table 4 are simply those for Bathurst, the capital; the

Table 4

INFANT MORTALITY RATES OF SELECTED TERRITORIES, 1950 AND 1957

(*Number of Deaths of Infants under 1 Year per 1,000 Live Births*)

TERRITORY	1950	1957
Fr. West Africa: Dakar only	115.4	103.1[d]
Gambia: Bathurst only	100.9	71.8
Ghana (Gold Coast)[a,b,e]	120.9[c]	n.a.
Malagasy Rep. (Madagascar)[a]	111.5	n.a.
Nigeria: Lagos only	86.3	80.1
Nyasaland[a]	n.a.	n.a.
Sierra Leone: Colony only[e]	178.7	144.5[d]
Zanzibar & Pemba[a]	83.2	35.9

See source and notes to Table 3.

Nigeria figures are for Lagos only; and those for Ghana relate solely to the "compulsory registration areas," which contain only about one tenth of the total population.

The evidence of progress in combating specific diseases is subject to equally important limitations. The chief of these, perhaps, is the fact that figures as a rule refer only to persons to whom the chance of treatment has been offered; therefore, they cannot be taken as representative of conditions at large. Even if all 30,000-odd doctors and medical auxiliaries were assigned to the job, they could not fumigate every home in the bush, inoculate its inhabitants against all the diseases that jeopardize their health, and teach them the rudiments of modern hygiene. Only a small proportion of the 30,000 are, of course, available for such an assignment. Consequently the figures cited must be thought of merely as gains made by skirmishing parties working on a limited front, not as the assurance of a total victory over the diseases in question.

Even so, some of the gains have been impressive. Here is a sampling, culled (except where otherwise stated) from recent government reports:

1. *Belgian Congo.* "[In] 1930, from among 2,779,448 natives examined by itinerant medical missions, 33,562 new cases [of sleeping sickness] were discovered, that is 1.2 percent. In 1953, among the 6,197,487 people examined, no more than 3,804 cases were found, that is 0.06 percent . . . In 1917, in certain regions there were many villages in which 40 percent of the population was sick, and it was not unusual to find villages where 60 or 70 percent of the inhabitants had sleeping sickness."

* * *

"Twenty-four years ago [1935] all children attending our hospital were suffering from one or more diseases, such as malaria, chronic anemia, yaws, helminthiasis (e.g., ancylostomiasis, ascariasis and filariasis), general malnutrition, scabies and impetigo. Now it is possible to find children without any of them, though most children still have subclinical malnutrition.

"Leprosy is still widespread: there are more than 3,500 cases of it among the 50,000 people served by the hospital, but the sulfone drugs are working wonders. More than 100 of the 1,000 patients in our leprosarium—most of them

afflicted with the once almost incurable type of the disease
—were sent home cured in 1958."[7]

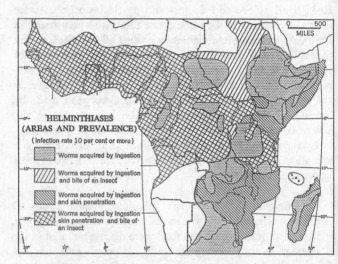

2. *Kenya.* During the late 1940s the incidence of river-
blindness (onchocerciasis) in young children living in
Nyanza Province was put at 35 to 40 per cent. As a result
of a sustained DDT-spraying campaign of the vector-breed-
ing streams and rivers in the region, Dr. A. J. Walker, Director of the Medical Services of the colony, was able to
report at the end of 1956 as follows: "No early stages of
Simulium neavei [the buffalo gnat, which is the local vector
of the disease] have been seen on crabs [the host], or adult
flies caught . . . since January when a residual focus was
found . . . It would thus appear that this ambitious scheme
of eradication . . . has been successful." Dr. Walker's
report for 1957 showed that his confidence was justified;
the vector had not been seen anywhere in the province.

[7] Dr. Stanley G. Browne, onetime medical superintendent, Baptist
Mission Hospital, Yakusu, Belgian Congo, in a personal communication.

3. *Northern Rhodesia.* "Figures of malarial cases in Broken Hill are available since 1936. The peak period was reached in 1945 with 43.11 percent of the admissions to the hospital being malarial cases, while this year [1956], the lowest figure yet recorded of 5.18 percent was achieved . . . These figures relate to Europeans and [Asians], but give an indication of the effectiveness of the work in the township as a whole."

4. *Sudan.* "No outbreak of [relapsing fever] was encountered [in 1954–55]: only 3 imported cases were spotted in Khartoum and treated. Delousing by DDT which

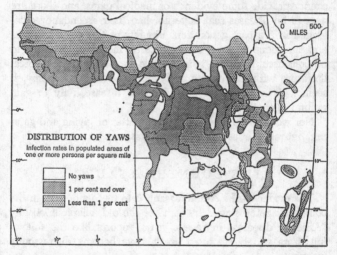

DISTRIBUTION OF YAWS
Infection rates in populated areas of one or more persons per square mile

☐ No yaws
▨ 1 per cent and over
▨ Less than 1 per cent

is applied at all posts of entry to Sudan on imported labour has removed the worry that this disease used to create in the past." How much worry it did create a decade earlier is evident from the figures cited for 1945: 17,392 cases and 444 deaths.

5. *Tanganyika.* Annual tabulations by the Government Medical Department show a decrease of more than 85 per cent in reported cases of smallpox between 1950 (6,390

cases) and 1957 (856 cases). The case mortality rate de-
clined sharply and steadily during the early 1950s, despite
a flare-up of the disease in 1953 and 1954. In 1957 the
rate was 4.4 per cent, against 21.0 per cent in 1950.

6. *Various territories.* "The cases of yaws in the [Af-
rican] Region have been estimated at twenty millions. Over
twelve million people have been examined, of whom seven
million have been cured by teams working with WHO collaboration."

There is no territory in the whole of tropical Africa that
cannot provide some evidence of medical gains, and there are
next to no diseases that have not had their ascendancy challenged in the past generation. But few of the gains are general, and none is as yet secure. Losses, moreover, continue to
be considerable and it is impossible to read current medical
literature without being gravely disconcerted: the enemy, it
seems, gives ground in one place, or disease, only to gain
ground in another.

Nor would it appear to be just a matter of giving and gain-
ing, but rather of assault and counterassault.

THE COUNTERASSAULT

The evidence of a counterassault is to be found, first, in the
comeback being staged by some of the old, characteristically
"African" diseases. In recent years, reports like the following, from widely scattered areas, have become distressingly
frequent.

1. *Sudan.* "A grave epidemic of cerebrospinal meningitis attacked the Bahr El Ghazal for the second successive
year. This Province was also visited by a severe outbreak of
smallpox which had not been brought finally under control
by the end of the year. Nor was control of smallpox in
Darfur fully successful and the epidemic there continued,
though at a lessened pitch.

"A raised incidence of sporadic cases of enteric fever and minor epidemics in Wadi Halfa, Dongola, Atbara, Abu Usher and Ed Dueim underlined the urgency of betterment of environmental sanitation throughout the country.

"There was an ominous rise in incidence of sleeping sickness in Yambio and Yei districts."

2. *Nigeria.* "From time to time . . . more virulent outbreaks [of yellow fever] do occur. Thus in 1946 an outbreak occurred at Ogbomosho; only eleven deaths were recorded, but since the area involved contained an urban population of some 100,000 people, and since proven cases wandered as far afield as Ilorin, Kafanchan and Gusau, the total number affected, if only in a mild form, must have been very much larger. In 1951–52 a much more serious outbreak occurred at Enugu, involving 5,000 cases and resulting in some 600 deaths. Another considerable, yet probably mild, outbreak was detected in retrospect along the north shore of the Lagos Lagoon. No case of yellow fever had been reported from the Lagos area between 1925 and the time of the investigation (1945), yet 17 per cent of all

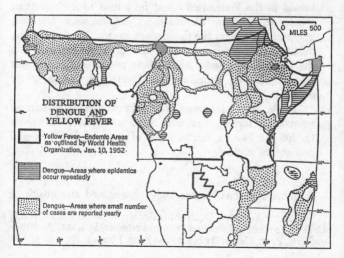

DISTRIBUTION OF DENGUE AND YELLOW FEVER

☐ Yellow Fever—Endemic Areas as outlined by World Health Organization, Jan. 10, 1952.

▤ Dengue—Areas where epidemics occur repeatedly

▨ Dengue—Areas where small number of cases are reported yearly children in the area had had the disease, the youngest being five. An epidemic of some size must have taken place in the district about the year 1941, and yet passed quite unrecorded."[8]

3. *Tanganyika.* "From 1949 to 1952 there was a progressive decline in the reported incidence of sleeping sickness. In 1953, however, there were indications that a general increase might be expected, and all precautions were intensified. Up to the end of October, 1954, over 1,000 cases had been reported, compared with a territorial total of 732 for 1953. More than 700 of these cases appeared in the Western Province. In May a new focus was discovered in the Lake Province not far from the Ruanda Urundi border, and a similar outbreak was reported from the Belgian Congo side of the border . . ."

4. *Federation of Rhodesia and Nyasaland.* "Smallpox was present in Northern Rhodesia in small outbreaks at the beginning of the year [1955] but later culminated in an epidemic beginning in April. The large mining towns on the Copperbelt were most seriously affected, and other outbreaks in the Federation could be traced to a Copperbelt source. In Northern Rhodesia, 3,538 cases were reported, 2,772 of them from the Copperbelt towns. There were 501 deaths. The overall mortality was 14.46 per cent, and in the Copperbelt district itself, 16.85 per cent. In one week in mid-June in Mufulira, there were 37 deaths in 42 cases. . . .

"I have seen more cases of kwashiorkor from the African township [Hartley, Southern Rhodesia] than I remember in the past, and a fair number of cases of beri-beri and pellagra in adults."

* * *

Bilharziasis has "increasingly endangered the health of

8 Professor A. Brown, Dean of the Faculty of Medicine, University College, Ibadan, in *Land and People in Nigeria,* by K. M. Buchanan and J. C. Pugh, University of London Press, London, 1955, p. 51.

human beings . . . in Southern Rhodesia during the past ten years . . . It is estimated that in the eastern part of the Colony, which includes Salisbury, 80 percent of the African population and 10 percent of European children are infected with bilharziasis. . . . [An] enormous increase in the number of dams and weirs and in the permanency of rivers [as a result of work sponsored by the Federal Department of Conservation and Extension] has led to a corresponding rise in the snail population. There is now a real danger of bilharziasis becoming as fatal [sic] as it is in Egypt, where it has existed for 5,000 years."[9]

At the same time, diseases not traditionally associated with most of the African tropics have spread. High on the list are tuberculosis, venereal diseases, pneumonia and poliomyelitis. Once again, it is very difficult to get reliable information for more than small sectors of any given territory. But where it is available, as in the cases that follow, it leaves no doubt about the inroads being made by these "foreign" diseases.

Tuberculosis

1. *Nigeria.* "2,591 pulmonary and 1,259 other cases with 406 deaths were seen in hospitals [during the period 1949–1950], but this does not give a true picture of the actual incidence. In Lagos, for example, 12.11 per cent of all deaths were attributed to tuberculosis."

2. *Uganda.* "This disease is widespread: about half the adult population react to the tuberculin test which shows that they are, or have been, infected."

3. *Federation of Rhodesia and Nyasaland.* "Tuberculosis in the African continues to be one of the biggest health problems facing the Federation . . . the special [curative]

[9] *Central African Examiner,* August 17, 1957, p. 8. The liver fluke disease of cattle, carried by water snails, has also, and for the same reasons, increased greatly in the past ten years or so.

accommodation for Africans was filled to capacity, over-
flowing into hospitals and clinics wherever beds could be
found or made available, but was still insufficient."

Other countries where the disease is widespread and
thought to be on the increase are Sudan, Kenya, Tanganyika, Angola and the Belgian Congo. "In all these countries," Dr. May reports, "tuberculin tests show from 50 to
90 per cent of positive reactions in adults."

Venereal Diseases

1. *Cameroons.* "The mission [of the U. N.] was informed that in some regions of the North, among the Fulani
and the few pagans of the plain, some 75 percent of the
population suffers from syphilis."

2. *Tanganyika.* Annual reports of the Government
Medical Department list the number of patients treated in
hospitals for gonorrhea and syphilis during recent years as
follows:

	1952	1953	1954	1956*	1957*
Gonorrhea	22,658	30,745	27,056	30,504	28,043
Syphilis	38,646	40,222	33,109	29,478	21,295

* Outpatients only.

Pneumonia

1. *Nyasaland.* According to the 1955 report on public
health issued by the Federation of Rhodesia and Nyasaland, pneumonia still remains "the number one killing disease" in the district of Ncheu in spite of modern drugs.

2. *Ghana.* "The principal causes of death through disease are pulmonary tuberculosis and the respiratory diseases," according to a Colonial Office report for the year
1954.

Poliomyelitis

In *Uganda*, according to a Colonial Office report, more cases of poliomyelitis than of sleeping sickness were notified in 1955. The report comments: "The change in the pattern of disease is interesting: whereas the so-called tropical diseases are gradually being brought under control, diseases common to more temperate countries are either actually increasing in incidence or are being reported in larger numbers."

How did this counterassault manage to get under way? Of the many contributory factors, the following would seem to be especially notable:

1. The opening up of tropical Africa. Since about 1900, Europeans and Asians have become domiciled in almost every part of the region, and wherever they have gone, their diseases have gone with them. But whereas most of them enjoy some degree of resistance to the more disabling forms of these diseases, the Africans living round about them do not. There is little doubt that it was the newcomers who lit the fuse for the explosion of venereal and respiratory diseases reported from many areas in the past generation.

2. The growing mobility of the African. Thanks to roads, railways and airlines, and the increasing demand for migrant labor, the African has become a highly efficient carrier of diseases, both new and old. Syphilis and tuberculosis acquired by men working on the mines are often carried, when their term of service is over, to places five hundred to a thousand miles away, hitherto free of either disease. Bilharziasis acquired in an old Sudanese focus of the disease can be carried overnight to the Belgian Congo or east Africa by the itinerant seller of ivory and metalware. Sleeping sickness can be carried from one territory to the next by infected tsetse flies hiding in the nooks and crannies of a truck or car.

3. The inadequacy of the African's defenses. These defenses are inadequate on several counts. In some instances they are

inadequate because—to all outward appearances at least—he
does not care enough about good health. It is a frequent
complaint of doctors and public health officers that even after
a man has been taught the "drill" of protection against a disease, he quickly falls back into his old infection-inviting
habits. In many instances the African's defenses are inadequate because he does not earn enough. He may not earn
enough to keep himself and his family in food, or to buy sufficient room space to avoid sleeping at close quarters with his
associates, or to buy footwear that will protect him from worm
infections and a change of clothes that will enable him to
avoid the consequences of getting soaked in the rainy season.
He is unlikely to earn enough to undertake anything in the
way of preventive measures like pond spraying.

More often the root of the trouble is neither unconcern nor
poverty, but ignorance. Most Africans are so accustomed to
being less than well that they frequently do not realize how
unwell they are until it is too late to do much about it. Doctors almost everywhere lament that "patients are generally
not brought into hospital until the last stages have been
reached and every other remedy has been tried without success."[10] Most Africans still do not see the point of supplying
themselves with pit latrines and a clean water supply, without
which it is scarcely possible, in most areas, to avoid contracting bilharziasis, the dysenteries (bacillary and amoebic) and
the typhoid fevers; or of sleeping in a well-ventilated atmosphere (instead of the customary fug), for want of which
many are daily contracting tuberculosis and bronchopneumonia. Increasing numbers of reasonably well-to-do Africans
know too little about bought foods and beverages to be able to
steer clear of nutritional diseases. Many of the most recently
reported cases of kwashiorkor, pellagra and beriberi in Southern Rhodesia have been attributed to "the inordinate consumption of white bread, buns, syrup and mineral waters."[11]

[10] *Colonial Office Report on the Nyasaland Protectorate for the
Year 1953*, H.M.S.O., London, 1954, p. 93.
[11] *Annual Report on Public Health, Federation of Rhodesia and
Nyasaland*, 1955, p. 18.

Observations such as these, recurring like a refrain in medical reports, suggest that possibly another of the African's inadequacies, when it comes to defending himself against disease, is his lack of confidence in himself and the folkways of his people. In many areas, certainly, he has virtually discarded his traditional food staples and beverages, along with his traditional wardrobe, such as it was. In many areas, too, his womenfolk are now weaning children after the nine-month period favored by most Europeans.

Although missionaries advocate teetotalism in the African convert with good reason, having all too often seen what happens to the man who acquires a liking for Western drinks, the fact remains that native beer, brewed from maize, sorghum, palm sap or sugar cane, contains protective elements that are not found in mineral waters and white bread. Traders, missionaries and government officials have equally good reasons for encouraging the African to wear Western-style clothes, but the fact is that over most of the African tropics there are no clothes like no clothes, or at least like the fewest possible clothes. The "Mother Hubbards" distributed by the early missionaries may have been replaced in these days by something a little more chic, but the forlorn spectacle of a dressed-up African woman caught in a tropical rainstorm is enough to convince anyone that she would look much happier, feel more comfortable, and run a smaller risk of catching pneumonia if she were less cumbered with soggy cotton and silk.[12] Again, cogent as many of the arguments may be for weaning a child at nine months, they do not cancel out the one great argument for leaving it at the breast for the more usual two to three years, namely, the fact that in most bush areas there is a scarcity of indigenous foodstuffs capable of nourishing infants adequately. In his paper written for this study, B. S. Platt notes that "the significance of weaning too early by traditional standards is well recognized. In some parts of Nyasaland the infant that deprives its predecessor of its

---

[12] It is only fair to add that the incidence of such traditional African ills as yaws and ulcerations is generally much lower in "clothed" than in "unclothed" communities.

full birthright of breast feeding is given a name which carries a stigma for the mother for conceiving again 'too soon.' The same idea is inherent in the term 'deposed child.' "

THE STRATEGY OF PREVENTION

It is clear, therefore, that the battle for the health of the African and, to a lesser extent, the non-African has still to be won, and that it is most unlikely to be won by nibbling tactics, no matter how efficient, or by an army of patched-up casualties, no matter how brave. To change the figure for a moment: though forest fires can always be put out, given enough men and equipment, even in tinder-dry conditions, there is no hope of stopping them from breaking out from time to time when the forest is tinder-dry. What is needed is a good fall of rain—a change of environment. So with the diseases of tropical Africa. The only hope of a durable victory lies in changing the cultural and physical environment to the point where disease cannot get away with aggression.

Such a victory will take a long time. The terrain over which the campaign will range is tough and in many places hard of access. The African's communication system is still far from satisfactory. The diseases to be fought are capable of putting up tremendous resistance. In most instances, they can be fought only one at a time, so that the strategy for the campaign against malaria must be quite different from that against, say, bilharziasis.

It will also take a vast amount of effort, both individual and cooperative: individual, because everybody needs to be able to recognize the vector and symptoms of a disease, and to do something about them; cooperative, because the good one man's efforts do will be annulled unless his neighbor can be persuaded to do the same. This effort must not be merely a matter of cooperation between neighbors. The vectors of malaria and sleeping sickness know nothing of political boundaries; they do as well in Uganda as in Ruanda-Urundi and can cross and recross the border unhindered. Region-wide cooperation of the fullest possible type is necessary if the fight is to be pressed home. So far, such cooperation has been limited for the most part to the exchange of epidemiological information between certain territories.

Victory will take education, too, for no fight is so hopeless as that fought in the dark, and there is still much gross darkness in tropical Africa on the subject of what makes for health and what for sickness. In many places it is still the medicine man's mumbo-jumbo that makes for health, and the sorcerer's for sickness.

But it is likely to be the money for the fight that will take the most getting. Not many of the people have it themselves; and if they had, they would be unlikely to subscribe it to some of the community projects that are part of the price of victory but that seem at times to have no bearing on the immediate needs of the subscriber. Nor can we justly blame them for being reluctant to support drainage or mass-inoculation campaigns while they have so many more urgent needs. Nor, again, can we justly blame local and central governments for their apparent tardiness in putting money into ditches and needles while they are short of roads, schools, hospitals and clinics. But if not from the people and their governments, where shall the money come from? The World Health Organization and the United Nations Children's Fund have barely enough money for pilot and pump-priming operations. The foundations have money only for training and research. The technical assistance programs of the United Nations and the United States are likewise not on a "military" scale. Consequently, short of a world-wide change of heart, funds for the fight for durable health are bound to be scarce.

But even in war, money isn't everything. The will to win, or the lack of it, has often made nonsense of logistics. And the will to win is not yet present in many Africans. As Kenneth Bradley observes in his working paper, "Disease and malnutrition have always been obvious evils to the African, so obvious and so much with him that, since he did not know how to overcome them, he long ago developed a philosophy to make them acceptable. They are the will of the gods, and the only hope of alleviation lies in propitiation and in a strict observance of the rites which the gods decree and of the customs of the tribe which the gods and ancestors are so anxious to preserve."

At the same time, the African's ability to acquire the will to win the battle of disease must not be underrated. Many Africans have already acquired it. Over much of tropical Africa today the tide of resentment against habitual sickness is running so strong that it promises soon to fill every creek and backwater. Governments are finding that many people are as interested in their preventive public health work as in their remedial work.

The preventionist still finds many serious obstacles in his path, but he is beginning to see how to overcome some of them.

How he goes about it is perhaps best seen in his fight against such "fly" diseases as malaria and sleeping sickness. To hospitalize all the victims of these diseases—conservatively, seven out of every ten persons—is self-evidently impossible, even if all Africans were willing to enter hospitals. If it were possible, it would still not be the answer, because the moment a patient left the hospital he would run the risk of re-infection. What is possible, and what the preventionist is trying to do, is (1) to so alter the physical environment of the vectors and hosts that they can no longer reproduce their kind in it; (2) to kill the vectors and hosts with insecticides; (3) to give individuals their own "built-in" protection or protective screen; and (4) to destroy in the patient the parasitic cause of his disease or diseases.[13]

In the existing economic and social context, very few of these things can be done on a generous scale. But where they are being done, they are amply proving their worth. Thus,

[13] Dr. Stanley G. Browne, a consultant to this study, reports that this "prevention by cure" is especially effective for such diseases as sleeping sickness, yaws and leprosy. "It satisfies both the clinician, out to help the sick individual, and the epidemiologist, who is primarily concerned with the good of the community. Furthermore, it demonstrates the concern of the public health authority and the value of its activities."

wherever tsetse-harboring bush has been cleared and steps have been taken to keep it from growing again, sleeping sickness infection rates have become almost negligible. To take a single instance: there are today large sections of the Niari valley (in the Republic of the Congo) in which African and European farmers live alongside each other oblivious of the tsetse fly's existence, whereas up to the late 1940s the valley was such bad sleeping sickness country that it was virtually uninhabited. Similar gains have been made in respect of malaria in the vicinity of Abidjan, Lagos, Douala, Léopoldville and a score of other cities as the result of draining or spraying nearby marshes and ponds. In the absence of such measures, most Europeans have escaped these diseases by the faithful observance of a few simple rules: "Never sleep without a mosquito net"; "Never skip an inoculation shot"; "Always have the pill box handy." To get Africans to keep such rules has, understandably, proved much harder. Many of them cannot afford the price of a piece of net or a box of pills; some of those who can are forgetful or careless; and not all live within reach of a pill supply or a medical syringe.

The measures required to combat diseases that follow in the train of human filth, such as the typhoid fevers, diarrhoeas and helminth infections (including bilharziasis), provide another example of the preventionist's strategy. Here there is but one road to prevention: cleanliness. Even so, the public health officer's job is anything but simple. It is not enough that he should build efficient disposal systems, public and private latrines and safe water supplies, and that he should treat snail-infested bodies of water with copper sulphate and so on. To insure continuing immunity to infection, he must also see that the work he does is never undone. This means persuading a lot of people—the better part of 167 million—to break with habits that are encrusted with tribal sanctions and endowed with symbolic meaning. It also means raising a lot of money, for in addition to the building costs involved, there is the cost of maintaining enough sanitary inspectors and their aides to see that everything is as it should be. However, for most Europeans and a slowly increasing number of Africans and Asians prevention is just a matter of observing a few more house rules: "Never go about barefoot"; "Never wade or wash in a stream or pond"; "Never eat raw vegetables or fruit of unknown origin"; "Never drink unboiled water" or, as many would have it, "Never drink water."

What is true of diseases having to do with ignorance of public hygiene is true in large measure of those having to do with ignorance of personal hygiene. Thus, a very large part of the characteristically high infant mortality and maternal mortality rates among primitive African groups can be traced to the failure of the midwife or the mother to observe the most elementary principles of cleanliness. "Until very recently," writes A. M. M. Nhonoli concerning the rural areas of Unyamwezi in Tanganyika, "there prevailed most unhygienic practices at childbirth and neither the mother nor the attendant old women knew even the rudiments of asepsis. The umbilical cord would be tied with any piece of cord or string picked up at the moment and the distal portion be sliced off with any old knife that came handy. . . . I have used the past tense throughout here, but the occasions when a more hygienic procedure is followed are still unfortunately few compared with what has just been described. No wonder that tetanus is common and that most, if not all, premature babies fail to survive."[14] The people of Unyamwezi are not very different in this respect from other African groups.

Needless to say, lack of cleanliness is not the sole reason for the high infant and maternal mortality rates. The endemicity of parasitic and other infections also counts for much.

What, in many cases, counts for more is the lack of proper food and feeding. It is even arguable that malnutrition is responsible for more untimely deaths and more habitual sickness among Africans than any other single factor. Theodore Gillman, Professor of Physiology at Natal University, Durban, has stated that two thirds of all African deaths on the Wit-

[14] "An Enquiry into the Infant Mortality Rate in Rural Areas of Unyamwezi," *East African Medical Journal*, Vol. 31 (1954), No. 1, p. 10.

watersrand are attributable to diseases associated with malnutrition; that up to 70 per cent of the African children attending certain schools are recognizably malnourished, 50 per cent of them needing nursing and medical attention, and nearly 10 per cent needing to be treated in hospital for "diseases directly or indirectly attributable to malnutrition"; and that "Chronic malnutrition from infancy, and even from conception, is . . . among the most important direct and indirect

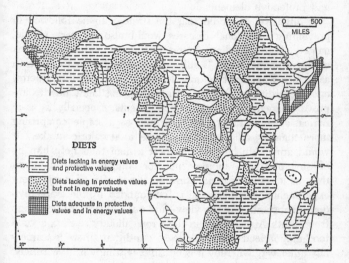

DIETS

Diets lacking in energy values and protective values

Diets lacking in protective values but not in energy values

Diets adequate in protective values and in energy values

factors sapping the vitality of the pigmented peoples of Africa."[15]

Though Gillman's figures are derived from South Africa and few similar surveys have been made north of the Limpopo, they apply, according to Platt, "in large measure to the continent as a whole," and particularly to those areas where the "process of sophistication" is well along. Certainly there are few areas where, on the evidence (very scanty, it is true, and based on available food supplies rather than on known

[15] "Chronic Malnutrition in Africa," *The Listener,* May 3, 1956, p. 538.

consumption), the ordinary African enjoys a perennially adequate diet. Dr. May, who has made some of the most comprehensive studies in this field, is of the opinion that, with the possible exception of the pastoralists living in the Somalilands and in the better-watered savannas of west and east Africa, and some isolated sedentary groups "which have not broken the boundaries of their primitive ecology," no African populations have diets that are adequate in both energy-producing and protective elements.

It might be supposed that the strategy to be followed in preventing nutritional diseases would also be very simple, namely, better feeding. Better feeding is, indeed, the crux of the strategy. But it is still not possible always to say with assurance what must be done to turn a poor diet into a better one. According to Gillman, "we still do not know how to improve [inadequate] diets by supplements, especially if, as in Africa, a single natural food is used as a staple comprising more than 75 to 80 percent of the total caloric intake." It would appear to be easier to hurt a man than help him by offering him such supplements, for Gillman goes on to say that, as a result of conducting hundreds of food supplement experiments on animals, he is "confounded by the ample evidence substantiating the view—first put forward ten years ago from South Africa—that, in the wrong dietary setting, a good food may indeed promote disease"; and that "there is scarcely any other way whereby it is possible, wittingly or unwittingly, to inflict such widespread bodily harm on so many people as tampering, incorrectly, with a nation's diet."

But it is not just a matter of finding and prescribing better foods. It is also a matter of making such foods available to every malnourished African; and this promises to be more difficult. At the present time the foodstuffs favored by most nutrition specialists are not available to the majority of Africans needing them, either because these foodstuffs cannot be raised where they are needed, or because storage facilities are inadequate to safeguard them from insects, rodents and fungi, or because they are quite beyond the means of those needing them.

Then again, it is also in part a matter, to which we come back time and again, of persuading the African to do new things, such as eating "alien corn" in alien ways.

How may such difficulties be overcome? In the opinion of Platt, Gillman and most other experts, it can be done only by developing and using all the resources of the area under attack by nutritional diseases. In this strategy the parts played by the food technologist, welfare worker, economist, educator, politician and administrator are likely to be quite as important as those of the medical man and nutritionist.

Combined operations of this kind have scarcely begun in most territories. Still too little is known about the habits and strength of the enemy. But plenty of scouting work is being done, and here and there raiding parties are already in the field. Thus, in Tanganyika "studies [are] now being made concerning the properties of . . . soils and extensive crop yield surveys will eventually contribute towards greater precision in the planning of food resources. The influence of the postwar years [of food shortage] on the future is seen in the programme of providing sufficient food resources for famine years by construction of food storage facilities and in the increase and wealth of the peasant producer which enables him to obtain articles of food of high nutritive value, such as milk and meat, which may not have been obtainable in the past."[16]

In parts of the Northern and Eastern Regions of Nigeria preliminary surveys have been made, according to Platt, of "the incidence of malnutrition and its dietary background. For the Western Region, the Carnegie Corporation has granted funds that are enabling the Nutrition Unit of University College, Ibadan, to study local foodstuffs and dietary patterns, especially the feeding of women and children. Very little was previously known of this subject, and the investigation will mean that reliable advice on the use of their local foodstuffs can be given to people in this area."

In the Belgian Congo strenuous efforts have been made, as

[16] *Tanganyika: A Review of Its Resources and Their Development*, edited by J. P. Moffett, Government of Tanganyika, Dar-es-Salaam, 1955, pp. 101-2.

part of the Ten Year (1950–1959) Plan, to increase the supply and improve the use of locally raised protein foods. In some areas the emphasis has been put on stock raising, elsewhere on fisheries, or on the cultivation of new crops. As production increases, it is hoped that local protein foods will gradually replace the skimmed milk which is now being widely used.

Similar work is in progress in the French Community. To quote from Platt again: "Successful experiments have been made using fish meal—generally supplied by the Food and Agriculture Organization—for child feeding in many territories in Africa. Children who had no appetite and would not take milk digested the fish very readily, with excellent results. If the fat content is kept low, this food can be given to babies as young as four months. Because of its concentration, only small amounts are needed, and the meal may prove a most satisfactory way of providing extra protein in the tropics."

As Platt points out, these are but examples. Reports of what has been done in the postwar years in the nutritional field by the Belgian, British, French and Portuguese governments are sufficient to fill several books and, in fact, do.[17] And everywhere it is being realized that good nutrition, far from being a purely medical matter, is the concern of all, from which none can stand aloof if the benefits of civilization are to be truly enjoyed by the African.

THE PROSPECT

The assault against sickness in tropical Africa has been going on long enough for some things to have emerged quite clearly.

The first of these is that the scale of the assault does not match the scale of the sickness. True, there have always been Davids ready to do battle with the Goliaths that stalk the

---

[17] A summary of the work done during the period is to be found in *Nutrition Research in Africa South of the Sahara*, Publication No. 19, Scientific Council for Africa South of the Sahara, London, 1957.

African earth, but mosquitoes, worms and viruses are not felled by slingshot. Reasons why the scale of the assault is inadequate are easy enough to find. There are the usual ones of ignorance, apathy and sloth; and they are important reasons. But perhaps more important than any of these is the difficulty of doing battle with an enemy that is ubiquitous and largely unseen—an enemy that can as easily lurk in a pail of water, a garment, a hut and a diet as in a child's feces, a mother's cough and a man's urine. There are no heroics, no *coups de grâce,* and no lasting victories in such a fight; only an unremitting daily foot slogging. "To fight and to fight when hope's out of sight" takes not only stamina but also dedication. It also takes money, and there's the rub. The African doesn't have it; his governments do not have nearly enough; the outside world has too much sickness of its own to feel passionately about the needs of people it has never met or about diseases from which it may not itself suffer.

The second thing that has emerged is that there is still a great deal to be learned about the enemy before anybody can be certain that a given strategy is the right one. Nor is it merely a matter of knowing whether hospitals take a heavier toll of his strength than health centers, or drugs than doctors, or good nutrition than good nursing. It is no less a matter of knowing whether the physical good that hospital care would do a woman suffering from bilharziasis would more than offset the psychological harm of being separated from her unweaned child; of knowing whether it is better to give a man a living wage, part of which he may squander in worthless food and drink and flashy clothes, than to feed and house him and his family adequately, and keep him in pocket money; and of knowing how far the gains accruing from a clearing and drainage campaign are canceled out by the losses of wildlife on which the inhabitants depend for their protein foods. And these are all matters in which almost any man may pose as expert—until he meets another.

What is equally clear is that about all we can hope for, in the present context of limited material resources, imperfect intelligence and inertia, is the continued coexistence of sick-

ness and health. For those—individuals and governments alike
—who are willing to pay the price in work, watchfulness and
hard cash, there will certainly be more health and less sickness.
Over increasingly wide areas it should be possible to speak
of the containment of more and more diseases. At the same
time there is no promise, either in the medical literature or in
the statistical trends, that the gains will be permanent. Many
of those already entered in the record are insecure. Not infrequently they are there by the accident of good government
—good, that is, in providing the funds needed for campaigns
against malaria, yellow fever and sleeping sickness, in promoting and administering these campaigns, and in coordinating them with public works, education, agricultural
and housing programs. Were the "accident" to cease, such
gains would soon be forfeit. It takes only a little neglect, a
little carelessness, to enable malaria-carrying mosquitoes and
trypanosome-carrying tsetse flies to repossess a district from
which their kin have been evicted. The advances made in the
control of a dozen other diseases, including the helminthiases,
the dysenteries and typhoid fevers, would likewise not long
survive the passing of good government. The same would almost certainly apply to most nutritional diseases, unless,
miraculously, the people found they could live as well under
a bad government as they could under a good one. Not even
good government can make some gains permanent, it seems.
It is now known that sleeping sickness may continue to be
present subclinically and in tsetse flies long after its eradication from a district has been officially announced. Plague may
continue to exist in wild rodents for years without ever showing up in man. Tertiary lesions may appear long after yaws
victims had supposed themselves cured.

Even where there is no likelihood of a disease staging a
comeback, there is a very real likelihood of the gains made
against it being offset by losses in a different quarter. The
growing urbanization of tropical Africa, with its almost inevitable accompaniment, overcrowding, is an open incitement to tuberculosis, poliomyelitis and meningitis to make
themselves at home in the land. Similarly, as the average Afri-

can tends to live better and longer, he can scarcely expect to avoid attack by "middle-age" diseases. From these, up to now, he has been largely free, if only because he has not lived to middle age. Among such likely attackers are diabetes (mainly in areas of "better" nutrition), arteriosclerosis, rheumatism, high blood pressure, kidney disease, obesity (especially in the towns), heart troubles and mental disorders. Most of these diseases are already being reported, though the extent to which the reports reflect better diagnosis rather than increased occurrence is not always clear.

Must we conclude from all this that the African is still unable to look forward to the time when he will be free, once and for all, of those diseases that for ages have incommoded, crippled, maimed, weakened, disabled and killed him—when it will be possible for him to speak of conquest, rather than containment, of disease? It is perhaps significant that the word "conquest" has, up to now, seldom appeared in the medical literature of tropical Africa; the most that is claimed is that a disease is under control—and control, like right of way, is a thing more often yielded than possessed. This does not mean that all thought of ultimate conquest should be discarded. But it does mean that it should be divested of wishfulness or, what often amounts to the same thing, the feeling that fighting is something only professionals do.

The fight against disease can never be won by professionals alone. There aren't enough doctors, public health officers, technologists, medical auxiliaries or administrators; and if there were, the cost of keeping them on a government's payroll would almost certainly be such as to doom that government to an early demise. Besides, there's a limit to what even an "unlimited" army of professionals can do. They can command a man to build a pit latrine, but they cannot always be around to see that he uses it. They may have cures for syphilis and malaria, but they cannot stop a man from believing that he has been bewitched and is dying.[18]

[18] In his working paper, Kenneth Bradley affirms, "No doctor . . . would guarantee that any patient in his wards might not disappear overnight, or just turn his face to the wall and die."

Further, the professional's reasons for engaging the enemy are sometimes open to question. The professional is the paid servant of the government, and some governments have a reputation—not altogether undeserved, it must be confessed—of using the African for ends he does not always perceive, let alone care for. When a district officer tells a headman to clear bush or drain swamps, there are usually some among those who find themselves doing the clearing and draining who wonder whether they aren't just paving the way for the D. O. to settle on the land himself. And when a medical officer insists on vaccinating every inhabitant of a village and taking X-rays of their chests, there are almost sure to be those who wonder whether he is doing it merely in the expectation of getting more work out of them—perhaps even sending the fittest of them to a distant mine or training camp.

But if not by professionals alone, how? By professionals working in cooperation with laymen—the common people, in fact? And, if in this fashion, how are ignorant spectators to be turned into efficient fighting units and these into disciplined teams who will do what they are told, and want to do it?

CHAPTER 4

THE RISE OF THE VOLUNTARY ORGANIZATION

The African has always been aware of the importance of the group. It is probably no exaggeration to say that he has always lived his life in the group, for the group and by grace of the group. Certainly he was a "joiner" long before the American. But, in the traditional milieu of African life, opportunities for "joining" were limited. For the most part they could be found only within the bounds of the family, kin and age set, clan and craft; in "the daily round" of raising children, honoring tribal obligations and maintaining order; in "the common tasks" of clearing bush, harvesting, hunting, fighting and propitiation. If there were other needs that could be met only by collaboration, they were either unfelt or unwilled. Ignorance is a powerful anesthetic, and there are no more effective paralyzers of the will than poverty and sickness. It might even be argued that the main reason why the old Africa was so long in outgrowing its "smallness" was its inability to get things going on a scale matching the need.

While Africa is still having difficulty matching the scale of its actions to the scale of its needs, it has been showing a remarkable capacity in recent years for adopting and improvising new forms of group enterprise. The timeliness of some of these enterprises may be open to question, but the utility of most of them, or the manifest good they are doing, cannot be denied. The range of their interest is wide; it embraces religion, politics, administration, education, civic and self-improvement, and recreation of all kinds. In scale, these enterprises run all the way from local to international—from village cooperatives to mine workers' unions affiliated to the International Confederation of Free Trade Unions and Boy Scout troops that form part of the world scouting organization. In character, they are voluntary, deriving their support from the freely donated time, effort and, in some cases, funds of those who believe in them.

COMMUNITY DEVELOPMENT

It is customary to speak of the expanding horizons of the African's world, and, up to a point, it is correct. Most Africans can "see" farther today than they could a generation ago, and most of them go much farther than they did then. The center of their world has not changed greatly in the last generation, however. There is probably not one African in a hundred—no matter how long gone "abroad" to the mines, cities and factories—who does not continue to think of his native village, town or ancestral land as the country to whose bourn every traveler, sooner or later, returns, and to whose demands he must ever be ready to pay heed. It is not surprising, then, if most of the new group enterprises, formal and informal, take their start and make their widest appeal at the local level.

There are other good reasons why most of them are based on the locality. To begin with, most of the African's needs are still for local things: a moisture- and vermin-proof storehouse for his grain; an all-weather gravel road for the transport of his surplus fruits and vegetables to the nearest town; an accessible, clean water supply that will cut down the unproductive portion of a woman's working day and eliminate the risk of water-borne disease; a dispensary that will help to lower the toll of needless pain and ill-health; a clinic that will reduce infant and maternal mortality; and an adult school that will make it possible to command higher wages, a more knowledgeable wife, and the respect of one's juniors. Unfortunately, though, most African governments are habitually hard-pressed for funds. The half-dozen dollars or so which they are able to collect annually from the African householder as his contribution to the territorial budget barely cover the costs of administration and maintenance. Accordingly, if needs of the kind mentioned above are to be met, much of the labor and native materials must be supplied by the householder. The world over, it is easier to get house-holders to support local projects than regional or national projects from which they may derive very little direct benefit.

Again, if tropical Africa is ever to be saved from its poverty, sickness and ignorance, it will be only as the ordinary people come to see that salvation is more a matter of works —their works—than faith, whether in their own culture or in their government's intentions and abilities; that salvation lies in self-help. Now, what people do for themselves, and how well and consistently they do it, is largely a matter of solidarity. And in tropical Africa solidarity is still compounded of kinship and common ties of language, land, livelihood, customs, beliefs and traditions. All these ingredients can still be found in the small bush community. In the big towns, mining compounds and plantations, they can be found in cellular form, but often there is very little communication between cell and cell. As for solidarity at the territorial level, it has barely begun to be compounded.

And, further, it is only at the local level that men and women, having no more than a glimmer of an idea of what they really need but often rather more than a glimmer of doubt about their rulers' intentions, can be made to see the point of any new government program and so be persuaded to become voluntary participants in it.

The need for a greatly enlarged program of local group enterprise is nothing new. It was there long before "community development" campaigns got under way. Many governments were, in fact, engaged in community development long before anybody was calling it that. In a sense, community development is another name for the primary goal of all enlightened government. Those who have seen something of the work of the district officer in British-administered territories or that of his Belgian, French and Portuguese counterparts will know that the development of a better community is precisely what he has been striving for for many years.[1]

---

[1] For those who have not, Kenneth Bradley's *The Diary of a District Officer* (T. Nelson, London and New York, 1947) will provide some rewarding, and amusing, reading.

What is new is the practice of community development as an economic, social and political creed, and the conviction of African governments that "the great mass of Africans [must be made to realize] that with the new knowledge and assistance brought by Western civilisation behind them, they can themselves by their own efforts improve their economic and social conditions . . . [and] that the new knowledge is not an enemy which will disrupt their society but an ally which will help them to overcome and make the most of the intractable environment of Africa," and the recognition that "development can only be fully understood [by the ordinary African] if it brings direct, visible benefits to him in the shape of improved wealth or improved services."[2]

In the years immediately after the second world war, several circumstances served to quicken these convictions and translate them into a language "the ordinary African" could understand. Among them the following were, perhaps, the most important.

1. The return to their homes of thousands of African soldiers, many of whom had been abroad and discovered for the first time that not everybody drank from the water they washed in; that ill-health was not essential to the business of living; that children need not die before they had begun to live; that even a very little book learning enabled a man to earn more money, raise more food and live longer; and that many of the things the African had been brought up to believe were "for his good" were simply not tolerated in other countries. From such men, in Ghana, Nigeria, French Africa, Kenya, Uganda and many more territories, has come much of the demand, and the drive, for local development programs.

2. The growing sensitivity of African governments to public opinion—colonial, metropolitan and foreign—and their own genuine desire to upgrade the ordinary African's living standards. To encourage their wards to go to war for them, some governments had named economic, social and political de-

2 Sir Andrew Cohen, the then Governor of Uganda, in a despatch (No. 490/52) to the Secretary of State for the Colonies, Colonial Office, London, July 22, 1952, p. 5.

velopment as the laurels of victory; before the war's end, almost all had announced plans for such development. Since the founding of the United Nations, the governments administering African trust territories have vied with the U. N. visiting missions to trust territories in the desire to justify their existence in the African's eyes.

3. The availability of money for development work. Part of this money was, in the view of the cynic, "conscience money" that governments ought to have used for this kind of work sooner. Much more of it, however, was either money that the Africans themselves were willing to put up in the form of voluntarily assumed levies on cash crops, head taxes, etc., or money, such as the British Colonial Development and Welfare funds, the Belgian Native Welfare Fund and Ten Year Development Plan, and the French Investment Fund for Economic and Social Development (FIDES), that the administering powers raised by additional taxation of their already heavily taxed metropolitan electors. In addition, sizable sums were put up by the large mining and plantation companies for the development primarily of their employees and families; by philanthropic agencies, such as the Belgian FOREAMI (Queen Elizabeth Funds for Medical Assistance to the Natives); and by the technical agencies of the United Nations and the United States.

4. The determination of ever-increasing numbers of young African men and women "to join the twentieth century," to rid themselves of their chronic ills, and to lead fuller lives. Every graduating class, whether it be from a secondary, primary or adult education school, swells the ranks of those so determined.

Forms, methods and aims. It is easy enough to say what community development is. In the words of the Social Commission of the United Nations Economic and Social Council, it is "a process designed to create conditions of economic and social progress for the whole community with its active participation and the fullest possible reliance upon the community's initiative. [It] implies the integration of two sets of forces making for human welfare, neither of which can do the job alone: (i) The opportunity and capacity for co-operation, self-help, ability to assimilate and adapt new ways of living that is at least latent in every human group; and (ii) The fund of techniques and tools in every social and economic field, drawn from world-wide experience and now in use or available to national governments and agencies."[3] Although there are shorter ways of saying the same thing, no African development agency would be likely to disagree with the thesis.

It is easy to say what community development does. It does, or seeks to do, virtually anything that will quicken a community's pulse. In most parts of tropical Africa this can be done as readily by digging a well or spraying a pond as by teaching a tongue, opening a clinic or organizing a sports club.

It is easy to say how community development works. It goes on the theory that development comes by seeing, seeing by believing and believing by the word, written or spoken. Its symbol is a pump; its agents, "primers"; its secret weapon, a dowser's rod. It cannot work in arid, unresponsive soil; it needs to feel the pull of desire. But once it has "struck water" and can demonstrate its worth to even a small community, its task is greatly lightened. It takes but a small success to start a lot of people talking, and in tropical Africa a talker seldom lacks for listeners.

It is also easy to say why—so far at any rate—community development in tropical Africa wins most of its acclaim in the rural areas. It is there, on the anvil of tribal solidarity, that common causes can still be shaped most easily, and dissenters most quickly "straightened out." It is the rural areas, with their characteristically small-scale organization of land and livelihood, that lend themselves best to the pint-sized projects most commonly undertaken by community developers. It is these same areas that need them most urgently,

[3] "Principles of Community Development," mimeographed report by the Secretary-General, E/CN.5/303, January 31, 1955, pp. 13–14.

of course, since the towns are almost always ahead of the villages in the matter of public utilities, welfare services and so on. Not least, it is the rural areas where most of the people live.

What is much less easy to speak of is the importance of community development in tropical Africa, whether as a means of ensuring development or enriching the community —which is not necessarily the same thing. Certainly no generalizations are yet in order. There are many places where community development is still unheard of; others where it has come and gone; still others where it has stayed, growing from strength to strength. Many very firm opinions about its importance have nevertheless been formed. One opinion is that community development is nothing but a cut-price cure for backwardness and frustration—and a not very efficacious one, since it substitutes good fellowship for good government and passing fancies for long-term policies. Another is that it is just a clever piece of window dressing done to draw a crowd of outside admirers. A third is that it is no more than a trick to keep colonial peoples colonial—a twentieth-century version of the "bread and circuses" formula. A fourth, and less easily disposed of, opinion is that the idea of "development" is completely incompatible with the idea of "community" as the Africans have understood it; that each new development is so much more fuel on a fire already threatening to destroy the old community order, including "those valuable human qualities which are the true foundation for any satisfying conception of welfare."[4] Lastly, there is the opinion of the community developers themselves, most of whom appear to feel that community development is the bootstrap by which lowly men and nations can lift themselves to higher ground, and become members of a larger world community while getting a firmer grip on their own.

In the face of such opposing views, perhaps the most prudent course is to describe some of the projects, both rural and urban, that have been or are being conducted. The

[4] T. R. Batten, "The Community and Development," *Corona*, September 1951, p. 334.

number of such projects is very large. Those selected merely illustrate the wide field of the community developer, its possibilities and pitfalls, its mixed soil, variable yield and amenability to differing techniques.

RURAL AREAS

A project at the district officer level. The Awgu Division of the Eastern Region of Nigeria provides an example of the small-scale, man-and-a-boy type of project beloved of the British. This project had its origins partly in the disillusionment of returned soldiers who found civilian life tame and stuffy; partly in the lack of economic openings commensurate with those available in the mining and industrial regions to the south, whither there was a steady flow of underemployed men; and partly in the growing estrangement of the schooled and the unschooled, the progressives and the traditionalists. Because of this, there is a certain representative, even symbolic, quality about the context of the project, if not about its size and scope.

How community development got started and what it has done and failed to do for the 150,000 people living in the 424 square miles of the Awgu Division has been described by I. C. Jackson,[5] one of the few Europeans who had anything important to do with it.

Since no community development project can succeed unless the leaders of the community are fully persuaded of its value and feasibility, the first thing to be done was to sweep away the benevolently despotic "native authority councils" that, along with the district officer, had been the government's field agents. The members of these councils were generally illiterate, inarticulate and incapable of understanding, let alone dealing with, the postwar stresses. In place of these bodies the government established, in 1948, a single native authority, or council, composed almost entirely of younger, educated men. The change-over was not made without words

[5] *Advance in Africa: A Study of Community Development in Eastern Nigeria,* Oxford University Press, London, 1956.

and loss of face, but within a year or so it had come to be accepted, largely because the people saw that their new leaders were capable of getting things done and the new leaders were anxious to get things done. By 1950 almost every village in the division had some community project in hand.

With the help of a very small pump-priming fund at the disposal of the district officer, a steadily rising local taxation rate and the occasional piece of expert advice from visiting members of the Public Works Department, the work went forward until, by the end of 1952, "Forty-one village water points—rain-water tanks, spring improvements, or wells—had been completed. Five leper segregation villages had been established. Six villages had reconstructed their markets in permanent materials. Five maternity homes had been started. Sixty miles of good motorable road, with the necessary bridges and culverts, had been completed, and a further forty miles awaited the day when the council would undertake its maintenance."[6]

However, the biggest need—that of a hospital—was still unmet. To build this would require the use of voluntary labor on an unprecedentedly large scale, and of people drawn not just from the "community" in which it was to be built, but from all over the division—from villages which had been "warring together until forty years before, and to this day . . . are still liable to have an affray over boundary disputes." Even so, it was built, along with the necessary utilities, by 1954. While it was the district officer who did most of the organizing and supervising, it was the local people who did most of the ordering, accounting and building. One group of men gave more than half the working days of 1953 to the job. The students of a nearby teachers' training college gave up part of their vacation to forward the work. One of the most enthusiastic workers was the local "congressman."

But hospitals, maternity homes, roads and even water tanks have to be maintained as well as built, and in Africa it is hard to whip up enthusiasm for maintenance of any kind, especially

[6] *Ibid.*, pp. 62–63.

the kind that takes money as well as labor. A hospital or a road, or even a water tank, invariably does take both, and the money has to come from the same people who have already given the labor. The next community project therefore was to raise the taxable incomes of the people of Awgu. This has proved a good deal harder.

> The earliest economic development was an attempt to introduce hand-loom weaving, and eight young men . . . were sent for six months' training at the expense of the native authority. On their return they were given workshops and houses, and loans to tide them over the initial period. Their response was to ask to be put on a regular wage. They refused a profitable government contract and preferred to weave yarn supplied by the Department of Commerce and Industries, which sold the finished cloth and gave the weavers a share of the proceeds. When this arrangement was stopped, and they were forced to use their own initiative in buying the yarn and selling the cloth, work came to a standstill at once, and the weavers dispersed.[7]

An attempt to develop pottery making on modern lines has "so far avoided the fate of weaving"; in other words, it, too, is having its troubles. "The new techniques demand a teamwork unnecessary under the old methods, and as production is done in bigger batches there is a long delay between the times of making the pots and selling them."

Somewhat more successful has been the campaign to get farmers to grow rice on low-lying land and to plant cashew trees on sandy land that hitherto produced nothing but firewood. However, there is not much enthusiasm anywhere in the division for development of an agricultural sort, and Jackson has sadly to admit that while "in one direction community development has achieved something considerable—the hospital; in the other direction there is nothing comparable." This, he contends, is not the fault of community development, which "can do no more than clear the path for the

[7] *Ibid.*, p. 66.

dynamic individual," but due rather to the absence of enough such individuals with technical training, and of enough credit and marketing facilities. Here, it seems, Jackson comes close to playing into the hands of his enemies, for is he not saying, in effect, that self-generating community development depends more on external stimuli than internal cohesion? And if this is so, is it likely that these dynamic individuals, once they have seen how much greener the grass grows in distant fields, will be content to go on cultivating those of the community? All too often the path that has been cleared for a dynamic individual leads away from those who cleared it. It takes dedication amounting to idealism for the dynamic souls of this world to spend themselves in the service of their less dynamic neighbors.

A program carried out by specialists. In some other British-administered territories, the government has held the reins of community development with a firmer hand, employing, where necessary, the art of the teamster to get things moving. The teamster technique is probably seen to best advantage in Uganda, thanks in large part to the driving power of Sir Andrew Cohen, Governor of the protectorate from 1952 through 1956 and in his earlier days community development policy-maker-in-chief to the Colonial Office. From the start he and his colleagues held that community development could become an effective instrument of economic and social policy only if certain conditions were satisfied. Among these, the most important were: (1) that the work should be done by trained specialists in community development, and not by grossly overworked district officers; (2) that it should be done in concert with the agricultural, cooperative, medical and other specialists already stationed in the district or province; (3) that African leaders, chosen from the new educated classes, should be "trained to help direct the programme in each area and to secure the co-operation of the people"; (4) that the program should be applied by and through local government bodies then being broken in and looking for "buyers" (and what could "sell" them better than a demonstration that they fostered economic and social improvement in rural areas?); (5) that the program should be carried through quickly and vigorously, since only in this way could the government hope to absorb the energies of those who were "at the same time most likely to help and if not properly occupied most likely to oppose and disrupt."[8]

How quickly and vigorously this policy was implemented in Uganda can be seen from the following miscellaneous items taken from the 1953 and 1954 annual reports of the Department of Community Development.

From the 1953 report:

> In 1952 the Protectorate Government contributed £ 10,-000 as additional provision for plans which African Local Governments might put up. In 1953 £ 100,000 was provided as the first instalment of £ 500,000 which is to be available over a period of five years . . .
>
> It is not practicable to include . . . full details of the many different projects which have been approved. The plan for the Toro District . . . may be regarded as a typical programme. Among the more commonly-chosen projects were those in which the people provide free communal labour for the building of schools, dams, roads, etc., while the funds are used to provide skilled labour, tools, cement, timber and other materials for finishing off the job. The provision of local workshops for making latrine stances, culvert pipes, doors and windows, etc.; the improvement of water supplies and their protection from fouling; the improvement and equipment of rural sports fields; educational visits and agricultural shows; the supervision of adult literacy campaigns; the provision of building materials for new leper settlements; the encouragement of local vernacular literature; encouragement for Boy Scouts, Girl Guides and other associations such as village clubs; the provision

[8] Despatch No. 490/52, p. 5. The year 1952 did not mark the beginning of community development in Uganda. For some years a Public Relations and Social Welfare Department had been as active as its limited resources of money and men would permit.

of materials for erecting shelters at bus stops—all these plans are common to several districts.

From the 1954 report:

> The Local Government and Community Development Training Centre at Entebbe accepted its first students on May 10th, just fourteen months after the builders had begun work, and a few weeks before their departure . . . The centre provides accommodation for 50 married students accompanied by their wives, 80 single men and 20 single women . . .

This training center at Entebbe offered courses covering all aspects of community development.

But breaking-in and training are only part of the teamster's art. No less important is the inculcation of staying power. In men as in horses, this is often more a matter of breeding than of training, and breeding takes time. Impressive as the Uganda program is, nobody either in or out of the government is suggesting that it is more than a blueprint—the "pedigree," if you will, of the cultivated, civic-minded, dedicated citizen. And among those who are most convinced of the propriety of what they are doing, there are some who are beginning to yearn for "a greater sense of urgency everywhere and a greater readiness on the part of those who have enjoyed the benefits of education and other opportunities that have been denied to so many to place service before self . . . not just by giving from a distance either advice or even money but by working with the community."[9]

It would be tragic indeed if, after taking so much trouble to get him to the water, the horse should lose his palate for it.

Programs to create communities. The Belgians approached community development—as most other aspects of govern-

[9] *Annual Report of the Department of Community Development for the Year Ended 31st December 1955*, Entebbe, Uganda, 1956, p. 22.

ment—more from the point of view of what they believed was good for the entire Congolese (Belgian-African) community than what was good for the Africans, most of whom are still living in anachronistically small communities. Accordingly, there has been more emphasis on "development" than on "community," though it does not follow that the community life of the Congolese people has not been as greatly strengthened as that of the peoples in British and other African territories. Indeed, it is arguable that, by putting social action on more of a business footing, the Belgians have been less bothered by their failures, less excited about their successes, less hesitant in their advance, and less restricted in their scope; that, in short, the Belgian Congo is likely to finish up with stronger communities than some of the other territories.

What the Belgians have been doing in their *paysannats indigènes* to strengthen peasant farming is described in the companion volume on *Land and Livelihood*. But the *paysannats* are more than farm projects. They are community developments of the most radical kind, since they are concerned with building communities where none worthy of the name existed, and in which the quality of life will be comparable to the best offered by the towns—communities that will be characterized by increased stability, higher living standards, and "an intensive social activity" that will lead to "a strengthening and an evolution of the social structure."[10] To this end, all *paysannats* have been supplied with social welfare centers around which the community side of their life is intended to revolve. Most of these centers consist of a social services building, a school, a collective storehouse, a collective workshop and a guest house. Some of the larger ones also have a hospital, and all of the smaller ones have dispensaries.

With so much expensive plant and equipment involved and so much at stake socially, politically and economically, the Belgians have contended that they were the ones to write the rules, decide the plays, and generally manage the players' affairs. Those who have joined a *paysannat* have, in fact, had

[10] United Nations, Economic and Social Council, "Principles of Community Development," E/CN.5/303, January 31, 1955, p. 75.

to do as they were told. They have had to take the land allocated to them, grow the approved crops in the approved rotations, and settle for whatever return on their cash crops the authorities named. Notwithstanding, the role of the African has been far from passive. Each *paysannat* "is established only after the administrator of the Territory has convened the councils of chiefs, and village heads, and has explained to them the purposes of the collective systems and gained the consent of the parties concerned . . . A *paysannat* council is held every three months to settle disputes, to keep the land records up to date and to settle changes, transfers and new applications for land."[11] Increasingly, Africans have been employed on the team that runs the agronomic and social affairs of the *paysannat*.

The results of the *paysannat* project have (1959) far exceeded official expectations, and not merely from a numerical point of view, though it is no small achievement to have put upward of 500,000 people into farm "collectives" and to have made them so popular that there are always more applicants than vacancies. Even more gratifying to the administration has been the fact that most of those who have come, have stayed; and that those who have stayed have developed an *esprit de corps* seldom surpassed in the old Africa or the new.

Much the same kind of pattern of government-inspired and government-directed rural community development has been established, more recently and on a smaller scale, in the French and Portuguese areas. As yet little such work has been done under government auspices in either Liberia or Ethiopia. In the newly independent countries of Ghana, Guinea and Sudan the pattern of government activity in this field continues to bespeak its metropolitan origin.

Community development by private industry. The community development experiences of business and industrial corporations have likewise been of large hopes, mounting difficulties and small successes. One instance must suffice—that of the Firestone Plantations Company in Liberia.

[11] *Ibid.*, p. 74.

Elsewhere[12] we have spoken of Firestone's great economic achievements at Harbel, near Robertsfield. The company's achievements in the social field, though notable, have not been of the same order. This has not been from want of effort or desire on the management's part: no company in Africa has tried harder to help its employees. But the fact is that after a generation of management that would be called enlightened in any of the world's free countries, the plantations are still more a transient camp than a permanent community. The majority of the workers continue to stay only for one season and then pocket their money and go back to their bush farms. They are unlikely to return to the plantations before the money runs out, and when they do return, they are unlikely to stay more than a year or so. While they can often be made to see the point of the company's generous medical services and may even have gone to the plantations for the purpose of getting the white man's free "needles," they still prefer the medicine man for many things. They can see merit also in the company's free education program, but what educated Liberian wants to stay around plantations tapping rubber or totting up the day's yield? The place of the educated man, even if he has had but two or three years' schooling, is behind an office desk, and not many of these are to be found in Harbel. Nor has anybody to convince him that security for old age and survivors is something to be prized, for the tribe has always made provision for the old and the survivor, and nobody has had to work thirty years to qualify for it. Need we wonder, therefore, that the path of the Firestone community developer is rather tiring, and as ill-lit as the paths of the bush about him?

URBAN AREAS

The problems of the community builder are multiplied when he takes them to the towns. In the country he does at least have straw for his bricks; in the towns and on the mining compounds (which are towns except perhaps in name and

12 See *Land and Livelihood,* Chapter 4.

administration) often the only straw available is that carried in by the winds of discontent. For the Léopoldvilles, Nairobis and Luanshyas of Africa are not communities: like all cities, they are places of catch-as-catch-can contest, of lonely crowds and anonymous individuals. This does not mean that the towns lack community nuclei, or that the nuclei cannot be enlarged. The very fact of there being towns means that those who live in them have many things in common besides loneliness and anonymity—among them idleness (especially at the weekends), the temptation to squander earnings and health, the discipline and boredom of repetitive work, and, not least, a skin color that frequently puts the town's choicer offerings out of reach.

The community developer who comes to town needs, therefore, to be a man of many parts. It is not enough that he be builder and architect; he needs also to be coach and player, master and servant, teacher and student, and, for good measure, alchemist, capable of transmuting dross into durable metal. He must also be able to play these parts with constancy and charm. Fortunately, there are such men.

The nuclei. The obvious starting point for the urban community developer is the nuclei. These, which exist in every town and compound, are composed of people belonging to the same tribe or kindred. Common language and background draw them together, just as Puerto Ricans, Germans, Poles and a hundred other groups are drawn together in New York. Common obligations and common circumstances tend to keep them together. Frequently, because of their separateness, they develop more cohesion and unity than the larger groups from which they are drawn. But like most exiles to the Babylons of this world, they spend a good deal of time remembering their far-away Zions. Weekend tam-tams in the compound of a senior tribesman, picnics, dances and pep talks form a major activity of many such tribal groups. Those that carry on "service" activities tend to confine them to such things as the provision of scholarships for the children of fellow tribesmen, loans to help a man with his taxes or bride wealth, and funds for the becoming burial of deceased members. Seldom do their interests reach out beyond the tribal group.

At the same time it is difficult for such groups of people to live long in a town or on a compound without becoming aware of the world about them and wanting to be of it as well as in it. Especially is this true of the younger members of such groups. Evidence of a change of orientation from "old-worldliness" to "new-worldliness" is to be had on almost every hand. The Boy Scout movement, the Red Cross and similar societies are being increasingly well represented in the larger towns and mining centers. So, too, are sports clubs. Many of the teams put up by these clubs are admittedly tribal in composition, but the trend is toward intertribal and, in some places, interracial teams. It is also true that most of the spectators are as partisan as American alumni, but, even so, their partisanship can be, and often is, demonstrated as vigorously for a town or compound team as a tribal one. The first loyalty of the 70,000 spectators that regularly fill Léopoldville's stadium is to the home team, be it African, European or interracial, and not to the players who happen to be their kin or speak their language.

Then again, most mines and almost all of the large towns today have community centers for the promotion of welfare and solidarity. On the social side, a good center, such as those found in the Rhodesian Copperbelt, is likely to number among its amenities a canteen, a beer hall, a cinema, a library, a games room, an auditorium (doubling as dance hall and theater), classrooms, special-interest groups (with a strong emphasis on the "Do It Yourself" type of work), music clubs and a counseling service. Some of the Copperbelt centers hold regular dances as formal as any student graduation ball. On the health side, a good center, such as may be found in a hundred towns from Dakar to Zanzibar, will have maternity and child welfare clinics, a dispensary, classrooms for instruction in public health and hygiene, and perhaps a domestic science section in which women and children are introduced to the principles of household management and nutrition.

In many localities the womenfolk are second only to the children and young people in susceptibility to this "new-worldliness." Unlike the men who come to town or mine, the women quickly find themselves with less rather than more work to do. Besides, African women, like the women of every land, can seldom resist the seduction of the shop window with its array of things that are pleasant to the eye and good for morale—especially if their neighbors, with whom they live in the closest physical proximity, have already yielded to it. A further reason for their susceptibility is sometimes the fact that they are not properly supported by their menfolk. "Many husbands think they are entitled to the whole of their earnings and so put clothes, bicycle gear and personal pleasures before house maintenance—even food."[13] Any delicacy of feeling such women may have had about the propriety of playing an unaccustomed role in the community is soon dispelled by hunger—their own and their children's.

All of the great civilizing agencies at work in urban Africa —governments, corporate bodies and voluntary organizations (secular and religious)—are now keenly aware of the importance of nourishing the nuclei.

No doubt much of their keenness is self-interested. It is the towns and the mines that are the chief generators of wealth. It is to the towns and the mines that men and their families must be drawn increasingly if budgets, balance sheets, contributions and offerings are to grow. And it is to them that the immigrants must become wedded if the efficiency of the generative mechanism is not to be impaired. The towns and the mines, therefore, must be humanized—we might almost have said communized. Further, it is the towns and the mines that are the great generators of prostitution, venereal disease, divorce and other social disorders that do so much to undermine the happiness of a community and the stability of its homes. And it is the towns and the mines that generate most of the political unrest. To regard them as concentration camps of cheap labor, as was often done in the past and is

[13] B. G. Ballenden, Welfare Supervisor, Rhokana Corporation Ltd., Kitwe, Northern Rhodesia, in conversation, April 1955.

still done in some quarters, is to invite the speedy disruption of their economy and the certain alienation of their inhabitants—their Communizing, in fact. At the same time, the disinterested concern that is to be found in these agencies for people who have been unceremoniously parachuted into the white man's world must not be underrated. The least anyone can do for such people is to give them the chance to survive the jump and find their bearings. Most of the agencies are attempting to do more than that.

To describe adequately what is being done for the urban dweller by the various administrations would be tedious, for in general it follows the pattern of community development in rural areas. If there is a difference, it is one of emphasis rather than technique. Where communities do not exist to begin with—and they seldom do in the rural sense—they have to be synthesized. It is this that largely explains the prominence given to housing and to educational, recreational and counseling services in the urban welfare programs of most governments.

Government activities. The provision made over the past two or three decades by the Belgian Congo government for the newly-come-to-town in its *centres extra-coutumiers* may have been more ample than that made by some other governments, but it has set a standard below which no African government can afford to fall. These centers in which Africans live away from the tribe and tribal jurisdiction are to be found near every large European town. Each is administered by a chief with the help of an assistant and a democratically elected council which advises the chief about local regulations, taxes, budgets and the uses to which the center's income is to be put. These councils have worked in close association with the European authorities, from whom they have learned the business of local government and the heavy responsibilities resting upon all those who minister to the welfare of their fellows.

One of the biggest responsibilities has been that of providing housing, because of the fantastic growth of most of the larger towns since the end of World War II. In a single five-year period the African population of Léopoldville, for instance, grew from 110,000 to over 275,000; by 1959 it was close to 350,000. To meet this responsibility the government has used various methods—none more community-minded than that associated with the name F. Grévisse, one of the contributors to this study and a former District Commissioner of Elisabethville.

In 1933 the *centre extra-coutumier* of Elisabethville had 9,000 inhabitants. By 1959 it had over 60,000,[14] most of the difference being accounted for by the postwar expansion of the Katanga copper industries. The Grévisse method was predicated on the inability of any one agency to deal with a "crisis situation" that was daily getting worse. Such a situation called for cooperation by the state, the municipality, the men needing the houses, and their employers. This cooperation was readily forthcoming. The state agreed to be responsible for providing the road net and utilities (*infrastructure*) of the city, and a loan fund for the purchase of building materials by those needing houses. The municipality agreed to look after the distribution of building plots, to let and supervise all contract work, and allocate materials to individual builders. It also made itself responsible for pouring the concrete foundations, building the walls and maintaining a supply of windows, doors, roofing and facing materials. Those needing houses and approved by the local authorities agreed to be responsible for all assembly and finishing work. Their employers agreed to give them a monthly lodging allowance sufficient to cover rental and loan amortization charges. In this way the builders became in time home owners, without having to dip into wages.

The African workers of Elisabethville were not slow to see the merit of such an arrangement. By the end of 1954, within four years of launching the Grévisse plan, they had built nearly 7,000 houses, providing accommodation for some

[14] The total African population of Elisabethville was as large again.

55,000 persons.[15] Grévisse reports that the loans made to them for this purpose amounted to 184 million Belgian francs, or approximately $3.7 million. To further encourage Africans to make their homes in the *centre extra-coutumier,* a mutual society of home builders was formed in 1952. By levying a 4 per cent tax on the money loaned to its members by the government, this society has been able to ensure that the house of any member shall pass, at death, to his heirs "free of all charges."

The increase in the ratio of women to men and the rise in the birth rate at the Elisabethville center may perhaps be taken as measures of the growing sense of security engendered by the Grévisse plan, and also of the growing acceptance by the African worker of the town as his "community." In 1933 there were only 57 women for every 100 men, and only 58 children for every 100 women. In 1948 the corresponding figures were 81 and 101. By 1953 they had risen to 89 and 167. Over the same 21-year period the birth rate at the center rose from 15.0 to 43.8 per 1,000, while the death rate fell from 20.8 to 8.6 per 1,000. The figures for more recent years tell the same story of growing family stability, and larger, longer-lived families.

After housing comes the slow and wearisome business of what, for want of a better word, may be called "habilitation." As the Belgians have themselves put it, most of the Africans who come to live in these centers find themselves "severed from traditional usage . . . Social education, material and moral help are, therefore, indispensable."[16] And with the Congo government "habilitation" has come to mean everything from educational, medical and health services, child care and allowances, home management counseling and recreational and trade-training facilities to social legislation (on

[15] This may seem to us like overcrowding, but not to Africans. Anyway, the authorities encourage them to build one or two extra rooms, the rental from which will enable them to pay off their loan more quickly.

[16] "Social Action in the Belgian Congo and Ruanda-Urundi," Belgian Government Information Center, New York, 1954, p. 45.

minimum wages, the rights of employees and employers, etc.) and professional organizations (including trade unions). Each *centre extra-coutumier*, therefore, has its school or schools, its health center (equipped with dispensary, clinics and classrooms, and attended by fully qualified medical personnel), its sports clubs, recreation center, adult groups and, perhaps most important of all, its *foyer social*, or social home.

The social home is where the battle for the African woman is being fought—where the biggest pitch is being made for the woman's acceptance of the town. The Belgians have argued that it is the woman who can do most to make or break a community, and who stands in most need of adjustment to urban life. Commenting, in a paper prepared for this study, on the work of the social homes, Nancy Berg says: "[They] give the African women training in home economics and child care so that they can better adapt to the material life of their community. In addition, they are a means by which the social service officers, through case work, counseling and personal contact, can help the women and their families to adapt to the social changes taking place in the urban areas. In brief, they are a means of easing the transition which Congolese society is making at the present time."

Each home has a complement of three or four European graduate social workers, including home economist and nurse; several locally recruited European auxiliaries, paid or unpaid; and ten or so African assistants (*monitrices*), not the least of whose functions is to learn enough to be able to extend the outreach of the home. Although the Belgians have had their staffing difficulties, the social home program has developed "at an impressive speed which shows no sign of abatement." By the late 1950s there were around fifty such homes in the Belgian Congo and Ruanda-Urundi.

Activity by corporate bodies in the field of urban community development has followed similar lines. More accurately, in many instances, it is the administrations that have been following. But whether as leader or follower, the contribution of these bodies has been remarkable.

Consider, for instance, what is done by the large industrial firms of the Belgian Congo. True, some of the services, such as housing, food rations and medical care, are decreed by government. But, without exception, they "have gone far beyond government requirements," until today the services offered by them are, in Nancy Berg's opinion, "probably as extensive and as well organized as any in tropical Africa." Those offered by the great transportation company Office d'Exploitation des Transports Coloniaux (Otraco) to its employees and their families living in Léopoldville may be taken as fairly standard.

There are two social centers located in the compounds of the workers. These centers, like the government centers, offer courses in home economics and child care for the women . . . However, the scope of their work extends far beyond these courses for women: the bulk of their activities is directed at the workers of Otraco. During the *permanence* [office hours] the social workers deal mainly with employee problems. . . . They visit hospitals . . . and make regular visits to the homes of workers in the compounds to check on living conditions.

There is even more to industrial social welfare than this, Nancy Berg reports:

When the wife of an Otraco worker becomes pregnant, she receives food rations in addition to those received normally as part of the family allowance of her husband's pay. She can go to the company clinic for medical attention, and to the company's *foyer social* to make clothes for the baby. When the baby is born, the company defrays hospital expenses. The mother and child receive extra food rations until the child reaches six months of age. The child attends the company school. Boys can obtain training as qualified workers in the company's schools after they finish primary school. There are evening courses for adults. The young men are given jobs at Otraco. When they decide to marry, they can ask the company for a loan with which to pay the bride wealth. The company will also make loans to its workers so that they can buy sewing machines and bicycles, or construct a house . . . Sports activities, movies and study groups for *évolués* are provided under the direction of male social workers.

When an employee or his dependents die in Léopoldville, the company covers the funeral expenses. Thus, the company is really a small welfare state providing security from womb to tomb.

Whatever may be said against paternalism of this kind—and plenty of people have much to say against it—the Africans seem to like it. The company certainly gains by it and a community springs from it, as another contributor, George W. Carpenter, points out:

> The company gains a skilled, contented, loyal and constantly improving labor force; its accident rate declines and productivity increases. Mechanization can be carried farther, and more and more difficult processes become feasible. The urban community gains responsible citizens and wholesome families. It is relieved of the burden of a large floating population of immigrants, unattached women, vagrant youths and wild children . . . Both the rural and urban communities have better sex ratios, and normal family life is encouraged instead of destroyed.

Many such urban communities now exist in the Belgian Congo. Aside from those of Otraco, which also has townships at Matadi, Thysville and Coquilhatville, the most notable are those of the Union Minière du Haut-Katanga at Elisabethville, Jadotville and Kolwezi; Symétain at Bunia and Kalima (Kivu), Géomines at Manono (Katanga), Forminière at Tshikapa (Kasai), Huileries du Congo Belge at Leverville (Léopoldville Province) and Compagnie du Chemin de Fer du Bas-Congo au Katanga at Luluabourg (Kasai), Jadotville and Kamina (Katanga).

Outside the Belgian Congo, several very fine corporation townships are to be found in the Rhodesias (at Luanshya in the Copperbelt, for example, and at Shabani in Southern Rhodesia) and at least one in Kenya (that of the East African Railways and Harbours in Nairobi).

The domain of the voluntary secular organization is much wider. It extends from ocean to ocean and from tropic to tropic. The town or compound that does not have at least one such agency is rare. It is also very badly off, for although the Red Cross, the "Y," the Women's Institute, "Les Volontaires" and similar organizations are habitually short of money and helpers, they symbolize service of a kind that is indispensable if community development is ever to become self-starting and self-propelling. So far the African's Africa has seen very few such developments. What few it has seen owe as much, it would seem, to religious as to secular influences.

THE INFLUENCE OF THE
CHRISTIAN CHURCH

Imponderables are always troublesome. Faith cannot be priced; the impact of a sermon, spoken or lived, cannot be measured. And because they are troublesome, there is a rather natural tendency to underrate them, if not to ignore them. But to do this with the influence of the Christian church on the community life of tropical Africa would be quite wrong, for several reasons. In the first place, every mission station has been the nucleus of a community (often a very small one) and a nucleating agent since missions began, which was long before most governments and corporations began. In the second place, the secular agencies have generally taken the view that the church was a useful aide-de-camp to be taken along wherever they went, to deal with all those awkward matters for which they had neither the time nor the understanding. In the third place, there are about 20 million Africans who call themselves Christians, who belong to one or other of the confessions, and who, in greater or less measure, live by what they confess. And in the fourth place, the churches have shown that while they have no monopoly of community spirit, their best variety of it retains its potency longer than most.

Not that the business of the Christian church is community development. Indeed, many Christians have long contended that, since they are "pilgrims and strangers" on this earth, it is a waste of time even to think about such a matter. And those Christians who are deeply concerned about community development would be among the first to admit that a purely "social" church was no church at all. The real business of the Christian church, as George Carpenter puts it, is to create "a fellowship of believers whose members assemble together for common worship, and share a common belief, experience, motivation and obedience."

But because this is so, no community having such a fellowship in its midst can expect to remain untouched by it. And since there are "fellowships"—congregations, assemblies, missions, etc.—in fully three fourths of tropical Africa, it is probably true to say that only in the solidly Islamic areas along the southern margins of the Sahara are there any people who are not being touched by the Christian church. It is also probably true to say that everything the church does and stands for has some influence, for better or worse, on the community it seeks to serve.

Consider, for instance, the kind of thing a well-equipped bush mission station does. It runs a school, where the children of the district learn not only to pray and sing but also to read, write and calculate, and where they encounter, for the first time in all likelihood, the notion that all people are not as they are—that there are different ways of looking at life, of spending one's energies and one's leisure. It runs a medical center, to which all who have need of doctoring, nursing, injections and drugs may come, whether they are members of the mission church or not. There they learn that sickness is a physical and psychological phenomenon, not the result of sorcery, witchcraft or "wishing" by ill-disposed persons; that it is possible to avoid about half of the customary sicknesses by keeping clean and about half of the rest by eating different foods and sleeping under a net. It runs a number of training programs, in farming and perhaps in printing, motor maintenance, carpentry and masonry, that open up possibilities of better living. It almost certainly runs a riot of recreations, from soccer and glee clubs to drumming and dominoes. And its doors are never closed to those seeking comfort or counsel, a go-between or a good listener.

The well-staffed, well-equipped urban mission station or church center is likely to offer even more in the way of community services—everything, in fact, from scout troops, sports clubs, sewing bees, pre-adolescent and premarital instruction groups, and prenatal and postnatal clinics to adult school groups and classes for the training of church members as office holders, speakers and counselors. All of these services, as Carpenter points out, will have this in common, "that they bring together in intimate fellowship a group of people within or related to the total congregation in a way that meets a particular need of the group and fosters their identification with the total life of the church."

The churches, urban and rural, have served other secular functions, too. They have taught the Africans to raise and administer funds, to take care of property, to keep accounts, run committees, organize conferences and speak in public—in short, to take the kind of responsibility that is indispensable to the development of a democratically ordered community.

The importance of the churches' specifically religious work in fostering the growth of community-mindedness is stressed by Carpenter. In fact, it is possible to contend that this is where a mission or a church plays its biggest community-building role, particularly when it serves an "immigrant" population, such as is found in a town or on a mine.

The African uprooted from the social complex of family and tribe in which his whole life has been cast greatly needs to know that he still belongs to a sustaining fellowship . . . This fellowship tends to strengthen the character and reinforce the motivation of the individual. It provides the sanction of group judgment and approbation in relation to personal moral judgments, actions and relationships . . .

Furthermore, the church brings to bear the religious sanction of divine purpose and judgment, and gives meaning to human life as part of God's creative and redemptive purpose in the life of the world. To the extent that these functions of the church are effective in the life of its members they become "new creatures" of enhanced value as members of society.

While both the Protestant and Catholic communions in Africa continue to exercise these functions with much fidelity, it is open to question whether they are doing so as effectively in the towns as in the rural areas, or as effectively in the rural areas as they once did. Nor are the "technical" reasons for this obscure, as Carpenter points out:

City churches tend to be large and heterogeneous in membership compared with the small Christian congregations of rural areas. The individual may therefore feel lost. . . . Many sophisticated Africans regard the message of the church as an old story so familiar as to be meaningless. . . .

The social atomization of humanity in the cities deprives the church of the prestige of social acceptance which it often has in smaller communities. . . . Protestant witness in many African cities is seriously weakened and impaired by sectarianism, the immediate and obvious effect of which is duplication of effort, a multiplicity of competing congregations and an excessive number of church buildings designed chiefly or solely as places of worship, with a conspicuous lack of suitable facilities for religious education and the group life of the church . . . Group activities of all kinds become secularized, because sufficient numbers of people with the same interest are not found in one congregation or even in one denominational group. As a result of all this the church becomes peripheral rather than central to the life of the community, and fails to be the focus of social integration . . .

Sectarianism and disdain of the church are not necessarily confined to town churches. "Sects and divisions may invade rural areas from the cities . . . Skeptical secularism becomes the practice, if not the conscious philosophy, of many young Africans in the cities, and that, too, has spread into rural areas. Moral vice and social disease are equally contagious in city and village. There is no quarantine between the communities."

Other reasons are less technical than spiritual, deriving from the nature of the enterprisers rather than of their enterprise. The Christian church in tropical Africa is still led in most areas by people of European descent, men and women possessed of high ideals, strong convictions and unquestioned dedication. They are also possessed of a book, a message and an authority that set them on high ground—the highest in the world, so they believe. They are therefore conspicuous people, constantly watched and talked about, and constantly being weighed in the balance of the African's shrewd judgment. To be found wanting, to fail to practice what the book teaches—human as this is—is liable to have grievous consequences, not only for the person at fault but also for his colleagues, the local church and, often, the community. The teacher who "blows off steam" at his class today is quoted throughout the district tomorrow, often in extenuation of his quoter's greater excesses. The pastor who tells his African callers to use the back door may find that they stop using any door.[17] Churches practicing any species of discrimination whatever need not be surprised to find themselves slowly losing ground to "splinter" churches that yield none of the expected fruits of Christian living.

Yet, its faults, limitations and failures notwithstanding, the Christian church must still be reckoned one of the great community-building and community-strengthening forces in trop-

[17] In some tropical African territories there are still more missionary homes where Africans are not regular or natural guests than where they are. See Peter Letchford, Canadian Secretary of the South Africa General Mission, in the *Christian Graduate* (London), September 1957, p. 131.

ical Africa. It is a generation since Dr. J. E. K. Aggrey, the famous Gold Coast educator, addressed a conference of Christian students held at the University of Toronto on the subject of what is best for Africa. But what he said then would be endorsed by many of Africa's present-day leaders: "Only the best is good enough for Africa. If you can show me a bridge, a hospital, raised by disciples of Muhammad or Confucius in my country; if you can tell me the name of a missionary from China or Turkey who has died for my people, then I will . . . accept the deletion of the name Christian from the title of this student's Federation. I put my hand before my eyes and I see in Africa, from north to south, from east to west, bridges and roads and hospitals and schools and thousands of men and women living a new life: and all that comes from Christ . . ."

These words would be endorsed by thousands of the common people—for whom let those of Aiyetoro speak.

Aiyetoro, the so-called Apostle Community of southern Nigeria, is a small urban community that owes absolutely nothing to either governments or corporations. Established in the late 1940s as an experiment in cooperative enterprise by a small group of Yoruba-speaking fishermen who had decided "to break away from the ancient, unchanging system of living,"[18] Aiyetoro had at the start only one source of revenue, smoked fish, which was marketed in Lagos, about a hundred miles away. From the beginning, all the money thus derived was turned over to the community treasury, any surpluses being set aside for development work and the promotion of new trades and industries. Within the span of a decade the community has grown from a hamlet of mud-and-thatch huts to a well-planned town complete with shade trees, playgrounds and all modern conveniences—all except bars, since the drinking of alcohol is prohibited, along with smoking and the making of unnecessary noise. Each year sees the people of Aiyetoro learning new skills, living better, putting more money in the treasury, and winning new converts to their way of life.

[18] *The Times British Colonies Review*, Third Quarter 1957, p. 19.

What, we may ask, is the secret of their success? They themselves say that there is no secret: all they have sought to do is to follow the way of the early Christian believers "[who] continued steadfastly in the apostles' doctrine . . . ; were together, and had all things common; and sold their possessions and goods, and parted them to all men, as every man had need . . . continuing daily with one accord in the temple . . . ; and . . . [who] did eat their meat with gladness and singleness of heart . . ."[19] Those who have seen the Apostle Community do not find it hard to accept their explanation—or to agree with the London *Times* correspondent who, in a moment of un-*Times*-like gusto, declared: "The people of Aiyetoro have pioneered a way of life in which they take great pride and which seemingly makes them well contented. They are certainly on the way to conquering the old enemies of mankind—disease, idleness, squalor, ignorance, and want."[20] No community developer could ask for more.

The kind of movement considered so far seeks, by doing a little for a lot of people, to tap the wellsprings of their desire for a better life and so to get them to bestir themselves on their own behalf. That is, it is a pump-priming movement. Needless to say, some communities can be primed more quickly than others. Some, like Aiyetoro, take very little priming. Others, like Awgu, prime easily enough, but have difficulty in staying primed. Their springs, seemingly, are shallow and subject to periodic exhaustion. And there are many communities throughout tropical Africa, which, for all their priming, have not yet produced anything more than a small, inconstant trickle of results.

Of course, there is no telling what a primed pump will yield. Before now, if we are to believe the witness of the movie screen, the fluid that has come out has been very different from and more intoxicating than the fluid that went in. But that is a chance all gamblers must take, and community development is nothing if not a gamble on the capacity of

19 Acts 2:42–46, A.V.
20 *The Times British Colonies Review*, loc. cit.

people for self-generating progress. Most of the time, however, it is true to say that like yields like. Where the emphasis has been on spiritual gains—freedom from fear, superstition and tyranny, or greater happiness, dignity and decency—the yield tends to be strongly religious and political. Where the emphasis of the priming agent, whether self-styled community developer, district officer or teacher, missionary or local chief, has been on material gains—more money, better houses, bigger crops and so on—the yield tends to be as strongly economic.

COOPERATIVES

Though the cooperative movement has found favor in many parts of tropical Africa, it has made most progress in the British and formerly British territories where it started. As long ago as 1913 a few African farmers in Uganda were marketing their cotton crop cooperatively. By 1930, 12,000 Chagga coffee growers were members of the five-year-old Kilimanjaro Native Coffee Planters Association (now the Kilimanjaro Native Co-operative Union, Ltd.).

In a sentence, a cooperative society—the physical expression of a cooperative movement—is a group formed by individual producers or consumers, or both, to carry on any mutually advantageous activity. Its chief distinguishing marks are: (1) that it is a voluntary association; (2) that it is run democratically, on a "one man one vote" basis; (3) that it exists to serve the greatest good of the greatest number of its members, and is therefore opposed to throat-cutting and coercion; and (4) that benefits from its operations accrue to members in direct proportion to the business transacted and not in proportion to capital invested.

The relevance of such societies to the African producer or consumer is clear if we recall some of the circumstances which habitually incommode him. First, his indebtedness. Almost everywhere in the world where the change-over from the old subsistence, moneyless economy to a cash crop economy has been made, it has been accompanied by the rise of the creditor and the debtor. Inexperienced and illiterate, the grower of such crops as cotton, coffee, cocoa and grain has been pretty much at the mercy of the buyer, shopkeeper and trader. In many cases, however, mercy was not the currency in which they dealt. Rather it was fast talking, sleight of hand, extortion and lies—the victim of which was soon likely to find himself owing money and so compelled to mortgage future harvests, leading to further indebtedness and ultimately to loss of all incentive. Second, his low standard of living. True, this is in part due to his characteristic indebtedness, but it has always been a low standard; consequently it has always been difficult, if not impossible, for him to accumulate goods or capital in excess of immediate needs. There has never been much room for errors and none for omissions. Progress, technical or material, was practically out of the question. Third, his inability to do anything very profitable with such occasional surpluses as he might find himself possessing. There were few ways of storing grain, fewer of meat. There were few means of transportation, none adequate. There was no marketing organization that could give him the benefits of timely buying and selling. For the urban African there has been the further circumstance of loneliness and loss of association with the corporate life of village and tribe.

For each of these conditions the cooperative society offers a cure. For indebtedness it offers credit associations from which money—government money, as a rule, to start with—may be borrowed at low rates of interest. It also offers the chance to learn thrift and the elements of business management, since it is the borrowers who are responsible for running the associations. For low standards of living it offers purchasing societies in which money—again, government money as a rule—is to be had for the purchase by a community of agricultural implements, stocks of seed and fertilizer, fruit trees, pedigreed breeding animals, and so on. Such societies will also give a member, from time to time, the chance to visit demonstration stations where his very own problems are being tackled rationally. For wasted surpluses, casual commerce and costly middlemen it offers the marketing society able to provide through its collective funds—initially government supplied, too, as a rule—the transport of produce to the market at a much lower cost, and to help the grower to get a higher price for his produce by arranging the sale without the services of the trader. It can also shield the producer from some of the worst effects of world market fluctuations, which in the case of cocoa, coffee, cotton and most of the other African cash crops are often considerable. For loneliness it offers companionship, teamwork and the chance, once in a while, for some fun.

How do such societies begin? Ideally, they should be the offspring of the people. For no matter how well-conceived and well-nourished government "babies" are, they are seldom greatly loved by those on whom they are foisted. There have been some very satisfactory societies of indigenous parentage. Thus, several of the women's societies formed since the end of World War II have had cooperation as their *raison d'être*. In southern Nigeria, for instance, "There are women's societies which run a bakery, a laundry, a weaving workshop, a calabash manufactory, a gari [manioc] mill, and so on. In these ways the women [have provided] themselves with necessary services, cut out the middlemen, and [raised] their own standard of living."[21]

But, on the whole, the initiative has come from without, since the people most in need of cooperatives are without means and quite unfamiliar with the ways of bankers, bookkeepers and businessmen generally. As a rule it has come from governments. In the case of the British government the initiative was taken reluctantly. To a large extent this reluctance, as J. G. Liebenow, a consultant to this study, has pointed out, was born of fear: fear lest "the cooperative might fall under the sway of an African who might find the temptation to line his pockets irresistible"; fear that "the cooperative might serve as a cover for political or nationalistic agitation"; and, in the multiracial areas, fear lest it should alienate the Europeans and Asians who were already running cooperatives.

[21] R. K. Gardiner and H. O. Judd, *The Development of Social Administration*, Oxford University Press, London, 1954, p. 77.

Since 1946, when the British government passed the enabling bill (the Co-operative Societies Ordinance), the initiative in each dependency has rested largely in the hands of the government-appointed Registrar of Co-operative Societies. It is his job (among so many others that he has been called "Commissar of Co-ops") to register new societies, approve their by-laws, supervise and audit their accounts, settle disputes and keep an eye on the selection, training and performance of his field agents, the Co-operative Departmental Inspectors. It is the inspectors who are largely responsible for encouraging the formation of cooperative societies; teaching the members and prospective members of such societies the rudiments of bookkeeping, auditing, business methods, and the law and economics of cooperatives; and checking and correcting accounts and, when necessary, writing up the books.

The range of economic interests to which the cooperative principle can be applied is virtually without limit. At different times and places it has been applied to manufacturing, welfare and crafts as well as to credit and thrift, producer marketing and processing, agricultural development and consumer goods.

A fairly typical example of a *manufacturing* cooperative is the Kasitu Valley Union in Nyasaland. This is a union—one of two such unions in the territory—of small cooperative dairy societies. Its business consists in taking the dairy societies' surplus milk and converting it into ghee, a more durable and more salable commodity. In 1957 this union processed and sold nearly 30,000 pounds of ghee. With the proceeds (about £6,000) it was able to give the producers more money than they would have got for their milk (always supposing they would have found a market for it), and at the same time to build up its capital reserve.

Welfare societies make a special appeal to women. One of the most popular cooperative projects undertaken by them is the building and running of maternity homes. In the Eastern Region of Nigeria there were already five such cooperatives in 1953, with a total membership of some 6,000; more than a thousand deliveries were made in the homes run by them. Since 1953 many other maternity cooperatives have been formed, in both the Western and Eastern Regions. In most cases the homes have been paid for by the women cooperators' own subscriptions, and their maintenance costs, including the cost of midwives, met by periodic mass "subscription" meetings. The only serious problem here—an understandable one in view of the fact that maternity, unlike accident or illness, does not come upon one unawares—is to get women to subscribe for the years in which they do not expect to be needing the home.

The *craft* society is not widely found in these days of mass-production techniques, and, so far as can be seen, it is not likely to have any great future. However, it is doing useful work in several communities, notably in Nigeria, where there is a strong tradition of craftsmanship. Prominent Nigerian representatives of this type of society are the Awka Carvers Union, the women's Akweti Weavers Society, the Benin Shoemakers, the Oyo Leatherworkers, and the Arochuku Embroideresses. The members pool their resources for the purchase of needed materials, tools and equipment (the Benin Shoemakers ordering their equipment direct from the United Kingdom), and in some instances market their products cooperatively.

Credit societies, sometimes called thrift and credit, or thrift and loan, societies, are among the most popular and most necessary of cooperatives. They are designed to relieve indebtedness; to provide short-term loans for land improvement, purchase of equipment, and maintenance during the "hungry" months; to promote the saving habit; and, not least, to give their members some understanding of modern business. One of the areas where they have come to assume a major role is the Eastern Region of Nigeria. In 1957 over 80 per cent of the more than 1,000 cooperatives in that area were either thrift and credit or thrift and loan societies.

Producer and *processing* societies are somewhat less numerous than credit and thrift societies, but they handle by far the largest volume of business. In 1957, for instance, the

3,800-odd such societies in British tropical Africa exclusive of Southern Rhodesia did an aggregate business of more than £42 million, or approximately two thirds of all the business done by all cooperatives. Although many of these societies, especially those in Kenya and Tanganyika, are largely or exclusively European in membership, there can be hardly any question that those serving the African serve him well. They take what he has but doesn't need, and often does not know how or where to sell, and turn it into something he doesn't have but needs desperately—a reasonably reliable income. By customarily paying it to him in two installments, the first on delivery of his crop and the second after it has been sold and all servicing charges have been cared for, they provide him with a useful curb to his improvidence. They also provide him with a useful goad to his ambition and self-esteem, since the better he farms, the bigger his crop, the larger his share in the equity, and the higher his standing in the community. Not least, they can provide those cooperators who are willing to deny themselves part of their earnings—as many are— with a capital fund for development or welfare work.

What a marketing cooperative organization can do for its members, and how it does it, is seen to good advantage in Ghana, where almost all of the farming is done by small holders or peasants, and where nine tenths or more of the farm revenue is derived from a single crop, cocoa. The marketing of this crop by primary marketing societies began, in a very small way, in 1929. Today about one fifth of the cocoa crop is handled cooperatively. The small primary society in a given district arranges for the collection and transport of its members' crop to the depot of the regional marketing cooperative union to which it is affiliated. This union, in turn, prepares and transports the crop to the headquarters in Accra of the Ghana Co-operative Marketing Association, Ltd., to which all of the unions serving the various cocoa-growing areas of the country belong. With funds loaned from the Co-operative Central Bank, this association pays each union enough to make an advance payment to each member of each affiliated society at the time the crop is collected. In 1951, a good year but by no means phenomenal, more than £ 4 million was paid to the 17,000 members of the societies in this way. A second payment of £ 120,000 was made later when the crop had been sold and all accounts settled. A further sum was put into a reserve fund maintained by the Co-operative Bank. During the same year the marketing association loaned £ 110,000 to members of societies for farm redemption and improvement, and for educational purposes.

Very few societies exist specifically and solely for the purpose of promoting agricultural development, because this calls for equipment beyond the means of the ordinary farm community. Usually this kind of development can be undertaken only by credit and thrift societies, or producer marketing and processing societies that have been established long enough to have accumulated a substantial capital reserve. Cooperative farm development therefore tends to be in the nature of a "plow-back" operation. One of the best examples of farm development financed in this way is provided by the Kilimanjaro Native Co-operative Union, Ltd., in Tanganyika. This union is made up of about 35 marketing societies, with an aggregate membership of over 35,000 coffee growers. Almost all of these belong to the Chagga people who live on the slopes of Mt. Kilimanjaro. As its profits grew, the union extended its operations beyond the mere marketing of coffee to the raising of its yield and quality. To this end, it built and staffed a school for the training of inspectors, instructors, nurserymen and growers. In the training special emphasis is given to such matters as the making and use of compost, anti-erosion measures, the control of pests and diseases, irrigation, and the improvement of cultural methods. By means of loans the union makes it possible for its more progressive members to exploit their training and to carry out its policy of retiring old and inferior trees. The headquarters of the union, in Moshi, is a building of which any town in rural America or Europe might be proud. It is open to members of all races, and contains a cultural center, a museum, a library, shops, offices, restaurant and garage. The union also prints its own books and pamphlets on coffee culture and runs its own interracial hostel and commercial school.

Possibly the least well-favored and least disciplined member of the cooperative litter is the *consumer* society. Where good consumer societies exist, as, for instance, in parts of British East Africa and the Federation of Rhodesia and Nyasaland, the chances are that some or all of the following circumstances contributed to their success: an ample supply of capital for premises and goods; local prosperity leading to lively demand for a wide range of goods and rapid turnover; good management; and not too much competition from the large trading companies. In point of fact, the majority of consumer societies are badly located, poorly housed, inadequately capitalized and stocked, indifferently run if not blatantly mismanaged, and no match in variety, quality or attractiveness for the department stores and bazaars of the nearby towns. Salt, kerosene, matches, tobacco, singlets, soap and scrap metal (for conversion into household and farm gear) comprise perhaps 90 per cent of their normal offerings.

Of all the modern business channels the cooperative one is probably the easiest to dig, and the hardest to keep open and clean. Almost everybody can see advantages in cooperation. The government official sees it as a way of capitalizing the African's instinct for teamwork, which none who have watched him in action as a hunter, tree feller, bush burner, road builder or dancer can deny. He also sees it as a way of lifting the African's lowly economic status, essential to the development of a stable middle class. The cooperator sees it as a way of escaping from the clutches of the money lender, the middleman and the petty trader, and of getting more for less. The educator sees it as a mold capable of carrying, besides the raw material of economic advancement, the essences of order, efficiency and self-help. The politician sees it to be a tool for the fashioning of leaders. But, as Europeans have long known and as Africans and Asians are now learning, the running of a cooperative calls for more than enthusiasm and a supply of cooperators. It calls for training programs, which officials often find easier to plan than provide. It calls for capital, which few cooperators have and most outsiders are shy of investing in novelties. It calls for discipline—regard for the spoken word and the written bond—which, as every educator knows, is more easily applauded than practiced. Not least, it calls for sophistication—the ability to buy and sell at the right time, skill in handling goods and money, and integrity in accounting for them—which is not conferred by political edict, or, for that matter, by the accolade of self-government.

TRADE UNIONISM

The success of any pump-priming operation depends on three things: an adequate supply of priming fluid, the ability of people to do the pumping and their belief in the utility of doing it. In tropical Africa, as we have seen, none of these things can be taken for granted. When the fluid—the money and material—is available, able pumpers are often lacking, and vice versa. And when both fluid and pumpers are available, there is not infrequently a scarcity of believers. The history, to date, of trade unionism in tropical Africa is one of slow priming, fitful pumping and small returns.

Although activities of the trade union type, including strikes, were being conducted in various territories as far back as the 1920s, it was not until the early thirties that the British government—the first to do so—recognized the right of workers in its African territories to organize trade unions. Even then workers were in no hurry to take advantage of their rights. Two years after Parliament had passed the enabling act, only three small unions had been registered in the whole of the British colonial empire. Most of the headway has been made since the mid-forties, and in territories administered, or once administered, by Great Britain and France. The increase in the number of registered unions in some of these territories has been considerable. In Nigeria, for instance, the number of such unions increased from 50 in 1941 to 135 in 1953 and to 177 in 1955. In French West Africa (where until 1946 labor was a commodity that could be acquired, moved about and dismissed at will) the number increased from 0 to 350 in a little over a decade. In Belgian Africa there were only some 5,000 trade unionists in 1950. By 1959 there were between 80,000 and 100,000. In Liberia there are a very few government-assisted unions. In Portuguese Africa and Ethiopia there were still no trade unions as late as 1959.

These unions are typically small. In 1955 the average nominal membership of the Nigerian unions was less than 1,000. The majority of the unions had fewer than 200 members. In the same year the average nominal membership of the Kenya unions was less than 500. The paid-up membership was certainly smaller, since almost all trade unions in tropical Africa are reluctant to drop from the rolls any person considered likely to be good for a dues payment, no matter how tardy. Even the large unions are small by European and American standards. The Northern Rhodesia African Mineworkers Trade Union, the largest of its kind in tropical Africa, has a membership of only about 20,000. The Railway African Union of Kenya, the largest in the colony, had about 9,000 members in the late 1950s.

Because they are small, they are weak—too weak, in some cases, to be able to exercise even the rudimentary functions of trade unionism. By the time the one or two necessary officials, say the chairman and secretary-treasurer, of a small union have collected their expenses and honoraria, there is very little dues money left for extension work. And in a small, largely illiterate group, it is seldom possible to find those who are skilled in negotiation, the making of agreements, and the settling of disputes.

Many unions are weak for another reason. They are forced rather than natural growths. Unlike European and American trade union movements, which came into existence on their own account and from a deeply felt need, most of those in tropical Africa are the products of paternalism, of belief that what is sauce for the metropolitan gander is sauce for the colonial gosling. While there may be good grounds for the belief, the fact is that chefs the world over are reluctant to accept the sauce-making recipes of others, and that for many people sauce is an acquired taste which comes only with maturity.

There are those who believe that the African worker is still too immature for trade unionism. There are others who believe that trade unionism which is government-inspired is bound, sooner or later, to be government-controlled. Neither school of believers has to look far for supporting evidence. Those of the first school point to the widespread dearth of leadership and of understanding of what unionism entails and of efficiency in the handling of union business and funds. They also point to the frequency with which such statements as the following occur in government reports on labor conditions: ". . . in certain instances unions have been started by a small number of people solely with a view to making good jobs for themselves as Executive Officers such as Secretaries and Treasurers." Or, to give another example, "His behaviour at best showed a greater interest in his own financial improvement than was consistent with his devotion to the cause of the miners, and at worst, exposed him to the charge that he deliberately used his position to enrich himself at the expense of union funds."

Those of the second school point to the fact that in many territories the most influential trade union officer is the one appointed and paid by the government; he not infrequently regards his primary tasks to be the maintenance of industrial peace, the discouraging of strikes and the fostering of unions of an amenable, nonaggressive type. They also point to the fact that in the Belgian Congo all unions have been under government control, not only in their formative period but throughout their life span; Belgian officials have examined their budgets and accounts, constantly checked their compliance with the manifold regulations, scrutinized membership lists for illegal admissions, taken part in the union meetings, and seen union minutes.

Another characteristic shared by most of the unions is their color-consciousness. It is not difficult to see how this came about in some instances. As James Griffiths, a onetime British Secretary of State for the Colonies, has pointed out,

> When the African . . . peasant is brought to work in a mine or a factory, it is as green labour: he is an unskilled labourer working under the close supervision of a "white" boss. He tends to think of himself not as a miner, or artisan, working with other miners and artisans, but as a poor "black" worker who has to obey the dictates of a supervisor . . . of a different colour. It is natural, therefore, that he should regard the trade union, not as an organization of workers to improve the conditions of their employment, but as a shield and protector against "colonialism." To him it seems that the appropriate grouping for the trade union is not the workshop or even the industry, but one that gathers within its fold all the "black" workers in defence against the "white" employers and workers alike.[22]

But not all the color-consciousness of unionism in tropical Africa can be explained as an incidental by-product of association between white employer and black employee, and its corollary, skilled white and unskilled black. Some of it seems to be the calculated end product of an attempt to keep employers white and the white skilled, and the employees black and the black unskilled. At least this is how it appears to such trade union leaders as Tom Mboya of Kenya and Lawrence Katilungu of Northern Rhodesia.

Being small, weak and on the defensive, most African unions devote a large part of their time to the redress of individual or collective grievances against plant managements, and to seeking to improve plant working conditions. Accordingly, in function, at any rate, they are not very different from the labor-management committees or works councils that many companies have set up. Union names frequently reflect their limited scope and no less characteristic anchorage to a place and a company. The United Africa Company Singlet Factory Workers Union and the Church Missionary

Society Bookshop African Staff Union, both of Lagos, are cases in point. There are still few industry-wide unions of the kind with which Europeans and Americans are familiar, and almost none in which specialized skill—that is, craft or trade—is the basis of union.

The difficulties notwithstanding, a number of powerful unions have grown up in recent years. This is particularly true of the Confédération Générale du Travail (CGT), which musters almost two thirds of all the trade unionists in the territories formerly constituting French West Africa; the Confédération Africaine des Travailleurs Croyants (CATC), which is strong in Senegal, Guinea, Dahomey, Yaoundé and Brazzaville; the Force Ouvrière, which includes a large proportion of European workers in the same general areas; and the west African Fédération des Cheminots Africains. The power inherent in the numerical strength of these unions has been enhanced by their willingness to join forces when the need arises. Thus, a coordinating committee of the west African branches of CGT, CATC, Force Ouvrière and the Cheminots is generally credited with having sped up the enactment and the implementing of the 1952 *Code du Travail d'Outre-Mer,* one of the most liberal pieces of labor legislation ever passed by the French government.[23] Although these unions, with the exception of the Cheminots, are offshoots of the great metropolitan federations of the same name, the power they wield is their own, and most of their leaders are African-elected Africans concerned more about doing something for those who put them in power than about upholding any doctrinaire position taken by the parent bodies. Thus, according to Thomas Hodgkin, the CGT, which in France has communist affiliations, is "regarded by most Africans as 'African' and [is] often so described"; while the CATC, which is

[23] "The extreme importance attached by the French African trade unions to the 1952 *Code du Travail* was due primarily to the fact that its intention was to secure equality of rights for African workers in such matters as the forty-hour week, holidays with pay and (partially) family allowances." Thomas Hodgkin, *Nationalism in Colonial Africa,* Frederick Muller, London, 1956, p. 130.

"closely associated with, and fostered by, the Catholic missions, has in fact a majority of Moslem members in French West Africa, and admits theists of all types (including Animists) to its affiliated unions."

Not the least reason for the power of these French unions is that they are large enough, being for the most part federations of unions, to have a decent income from dues. This enables them to maintain both a field staff and a headquarters staff. With the former they can keep their members well informed of the work of their union and so disposed to go on supporting it. With the latter they can keep government and management apprised of their demands, and see to it that these demands are continually put before the public in speech, newspaper and pamphlet. These unions have seldom had any difficulty in making the headlines or in getting "summit-level" hearings.

Because they are very largely a product of the local economic environment and owe little to external movements and financing, the trade unions of British, and ex-British, tropical Africa, even the biggest of them, are of smaller stature than those of French provenance. All the same, there are some sturdy middleweights among them, notably the Northern Rhodesia African Mineworkers Trade Union and the organization of European workers called the Northern Rhodesia Mine Workers Union. The latter, under its agreement with the Copperbelt mining companies, controls the range of jobs undertaken by its members and so, by elimination, those that can be undertaken by the members of the African union. There are also strong mineworkers' unions in Ghana and Nigeria. Other occupational groups served by fairly large unions are the railway workers (e.g., in Sudan, Nigeria, Ghana and British East Africa), public utility workers (e.g., in Ghana and Nigeria), teachers (e.g., in Ghana and Nigeria), and local government workers (e.g., in Ghana, Nigeria and Kenya).

In several territories attempts have been made to develop a central organization on the model of the British Trades Union Congress for the purpose of acting as a general staff to the entire trade union body, and dealing, on its behalf, with the territorial government. To date, Ghana and Sudan are the only territories, either British or ex-British, to have succeeded in their attempts. Since 1957 the Sudan Government Workers Trade Union Federation has had the support of most of the 100 or so unions—unions that cover everybody from bakery assistants and dock workers to schoolteachers and civil servants. Since 1959, the Ghana Trades Union Congress has had the support of most of its 24 national unions that now "represent not only a substantial part of the population, but one of the important factors in the nation-building process." Elsewhere, such federations as have been established manage to flourish only during times of crisis. At other times they have been weakened or rent by personal rivalries, disagreements over means and ends, administrative inefficiency and conflicting loyalties, as between the International Confederation of Free Trade Unions (ICFTU) and the leftist World Federation of Trade Unions (WFTU). There have been one or two crises during which they were forcibly restrained from flourishing by their territorial governments. This was the case in Kenya during the Mau Mau emergency, when enough union leaders and members were detained on allegations of complicity with Mau Mau to leave the local federation temporarily impotent.

Broadly, the interests which the trade unions of tropical Africa seek to further are of two kinds: defensive and aggressive. There are grievances to be settled; wrongs, real and imagined, to be righted; exploitation to be eliminated. There are also rights to be won: the right to strike; the right to bargain and to be heard in the councils of employers; and the greater right—or so most colonial trade unionists conceive it to be—to frame one's own industrial laws and administer them, which implies the right to be politically autonomous.

The incidence of these interests is still patchy. Some union members can give no reason for their membership beyond the fact that they were asked to be members and that it is pleasant to belong to any group that helps to fill the empty hours of a migrant's life. Others have yet to grasp the idea that membership confers obligations (including the regular payment of dues) and the privilege of working for a cause bigger than a grievance. Even among mature trade unionists there are frequently wide disparities of interest. Thus, speaking generally, says Hodgkin, "there is a marked tendency for the demands of French African trade unionists to be dominated by the idea of equality, in the sense of equality of wages and conditions and equality of trade-union rights for African and European workers." British African trade unionists, on the other hand, "are concerned less with *equality* of rights, and more with the rights of *African* workers as such"—a fact which, as Hodgkin goes on to observe, "necessarily gives their demands a strongly nationalist flavour," and their activities frequently a political appearance. Where African trade unionists have come to grips with the world of work and their own shortcomings as workers, however, they have not been slow to perceive, and promote, the true functions of unionism.

To find out what unionists held these functions to be, the Institute of Extra-Mural Studies of the University College of the then Gold Coast conducted an inquiry in 1953. In descending frequency of selection by the group of unionists surveyed, the functions considered most appropriate to a trade union were as follows: negotiation on wages (selected in 79 per cent of the total possible number of times), prevention of dismissals (78 per cent of the total possible times), increase of production (73), prevention of victimization (72), settlement of individual complaints (59), holding of strikes for the purpose of getting higher wages (42), obtaining of cash benefits (42), organizing of social activities (38), organizing of political party activities (17), and holding of strikes for the purpose of bringing about political changes (10).

Several things about this list call for comment. The low rating of political functions is surprising, all the more so when we recall the prominent part which the unions played in the 1950 political disturbances and the fact that in 1953 political change—"Self-government now"—was regarded as the key that would open the gates of Utopia. The modest store set by

Nobody can travel in tropical Africa without soon being made aware of the importance attached to learning. Ask a dozen high school students what they want to do, and at least half of them are likely to reply, "Go to college." Ask a dozen college students what they consider to be their country's greatest need, and at least ten of them will unhesitatingly say, "More education." In education they see the key to greater output, higher consumption, healthier living and better government. (*Above:* University College of Ghana.)

Photographs by Omar Marcus

The desire to be educated and to educate is not confined to the young and lettered. The enthusiasm of the illiterate adult is frequently as great, especially if he has children who are going to school. (*Top left:* literacy class, Ghana. *Top right:* community development teacher, Uganda.)

Although government agencies are taking on more and more educational responsibilities, the churches continue to be a powerful force in stimulating and satisfying the desire for modern knowledge. (*Top:* government secondary school, Mozambique. *Bottom:* Catholic church, Congo.)

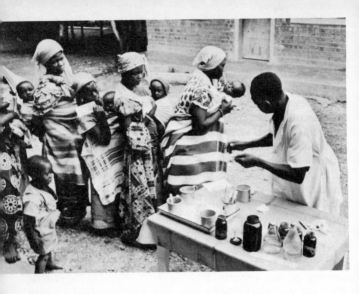

No kind of modern knowledge is more necessary, or more sought after, than the knowledge of how to cure sickness, and how to stay well when cured. (*Top:* vaccination of mineworkers' children, Congo. *Bottom:* hospital nurses in Addis Ababa, Ethiopia.)

cash benefits is in sharp contrast to union practice in the United States and Europe. "Presumably this can be explained," a published account of the inquiry observes, "by the widespread family system which renders union financial assistance in times of unemployment, sickness and other distress less urgent than in more urbanized societies."[24] The disinclination of those questioned to employ the strike as an instrument of union policy is something new, since in colonial Africa, as elsewhere, the strike has traditionally been looked upon as one of the stoutest "defences of the poor," and "the only argument with which workers can collectively press their economic claims and challenge managerial autocracy."[25] It is all the more surprising since, in at least two African territories—Nigeria and Sudan—general strikes proved to be "the midwives of trade unionism, and have acquired a special sanctity on that account."[26] Possibly the Gold Coast unionists were still remembering their own general strike of 1950, which, useful as it may have been to the politicians of the Convention People's Party in whose interest it was called, brought them only discredit, confusion and the dissolution of their congress. The emphasis on protection—job security, prevention of dismissals and victimization (which was defined as punishment short of dismissal)—suggests that the trade unionist is as interested in having steady employment as he is in having good employers. Perhaps most unexpected of all is the high priority given to increased production. Usually in tropical Africa it is the employers who are concerned about productivity levels and the difficulty of getting the workers to raise them. It is therefore a matter for encouragement that for every 79 times a Gold Coast unionist bestirred himself in the cause of wages, he bestirred himself 73 times in the cause of productivity. Just how far he was willing to carry his concern for the latter cause, the surveyors did not tell.

Whence comes the sense of responsibility disclosed by the ranking of these trade union interests? In part it comes, as

[24] *The Times British Colonies Review*, Winter 1953, p. 24.
[25] Hodgkin, *op. cit.*, p. 133.
[26] *Ibid.*

hinted earlier, from the hard school of experience in which men have been made to see the emptiness of hopes divorced from reality, and of platforms lacking proper economic support. In part it comes from exposure to the experience of others, especially the hard-bought experience of trade unionists in France and Great Britain. Their cautionary voice is being listened to with increasing respect in the lands of tropical Africa. In part, too, it comes from the training in trade unionism which unionists and others are getting from the unions themselves, from the labor departments of government, from such international bodies as UNESCO and the ICFTU, and, not least, from the extramural departments of African universities. Indeed, in the case of Ghana, it might be claimed that the Institute of Extra-Mural Studies of its University College has been the biggest single factor in the growth of trade union responsibility. Since 1948 the institute has been explaining assiduously, insistently, persuasively and —if we may believe its now-departed government critics—at times inconveniently and embarrassingly what trade unionism stands for, and seeing that it shall not want for leaders or for discerning followers. To this end, the director and his African and European associates have conducted evening classes on trade unionism wherever the local people could be induced to attend them; weekend (and longer) residential courses at which trade unionists from different parts of the country could swap problems and answers, learn to show becoming respect for other men's judgments and modesty for their own, and to distinguish fact from emotion, reason from sentiment; and interterritorial seminars attended by trade unionists from inside and outside Africa for the purpose of acquiring finesse in the arts of negotiation, collective bargaining, consultation and arbitration, and in the no less necessary art of making friends of management and influencing governments. The University College may have sponsored more formal activities during the past decade or so, but none more formative or, we venture to think, more widely appreciated.

But this is not to say that there is nothing wrong with African trade unionism that a few well-spaced extramural departments, or UNESCO or ICFTU teams, cannot put right. For one thing, in some territories there are still no trade unions to put right; and if there were, it is doubtful if the governments of those territories would view with favor the idea of campus-based crusades to make trade union sympathizers of all working men. And for another, the function of adult education is not to serve as either the receiving or transmitting antenna of trade unionism, but only "to teach people to weigh opposing points of view, and to think critically and constructively for themselves";[27] and there is no guarantee that the results of such weighing and thinking will be the same among the Somali and Azande as among the Fanti and the Ashanti. Not all intellectually awakened men, even in the United States, care enough for the hazards of the trade union course to be willing to run it. In tropical Africa there are millions of workers in whose minds the notion of union with strangers for the sake of personal or group advantage still has no place. Furthermore, it is unlikely that the advent of such a notion "will be materially hastened by stirring up various 'forms' of activity where, in fact, no activity exists."[28]

We can be quite sure that trade union activity will grow rather than decline, for it yields economic and political dividends esteemed by all those who seek to capitalize their people's potential on the floor of the world's exchange. As Hodgkin has put it,

> [Trade unions] are a means of providing political education, in the broadest sense, for a section of the community that has little opportunity to play a prominent part in

[27] David and Helen Kimble, *Adult Education in a Changing Africa: A Report on the Inter-African Seminar Held in the Gold Coast from December 10 to 23, 1954,* International Federation of Workers' Educational Associations, London, 1955, p. 22.

[28] Nelly Xydias in *Social Implications of Industrialization and Urbanization in Africa South of the Sahara* (prepared under the auspices of UNESCO by the International African Institute, London), UNESCO, Tensions and Technology Series, Paris, 1956, p. 305.

nationalist political parties. They tend to substitute a new relationship based upon common economic interests for traditional tribal ties. At the same time they make it possible for the collectivist values of traditional African society to be restated in modern language, in opposition to the naïve Benthamism (or Burnhamism) of many Westernizing nationalists. Or—to put the same point differently—they counteract the nationalist tendency to present political independence, or liberation from European control, as an end in itself; and draw continual attention to the facts of poverty, hunger, disease, slums, insecurity and social waste, which will not be altered simply by the transfer of political power from Europeans to Africans.[29]

To the extent that they do this, they are at one with the cooperative and community development movements, and as deserving of sympathetic encouragement. Already, as we hope to show in the next chapter, some unions have influenced the character and outlook of African nationalism in important ways.

[29] *Op. cit.*, pp. 137–38.

CHAPTER 5

NATIONALISM AND POLITICS

Like most of the other fighting words of our time, nationalism means different things to different people, including political scientists and lexicographers. As with colonialism, democracy and freedom, it is more readily defined by what is done in its name than by what it is. And in tropical Africa a great many things are being done in its name. There are "nationalistic" movements in religion, education, economics and art, as well as in politics. And in politics there are movements that seek to promote nationalism on different scales, with different coverages, and for different objectives. There are, for instance, the tribal nationalisms of the Yoruba, Ewe, Ganda, Luo and Kikuyu; the territorial nationalisms of Nigeria and, until its emergence as an independent country, Ghana; and the interterritorial nationalisms of Togo, the Cameroons, the "United States of West Africa" and "Pan-Africa." There are white and brown as well as black nationalisms, the European and Asian settlers in Kenya and in the Federation of Rhodesia and Nyasaland being no less interested in their rights as nationals than are their *évolué* African neighbors. There are Christian and Moslem nationalisms, incipient and mature nationalisms, "democracy-oriented" and "fascism-oriented" nationalisms. There are also nationalisms that are directed toward such limited goals as multiracial partnership, the abolition of color bars and other forms of discrimination; and those that are directed toward the severance of all imposed political bonds and the winning of unconditional sovereignty.

In view of all this we shall not waste time devising definitions, beyond suggesting that African nationalism is what African nationalists like, and that African nationalists are those, of all racial origins, who believe in the right to govern and be governed in the way of their own choosing, and to resist, by whatever means in their power, those who would withhold that right.

GROWTH FACTORS

We do not have to go far to find reasons for the unparalleled growth of nationalist movements in our day, for this is the day of nationalism. It has its sweet singers on short-wave radio stations, its lobbyists in the labor unions, its strategists in the council chambers of the United Nations. There is barely a characteristic of the life of any non-self-governing territory that does not, from time to time, provide these singers, lobbyists and strategists with the theme of an attack on colonialism, or a defense of self-government, even though it be bad government. And, after all, what can the modern world offer African man that is at once as beguiling and as challenging, as pleasing and as flattering, as the creed of nationalism?

For convenience the growth factors may be divided into two categories: predisposing and precipitating. They may overlap here and leave a few gaps there, but they will probably serve as well as any to remind us that every child of the human spirit is the progeny of the general and the particular, is cradled in time and in place, and owes as much to the nurture it gets as to its nature.

PREDISPOSING FACTORS

Internal

Economic. The coming of the European as miner, manufacturer, trader, administrator and settler on the land has had profound results for the African. As earlier chapters have shown, it has loosened the shackles of his social order, brought him into touch with men of diverse backgrounds, given him a new idea of the material and intellectual possibilities of life and the means of realizing some of them. It has also created a host of new ways of earning a living, and of acquiring wealth and status. It has, in fact, created a new—middle—class composed of traders, well-to-do farmers, teachers, lawyers, doctors and clergy. How this came about James S. Coleman recounts in a paper prepared for this study:

> In many instances this new class is made up of persons drawn from the lower strata of traditional African society, partly because of indiscriminate missionary education and partly because of the social mobility and freedom allowed the non-conformist under the European *pax*. This new class —lacking status in the traditional structure and in general denied participation in the European superstructure—has everywhere tended to provide both the leadership and the financial support for nationalist movements. The unwitting contribution of colonial governments and extra-territorial enterprises to the development of this new class has tended to be overlooked. By providing salaried employment to clerks and artisans—indispensable to the conduct of colonial government and large-scale commercial activities—an opportunity was created for the accumulation of capital later used by those groups either to undertake professional training or, what was frequently more desirable, to set themselves up as traders . . . A study of their biographies reveals that most African nationalists received their initial boost as employees of either the colonial government or one of the large extra-territorial firms.

Besides opportunities, the new economic order created fears and grievances. There was the fear of change from subsistence to cash crop farming, from communal forms of ownership to private ownership—sometimes to ownership of nothing— and from bush life to town life. There was the fear of want of food, security, companionship and redress. There was the grievance of land alienation in some areas (notably in Kenya, where more than 10,000 square miles of highly attractive farm land was early reserved for European settlement). There was the grievance, mostly in the same areas, of race prejudice. And there were the grievances, almost universal, of low wages and the exploitation which they frequently betokened, of poverty in the midst of abundance, and of the difficulty of discharging family obligations in a money-wise world. It is of such stuff, as Chapter 4 suggests, that the cloak of trade unionism is made —a cloak that fits the nationalist as well as it does the unionist. Indeed, it is difficult for the man who dons this cloak not to look like a nationalist. Thomas Hodgkin tells why this is so:

African nationalism, like other nationalisms, is in part a revolt against an inferior economic status. In all the main regions of agitation . . . demands for economic development have been written into political programmes, and have swayed African opinion in times of tension and upheaval. These have included demands for higher prices for farmers; for higher wage and salary levels for manual and clerical workers, for a larger share in internal and foreign trade for African merchants (as against European, Lebanese or Indian firms); for the nationalisation, or profit-squeezing, of foreign concessions; for more rapid industrial development; and (in countries of European settlement) for the breaking up of European estates and their redistribution among African peasants. The fact that the economic claims and interests of different sections of African society . . . may be divergent is of subordinate importance, so long as for all sections the colonial régime is regarded as the main obstacle in the way of economic advance.[1]

Frequently the unionist not only looks and talks like a nationalist, he *is* a nationalist—and a leader at that. Among those who have used trade unionism as a means to political power are Dr. E. M. L. Endeley, former president of the Cameroons Development Corporation Workers Union, who became Leader of Government Business in the British Cameroons, and Tom Mboya, General Secretary of the Kenya

[1] *Nationalism in Colonial Africa*, Frederick Muller, London, 1956, p. 115.

Federation of Labour, who is today one of the most influential African politicians in his country.

Social. New economic classes become new social classes— if not in the eyes of the conservatives, in the eyes of the progressives. The prestige that has come to be associated with the abundance of things a wealthy educated man may possess has been a powerful factor in enabling such men to assert the leadership of nationalist causes. And because Western education is the master key to "Western" wealth and power, it is without doubt the most important single factor in the recently accelerated growth of African nationalism. Coleman notes that "Early missionary education provided the African recipients with a background which was a technical prerequisite of their pursuit of higher education. Without higher education it would have been impossible for Africans seriously to have challenged the colonial system. It is the doctors, lawyers and others with higher Western education who occupy the top rung in the new nationalist leadership—even in the Moslem areas of northern Nigeria."

The association between the availability of post-primary education and the vitality of nationalism is very close. Almost without exception the territories which have had the longest and most ample experience of such education are the territories with the most articulate nationalisms. Within those territories, it is the groups which, either by accident or design, have had the best education that are the banner-bearers of nationalism—a fact which may explain, in part at least, why the Yoruba and the Ibo of southern Nigeria are politically more articulate than the Hausa and Fulani of northern Nigeria, the Creoles of Sierra Leone Colony (Freetown region) more than the indigenous peoples of the Sierra Leone Protectorate, the people of Buganda more than the people of Bunyoro, Toro, Acholi and Karamoja in Uganda, and the Kikuyu and Luo more than the Masai and Teita in Kenya.

It is easy to see why the association between the two should be so close. While primary education is essentially a technique for making oneself understood, post-primary education is essentially a training in the art of understanding others—their times and inventions, their thought and influence. Not the least of the uses of post-primary education is that it promotes the habit of criticism of oneself and one's teachers, of speculation concerning the fitness of things, and of experiment in the hope of increasing that fitness. Though the field of African social experiment is large, the paths across it are convergent, and all can be made to serve the purposes of the political reformer. The organizing experience gained by a man in running a district welfare association can easily be put to advantage in developing a party system. The village group that is willing to discuss the pros and cons of land consolidation or well digging can as easily be used to tout the idea of self-determination or universal suffrage. The man who is good at public speaking or writing can as easily persuade his audience to lay down their tools in defense of political rights as of economic ones.

Religious. The disruptive effect of the Christian religion on African society is discussed elsewhere; here we are concerned only with the extent to which the Christian religion has influenced the growth of African nationalism. And on this subject opinion is divided. On one side there are those who maintain that missionary insistence on the rejection by converts of the religious sanctions of chieftainship and of such practices as dancing, polygamy and clitoridectomy has provided the African nationalist with one of his strongest weapons. Economic exploitation is bad; social discrimination is worse; but could anything be more humiliating than the denial of a people's birthright—its traditions—by unknowing strangers?

On the other side, there are those who argue that the sum total effect of missionary enterprise has been to dull rather than whet the cutting edge of African nationalism. And it is true that many of the fundamentalist missions have held, with St. Paul, that on earth man has no continuing city; that his citizenship is in heaven, whence eventually will come both his temporal and spiritual salvation; and that meanwhile he should "come out and be separate" from all unnecessary earthly entanglements. On the same side are those who argue that the growth in recent years of separatist, or splinter, church groups is incompatible with the spirit and purpose of nationalism and may, in fact, be related to the failure of nationalists to give them "the kingdom."

Some, however, see in the phenomenon of the separatist church an assurance that the African will go along with any man who promises him more than the next, especially the man who does it to the accompaniment of religious music, symbolism and ceremonial. In evidence they cite the leaders of the Convention People's Party in the Gold Coast who in the early 1950s won sympathy and support by singing "Lead, Kindly Light" at their mass meetings, and reciting nationalist prayers and a nationalist creed in which Kwame Nkrumah took the place of Christ, and the Governor, Sir Charles Arden-Clarke, the place of Pontius Pilate. They also point to the nationalistic overtones of many of the separatist churches in southern Africa. Some of these, notably the "Ethiopian" churches, stand for, and have in fact achieved, independence of control by European clergy. Others, notably the "Zionist" churches, owe an almost unquestioning allegiance to a leader inspired by apocalyptic hopes of a total reconstruction of society. And almost all of them stand for the principle of "Africa for the Africans."

Then, too, there are those who see in nationalism a flowering of the Christian ethic, for does not the New Testament repeatedly affirm the sovereignty of the human spirit, and the equality before God of all men, whether Jew or Gentile, Greek or barbarian? Certainly biblical texts have been used with great frequency by nationalists to advance their political ends. Moreover, the indigenous church has provided many African leaders with a forum and a following, and "an area of relatively free expression not found elsewhere," as Coleman puts it, "that have been subtle contributions to the development of African nationalism." More than one Western church leader has argued, with R. W. Stopford, that "almost everywhere in Africa the church has been ahead of the government in developing self-governing institutions."[2]

By contrast, the influence of Islam on the growth of African nationalism has so far been very small, and negative at that. In George Carpenter's words: "The characteristic pattern of the Islamic state has been a personal despotism resting on mass loyalty grounded in religion, on fear, and on military force . . . The pattern is quite incompatible with the complex administrative structure and varied technical competence required for the multiple functions of modern nations; it cannot engender a patriotic loyalty transcending religious and cultural differences; it does not provide scope for potential leaders nor assure security to competent servants of the state."[3]

Political. Territorial nationalisms are the product of the European "presence." "That presence," Coleman says in his working paper, "has provided a framework in which certain common sentiments and a sense of common destiny could develop: a territorial system of law and order permitting relatively free circulation of goods and peoples and the consequent development of a common set of assumptions and expectations regarding political authority; a common territorial currency, language, communications media and political institutions; indeed, even a common set of grievances."

"Unintended by-product" of the European presence is perhaps a more precise way of putting it, for when the colonial powers first began to talk of self-government in tropical Africa, they had in mind native-style rather than Western-style autonomy. "Real national self-government," declared Sir Hugh Clifford, Governor of Nigeria, in 1920, can be realized only through the "local tribal institutions and the indigenous forms of government." The concept of independent African nation-states larger than the tribe or the language group was not

[2] "Nationalism in Africa," *East Africa and Rhodesia,* September 9, 1949, p. 9.
[3] "The Role of Christianity and Islam in Contemporary Africa," p. 98 in *Africa Today* (edited by C. Grove Haines), Johns Hopkins Press, Baltimore, 1955.

anywhere officially contemplated in those days. Nor is it yet contemplated in parts of tropical Africa. "There is, of course, nothing unprecedented about this," Coleman notes. "The British did not plan Burma, nor the Dutch the Republic of Indonesia."

But unintended though the birth of territorial nationalism may have been, the cradle in which it was laid could scarcely have been better adapted to its early needs. The existence of a central territorial framework of government compelled politically conscious Africans and Europeans alike to think in territorial terms. With the birth of political parties, they were obliged not only to think, but to organize and act in territorial terms if they wanted to act meaningfully.

The European presence did more than provide a cradle for African nationalism. It provided a climate for it. This climate may be measured in various ways. It can be measured by the degree of legitimacy possessed by a given nationalist movement, that is, by reference to the declared objectives of a given colonial policy. It can be measured by the number of freedoms, e.g., of communication by speech, press, etc., of assembly and association, and of movement (entry, emigration), enjoyed by a given people, African and non-African alike. It can be measured by the number of students who are sent abroad for advanced training, and by the availability of such training at home; by the degree of "upward mobility" of Africans in government and private employment, and by the extent to which the new elites are permitted to compete, economically, socially and politically, with the old elites. Not least, it can be measured by the sensitivity of the government to political pressures and public opinion, internal and external. On any of these counts, some African territories can be shown to provide a consistently better climate for the growth of nationalism than others. Some can be shown to have a rather more attractive climate than was formerly their luck; a few to have a distinctly austere climate; and one or two a climate that is positively inclement.

Writing of the mid-1950s and using the criterion of legitimacy, Coleman graded the territories in the following descending order of "congeniality" to the nationalist cause, or, what amounted to much the same thing, of nationalist progress:[4]

1. British West Africa, including Cameroons under United Kingdom trusteeship; Senegal and French trust territories
2. The rest of French tropical Africa (since 1947); Uganda; Northern Rhodesia; Kenya (prior to the 1952 Mau Mau troubles); Tanganyika
3. Southern Rhodesia
4. Belgian territories

On any of the other counts, the rating would have been much the same, for just as legitimacy is an abstraction which, to be understood of the people, must be expressed in "concrete" freedoms, so public opinion and political pressure cannot exist without the exercise of such freedoms.

External

In a sense, all internal growth factors have their roots outside the territory, and so are as much external as internal. At the same time, a useful distinction can, we believe, be made between those factors which, while external in origin and inspiration, operate indigenously, that is, those that have given the nationalist his "case," and those which operate extra-territorially and merely fortify or frustrate him in the prosecution of it. It is perhaps the distinction between the players on the field and their anything but bipartisan cheerleaders on the side lines.

Among such external factors six are worthy of examination. These are the independent native states of Haiti, Liberia and Ethiopia; the United States; the metropolitan countries; communism; the liberation of colonial Asia; and the United Nations.

[4] The Portuguese and Spanish territories were not listed by Coleman, presumably because there was nothing to list.

The independent native states. The existence of independent native states and their ability to keep going, often with very little outside encouragement, have long drawn the respect of the politically awakened colonial African. In many of the non-self-governing territories the names of Toussaint L'Ouverture, Edward W. Blyden, Arthur and Edwin Barclay and Haile Selassie are much better known than those of the colonial governors, or their metropolitan masters. And it is not without significance that the first and major literary work of Nnamdi Azikiwe, eastern Nigeria's leading statesman, bore the title *Liberia in World Politics*.[5] The fact that these states "were recognized as legitimate and theoretically endowed with sovereign equality in a modern states system," says Coleman, "widened the vision of thoughtful Africans regarding 'the possible,' which awareness tended to sharpen their discontent with a colonial status."

The United States. Of the various American contributions to the growth of African nationalism, those made by religious and quasi-religious organizations have been among the more influential.

In the nineteenth and early twentieth centuries many missions were strongly millennial in their outlook. While there was nothing exclusively American about millennialism, it was from the America-based Watchtower movement, the missionary arm of Jehovah's Witnesses, that Africans "caught" what was perhaps the most infectious of all forms of millennialism. To a world "living in a time of unparalleled woes," it offered the following assurances: first, that "the Kingdom of God is at hand"; second, that this kingdom will be an earthly kingdom; third, that it will be a kingdom in which not only tears and death, but poverty, tyranny and even barrenness shall be unknown; and fourth, that only Witnesses will be citizens of it. Such teaching could hardly fail to affect the attitude of those

---

[5] In this two-volume study Azikiwe does not ignore the mistakes and shortcomings of the Liberian experiment, but the burden of his argument is that, all things considered, the country has shown that it is capable of governing itself.

who accepted it toward civil authority. What was the point of supporting a godless government, especially when it might any day be ousted by a theocracy? The voice of the Witness therefore tended to be one of muted opposition, if not of open rebellion.

Though the Watchtower movement was not, and is not, nationalist in the usual sense of the term, it has been regarded by many governments as being as subversive as any nationalist movement and therefore liable to repression. In at least three territories, Nyasaland, Northern Rhodesia and the Belgian Congo (where it is called Kitawala), the movement has been under a long-standing government ban. Nothing serves the bona fide nationalist better than other people's repression, and there is little doubt that many African Witnesses have been repressed—even persecuted and killed—for their convictions.

Probably more influential—Hodgkin calls it "the most important single outside stimulus" to African nationalism[6]—was the movement to which Marcus Garvey gave his name. In Garveyism the alloy of pan-Africanism was smelted into the iron of "Ethiopianism." Garvey's Universal Negro Improvement Association (founded in 1914), his African Communities League, his *Negro World*, and his international conventions for Africans and non-African negroes became as much a part of Garveyism as his African Orthodox Church. Garveyism may not have been a very well tempered weapon with which to beat the colonial powers, but it was a popular one in British and French West Africa and the Cameroons after World War I, and it was "successful in spreading the idea of independent African churches as an instrument of African liberation."[7] Even today the name of Garvey is greatly respected by many of the older nationalists, including Dr. Kwame Nkrumah.

There have been other American "instruments of African liberation." Among these were those negro writers who, from World War I onward, made African history and art, and African culture generally, their special field of interest.

[6] *Op. cit.*, p. 101.
[7] *Ibid.*, p. 102.

While their primary reason for doing so may have been the "desire to destroy the inferiority complex of the American negro by giving him a past which he could honor and respect," Coleman says, "this literary movement had a secondary impact upon thoughtful Africans which was an element in their own nationalist build-up." Many of the more attractive, if not always warrantable, interpretations of their history and culture were widely circulated, and as widely quoted. High on the list of the interpreters were Charles Morrow Wilson, Carter G. Woodson, W. E. Burghardt Du Bois and Ralph J. Bunche.

Nor was it simply a literary and intellectual movement. The five Pan-African Congresses organized by Du Bois and others along the lines of the Garvey conventions did almost as much to foster African negro nationalism in its early days. So, too, did the American negro press, which from the time of the Italian invasion of Ethiopia gave increasing publicity to African causes, and hospitality to African students of journalism —Nnamdi Azikiwe among them. Such groups as the National Equal Rights League of Democracy Congress of America, the National Race Congress of America, the National Association for the Advancement of Colored People, and the Council on African Affairs influenced African nationalism by the comfort and encouragement they gave to African students in the United States and their frequent, well-publicized pronouncements of the evils of colonialism.

These activities and the intellectual ferment which they symbolized served to sharpen the racial consciousness of the new African elite, and to provide them with an external movement with which they could identify themselves and from which they could derive strength, leadership and confidence in the rightness of their cause.

Nor must we forget the "instrumental" role of the United States in relation to African students. No African can be in the United States long without having his race consciousness sharpened by "the apparatus of social and economic discrimination" he encounters, and the stories he hears from American negroes, with whom he tends, either from necessity or inclination, to consort. This sharpening process is especially apparent in the case of the student who tries to work his way through school, and the one who has come from a part of Africa where there is little, if any, discrimination. Not all Africans take the calculated insult and the down-the-nose look with the good grace of a Kwame Nkrumah, and at times during his ten-year residence in America even he found it difficult to believe "that anyone could refuse a man a drink of water because his skin happened to be a different color."[8] On the other hand, no African student can be in the United States long without becoming infected by its social mobility, its impatience with authoritarianism, and its readiness to take a tilt at all foreign windmills (and some domestic ones, too), or without sensing that its dominant ethical assumptions and ideals are still Lincolnian. If we could cast up a balance sheet of African student experience in America, it would almost certainly have more entries on the credit than the debit side. At any rate it is uncommon to meet an African alumnus of an American institution who does not speak gratefully, and proudly, of the years he spent in it.

The metropolitan countries. The influence of the metropolitan country on the rise of "colonial" nationalism appears to have been in direct proportion to the effective strength of anti-colonial opinion in that country. It has therefore been greatest in the British territories, least in the Spanish and Portuguese, and greater in the French territories than the Belgian. The influences at work have been of four main kinds: humanitarian, religious, trade unionist and political. On the humanitarian side, we may cite the activities of the (British) Anti-Slavery and Aborigines Protection Society, which while it neither indicted imperialism nor advocated self-government, did much to increase the African's self-esteem. It also helped to ventilate his grievances at the court of public opinion.

On the religious side, the Protestant churches of the United Kingdom, France and Belgium and their affiliated Christian councils and missionary conferences have from time to time,

8 *Ghana: The Autobiography of Kwame Nkrumah,* Thomas Nelson & Sons, New York, 1957, p. 43.

and with increasing frequency in recent years, spoken out strongly against the denial of the basic human rights of liberty, equality and brotherhood.

The trade unionist influence has been most conspicuous in French areas, thanks, in large measure, to the exertions of the Confédération Générale du Travail, the Confédération Africaine des Travailleurs Croyants, and the Force Ouvrière, which are patterned on the metropolitan trade unions of the same name, and, as shown in Chapter 4, are deep-dyed in egalitarianism. In British Africa, the metropolitan link, formerly loose and unavailing, has become much closer since the end of World War II. Some African unions have been actively courted by the Trades Union Congress and, upon occasion, subsidized by it. From time to time, the congress has also loaned its legal specialists to unions involved in strikes and arbitration, and advised them on matters relating to their economic and political advancement. And while it may not always preach what the unions like to practice, its benedictions are a constant source of comfort to their nationalist hearers.

On the political but non-communist[9] side, the Fabian Colonial (now Commonwealth) Bureau, the Congress of Peoples Against Imperialism, the Movement for Colonial Freedom, and the Africa Bureau—to name only a few of the more notable British pressure groups—have proved themselves to be doughty critics of their country's colonial policies and willing tutors of aspiring nationalists. Upon occasion, they have proved to be no less doughty critics of the more aspiring nationalists.

As in the United States, the Africans on whom these movements have made the most direct impact are the students. And since it is to the United Kingdom that most of the students have gone, it is there that the impact has been greatest. In the mid-1920s a few British West Africans then studying in the United Kingdom organized the West African Students Union. For nearly two decades this union served as a seedbed

[9] Because of its international nature and direction communistic influence is dealt with lower down, under a separate heading.

for the germination of African nationalist ideas and programs. It was here that many of today's leading west African politicians dreamed their first dreams of "positive action," "people's parties" and "self-government within the shortest possible time." In the post-World War II period, as loyalties and ambitions became increasingly territorialized, the nationalist cause was strengthened by the formation of "national" student unions (e.g., the Gold Coast Students Union), and by metropolitan branches of such west African political organizations as the Action Group (Nigeria), the National Council of Nigeria and the Cameroons, the Uganda National Congress, and the Kenya African Union. Almost every one of these groups was in turn strengthened by the ministrations of those British political groups—notably the Fabian Colonial Bureau —that were working toward the same ends.[10]

Because of their much smaller numbers, African students in France long had difficulty in organizing and maintaining "seminaries" of this sort.[11] Of those that have been established in recent years, the most influential is probably the student union of the Rassemblement Démocratique Africain, which publishes its own journal, La Voix d'Afrique Noire. As for Belgium, Portugal and Spain, until the past few years they had no Africans to form such unions, for there were no African students in their metropolitan centers of higher learning. Even today the number of such students is small—in 1958 there were no more than 100 in Belgium and 50 at the most in Spain and Portugal—and their corporate life almost nil.

Where these metropolitan organizations have helped most is in convincing the African nationalist that, at least in the United Kingdom and France, he was not up against a "monolithic" community; that there was in fact as much concern

[10] During the second world war members of the West African Students Union met regularly with Fabian leaders to formulate questions for Labor M.P.s to put before the House of Commons regarding specific African grievances and needs.

[11] As late as 1945 there were only about 100 French African students enrolled in metropolitan universities. Around 1950 there were about 1,250. The corresponding figures for British African students in metropolitan universities were 500 and 3,500.

with the dignity and rights of man in the metropolitan countries as in his own; and that he could count on a vast fund of altruistic support for his program, even among the governing classes. The fact that he faced an ideologically differentiated—not to say divided—community in which "politically significant groups sympathized with him, aided and encouraged him, and provided him with formulas and techniques for realizing his objectives," says Coleman, "has tended not only to fortify him in the pursuit of his objectives, but also to attract him in many instances to a programmatic nationalism."

Communism. If communism is not the most powerful of forces within the African nationalist movement, it is not from want of effort. This effort has been sustained and intelligent, and devoted to the twin purpose of seduction and disaffection. While most of the effort appears to have been directed by national communist parties and front organizations, notably those of the United Kingdom and France,[12] some of it has undoubtedly been directed by international agencies. The primary target of the metropolitan Communists has been the African students in their midst. Their tactics, as Coleman describes them, have followed the customary lines: "solicitation regarding lodgings, social relations and entertainment; unconditional support of all nationalist objectives; arranging of summer tours behind the Iron Curtain; and the stimulating vision of a return to Africa armed with funds and the potential might of the Soviet Union to become leaders in African Soviet Republics."

Although few were won by this wooing, many were moved by it to the point of a benevolent interest. Prominent among those Africans whose nationalism was fed, in part at least, on a diet of communist comfort and dialectic, are Jomo Kenyatta (who spent some months in Moscow in 1931), I. T. A. Wallace-Johnson, co-editor with Nnamdi Azikiwe of the *African*

---

[12] The Belgian Communist Party has been unable to play the same role because few Congolese students have resided in Belgium, and those who have have been carefully chaperoned. Neither Portugal nor Spain has a communist party.

Morning Post (Accra) in 1934–1935, founder of the West African Youth League, and leading radical nationalist of Sierra Leone for over twenty years; Ladipo Solanke, founder and long-time leader of the West African Students Union; Dr. Félix Houphouet-Boigny, founder and first president of the Rassemblement Démocratique Africain, which in its early days (about 1945) had close connections with the French Communist Party; and Kwame Nkrumah, who still speaks of himself as a "Marxist socialist."[13]

The international—Moscow-directed—agencies have worked rather differently. Their objective, seemingly, has been to foster revolt within key African areas. For a time the World Federation of Trade Unions (WFTU) had several members in British tropical Africa and affiliates, through the Confédération Générale du Travail (CGT), in French tropical Africa. Though most of the memberships have lapsed, interest in the WFTU is far from dead. Representatives from both British and French territories continue to attend most of the congresses organized by the WFTU. Other agencies that have been used to further Russian ends are the International Students Union and the International Federation of Democratic Women. For a time, too, the Russians were using front organizations, such as the Free Council of Democratic German Youth, to bring African students on scholarship to universities located behind the Iron Curtain. But this did not prove to be a very profitable investment of their funds; too many of the scholarship holders went solely "for the ride."

The liberation of colonial Asia. The political "coming out" of Asia during the past generation has been followed with the keenest interest by African nationalists. As early as 1927 Ladipo Solanke affirmed that "It took the white race a thousand years to arrive at their present level of advance; it took the Japanese, a Mongol race, fifty years to catch up . . . there is no reason why we west Africans should not catch up with the Aryans and the Mongols in one quarter of a cen-

[13] *Op. cit.,* p. 13.

tury."[14] Solanke's time scale, like his ethnology, may have been on the rough-and-ready side, but few of his African contemporaries would have quarreled with it; and none would have quarreled with the conviction that what the people of Asia could do, the people of Africa could also do. Nor could any say that the people of Asia were not "doers," when almost every year of the past score and more has seen a new independence movement gather speed or a new Asian name added to the scroll of sovereign states.

Of all the Asian independence movements, the Indian movement has undoubtedly stirred the imagination of African nationalists the most. And it is not difficult to see why. First, there was the personality of Mahatma Gandhi. The message cabled by the National Council of Nigeria and the Cameroons (NCNC) on his death expressed the sentiments of all African nationalists, for whom Gandhi was "the bearer of the torch of liberty of oppressed peoples," and whose life had been "an inspiration to colonials everywhere." Second, there was the passive nature of it. Most of the African nationalists had been raised in the conviction—part-religious and part-political— that the really durable victories are the bloodless ones, and that a good cause is advanced much faster by going to prison for it (as many Indian and African leaders have done) than by dying for it on a battlefield. Third, there was, and still is, the kinship between Indian and African students living in London and elsewhere—a kinship fostered in the early days by the interest of Indian nationalists in the West African Students Union and in the short-lived but influential journal *Pan-Africa* (to which many of them contributed articles), and, more recently, by the presence of Indian groups along with African ones in the Movement for Colonial Freedom. Fourth, there has been the consistent condemnation by Indian government spokesmen of African colonialism and race discrimination. This condemnation has been widely voiced in the press, on short-wave radio programs beamed to African countries, and at international conferences. At the Colombo Conference

[14] "United West Africa," an unpublished manuscript cited by James S. Coleman.

of Asian Prime Ministers in early 1954, Prime Minister Nehru, the most consistent and respected critic of them all, himself a "prison graduate," affirmed that "colonialism is a violation of fundamental rights, and a threat to peace," and in the following year at the Afro-Asian Conference in Bandung he pleased his African admirers even better by affirming that it is an "intolerable humiliation for any nation of Asia or Africa to degrade itself by becoming a camp follower of one or the other of the power blocs . . ." Fifth, there has been the generosity of the Indian government in providing scholarships and travel grants to African nationalist leaders, actual and potential, and in encouraging its own elite to learn about Africa. (Since 1954 there has been an African Studies Program in the University of Delhi, in which work up to the doctoral level is offered.)

In Coleman's view, "the continued assertion by India of the role of leader of the newly independent and colonial areas of the world will mean a continuing Indian influence upon emergent African nationalism and in favor of neutralism." He also believes that "the real significance of the Indian factor is that it has given and continues to give African nationalists a sense of power derived from external allies, as well as conviction that their cause will triumph." On the other hand, there are those who argue that the leadership of India is in danger of being completely "neutralized" by the unfortunate image of that country created by Indians living in tropical Africa and by those with whom African students come into contact in India. Increasing numbers of Africans find themselves out of humor with the hard bargaining and not always scrupulous practices of Indian traders, and contemptuous of the inequities of the Hindu caste system.

The United Nations. Since 1945, the United Nations has also been a predisposing factor of some magnitude. By the sympathy and support it has tendered to aspiring nationalists and nationalist groups it has forced African governments to recognize their accountability at the court of world opinion. It is true, as Vernon McKay has pointed out, that much of what the United Nations has done has been ignored by the governments concerned, but "the trust territories and, indirectly, the other territories in Africa have benefited from the fact that every year the colonial powers present their records and defend their policies before the United Nations—a continual international justification which helps them to reappraise and perfect their methods of administration."[15]

More important perhaps from our present point of view is the manner in which the work of the United Nations has affected the political behavior of Africa's people, Asian and European no less than African. This it has done mainly through its 12-member Trusteeship Council, which annually receives petitions from, and examines conditions in, the territories falling under its surveillance and triennially sends missions to these territories. The publicity given to the petitions and petitioners has been especially significant. It has raised the morale of nationalist leaders both in and out of the trust territories, and enormously helped their credit rating with their followers. It has also turned more than one unknown petitioner into a leader overnight. Whether or not publicity of this kind does more good than harm, it has unquestionably accelerated the growth of African nationalism in a number of areas; in some it may even have precipitated it.

PRECIPITATING FACTORS

We have already suggested that it is difficult to draw a firm line between factors that predispose and those that precipitate. The trouble is that in the climate in which African nationalism is being raised, one day's predisposition may become the next day's precipitation. But this is no reason for not recognizing the difference between the two, for it is real enough, especially in politically critical situations.

As any social psychologist will affirm, the members of a group living in a "critical situation" are highly suggestible.

---

[15] "The Impact of the United Nations on Africa," p. 384 in *Africa Today* (edited by C. Grove Haines), Johns Hopkins Press, Baltimore, 1955.

Their passions are easily manipulated, directed and ignited. The more critical the situation—that is, the greater the stress of life, its frustrations and confusions—the greater the ease with which these passions can get ignited. The tinder—or, to change the figure, the precipitant—of nationalist passion can be of several kinds. It can be economic. It can be supplied by a company's refusal (justifiable though it may be on the grounds of productivity) to respond to a labor union's request for increased wage rates. The miners of the Rhodesias and elsewhere have more than once used such a refusal as the occasion for a display of nationalist fervor. It can be racial. It can be supplied by an unpopular decision (right though it may have been) by the referee of an interracial soccer game—as happened in Léopoldville in June 1957 after a European team was awarded a penalty that led to the defeat of the opposing African team, and subsequently to the injury of several Africans and Europeans. It can be religious. It can be supplied by a mission's condemnation (high-principled though it may have been) of a cherished African practice. There are many, including some Christian Kikuyu, who believe that the Church of Scotland's denunciation of the Kikuyu custom of clitoridectomy had as much to do with forwarding the nationalist aims of the Kikuyu Central Association as the land question.

Most of the really powerful precipitants, however, would appear to be derived from other compounds, such as constitutional change or the prospect of it, astute leadership and provocative journalism.

Constitutional change. No political atmosphere is more unstable than the one that echoes with the "uncertain sound" of the lawmaker's trumpet. Such an atmosphere is at once a source of bewilderment to those who live in it and an incitement to their nationalist leaders to fill as best they may whatever vacuums appear in it. It is, further, a breeder of baleful miasmas—the chief of which probably is a fear lest the uncertainties be so resolved by the governors that the disabilities of the governed shall be increased rather than diminished. In

Coleman's view this fear of new disabilities resulting from political change has been "one of the most powerful precipitants of political activity." Among the evidences advanced by him in support of this view are the chain-reaction awakening of the peoples of British and French Togoland on learning of the differing statuses they would have under the British, French and United Nations schemes proposed in the early 1950s for the solution of their political problems; and the very remarkable, almost violent, outbreak of northern Nigerian nationalism following on constitutional developments that created the vision of domination by the southern Nigerians. The crucial point, says Coleman, is that "although nationalism is primarily a movement to bring about change, it tends to be precipitated by the prospect of change."

Astute leadership. But the threatening atmosphere of political uncertainty and disability, real or imagined, does not automatically rain nationalism. To use the rain-maker's jargon, a nucleator is needed: a leader who can release the latent energies of his people and give direction to their disorderly emotions, loyalties and desires.

It is still an open question whether it is men who make movements, or movements men. While we have no intention of debating it, we believe that, in the realm of tropical African politics at least, a case could more easily be made out for the former than the latter. Almost all of the stronger nationalist movements have been sired by individuals, or small groups, and have been characterized by stronger loyalty to the sires than to the things for which they stand. This is as true of such post-World War II movements as the Parti Démocratique de la Côte d'Ivoire (sired by Dr. Houphouet-Boigny) and the Convention People's Party (sired by Kwame Nkrumah and still referred to by him as "my party") as it is of the much older Aborigines' Rights Protection Society (long dominated by the remarkable Gold Coast lawyer W. E. G. Sekyi) and the Senegalese *section* of the French Socialist Party, organized and led during the 1930s by the equally remarkable

Wolof lawyer Lamine Gueye. Nor could it very well have been otherwise in a world where until recently the masses were politically inarticulate, unaware and impotent, and where a man had to be exceptionally well qualified to get anywhere beyond the village limits.

As different as the leaders of nationalist movements are, the more successful of them have generally had at least three things in common.

In the first place, they have either been or made themselves economically independent of the government, deriving their support from business, professions, farms, plantations, trade unions, journalism and so on. Nnamdi Azikiwe, for instance, is a banker, company director, newspaper owner and editor. His compatriot and political opponent, Obafemi Awolowo, founder of the Action Group of Nigeria, is a barrister. Dr. Félix Houphouet-Boigny is a physician and the owner of extensive cocoa plantations. Dr. E. M. L. Endeley, for many years the leading politician in the British Cameroons, is a physician, landowner and corporation director. Sir Milton Margai, long-time leader of the Sierra Leone People's Party, is also a physician and the owner of a lucrative nursing home. Sayed Ismail Ahmed El Azhari, who was the first Prime Minister of the Republic of Sudan, is a secondary school teacher by profession. Though Kwame Nkrumah could by no stretch of the imagination have been called a man of means in his "nationalist" days, he, too, managed to stay out of government employment until he became Prime Minister—thanks largely to his academic qualifications. Most of the leaders, in other words, have not had to wrestle with the specters of intimidation and hunger; they have been free to speak their mind.

At the same time, and this is our second point, most of them have sprung from, or have been able to identify themselves with, the people they endeavor to lead. "'Sons of the soil' have had a special legitimacy," in Coleman's words. True, some of them, like Jomo Kenyatta, Nnamdi Azikiwe, Kwame Nkrumah and Dr. Hastings Banda, were away from the "soil" for long spells, but their return to it was usually very well publicized—often to the accompaniment of libations and affirmations of their weddedness to it and its people.[16]

In the third place, most of them have been clever men. Almost without exception they have shown themselves to be shrewd judges of the temper of their people, and of the amount of taxing and shoving they will take. They have, likewise almost without exception, been accomplished performers on the platform, with a turn for flamboyancy that few African audiences can resist. And, to give them their due, they have seldom showed reluctance to go to prison. In Africa, as in Asia, the fraternity of the "prison graduate" is a noble one and greatly respected by the common people. Membership in it never yet hurt any nationalist leader.

Provocative journalism. The nationalist newspaper,[17] according to Coleman, has been "one of the most effective instruments in the hands of the new leadership for the exploitation of political uncertainty and threatened disabilities . . . It performs the indispensable function of linking leadership and following. In emergent Africa no aspiring leader can seriously make a claim to power without having his own newspaper. The areas of relatively advanced nationalism coincide with areas in which the African-owned-and-edited press is most advanced."

On several occasions the African press has provided the build-up for a crisis atmosphere. One such occasion is described in the *Report of the Commission of Enquiry into Disturbances in the Gold Coast, 1948:* "Beginning about September 1947, the press in general, which had hitherto exhibited a reasonably balanced opinion on affairs, gradually degenerated into an instrument of abuse of the Government. Immediately before and after the unhappy events of February 28, 1948, its tone and content were calculated to inflame the

[16] It has often been said that no small part of Kwame Nkrumah's early popularity arose from the mystique, cultivated assiduously before his marriage to an Egyptian in 1958, that he was married to the people—that every woman in Ghana was his "bride."
[17] See Chapter 2 for a discussion of the African press in general.

populace, to keep alive public tension and to provoke further mischief."[18] Though this expresses the opinion of the administration, none of the journalists concerned would have denied that their editorials were in fact inflammatory, and intended so to be.

Two other such occasions were those of the Uganda disturbances of 1949 and 1954. Of the April 1949 disturbances the Commissioners of Inquiry had this to say: ". . . Next to the leaders of the Bataka Party and the Uganda African Farmers' Union responsibility for the disturbances must be laid at [the] door [of the vernacular newspapers],"[19] all but two of which were consistently and virulently anti-administration. The 1954 disturbances, associated with the Kabaka's exile, were laid at the door of the same papers by many people not connected with the administration. And there are those who feel that of all the factors contributing to the restiveness of the Kikuyu in the immediate pre-Mau Mau period, the vernacular press was the most potent. "[African vernacular papers] were all from the first, with the exception of the *African Star*, strongly nationalist view-sheets . . . By [the time of] the declaration of the Emergency there were about forty [of them], mainly in Kikuyu . . . mostly highly seditious and taking a bitterly anti-White 'Quit Kenya' line."[20]

Where there is little or nothing in the way of an African-owned press, and where either governments or foreign corporations have been able to develop what is usually referred to as "responsible journalism" (as in the Rhodesias, Tanganyika, the Belgian Congo and French tropical Africa), the role of the newspaper in parlaying incidents, criticism and discord into "crisis situations" has been almost negligible.

It is not only the African-owned-and-edited papers that go

[18] *Op. cit.*, H.M.S.O., London, 1948, p. 32. February 28, 1948 was the day on which two Africans were killed and five others were wounded following the refusal of a contingent of ex-servicemen to halt a grievance march on Christiansborg Castle, the Governor's residence outside Accra.

[19] *Report of the Commission of Inquiry into the Disturbances in Uganda during April 1949*, Entebbe, 1950, p. 100.

[20] *New Commonwealth*, August 19, 1954, p. 171.

in for provocative journalism. Some of the European-owned-African-edited papers are anything but sedative. However, unlike the African-owned papers, the cause of their provocation is not always the same. One day it may be the irresolution of the government to carry out announced constitutional changes. The next day it may be the alleged malfeasance of some nationalist leader. The day after it may be the snobbishness of the local expatriate population. Among the more notable exemplars of this type of journalism are the *Daily Graphic* of Accra, the *Daily Mail* of Freetown and the *Daily Times* of Lagos. Consistent supporters of constitutional government, "they have demonstrated remarkable objectivity in news coverage and editorial comment, including biting criticism of the British administration as well as of nationalist leaders," Coleman reports. "In particular, the *Daily Times* of Lagos has been called simultaneously pro-nationalist by British administrators, pro-North or pro-British by southern nationalists, pro-NCNC by the Action Group, and pro-Action by the NCNC." Most of the other European-owned newspapers, whether edited by Africans or Europeans, have generally refrained from provoking either the European or African reader to do very much beyond writing letters to the editor. On balance they have probably done more to slacken than to quicken the pace of nationalism.

THE ROLE OF THE POLITICAL
ASSOCIATION

To thrive, nationalism needs more than "precipitants." It needs support, direction and momentum; in other words, it needs vehicles. In colonial Africa, as in other non-self-governing regions, many types of vehicles have been tried out in their time:

> [from] self-appointed committees of intellectuals, advocating limited reforms; pressure-groups, constructed by particular interests—chiefly, religious, regional, economic—for purposes of political action; *mafias* and underground move-

ments, seeking to displace the colonial State, and using, or prepared to use, violence and armed revolt for the purpose; [to] loosely organised "congresses," demanding national independence or democratic rights; and, finally, political parties in a stricter sense—i.e., associations possessing a definite machine, a constitution and a platform, working within the framework of some kind of parliamentary system, and concerned to win the support of an electorate.[21]

Of these the most consequential by far have been the congress and the party. Both have been represented in colonial Africa for many years. The National Congress of British West Africa was organized in 1917; the Nigerian National Democratic Party in 1923; the Kikuyu Central Association (of Kenya) in 1928; the Senegalese *section* of the French Socialist Party (SFIO) in the 1930s. In the 1930s also a number of youth movements, congresses and leagues came into existence. In different ways and degrees, all of these were concerned with the need for more liberty to run their country's affairs in their own way, and more opportunity for becoming competent to do so. They may not always have followed the wisest paths or been run efficiently, but they made wonderful proving grounds for men and ideas, strategies and tactics. On their membership rolls were the names of many who were subsequently highly influential leaders of nationalistic causes, among them Lamine Gueye, the founder of the Senegalese *section* of the SFIO, who gave his name to two of the most liberal, and liberating, laws passed by the French Assembly since the end of the war; Joseph Casely Hayford, one of the prime movers behind the National Congress of British West Africa, whose influence as lawyer and journalist won him a place among the founding fathers of Ghana; and Jomo Kenyatta, the first secretary of the Kikuyu Central Association, who, on his return to Kenya from Europe in 1946, was hailed among his own people as the greatest leader Africa had so far produced.

The real burgeoning of organized political activity came in

21 Hodgkin, *op. cit.*, p. 139.

the 1940s. Of the two types of political association, the congress initially enjoyed the greater vogue, as it still does in some territories. What was needed to impress the colonial powers with the strength of the sentiment for self-rule was an association that could claim to speak for all the people; one that was free from the reproach of privilege and partisanship; one, moreover, that was powerful enough to run country-wide press campaigns, mass demonstrations and, if need be, country-wide boycotts and strikes. For this, the congress was better fitted than the party. In any case, as J. G. Liebenow points out in a written comment, the *raison d'être* of *African* political parties was lacking in most (including most British) territories, since there were very few elective offices at either the territorial or local levels down to the end of World War II.

THE CONGRESS

The more important congress-type organizations dating from this period are the following:

1. The Graduates General Congress of Sudan. Although founded in 1937, it did not commit itself to a forthright political program until 1942, when it began to press for the granting of "the right of self-determination, directly after the war." Its name notwithstanding, the congress claimed to speak for all Sudanese people; and it is true that from 1943 onward membership in the congress was open to all who had graduated—even from primary school.

2. The National Council of Nigeria and the Cameroons (NCNC), founded in 1944. The objective it set itself was "internal self-government for Nigeria, whereby the people of Nigeria and the Cameroons under British Mandate shall exercise executive, legislative and judicial powers." Its membership was open to "tribal unions, trade unions, political parties, professional associations, social and literary clubs, etc."

3. The Kenya African Union (KAU), formed the same year as a supratribal version of the dissolved and outlawed Kikuyu Central Association. Until it, too, was dissolved and

outlawed (at the time of the Mau Mau troubles[22]), it was
the one legal African political organization in Kenya and,
Coleman says, sought to represent itself as an "all-Kenya
'united front' movement." Under its president, Jomo Kenyatta,
it stood for "self-government by Africans for Africans" and for
electoral and land reform directed to that end. But in spite
of its name and purpose, it remained to the end an essentially
tribal—Kikuyu—movement.

4. The Nyasaland African Congress (NAC), likewise
founded in 1944. Originally there was nothing more nationalistic about its aims than the intention to recommend and lay
before the Nyasaland government bills for the benefit of Africans, and to seek to keep the government from passing dis-
criminatory bills. However, since 1951, thanks first to the idea
and later the fact of federation with the Rhodesias, the congress has been working for immediate self-government on the
Ghana model, the control of all non-African immigration, and
the reversion of all alienated lands to "the ownership of the
African people."

5. The Rassemblement Démocratique Africain (RDA),
founded in 1946, for the purpose of promoting "equality of
political and social rights . . . local democratic assemblies;
and a freely agreed union of the peoples of [French] Africa
and the peoples of France." Its membership was open to
"every national group, to men of all social conditions and
every territory." In a sense, it was as much a party as a congress, for it competed in the territorial elections.

6. The Northern Rhodesia African National Congress

---

[22] Coleman is disinclined to regard Mau Mau solely as a manifestation of nationalism. Rather he sees it as "a complex mixture of
nationalism with a strong traditional bias on the part of Westernized
leaders, and nativism, manipulated by the leaders, on the part of the
masses. Both have been generated to an especially high level of
intensity as a consequence of the acute and largely unassuaged sense
of frustration on the part of the Westernized elite, growing out of
the . . . almost total absence, until recently, of meaningful career
and prestige opportunities within either the old or the new systems,
and of the masses, resulting from the land shortage and the overcrowding on the reservations."

(NRANC), founded in 1946,[23] and, like the NAC, having quite modest aims (the breaking of tribal bars, for instance) to begin with. However, in 1949 it became, says Coleman, "the principal instrument for organizing the anti-federation fight" in the colony.

7. The United Gold Coast Convention (UGCC), founded in 1947, for the purpose of ensuring by "all legitimate and constitutional means [that] the direction and control of government should pass into the hands of the people and their chiefs in the shortest possible time." Its membership was open to "the people and their chiefs."

8. The Uganda National Congress (UNC), which, since its founding in 1952, has "led the agitation for . . . greater self-determination in Uganda," according to Coleman.

9. The Tanganyika African National Union (TANU), founded in 1954.[24] It stands for the recognition of Tanganyika as an "African country" and the attainment of self-government by the speediest possible route.

10. The Southern Rhodesia African National Congress (SRANC), founded in 1957. Southern Rhodesia has had several congress-type organizations in the postwar period, but, for one reason or another (including inadequate leadership and governmental restraint), none of them has done very much to further the political ambitions of the African. The recently reconstituted SRANC differs from its predecessors in at least one important respect, namely, that its membership is open to people of all races—"Africans" being taken to cover all those who have made Southern Rhodesia their home. It also has an able and seasoned "congress" leader in Joshua Nkomo. Its aims are very much like those of other African congresses: the abolition of "imperialism, colonialism, tribalism and all forms of oppression," "the promotion and maintenance of the na-

[23] More accurately, the Federation of African Societies of Northern Rhodesia, which had existed since 1945, was then renamed the NRANC.

[24] Its forebear, the Tanganyika African Association, had been in existence since the early 1940s, but it was neither "national" nor noticeably nationalistic in sentiment.

tional unity of the people of the colony," the establishment of better human relationships, and of "parliamentary democracy, based on universal adult suffrage, since this alone can produce a government responsible to all the inhabitants of the country and aware of the needs of all."

THE PARTY

But nationalists, in common with other people, find it easier to sing the praises of unity than to work at being united. They, too, have their personality problems, vested interests, private feuds and ambitions, and ideological differences. Frequently the only thing that unites them is belief in the need for change. When governments begin to recognize this need and do something about it, the façade of unity collapses, to disclose the existence of often quite large "back-room" differences. This is what has been happening, notably in French tropical Africa, Commonwealth West Africa and Sudan. In each of these territories constitutional reform has been followed—in some instances anticipated—by a shift of political attention from the congress to the party. In Sudan, for instance, the beginnings of a modern party system date from 1948, the year in which the "transitional constitution" went into effect, a constitution that provided for an all-Sudanese legislature and a partially "Sudanized" executive. In Ghana, the Convention People's Party (CPP), a chip off the congress (UGCC) block, dates from 1949, just prior to the widening of the franchise and the establishment of responsible government recommended by the Coussey Commission.[25] In Nigeria, the start of the Action Group and the Northern People's Congress (a party, its name notwithstanding), and in Sierra Leone, the start of the Sierra Leone People's Party (SLPP), were likewise closely synchronized with constitutional developments. And the further along the track of constitutional reform a country gets, the more its national unity suffers. Thus, whereas the

[25] A commission appointed by the British government to formulate plans for constitutional reform, and named for its chairman, the eminent African jurist, Mr. Justice (now Sir Henley) Coussey.

Gold Coast had only one party in 1947, there were seven in the country in 1957. Nigeria, which had none in 1947, had six major parties and several minor ones in 1957.

In east and central Africa, where the pace of constitutional reform has been slower, there has been less wear and tear of such unity. Indeed, in the Portuguese and Spanish territories, what wear and tear there has been is less the work of the ruled than of their rulers, who still have no great liking for African nationalism, let alone for African congresses. Although some of the longer-established congresses in British East and British Central Africa think of themselves as parties (the Northern Rhodesia African National Congress voted in 1954 to convert itself into a political party), so far their political sway among their own people has not been seriously contested.

Important as it is, constitutional reform is not the only reason for the decline of the congress and the rise of the party. Also important, in Hodgkin's view, is the dissatisfaction of many of the younger nationalists with "what seemed to be the old-fashioned agitational methods, and personal ascendancy, of the generation of nationalist leaders that the tide of revolt of the early post-war years had carried to the front."[26] This, he believes, was partly responsible for Kwame Nkrumah's challenge of J. B. Danquah's leadership in the then Gold Coast, and Obafemi Awolowo's challenge of Nnamdi Azikiwe's leadership in western Nigeria. Nor has the dissatisfaction always stopped at the ways of leaders and the means employed by them. Not infrequently it has extended to the ideas that have moved them—or failed to move them. To quote Hodgkin again:

It was primarily ideological divisions that split the RDA. At the outset . . . the Senegalese socialists broke away. In 1950 the conflict between the Right wing, led by the President, M. Houphouet-Boigny (and including most of the RDA parliamentary representatives), who favoured a policy of compromise with the French administration, and the Left, led by the Secretary-General, M. d'Arboussier, who fa-

[26] *Op. cit.*, p. 150.

voured *la lutte à l'outrance* and continued co-operation with
the French Communists, came to a head—leaving the Right
in control of the machine, while the Left retained its influence in Senegal and the Cameroons, and among trade
unionists and students.[27]

The decline of the NCNC at the end of the 1940s can also
be attributed in part to ideological schism. There is a world of
difference—economic, social and political—between northern
Nigeria and the Eastern and Western Regions of southern
Nigeria. The Ibos of the Eastern Region and the Yorubas of
the Western Region, while willing to take what is offered them
by Europeans, are seldom willing to take each other's offerings.
Once the NCNC came to be represented as an Ibo-sponsored,
or at least Ibo-dominated, idea, it lost a lot of its attraction
for the Yorubas.

Much the same is true of the Graduates General Congress.
Sudanese radicalists found themselves opposed by gradualists,
and the followers of one religious faction (Khatmiyya) by the
followers of another (Ansar), and separated from one another
by so broad an intellectual divide that there was little chance
of any traffic moving across it. It was this, in part, that led
in 1945 to the formation of the 'Umma Party—the party that
stood for independence from Egypt, no less than from Great
Britain.

Some of the parties are not chips off the old congress block
but splinters off the chips. Notable examples of such are the
Bloc Démocratique Sénégalais (BDS), which broke away
from the Senegalese *section* of the French Socialist Party in
1949 on the initiative of Léopold-Sédar Senghor and other
new-generation African socialists; and, in the Gold Coast, the
Moslem Association Party, the Togoland Congress and the
National Liberation Movement of Ashanti, all of which were,
in effect, breakaways from the Convention People's Party, and
most of whose leaders were drawn from the same party.
Several parties are "reconstituted" chips, formed by the amal-

gamation of splinters. In this category come the Ghana Congress Party, established in 1952 as "a merger between the rump of the UGCC, the moderate National Democratic Party, and a few individual CPP dissidents"; the Front pour l'Action Civique du Tchad, "formed as an electoral alliance between the local section of RDA and the local Socialists against the dominant Union Démocratique Tchadienne"; and the Sudanese National Unionist Party, established in 1953 as the result of "a merger between the Ashigga and other minor parties and groups supporting the principle of a constitutional 'link' with Egypt."[28]

Then there are parties that came into being independently of existing congresses and parties. As Hodgkin says,

Many of the most effective parties, both in British and French West Africa, have been brought into being through the initiative of a semi-political association which was already well established, and could thus provide the new party with a ready-made leadership and body of support. This kind of historical connection existed between M. Houphouet-Boigny's Syndicat Agricole Africain and the party organised in 1945 under his direction, the Parti Démocratique de la Côte d'Ivoire. The Kamerun National Congress (formerly the Cameroons National Federation), of which Dr. Endeley is President, had a similar link with the 11,000-strong Cameroons Development Corporation Workers' Union, reorganised on Dr. Endeley's initiative in 1947. In Nigeria Mr. Obafemi Awolowo's Action Group (1951) was the offspring of the Yoruba cultural association, Egbe Omo Oduduwa (i.e., 'society of the descendants of Oduduwa,' the legendary ancestor of the Yorubas), a body which Mr. Awolowo inspired, created (in 1948) and led; while the Northern People's Congress (1951) led by the Sardauna of Sokoto, was simply a Moslem, predominantly Hausa, cultural society—the Jami'a—renamed and adapted.[29]

[28] *Ibid.*, pp. 153–54.
[29] *Ibid.*, pp. 154–55.

And in Sierra Leone, the Sierra Leone People's Party, founded in 1951 and led by Dr. M. A. S. (now Sir Milton) Margai, had as its parent the Sierra Leone Organisation Society, the primary aim of which was to promote the cooperative movement.

Then again, as Hodgkin goes on to point out, several parties have come into existence as a result of outside encouragement. In some instances, notably the French African socialist parties, the encouragement has come from political leaders and parties in the metropolitan country. In a few instances, of which the Northern People's Congress of Nigeria is perhaps the most striking, the encouragement has come from the colonial administration.

But whatever their origin, nearly all of the parties have two very important features in common. In the first place, they have a great capacity for taking Africans and making nationalists of them. This is as true of the "special-interest" parties, such as the Moslem Association Party and the (Ashanti) National Liberation Party of Ghana, as it is of the "personality" parties, such as the Ghana Congress Party, and the "people's" parties, such as the CPP of Ghana, the NCNC of Nigeria and the Union des Populations du Cameroun (UPC) of the French Cameroons. The first of these may be, and often are, more interested in developing or protecting an ethnic nationalism than a territorial one, and the second may be, and often are, less assertively nationalist than the third, but all three are energized by the desire to serve as the instrument for uprooting colonialism from the body politic and establishing national independence.

In saying this, we are not suggesting that where the party goes today, there the seeds of nationalism will germinate tomorrow. As with all seed, some falls on dry, unresponsive ground, and some is swallowed up by the cares and pleasures of daily life. For that matter, not all the seed that germinates is fruitful, for many who call themselves nationalists know only their party's slogans—"Free-*dom*," "Islam," "S.-G. will make us all rich." Understanding of what the slogans imply in con-

One of the most powerful weapons being used in the assault on ig-norance is the radio. Battery receivers of the heavy-duty "saucepan" type enable educational agencies to reach deep into the roadless, schoolless bush. (*Above:* near Lusaka, Northern Rhodesia.)

Most Africans have always been poorly housed. Most town-dwelling Africans still are, but thanks to the work of public and private corporations, better housing is being provided, as these pictures indicate. (*Top:* Bukavu, Congo. *Bottom:* Nairobi, Kenya.)

The pace of change is nowhere faster than in the field of government. Colorful and humane as the indigenous systems often were, they have little place in a world that has been unhorsed by nationalism. (*Top:* ceremonial occasion, northern Nigeria. *Bottom:* Ghanaian legislators.)

The new African polity has many architects, but none greater, in the opinion of the Ghanaians and, indeed, of many others, than Dr. Kwame Nkrumah—who, as John Gunther has aptly said, "personifies the hopes of black nationalism everywhere on the continent where people are educated enough to have heard of him." (*Top:* President Nkrumah, of Ghana. *Bottom:* Legislative Assembly in the Gold Coast on the eve of independence.)

straint, loyalty and sheer hard work is usually much later in coming, and may not come at all. Party membership figures (some of which, notably the RDA's, are enormous) therefore tell very little about the strength of any given cause or the degree of sophistication of those identified with it. More important, by far, is the quality of party leadership.

The second widely shared characteristic of African political associations is their role as leadership cramming schools. Almost all the angry young men of postwar Africa have looked upon the party as the vehicle likely to convey them most quickly to power. Its often elaborate structure, simulating that of a government-in-being (complete with cabinet, caucuses and committees), enables the man with talent to be spotted quickly. Its customary dearth of funds means that the man with talent finds himself called upon to exercise it in different ways—as organizer, administrator, planner and tactician. And in a still largely illiterate world its purpose is advanced more rapidly by personal advocacy than by printed word or recorded voice, so that the party not infrequently becomes more closely identified with the salesman than the product he is selling. At times it would almost look as if the salesman has "sold" himself. At any rate, there was a time when the creed of the Convention People's Party of the Gold Coast read "I believe in Kwame Nkrumah . . ."—which, of course, was not necessarily the same as believing in national sovereignty and democratic government. Among those who have been through the cramming process and emerged as leaders, not merely of a party, but of a people, we must name, besides Kwame Nkrumah, Nnamdi Azikiwe in the Eastern Region of Nigeria, Dr. Houphouet-Boigny in the Ivory Coast, Léopold-Sédar Senghor in Senegal, Sekou Touré in Guinea, Sylvanus Olympio in Togo, Joseph Kasavubu and Patrice Lumumba in the Belgian Congo.

Not all African political associations work solely for political ends, however. Some have been quite as concerned with economic ends. Indeed, Coleman quotes Senghor as saying around the year 1955 that "the main complaint" French West Africans had with the French connection was "economic in character and not political." While not all of Senghor's compatriots (certainly not Sekou Touré) would agree with his judgment, it is one that finds support among many foreign observers. Melville Herskovits, for instance, has said that the outstanding thing about the discussions he had with a number of Africans during a visit to Dakar around the same time was "the way in which they accept the present political situation and tend to think in terms of economic rather than political activity." Indicative of this preoccupation with economic matters was the sustained drive by French West African politicians to bring about a literal translation of the 1946 constitution, especially those portions of it dealing with equality of opportunity and conditions of employment, including such fringe benefits as family allowances, for African and European.

But it should not be supposed from all this that the African leaders in the former French areas have shown themselves less capable of pursuing political ends than they were economic ones, or conversely in the case of those in British areas and elsewhere. Big sticks can be used for many purposes, and it is quite evident that the political associations, whether congresses or parties, of tropical Africa are becoming increasingly adept in using them. It is no less evident that these associations will be using them for an increasing variety of purposes, as the impediments in their path are cleared away.

IMPEDIMENTS IN THE NATIONALIST'S PATH

Nationalism has made such strides in tropical Africa in the postwar period that it is easy for us to forget the impediments it has encountered. These impediments have everywhere been considerable; for the fact is that much in the environment of tropical Africa is unfavorable to the progress of nationalism. Some things are downright hostile to it.

NATURAL IMPEDIMENTS

In the companion volume we speak at length about the intrinsic qualities of the land and life of tropical Africa. Suffice it to say, therefore, just three things under this heading.

The scale of the region. To harness the vast rivers, tame the immense forests and savannas, and control the great deserts, plagues and pests of tropical Africa calls for correspondingly large-scale thinking, planning and acting. African man, however, remains for the most part a small-scale thinker, planner and actor. He is a Lilliputian in a land of giants. But unlike the Lilliputians he has not yet developed much facility for working with his fellows on large-scale projects; accordingly he is still unable to make the giants subject to his will. A nationalism that is impotent to control the sources of power and remove the sources of weakness in its system is a frail thing. It is perhaps too frail to stand exposure to the harsh winds of a world of power blocs, high interest rates and soaring efficiency levels.

Resources. Unquestionably great as the resources of the region are, their distribution bears little relation to the incidence of nationalism. Indeed, at times it would almost look as if the resources are greatest where the manifestations of nationalism are fewest, and smallest where they are most numerous. Certainly there are few, if any, territories richer than the Belgian Congo, where, down to 1958, nationalism was little more than a "patriot dream that sees beyond the years." And there are no poorer territories than Somalia (for what does it have but some small crop surpluses, some poor-quality livestock, some salt and the smell of oil?), where nationalism is to have its fulfillment in nationhood in 1960. Though Ghana is better off, it is far from rich. Already it has discovered that more than a change of name and status is needed to lift the incubus of dependence on a single commodity.

Then, too, the resources are, in general, of such a kind that they cannot be exploited without large amounts of capital being sunk into them—capital that is scarce in most of the areas concerned and hard to come by abroad, often for no other reason than that the controllers of it are nervous about what may happen to it in nationalist hands. Nowadays it takes several million dollars to develop a sisal or rubber plantation of economic size, and many times more millions to install a "Volta"-sized power plant.

The number of ethnic groups. In a region where there are probably not less than 600 groups of people who do enough things so differently as to be recognizably distinct from one another—in many cases as distinct as Spaniard, Swiss and Swede—it is easy enough to talk of the grounds for self-determination, but it is much harder to see how nation-states can be established on those grounds. Anti-colonialism does not of itself constitute grounds for the building of a nation-state; the very act of setting up such a state removes the grounds on which it is set up! For nationalism to flower in nationhood that is at once viable and strong, something more than a shared hatred of colonialism and a shibboleth is needed. What is needed just as much (apart from a broad-based economy) is the means of rallying the voluntary support of enough people to make self-government possible and of keeping it under the changing banners of party politics, through all the exactions and tyrannies of small men raised to great power, and in face of the duplicity, lies and ignorance of those outsiders who come to praise but stay to blame. Thus, what is needed as much as anything is adequate means of communication and persuasion. In many areas, including some of those in which nationalism is a burning issue, such means barely exist—and this not so much because of unwillingness on the part of the ruling powers as because of the staggering dimensions of the task.

Consider, as a case in point, the problems of communication and persuasion in British East Africa. In the four territories of Kenya, Tanganyika, Uganda and Zanzibar there are at least 200 distinct indigenous groups, in a population of about 20 million. In Tanganyika alone there are over 100 such groups, in a population of not more than 9 million. Nearly all of these groups have their own language or dialect. Most of them have their own ways of doing things, behaving and thinking, their own valuation of what is good and bad, right and wrong. And their ideas on such matters are not infrequently divergent. What is regarded as good government by a Lango is likely to be regarded as intolerable interference by a Masai; and a Masai's idea of independence is usually very different from that of a Kikuyu. To preserve what is good and eradicate or neutralize what is evil, most of these groups would still be willing to go to considerable lengths.

Consequently, any government or party that seeks to get the people of British East Africa, or even of Tanganyika, to the point of consensus, whether in the realm of economy, morality or government, need not look for an easy victory, or be in a hurry. To get a consensus at all, it will need to stop its ears to the cries of the more determined nationalists who claim that every man has an inalienable right to live as he pleases, and to be communicated to in his own tongue. For how is the government of a country like Tanganyika, with a per capita income of approximately $50 a year and a rather modest physical endowment, to tackle the problem of reaching and persuading over 100 different ethnic groups? By recruiting a task force of anthropologists to plumb "the psychocultural base of their ethnocentrisms," and measure the hazards of fiddling with them? By training a corps of linguists to communicate to each of the groups its social and political plans and the impossibility of bringing them to pass without higher taxes and higher productivity? By printing its literature on the development of cash crop farming, coffee cooperatives, child care and multiracial rule in all of these languages? By building in each language area elementary, secondary and technical schools where vernacular training can be had in the strenuous business of running a country with enough skill to become self-supporting and respected in a highly competitive world? Of course not. Neither the Tanganyika government nor any other in tropical Africa commands the kind of money needed for such enterprises. Most of the languages spoken in the region have never been reduced to writing, and, with the exception of Swahili, those that have are almost entirely without reading matter, except for the Bible or parts of it. Furthermore, many of the things a teacher, doctor, agronomist, social worker, administrator or politician wants to say to these people cannot be expressed in their languages; the words for them do not exist.

ACQUIRED IMPEDIMENTS

Other impediments—acquired rather than natural—also stand in the path of those who wish to settle for nothing less than self-determination and sovereignty.

First of these is the existence of more than one kind of nationalism and nationalist—a subject referred to at the beginning of this chapter. To the outsider all nationalists, like all imperialists and politicians, are apt to look alike. But we greatly oversimplify the case if we suppose that all nationalists in tropical Africa stand for the same things. Almost every territory has its own special brand. Some territories have more than one brand. In Nigeria, for instance, there are nationalists, like Nnamdi Azikiwe, who have stood all along for state-wide sovereignty. There are those, including many of the most influential Moslem leaders, whose political ambitions would have been satisfied with the granting of autonomy to the three—Western, Eastern and Northern—regions of the territory. And there are those, like the members of the Ibo Union, who believe that the only feasible nationalism is one based on tribal cohesion. In the areas where French influence is strong, there are nationalists, like Dr. Houphouet-Boigny, who believe their goal was as good as reached with the granting of self-government within the framework of the French Community and those, like Sekou Touré, who have seen their goal as complete independence from the French Community. In the British territories there are those, like Tom Marealle, of Tanganyika, who see no contradiction between nationalism and multiracial partnership, and those like Jomo Kenyatta, of Kenya, who contend that in Africa only Africans have a right to be nationalists.

There is yet another brand of "African" nationalism—the non-African. Europeans and Asians may form rather small minorities, but many of them are more than a match for the African when it comes to nationalistic fervor and political acumen. Africa is their home, and has been for two to three generations in many cases. They neither have nor want another home. They have worked for what they have and they see no more reason for giving it back to the Africans than the up-state New York farmers do for giving back their lands to the Mohawks. They neither want to impose their way of life on their neighbors nor to have theirs imposed upon them. They merely wish to maintain their separate identity—which is exactly what most African nationalists are interested in doing. Like the African nationalists, they have different views on the degree of identity that is desirable and feasible, and the means of securing it. In some cases the differences of viewpoint are not serious. Thus, in the Federation of Rhodesia and Nyasaland the aims of the new Central Africa Party, formed in 1959, read very much like those of the United Federal Party: both parties look forward to multiracial partnership, the main difference between them being one of schedule. In other cases the differences would appear to be fundamental. Thus, it is difficult to see how the white supremacists of the Dominion Party in the same Federation could ever come to an accommodation with the CAP or the UFP. Like most African nationalists, too, the European and Asian nationalists are becoming increasingly impatient of political paternalism—"the government knows best" kind of philosophy— and increasingly set upon replacing it by something more adult.

In the eyes of many indigenous African nationalists, the attitude of the European and Asian nationalists in their midst is now a more serious impediment to their political progress than the "paternalism" of the metropolitan powers.

CHAPTER 6

THE MACHINERY
OF GOVERNMENT

Until the "partition" of the late nineteenth century, tropical Africa had, for hundreds of years, been governed almost exclusively by Africans. Most of the governments, it is true, were only tribe-sized and, to a Westerner's eye, wretchedly poor and indifferent to human suffering, but they had, to an African's eye, the overriding merit of being indigenous. They were "of the people." To a degree, also, they were governments by the people. For while the heads of these governments—the chiefs, the elders, the kings and the priests—may frequently have had total powers, their subjects had no difficulty in recognizing abuse of such powers when they saw it, and in doing something about it.

The relationship between government and people in tribal society was usually close, and the aims of one were the aims of the other. The staking out of virtually the whole area—only Liberia and Ethiopia were excluded—among the major European powers altered all this. Not only did European rule make the aim of government more difficult for the African to understand, it also put the business of government on an entirely new plane. Government ceased to be a matter of preserving the *status quo,* and became one of promoting and enforcing an alien, and often unwanted, way of life. In place of maintenance, it offered expansion; for tribal autonomy, it offered colonial dependence; for personal negotiation, rule by proxy; for liberty to make war, constraint to keep the peace; and European punishment to fit almost every African offense, civil and criminal alike.

The machinery of government became more complicated. In most of the indigenous systems there had been no government machinery to speak of. With some notable exceptions (which include the Ganda, the Chagga, the Ashanti and the Dahomey), government was primarily a matter of compliance with word-of-mouth orders or with the "sense of the meeting." Since every man's status and attendant responsibilities were known to every other man, no man needed a policeman, or a tax inspector, or a security agent to tell him what he had to do. For the man who did fall short of his responsibilities, there were sanctions; but since he would know as well as his accusers what these were, they likewise required no very elaborate machinery for their enforcement. The indigenous systems were bookless, printless and paperless; they needed no files, no archives, no gear of any kind, and no clerks, messengers or administrators. Their only communication system was the "bush telegraph." Their headquarters were where the chief or his council happened to be: they could operate as efficiently under a tree as in a house.

THE QUESTION OF DESIGN

The running of machinery presupposes the existence of designers, and their ability to design what other people can be made to want, and to run efficiently. Tropical Africa has always been as hard on the designer of machinery as it has been on the user of it. It was especially hard on the early European designers of government machinery.

For one thing, the designers—Belgian, British, French, Portuguese and Spanish alike—knew next to nothing about the region or its peoples. They seldom had accurate maps. They almost never knew where one tribe or kingdom ended and another began. As a result, tribes having nothing in common with one another frequently found themselves lumped together in the same administrative area, while people of common tribe and tongue found themselves living on opposite sides of a boundary and compelled to learn the quite different ways, laws and languages of their newly acquired rulers. The designers knew even less about the customs of the people, with the inevitable result that many well-disposed tribes were frequently alienated by their ruler's apparent lack of feeling for their culture, and many who were ill-disposed to begin with became openly hostile.

For another thing, the designers had very little money to work with. The partitioned territories were poor; they had already been bled of their two most accessible sources of wealth, slaves and ivory. It was to be many years before their budgets were bigger than those of a small-sized American town. Even today, very few of them are self-supporting, and the average per capita income of the region as a whole is still well under $100 a year. Consequently the designers had to come up with something that was low-priced, for while the metropolitan taxpayers may have appreciated the prestige (and not all of them did) of belonging to a colonizing and civilizing power, they could hardly be expected to appreciate having to pay for the prestige.

Then again, the designers could make very little use of indigenous government systems. Except in a few areas where the possibilities of indirect rule existed, the indigenous systems were usually incapable of being remodeled.

This being so, the designers found themselves pretty well obliged to work with the metropolitan models, adapting them as best they could to the different environments encountered in the various colonial territories. What Lord Hailey has said of the colonial policies of the "partition" powers applies no less to their whole governmental effort: it was "the result of the projection into overseas areas of certain domestic characteristics and philosophies of life."[1] There was, naturally, no guarantee whatever that either these characteristics or these philosophies were capable of flourishing on tropical soil. On the contrary, there was an excellent chance that they were not. Not only were the resources of men and money at the disposal of these governments small, but the environmental conditions—physical, social and psychological—were exceedingly trying, and the opportunities for abuse of authority vastly greater than those with which the government official was presented in Europe.

[1] *An African Survey: Revised 1956*, Oxford University Press, London, 1957, p. 542.

It follows that the machinery had to be kept as simple as possible. The simpler it was, the easier it was for the European to run and the African to comprehend, the more likely it was to be kept in working order, the cheaper its maintenance, and the longer its working life—and that of the Europeans in charge of it.

It also follows that a great deal of thought had to be given to the kind of people to run the machinery of government. The best-designed administrative machinery in the world quickly becomes ineffective in the hands of the inept, unjust, indiscreet, intemperate or intolerant. While the colonial governments of tropical Africa have had such men, on the whole they have been served uncommonly well by their public servants, junior and senior alike. Indeed, such success as the European administrations of tropical Africa have enjoyed over the years probably stems as much from the quality of the men attracted to them as from the quality of the machinery. Or, to put it in another way, the designers have been keenly aware ever since the beginning of the partition period that the whole of government is much more than the sum of its working parts and that a government can be only as good as those who run it.

Whatever faults the European administrations in tropical Africa may have had—and they have had plenty if we are to believe all that their critics have said—complexity has not been one of them. It is unlikely that in the whole of human history there were ever so many people governed by so few with so little fuss as during the heyday of African colonialism. At no time during its non-self-governing epoch did Ghana, with an area nearly that of Oregon and a population of not less than 4 million, have more than about 2,500 British civil servants, or more than about one tenth that number of commissioners (provincial, district and assistant district) and police officers. Even on the eve of its independence, when the civil service list was swollen with expatriates busy "Sudanizing" the country, Sudan had no more than 7,000 people in the entire political service, of whom only about 1,000 were expatriates—and this is a territory of almost a million square

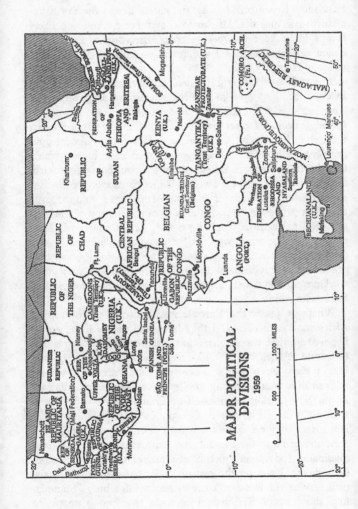

MAJOR POLITICAL
DIVISIONS
1959

miles with a population (at the time it became independent) of not less than 9 million. Those who care to wander off the highways of tropical Africa may still come upon *cercles, bomas* and *postos* whose officers in charge, barely ten years out of school, maintain law and order, almost singlehanded in some cases, over territories the size of Connecticut or Massachusetts, and enjoy the esteem—often the affection—of the 100,000 and more people who constitute their charge. For that matter, it is impossible to go anywhere, even in these impersonal times of quick transit and rule by loudspeaker, without being struck by what one man can do to put across a new government edict, or a new tax, when he happens to have the right look in his eye. (It must also be admitted that the man with the wrong look can do very little, except earn the fear and hatred of those he works with.)

THE WORKING PARTS

Notwithstanding the modern proliferation of government agencies, the business of government remains what it has always been: the making of laws, the applying of them, and the settling of disputes arising from their application. Its main working parts are, therefore, three in number: legislative, executive and judicial. But since the divide between the executive and judicial functions of most government administrators in tropical Africa is fine to the point of being undemarcated (and perhaps undemarcatable), these two parts will be fused in the following discussion, and designated as administrative.

LEGISLATIVE

Several of the territories under review are still dependencies, of one kind or another, of European powers. In each such territory control of legislation and of legislative institutions is in the hands, not of the local people (whether African, Asian or European), but of the metropolitan government and its local agents. The attitude and activity of the legislators differ widely from territory to territory, since no two

European powers have exactly the same idea about the purpose of government, or the methods needed to achieve it in a given economic and social context. There are scarcely less wide differences in the attitude and activity of those legislated for; not infrequently, the only things they have in common are a dislike of all imposed legislation, and the desire to do something about it.

Because the colonial powers have all along based their legislation on different political, and often different social, premises, it will be necessary to deal with their activities in this field under separate headings.

Belgian territories. Until 1959 there had been comparatively little remodeling of the legislative machinery of the Belgian Congo since 1908, when the Belgian government took over its control from the Congo Free State. In almost all major respects the *Charte Coloniale* carried as much weight with the legislators of 1958 as it had done with those who wrote it fifty years earlier. The power of legislation for the colony continued to be delegated from the Belgian Parliament to the King, who exercised it by royal decree. The Parliament continued to retain certain powers. Among other things, its authorization was still required for colonial loans and agreements with commercial companies and companies seeking concessions, and it still passed on all budgetary matters. The Belgian Minister for the Colonies continued to issue to the Governor-General of the Colony instructions on the main lines of policy to be followed, and remained largely responsible for the appointment and dismissal of administrative officials. He likewise continued to advise the King (who might or might not take his advice) on all senior appointments (e.g., Governor-General, Vice Governor-General and governors of provinces) and to be advised, in turn, by the Colonial Council. This body, though somewhat less "official" in composition than when first established, also continued to serve the functions outlined in the *Charte;* that is, it continued to give the Minister its opinion on all proposed legislation, and to make its own legislative and administrative recommendations. If the Minister wished to override the council's recommendations, he might, but he had to give his reasons for doing so.

As in the early years of the century, the office of Governor-General continued to be one of great prestige with little power. Only in emergencies might its incumbent introduce new legislation or suspend laws in being. In either case his legislative actions became a dead letter if they were not confirmed by royal decree within six months. The legislative powers of his gubernatorial colleagues, the governors of the six provinces, were nominal. Even some of the routine executive business conducted by the Governor-General and his six colleagues in the Government Council, such as the granting of land concessions and the annual recruitment of the *force publique*, or militia, required the sanction of a decree.

In other words, there was virtually no devolution of legislative authority in this half-century period. And it is a little difficult to see how there could have been any, without the setting up of a representative legislature in Léopoldville. Of the need for such a legislature, the Belgian government remained unconvinced until the troubles of late 1958 and early 1959, when it declared its intention of organizing a democracy in the Congo "capable of exercising the prerogatives of sovereignty and of deciding upon its independence." To this end it established a 12-member Legislative Council that was intended to serve as "the first form of a Senate," and replaced the old Government Council by a General Council that was intended to serve as "the preliminary form of a Chamber of Representatives."

The Trust Territory of Ruanda-Urundi has been governed on the lines of the Belgian Congo proper. Its Vice Governor-General—the ranking Belgian authority in the territory—has had the same limited legislative power as the Governor-General of the Belgian Congo. The Vice Governor-General's council (created in 1947) played an almost purely advisory role, even after it was transformed into a General Council in the mid-1950s. Legislation introduced into the Belgian Congo did not automatically go into force in Ruanda-Urundi, however;

in deciding the propriety of such legislation the Vice Governor-General was given wide discretion. While for many administrative purposes Ruanda-Urundi has been treated as part of the Belgian Congo, it has had its own judiciary and its own budget, the funds for which have been quite distinct from those of the Belgian Congo.

Commonwealth territories. The British have always believed in being master in their colonial house and in staying master of it as long as they deemed their presence there to be desirable. Thus it has been the practice of the British government to control the external relations and policies of each African colony, and to assume responsibility for the protection of each colony in time of war. Equally, it has been its practice to reserve the right to make laws for the colony, to appoint the Governor and decide the extent of his executive powers, and reverse his decisions whenever it saw fit. It has also made a practice of controlling the appointment of all other senior posts in the civil and defense services of each colony, of supervising the administration of justice, of appointing and dismissing judges, and of having the final word in the matter of a colony's annual budget.

At the same time, the British government has seldom failed to relax its legislative grip on a colonial government as its leaders, African and non-African, have given proof of ability to provide impartially for the welfare of all their peoples.

Quite early in the history of Britain's African colonies provision was made for the governors of them to receive advice on the exercise of their powers from legislative bodies known as assemblies or councils. The membership of these bodies was, to begin with, mainly "official"; that is, it consisted of men appointed by the government, and, for the most part, government (civil service) men. The "unofficial" minority was made up largely, if not always entirely, of representatives of special interests (mining, business, industry) or special groups (racial minorities, European settlers). Initially, African interests were represented by Europeans, usually missionaries; but increasingly they have come to be represented by educated

Africans. The official members were nominated; the unofficial, either nominated by the Governor or elected.

Over the years, the "unofficial" membership of these legislative bodies has been increased, the basis of its selection broadened, and its role enlarged. Also, the legislative power of these bodies has been increased by a continuous process of devolution. However, their power has always fallen short of that of the British Parliament. T. R. Batten has characterized the "standard model" (not that there is really such a thing in British colonial constitutional practice) as follows: "It may debate and vote on legislative proposals put before it. It may criticize annual estimates. And it may question the government on detailed matters concerning its administration. Criticism from unofficial members may often lead government to modify its original proposals, but it need not do so. The official members have to vote for the government proposals, and where they form the majority they can always outvote the unofficial members."[2]

While the legislative council has everywhere been "the most conspicuous feature in the progress of the British dependencies towards the stage of Responsible Government,"[3] this progress probably would not have been as steady or as efficient without the help of a second legislative institution early introduced by the British into their colonial administration, namely, the executive council. For this council, in Lord Hailey's words, "may be said . . . to have provided the bridge over which the Legislative Council passes on its way to gain control of the executive agencies of rule."[4] In some territories the bridge was built before there was any traffic to use it, that is to say, before the legislative council was set up. Usually the two were set up side by side. The members of the executive council, drawn initially from the ranks of the senior government officials in the colony and of recent years, in some cases, from the unofficial members of the legislative

---

[2] *Problems of African Development,* Oxford University Press, London, 1949, Part II, pp. 128–29.

[3] Lord Hailey, *op. cit.,* p. 288.

[4] *Ibid.*

council, are expected to advise the Governor on problems of administration, the preparation of the budget, and on all bills to be put before the legislative council. As in the case of the latter, the Governor is under no obligation to accept the advice tendered to him. Even so, no Governor can feel happy about refusing advice which represents the opinion of a considerable portion—perhaps the majority—of the articulate people in the colony. Accordingly, not the least of a Governor's tasks is to modify his, or his government's, proposals enough to win a qualified assent to them; and failing that, to persuade his opponents that while they are fully entitled to fight for the minority or special interests they represent, he must always be guided by what he considers to be the interests of the colonial community as a whole.

At first the "unofficial" as well as the official members of these British colonial legislative bodies were Europeans. In the years following World War II, African representation increased substantially in almost every colonial territory. As early as 1946 the unofficial members of the Gold Coast Legislative Assembly, most of whom were directly elected, had a clear majority over the official and nominated members. By 1954, three years prior to the granting of its independence, the colony had a wholly elected legislature, with an all-African cabinet of ministers chosen from its members. Some "reserve powers" were still vested in the Governor, but they were not once exercised during the years in which they were in force. On independence day (March 6, 1957) the Gold Coast—now Ghana—also took over the government of the neighboring territory of British Togoland, hitherto administered as a U. N. trust territory.

In 1947 a new constitution gave the Legislative Council of Nigeria an unofficial majority for the first time. However, only a minority of the "unofficials" were directly elected. The same constitution also gave the Houses of Assembly of the three regions and the House of Chiefs for the Northern Region, all of which it brought into being, large unofficial majorities. But while these bodies were given some financial powers, they were given no legislative powers; consequently most of their time was spent in rather fruitless discussion. Later, in 1952, another constitution gave the country an African ministerial system, and the House of Representatives (as the federal or central Legislative Council came to be called) and the three regional assemblies a majority of elected members.

For various reasons, including the country's much greater size and ethnic and religious complexity, Nigeria found it impossible to keep up with the tempo of legislative reform in the Gold Coast. The demand for responsible government, though loud and insistent, was only tardily matched by the unity needed to underwrite it. Many of those campaigning for it were united only by opposition to continued British control. As the prospect of its removal in 1960 has come closer, the spirit of regional particularism, if not of separatism, has tended to become fiercer.

Good progress toward responsible government has also been made in the Trust Territory of the British Cameroons (which shares Nigeria's legislative system and has been treated, for all practical purposes, as an integral part of the adjoining areas of Nigeria), and in the British West African territories of Gambia (where since 1954 both the legislative and executive councils have had "unofficial," and largely elected, majorities) and Sierra Leone (where the same has been true since 1951).

In east and central Africa, with the two exceptions of Sudan and Southern Rhodesia, the devolutionary process has taken place rather more slowly. Thus it was not until 1944 that the first African was nominated to the Kenya Legislative Council, and as recently as 1958 there were fewer than 20 Africans in a council of more than 80; neither the Legislative Council nor the Executive Council had an unofficial elected majority.[5]

It was not until 1945 that Africans (three in number) were

[5] While the "Macleod" constitutional proposals of early 1960 envisaged the possibility of the Legislative Council having an unofficial majority, they made no provision for allowing that majority to nominate its own ministers. The Governor would remain the head of government and would retain complete freedom in the selection of the Council of Ministers (which provides the bulk of the membership of the Executive Council and is "the principal instrument of government").

appointed to the Uganda Legislative Council, and not until 1946 that the first two Africans were appointed to the Tanganyika Legislative Council. The dates for such appointments in Northern Rhodesia and Nyasaland were 1948 and 1949 respectively. Only the two Rhodesias, out of all the east and central African dependencies, yet (1959) have a legislative body with an unofficial elected majority. Uganda, with a council composed of 62 members (exclusive of the Governor and the Speaker), of whom 32 are on the government side, comes nearest to doing so. Tanganyika has been promised such a majority beginning in 1960.

As for the Bechuanaland Protectorate, it continues to get its laws in the form of proclamations issued by the British High Commissioner. The names of the highest governmental institutions—the Native Advisory Council, the European Advisory Council and the Joint Advisory Council—bespeak the strictly limited extent of their powers. (In late 1959 there was talk of turning the Joint Advisory Council into a Legislative Council "with powers to legislate for peace, order and good government . . . subject to the assent of the High Commissioner, who would also have power to ensure the passing of any law which he considered necessary.") The position of British Somaliland is somewhat better, for since 1957 it has had a Legislative Council which could initiate laws, and since 1959 the doors of this council have been open to Somalis. In the Protectorate of Zanzibar, however, legislation is still largely by decree of the British Resident, working in cooperation with the Arab sultan.

In the opinion of the British government it is likely to be a while before some of these territories are ready for legislative responsibilities comparable to those possessed by Ghana on the eve of its independence. But whether the time is long or short, whether the place is east, west or central Africa, it remains the avowed intention of the British government to hand over eventually all legislative powers to its dependencies. So far (1959) the handing-over has taken place only in Sudan (1956) and Ghana (1957). In British Somaliland it will take place in 1960 (on the understanding that if its electors so desire—as they have said they do—they can join with Somalia); in Nigeria, October 1960; in Sierra Leone, April 1961; in Tanganyika, December 1961. In Southern Rhodesia the process began much earlier (the country has had responsible government since 1923) but has not yet been consummated; all measures that could be regarded as differentiating between Africans and non-Africans continue to come under the jurisdiction of the British Secretary of State for Commonwealth Relations. In the related case of the Federation of Rhodesia and Nyasaland (which came into existence in 1953 as the result of fusing the two protectorates of Northern Rhodesia and Nyasaland with the colony of Southern Rhodesia), legislative powers are divided between the federal legislature (in Salisbury) and the three territorial legislatures (in Salisbury, Lusaka and Zomba), but subjects regarded as being of special concern to Africans, such as the system of land rights and the procedures of native (African) administration, remain entirely within the sphere of territorial legislation, which, in the case of Northern Rhodesia and Nyasaland, continues to remain within the jurisdiction of the Colonial Office. Judging from the present temper of British public opinion, it is unlikely that the Federation will be granted the status of a self-governing dominion until its electors have shown themselves willing to treat all civilized men in the Federation as equal, and to give all Federation men an equal opportunity to become civilized. Of such willingness there is much talk, but still rather little sign.

The French Community. Carrying their metropolitan preference with them wherever they have gone, the French have worked on the principle that the fewer people there are, within reason, to handle the machinery of government, the better it generally works. They have, accordingly, long been drawn to centralized systems of rule in which lawmaking is the prerogative of the authorities—whether civil or military—in Paris. This preference continued to find expression in some of the legislative arrangements made by the French for their tropical African territories down to the birth of the French

Community in September 1958. After 1946 all these territories sent deputies to the French National Assembly, senators to the Council of the Republic, and councilors to the new
Assembly of the French Union. By 1957 they were sending
33 African deputies (out of a total of 39 deputies sent from
these territories) to the National Assembly, 23 African senators to the Council of the Republic, and 37 African councilors
to the Assembly of the French Union. In the first postwar
decade French criminal law and trial on criminal charges by
ordinary French courts were extended to all the inhabitants
of French tropical Africa, instead of being restricted, as they
were before the war, to the few thousand Africans who had
become French citizens. On the other hand, "in conformity
with the principle of leadership entrusted to Metropolitan
France during this transitional period, 'legislative powers with
regard to penal law, civil liberties, and political and administrative organization in the Overseas Territories' [continued to
rest] with the French Parliament."[6]

As if to dramatize the constitutional unity of the overseas
and metropolitan provinces, the postwar, pre-de Gaulle governments of France made increasing use of African deputies
at the ministerial level. Lamine Gueye was Under Secretary
of State to the Presidency of the Council in the Blum cabinet
(1947); Fily Dabo Sissoko, deputy from the province of
French Sudan (French West Africa), was appointed Under
Secretary of State for Commerce and Industry in 1948; Joseph
Conombo, deputy from the province of Upper Volta (French
West Africa), was appointed Secretary of State for the Interior in 1954; Léopold-Sédar Senghor, deputy from Senegal,
was appointed Secretary of State for Scientific Research in
1955; Hammadoun Dicko, deputy from French Sudan, was
appointed Under Secretary of State for Industry and Commerce in 1956; and Dr. Félix Houphouet-Boigny, deputy
from the Ivory Coast, held ministerial rank in several succes-

[6] "Democracy in French Africa South of the Sahara: The Development of Local Assemblies," *African Affairs* (French Embassy, Service de Presse et d'Information, New York), February 1955, p. 4.

sive French governments, and continued to do so in the de Gaulle government.

Between 1946 and the demise of the Fourth Republic in 1958 French tropical Africa made very considerable progress in the direction of greater legislative, as opposed to merely administrative, autonomy. In 1946 territorial assemblies were established in the territories of French West Africa, French Equatorial Africa and in the two Trusteeship Territories of the French Cameroons and Togo. In Madagascar five provincial assemblies—one to each of the then five provinces—were set up. These assemblies were modeled on the General Councils which exist in the metropolitan *départements*. While they had some executive power (more especially in regard to budgetary matters), and had to be consulted by the administration on a wide range of subjects, they had next to no legislative scope; in most fields they could merely pass resolutions for submission to the Minister of Overseas Territories.

Under the *loi-cadre*[7] of June 23, 1956 the territorial assemblies could be given much the same powers in internal affairs as the legislatures in, say, pre-independence Ghana. Beginning in March 1957, when the provisions of the law went into effect, these assemblies were elected by universal adult suffrage on a single electoral college; and they had fully responsible executive councils, or cabinets, drawn from their members. Until the end of 1958, though, their powers were not such as to make them in any way independent of Paris, or of Paris' territorial representatives in Dakar, Brazzaville and elsewhere. The division of responsibility between the territorial and metropolitan governments on the eve of the Fifth Republic has been summarized by Hella Pick as follows:

> Before the *Loi-cadre* far greater powers resided at Dakar and Brazzaville than now, but even so the *gouvernements-généraux* in these two centers still retain enough power, especially in financial matters, external trade, control of the

[7] So called because the law provided a "framework" (*cadre*), or the general principles, to be followed in developing the governmental institutions of the overseas territories of France.

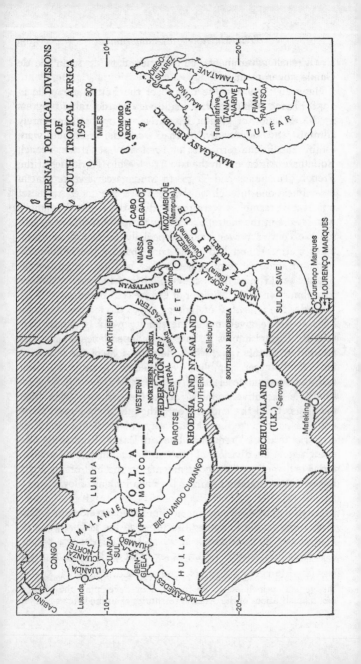

police, communications and other common services, etc., to make them an important factor in territorial development. These *gouvernements-généraux* are controlled, not by African elected members, but by French High Commissioners who act in a dual capacity, both as head of their respective groups and as representatives of the French Government . . . The functions of the *gouvernement-général* are exercised through the *Services d'Etat*, which now work in the territories side by side—sometimes at cross purposes—with the territorial public services; the latter are responsible not to the Governors, but to the elected Ministers. The *gouvernements-généraux* . . . and *Services d'Etat* are responsible to Paris. Their work is, however, debated by the *Grands Conseils* of [French West Africa and French Equatorial Africa], consisting of members drawn from the territorial assemblies . . . The *Grands Conseils* have no legislative powers.[8]

While all this undoubtedly made good the claim of the French to have started their tropical territories on the road to decentralization, the fact is that Paris itself continued to retain the power to legislate for French Africa on many issues; it also continued to supply and control the capital budgets of French West and French Equatorial Africa, and the individual territories; and to pay for the cost of the "state services."

It is also a fact that the French set themselves a very different objective from the British in promoting decentralization. For, whereas the British have everywhere been moving toward autonomy, the French have been moving toward interdependence, or as Dr. Houphouet-Boigny and his friends prefer to call it, the *communauté Franco-Africaine*. In the *loi-cadre* these men saw the constitutional frame of such a community. All that was needed, in their view, to fill in the frame was the granting of a still greater degree of autonomy to the individual territories, and, its corollary, the diminution of the

[8] "French Africa on the March," *Venture*, London, January 1958, p. 7.

powers—perhaps even disappearance—of the quasi-federal administrations at Dakar and Brazzaville. These autonomous territories would then federate with France. This, in fact, is what all of them, with the exception of Guinea, elected to do in the referendum of September 1958.

As a result of this referendum, the "Community" territories became "autonomous in the management of their own affairs." However, they continued to "[place] in common with France certain responsibilities such as defense and external affairs," and to preserve "special and reciprocal ties with the Republic, particularly in the financial, economic and political fields."[9] In 1959 two legislative bodies were set up, the Executive Council of the Community and the Court of Arbitration, to help the Community find its feet. The former of these, composed of the prime ministers of all the member states and the French ministers responsible for Community affairs, is "the supreme organ of the Community on the government and administrative level." The latter is charged with "settling any disputes that may arise between the member states of the Community." (A third—purely advisory—body, the Senate of the Community, was also established.)

The utility of these new instruments has yet (late 1959) to be demonstrated. Most "Community" decisions had, down to that time, been made by the President of the Republic—a fact which perhaps partly explains why the African leaders in these states now have such widely differing views about their future relationship with the Community. On the one hand there are those who believe with Houphouet-Boigny that the Community must transform itself into a "multiracial federation" with strong metropolitan ties if it is to survive. On the other hand there are those who look, with Léopold-Sédar Senghor, toward a "Commonwealth à la française," a federation of sovereign African states. Fortunately, the constitution of the French Community does not exclude the realization of either goal.

[9] Maurice de Murville, French Minister of Foreign Affairs, speaking in the General Assembly of the United Nations on September 30, 1959.

Portuguese territories. The Portuguese constitution, which since 1951 has applied to all the overseas provinces (e.g., Portuguese Guinea, Angola and Mozambique) as well as to Portugal proper, "assigns a much higher range of authority to the executive than to the legislative institutions of the government."[10] Unlike the British, French and Belgian constitutions, it provides no parliamentary arena where a man may habitually and freely say what he feels about his government's conduct of its African affairs; nor does it provide him with an opportunity of radically influencing his government's legislative program. As a member of the National Assembly in Lisbon, about all he can hope to do is to give his judgment on such matters as the authorization of development loans, and the respective roles of metropolitan and overseas governments in the granting of concessions.

Almost all real power lies with the Overseas Minister. He is charged with responsibility for all matters affecting the higher or general interests of the nation's overseas policy, or those common to more than one province. More specifically, this means that he is responsible for the whole financial administration of the overseas provinces; for determining the legality or desirability of all colonial measures proposed by his government; for authorizing all loans which are not repayable from current receipts; and for seeing that no legislative enactment can come into force, even though approved and promulgated by the government, until he has ordered its publication in the *Boletim Oficial* of the province or provinces concerned.

It is true that the Minister can draw upon the good offices of a large number of advisers and advisory bodies—such as the inspectors, whose business it is to keep in close touch with all that is going on in the overseas provinces, and the Overseas Council, which hears appeals brought before it from the overseas provinces and offers the Minister advice on such matters as he may lay before it. It is also true that the Overseas Council is the supreme administrative tribunal in matters affecting the overseas provinces. But the Minister is not

[10] Lord Hailey, *op. cit.*, p. 353.

bound to accept its decisions even when he is bound to consult the council, and in cases of urgency he is under no obligation to consult it. The legislative powers of the Governor-General of an overseas province are consequently small. All the same, in the exercise of them he is expected (though not compelled) to be guided by the judgment of the legislative council of the province and the government council. Among other things, he is expected to discuss his budgetary plans with the legislative council and secure its approval of them; and he must submit the budget itself to the vote of the government council. Even in regard to African affairs, which are his special responsibility, his powers are more executive than legislative. For the most part they have to do with controlling the manner in which the government's native policy is implemented, and in making sure that the laws concerning individual rights, freedom of labor, and native usages are enforced.

The powers of the government councils and legislative councils are even more restricted than those of the Governor-General. Indeed, the powers of the small, eight-member government councils are really no more than advisory. Those of the larger legislative councils, which have existed since 1955 (in Angola and Mozambique), are legislative only to the extent that the council members are able to influence the legislative intentions of the Governor-General. Thus, "in legislative matters [the Governor-General] is, in principle, guided by the vote of the Legislative Council, and if he disagrees with that vote, the disagreement must be immediately reported to the Minister, with whom the final decision will rest."[11]

Spanish territories. As in earlier times, the people of Spain continue to regard Fernando Po and Rio Muni (or continental Guinea) as if they were part of the motherland. Legislation is effected by decree from the metropolitan Dirección General de Marruecos y Colonias; the local budget is drawn up and approved by the metropolitan Cortes. There is no local institu-

[11] F. C. C. Egerton: *Angola in Perspective,* Routledge & Kegan Paul, London, 1957, p. 115.

tion possessing legislative power. The authority of the Governor of Fernando Po is almost wholly confined to the realm of administration; and that of the local *junta*, or council, is purely advisory.

Liberia. The governmental machinery of the "free, sovereign and independent republic" of Liberia bears a marked likeness to the American model of the mid-nineteenth century. (The Liberian constitution dates from 1847.) It is directed by an elected President, and an executive branch and a judiciary of the President's own choosing. It is cared for by two legislative bodies, the Senate and the House of Representatives. While, as in the United States, the President and the executive branch can do many things on their own initiative, they need the approval of the legislature for all legislation proposed by them. However, this approval is rarely withheld, because, unlike the United States, Liberia has been a one-party country for eighty years. To be a member of the legislature it is necessary to be a member of the True Whig Party; up to now it has been practically impossible for any opposition candidate to obtain more than a token support. And within the ruling party, power has, up to now, been very largely in the hands of the Americo-Liberians, who form less than 2 per cent of the population. In the past decade or so a few indigenous Liberians have had seats in the legislature and posts in the executive and judicial branches of government, but their ability to influence the course of legislation in Monrovia remains small—almost as small as the ability of the Monrovia government to influence the course of customary legislation in the hinterland.

Ethiopia. For centuries Ethiopia had the simplest legislative machinery of any territory in Africa, perhaps in the world. It could even be contended that it had none and needed none, since all the legislating was done by the Emperor. There are many who feel that, the existence of legislative machinery notwithstanding, the Emperor is still the law of the land—"the true embodiment of everything that's excellent."

While this feeling flatters the Emperor, it does not entirely please him. Over the quarter century and more of his rule, he has made several moves to get "[his] beloved people . . . to share in the responsibilities of the public affairs of [the Ethiopian] government."[12] In 1942 he gave his nation its first constitution and nominated parliament. In 1955 he gave it a new and more liberal constitution, which, among other things, provided for a Chamber of Deputies elected by universal suffrage, a Senate Chamber, an independent judiciary, and defined the powers of both Parliament and Emperor. In 1957 he gave the country the first free election in its history.

But the Emperor continues to guard the substance of power, even though his people now have some of the forms of it. He has the right of absolute veto over all legislation, the right to appoint and dismiss judges, cabinet ministers and senators, to legislate by decree when Parliament is not in session, and to dissolve it when it is.

Sudan. Until January 1, 1956 Sudan was administered jointly by the British and the Egyptians, the British doing rather more of the administering. In the months following its declaration of independence, the Republic operated under a transitional constitution based on the self-governing statute which brought it into being. This constitution provided for government by cabinet (headed by a Prime Minister elected by the House of Representatives from among its members) and by a five-man Council of State invested with the powers and prerogatives of chief of state. It was intended to last only until a new parliament, to be elected in 1958, could sit as a constituent assembly and approve a permanent constitution.

In preparation for this event, a National Constitutional Committee was appointed in September 1956. At that time the draft constitution was expected to provide for a unitary state with an elected chief of state, a bicameral parliament,

[12] H. M. Haile Selassie, in a speech to the newly elected legislators, November 1957.

a cabinet headed by a Prime Minister appointed by a chief of state and responsible to the lower house, and legislative machinery closely resembling that put into operation and left in operation by the British, for all of which there was apparently wide support. But, as has been the case in more than one country newly come to autonomy, the expected has not happened. Before the committee had completed its work, the army took over the government. On November 17, 1958 the Council of State and cabinet were dismissed; parliament and all political parties were declared dissolved; and the provisional constitution was suspended. At present (1959) the constitutional authority is invested in the "Supreme Council of the Armed Forces."

ADMINISTRATIVE

Central Government

Belgian territories. The running of the Belgian Congo during the past half century may be likened to the running of a large, efficient and profitable company, which in a very real sense it has been. The head offices of the company have been the Ministry for the Colonies in Brussels. The board chairman has been the King; its director, the Minister for the Colonies; its executive secretary, the Governor-General. Only executive appointments at the lowest level, that of "fourth-class agent," have been made by the Minister or Governor-General; all the rest have been made by royal decree (*arrêté royal*).

The company's chief "field office," or general secretariat, has been at Léopoldville. Its operations have been divided into a number of directorates, or *directions générales*. These covered the following fields: political and judicial affairs; native affairs, including education, labor and social security; finance, customs and excise; economic affairs, land and mines; agricultural and animal husbandry; public works and communications. The head of each directorate has been responsible to the Governor-General for carrying out the administration's policy in the field or fields concerned.

Because of the size of the territory, most of the government's operations were "provincialized." Thus, each of the six provinces of the Belgian Congo (Léopoldville, Kivu, Kasai, Equateur, Katanga and Orientale) was under the management of a Governor, with its own Provincial Secretariat, Provincial Commissioner (the Governor's deputy), district commissioners and other administrative officers, and its own technical and advisory staff. Besides running the secretariat the Governor, or his deputy, was expected to visit each dis-

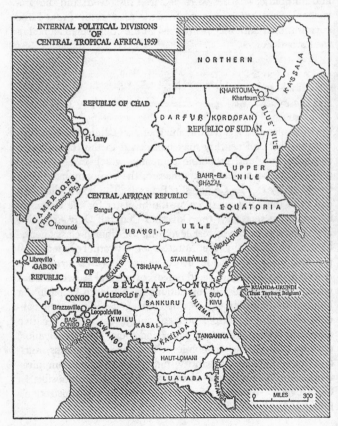

trict in his province at least once a year. Each commissioner of a district was expected to make a detailed inspection of his area at least twice a year and to supply the Governor with a detailed report on his observations. He was assisted in his advisory work by members of the provincial land, agriculture, public works and veterinary services. His administrative assistants were expected to spend almost two thirds of their time in their *territoires* keeping in close touch with native government authorities and guiding their development. The "fourth-class agents" were responsible for all census work and for such other activities (local public works, compulsory cultivation programs, etc.) for which no technical personnel was available.

Down to the end of 1958 very few Africans had held executive positions in either the general or provincial secretariats. Since 1921 there have been African *agents auxiliaires,* but these have been employed almost exclusively in teaching or in routine work in the post office, customs and medical departments of the government. However, the scale on which the establishments in the provinces were being organized in the late 1950s and the promulgation in 1959 of a "new unified statute for public servants [giving] the Africans access to all the grades of the administration" clearly indicated that the government wanted to see a progressive devolution of executive authority.

The judiciary has consisted of "European" and native courts. The former comprised (1) police courts, which were presided over by an administrator and were empowered to deal with those criminal offenses, committed by Africans, for which an imprisonment of not more than two months was held to be adequate (or was, in fact, the maximum) punishment; (2) district courts, which were presided over by an administrator and were empowered to deal with all criminal offenses committed by Africans; (3) prosecutor courts, which had unlimited civil jurisdiction and appellate criminal jurisdiction in regard to first-instance decisions of the district courts, and which also had jurisdiction for all criminal offenses committed by non-Africans; (4) courts of appeal (two in number), which were subject in civil matters to the overriding jurisdiction of the court of cassation in Brussels. The personnel of the courts of appeal, as of the prosecutor courts, was made up of professional lawyers.

The native courts served two purposes: they were intended to make good the gaps in the "European" system of justice, and to enable the African to perpetuate those aspects of his own juridical systems that were regarded as having intrinsic value and as forming, in Lord Hailey's words, "an appropriate bridge between African social life and that of Europe."[13] The criminal jurisdiction of these courts (which, like the "European" courts, were hierarchical in structure) was normally confined to offenses against customary law, whether committed in or out of the "customary" setting. Their civil jurisdiction extended to all matters not involving written law.

For almost all administrative purposes the Trust Territory of Ruanda-Urundi has been a seventh province of the Belgian Congo. Such differences as there are are mostly nominal. Thus, the chief executive is called Vice Governor-General instead of Governor. And instead of being divided into districts and territories, Ruanda-Urundi is divided into residencies and territories. In actual fact, the two residencies are the districts of Ruanda and Urundi. The judicial system is broadly similar to that of the Belgian Congo.

Commonwealth territories. Consistency is a word not often heard in British colonial circles. Looking at the British record in legislation, the cynic might be tempted to say that it is a word not often respected. But he would be wrong, for while the British may not rate consistency as high as, say, flexibility, they have never had anything against it. It is simply that they see no virtue in being consistent in the presence of inconsistent circumstances—as those they face in the field of colonial lawmaking and legislature making undoubtedly are. In their view no two African territories can be legislated for in

13 *Op. cit.*, p. 620.

the same way at the same time, or even in the same way at different times. But when it comes to applying the law and seeing that it is kept, the British have shown themselves more than a match for any of their consistent colonial colleagues. Inconsistency of administrative procedure, legal interpretation or personal dealings is apt quickly to acquire uglier names —inefficiency, complacency, lack of integrity, corruption—that can destroy a government's reputation as easily as a person's. In the day-to-day handling of their colonial business, therefore, the British have generally inclined to the view that what is good for Gambia is good also for Uganda and Nigeria.

In large part the credit for this view must go to the Colonial Office. Most of its members have never been to Gambia, Uganda or Nigeria, and approach the problem of governing colonial peoples without the prejudices they would be almost certain to derive from living among them. Being a branch of the British civil service, the Colonial Office is staffed by career men; and being for the most part able and dedicated, these men see themselves both as creditors to a proud colonial past and as debtors to a no less proud future, whether colonial or otherwise. Nothing breeds consistency of outlook and action like the sense of being caught up in history—unless it is being in a public service where promotion is wont to go to the "reliable blokes" and the "sound fellows"—the consistent ones, in short. This is not to say that the Colonial Office, as managing director of Britain's colonial holdings, has reduced the business of management to a simple formula, let alone a logical one, but only that it has been in the business long enough to have decided which of several types of colonial management gives the most satisfactory results, from its point of view.

As an example of the type of management organization developed over the years by the Colonial Office, the Protectorate of Uganda will probably serve as well as any British African territory. In Uganda the Colonial Office has been dealing all along with an essentially "African" territory; it has been able to follow its bent without running into the kinds of troubles that have dogged its steps (and those of the local

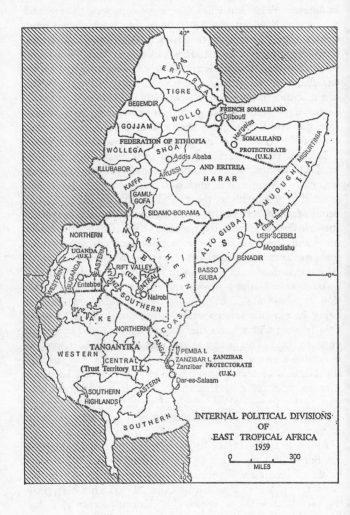

INTERNAL POLITICAL DIVISIONS
OF
EAST TROPICAL AFRICA
1959

0   300

MILES

Europeans) in such "settler" territories as Kenya and the Rhodesias. At the same time, it has had to deal with one of the most delicate management problems found anywhere in colonial Africa, namely, that arising from the presence, in the province of Buganda, of a people far more highly developed politically than most of their tribal neighbors and the inheritors of a centuries-old tradition of sovereignty.

The basic components of the central government system developed by the Colonial Office in Uganda are simple. They consist of a Governor's office, a secretariat, a number of ministries (11 in 1959), a somewhat larger number of departments, each with a directorate in either Entebbe (the administrative capital) or Kampala (the commercial capital) and most with "branch offices" and field staff at centrally located places in the provinces.

For administrative purposes the protectorate is divided into four provinces (Buganda, Eastern, Western and Northern) and 16 districts. With the exception of Buganda, each of the provinces is administered by a provincial commissioner and district commissioners who work under the supervision and control of the provincial commissioners. "They are the principal executive officers of Government in their areas. Without interfering in technical detail, they are generally responsible for the efficient conduct of public affairs, and provincial and district teams have been set up under their chairmanship to act as informal consultative bodies for the shaping of policies and schemes of local application. The teams comprise representatives of the technical departments and, at district level, representatives of the African local authorities."[14]

Justice is administered through the following instrumentalities: African courts, which operate at the local level for the most part; subordinate courts, of which there are 16, and the business of which is handled by resident magistrates; Her Majesty's High Court, which has full jurisdiction, civil and criminal, over all persons and matters in Uganda and which works both as a court of first instance and as an appellate

[14] *Uganda, 1958*, H.M.S.O., London, 1959, pp. 146–47.

court from subordinate courts, both protectorate and African; and Her Majesty's Court of Appeal for Eastern Africa, which hears civil and criminal appeals from the High Courts of Uganda and its east African neighbors. From these courts of appeal a further appeal lies, in certain cases, to the Judicial Committee of the Privy Council in Great Britain.

The law of the land is based on "the common law of England, the doctrines of equity, and all statutes of general application in force in England on 11th August, 1902," the date of the Uganda Order in Council that outlined the constitutional framework of the country. However, "in all cases 'to which natives are parties, every court shall be guided by native law so far as it is applicable and is not repugnant to justice and morality' or inconsistent with Protectorate laws." It is also laid down that "substantial justice" should always be done "without undue regard to technicalities of procedure."[15]

In most respects Buganda is administered rather differently from the other three provinces. Its indigenous government systems, both central and local, were found to be so greatly superior to the average that the British had little difficulty in adapting them to the requirements of modern government. In matters affecting the welfare and justice of its own Baganda people, the Kabaka's government performs the functions performed in the other provinces by the provincial and district commissioners and their staffs, and in recent years it has assumed responsibility for certain services previously rendered by the protectorate government. It is, in effect, a central government within a central government. The Resident, as the chief representative of the protectorate government is called, maintains a headquarters staff in Kampala, but his executive powers nowadays fall far short of those of the provincial commissioner.

There are, needless to say, differences between the way Uganda is run and the way Gambia and Nigeria are, to say

[15] *Ibid.*, p. 95. "Common law" is not the law in all British and ex-British territories. In Southern Rhodesia, for instance, the law is more Roman than English, largely because it was developed in the Union of South Africa, whose early settlers were Dutch.

nothing of the "settler" territories. No two territories have followed the same departmental or ministerial pattern (some have not yet introduced ministries); and no two territories make identical use of their personnel and funds or raise their budgets in identical ways. But nobody who has studied the annual reports of the territories administered by the Colonial Office can fail to have been struck by the family likenesses between them. And nobody who has been entertained by officials of the central government in any part of British colonial Africa can fail to have noticed that the houses they live in and the furniture with which they have been supplied are as alike as their in-trays. But perhaps these likenesses are the product not so much of consistency as of economy, and a desire to make the expatriate feel as much at home in Gambia where he may start his career as in Nigeria or Uganda where he may end it.

The French Community. Having set itself different goals from those of the British Colonial Office, the Ministry of Overseas France found it necessary to use different means of pursuing them. The "deconcentrating" (as Hubert Deschamps calls it in his working paper) of legislative power in the years immediately preceding the Fifth Republic did not lead to any major departure from the traditional managerial practice of always keeping the circumference tied to the center.

Under the Fourth Republic the chief executive in each of the "overseas territories" (French West Africa, French Equatorial Africa and Madagascar) had the rank of High Commissioner. In the "associated territory" (that is, U. N. Trust Territory) of the French Cameroons, he also had the rank of High Commissioner, and in Togo he had the rank of Commissioner. As governors-general, the high commissioners for French West Africa, French Equatorial Africa and Madagascar were the representatives of the French metropolitan government in their territories and the "depositories" of the power of the Republic, charged with the responsibility of coordinating all the public services in their territories and exercising the supervisory powers of the metropolitan government over

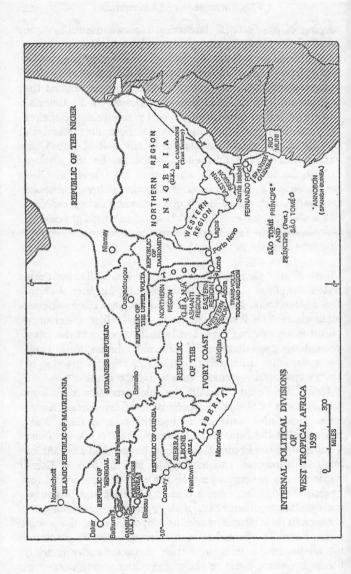

INTERNAL POLITICAL DIVISIONS
OF
WEST TROPICAL AFRICA
1959

0   300

MILES

such subordinate local bodies as municipalities. They were responsible for filling all posts with the exception of those reserved to metropolitan control; they also had the right to deal directly with the Ministry of Overseas France. They were responsible for the defense and the internal security of their territories and were in particular empowered to declare a "state of siege," a power which was exercisable in metropolitan France only by the Assembly or the President. Each High Commissioner was assisted by a Secretary-General, a Grand Council and various offices and departments—the whole of which was referred to as the Government-General. The Government-General of French West Africa was located at Dakar, that of French Equatorial Africa at Brazzaville, that of Madagascar at Tananarive.

The French Cameroons and Togo were administered—as they continued to be until their autonomy was secured in 1960—on a similar basis. However, being trust territories, they had rather more freedom of action than the other territories. Thus, under the trusteeship agreements, their consent was required if the metropolitan government wished to create fiscal monopolies or to establish public enterprises which might involve a departure from the regime of equal economic treatment of the nationals of all member states of the United Nations.

Each of the eight constituent territories of French West Africa (Mauritania, Senegal, French Sudan, French Guinea, Ivory Coast, Dahomey, Upper Volta and Niger), each of the four constituent territories of French Equatorial Africa (Gabon, Middle Congo, Ubangi-Shari and Chad), and each of the six provinces of Madagascar (Majunga, Tuléar, Diégo-Suarez, Tamatave, Tananarive and Fianarantsoa) had its own Governor (*chef de province* in the case of Madagascar), secretariat and public services. Each territory or province was divided into either *cercles* (as in French West Africa) or *régions* (as in French Equatorial Africa) under an administrator usually referred to as the *commandant de cercle* and corresponding roughly to the provincial commissioner of the British system. Each *cercle* or *région* was divided into either *subdivisions* (as in French West Africa) or *districts* (as in French Equatorial Africa and Madagascar). The *subdivisions* or *districts* were themselves divided into *cantons,* which, in turn, were divided into *quartiers.*

The executive powers of a French overseas Governor have always been small compared to those of a Governor-General, to whose authority he is at all times subject. In the last years (1956–1958) of the Fourth Republic the Governor became increasingly subject to a second authority, the ministers of the elected assembly in his territory; for under the *loi-cadre* of 1956 these ministers were given considerable executive as well as legislative responsibility. The Governor-General continued to work, not through the territorial public services, but through the federal *Services d'Etat,* which were responsible only to Paris.

Just as the administrative responsibilities of the Governor were subordinate to those of the Governor-General, so those of the territorial assembly (or, in the case of Madagascar, the provincial assembly) were subordinate to those of the Grand Council of the Government-General. This is seen in the funds allocated to the two governments. Thus, in some years prior to 1958 the budget of the French West African government was anything up to twice as big as the aggregate of the eight territorial budgets. It is also seen in the taxing authority of the two governments. Thus, the Grand Council decided the basis of assessment of all taxes (including those paid into the territorial budgets), while the territorial assembly decided only the actual rate at which the "territorial" taxes were to be levied. Then again, it was the Grand Council of the Government-General, rather than the territorial assembly, that did the disposing of all development money provided by such metropolitan agencies as FIDES (Fonds d'Investissement pour le Développement Economique et Social) and had the responsibility of seeing that all development so financed was satisfactorily carried out.

As of late 1959, few significant changes had been made in the administrative machinery of the now autonomous territories of the French Community. Most of the changes amounted to little more than changes of name and personnel. Even independent Guinea was seemingly content to jog along with the "model" it had inherited from the French—which was, perhaps, not surprising. After all, the making of new models, whether of automobiles or of administrations, takes money and skills, both of which are still scarce in Guinea; and there is always the possibility that the new model will be less serviceable than the old.

Portuguese territories. In line with its assumption that the overseas provinces are an integral part of Portugal, the Portuguese government has been trying for many years to put their administrative organization onto the same footing as that of the metropolis. To this end the Organic Law passed in 1955 decreed that, sometime in the future, the basic unit of the administration should become the metropolitan *concelho*, or council. But, as Egerton has noted, "the *concelho*, being an institution to which local self-government is committed, presupposes a certain degree of capacity for such self-government, and the existence, within a reasonable area, of a considerable population of fully qualified citizens."[16] While there are such areas in Portuguese Africa, notably the municipalities of Luanda and Lourenço Marques, they are small in size compared to those where there are no such qualified citizens. For the time being, therefore, the overseas provinces must continue to be administered largely on the basis of the *circunscrição*. This is a more or less arbitrarily chosen area— sometimes very large—which is incapable of self-government. Each *circunscrição*, or circumscription, is divided into *postos*, or posts, usually from two to six, each *posto* being in charge of a *chefe do posto*, or chief of post.

From the administration's standpoint, the council ranks with the circumscription. Both are headed by an *administrador*, who centers in himself wide powers in every line of European administration, and supervises native policy. He serves both as magistrate and manager, and is appointed by, and re-

16 *Op. cit.*, p. 116.

sponsible to, the Governor-General. In both cases his work is coordinated by an officer holding the rank of *intendente* (usually in the senior grade of *administrador*) and carried out with the aid of chiefs of posts.

Until 1955 the circumscriptions were grouped in districts and these, in turn, in provinces or subprovinces, of which Angola had five (six if the Luanda region, which was administered differently, is included) and Mozambique had four (five if the Lourenço Marques region, also administered differently, is included). The Organic Law, however, has grouped the councils and circumscriptions directly into districts corresponding to the old provinces or subprovinces, and where the interests of the Africans were believed to require it, into new intermediate-sized units known as *intendências*. Angola, for instance, now has 13 districts and four *intendências*. Each district is administered by a Governor, a Secretary-General, administrators and chiefs of posts, and has its own departmental services covering such matters as registration and census, native labor and immigration, and native justice.

The administration of the provincial, that is, the central, government is in charge of the Governor-General, assisted by a Secretary-General of his own nomination and, if he wishes to use them, two provincial secretaries. To these secretaries he may, by what is called a *portaria*, delegate such of his administrative responsibilities as he sees fit. The major government services organized departmentally at the provincial level are education, finance, justice, health, agriculture, industry, mines, veterinary affairs and survey.

With slight modifications, the civil and criminal codes of the Portuguese territories are those of metropolitan Portugal. All offenses (other than those committed by officials or alleged against them, which are dealt with by an Administrative Court) are brought before either the Ordinary Courts or the Special Courts which serve both as higher courts of first instance and courts of appeal. The supreme court of appeal—the High Court—is located in Lisbon.

Liberia. In so far as one man can be said to manage a still rather unmanageable country, President Tubman is that man. For he is popularly, and reliably, credited with knowing everything of consequence that goes on; with seeing everybody who seeks an audience; and with keeping a check on the doings of all his lieutenants. He is said to scrutinize all expense items in all departments exceeding $100, and even smaller amounts toward the end of the fiscal year, when his departmental heads are inclined to look around for ways of spending any credit balances they still have. Only the most routine actions may be taken by any member of the administration without prior consultation with him.

In the handling of the executive business of the country, the President is able to draw upon the resources of ten departments, the heads of which constitute, with him as chairman, the membership of the cabinet. The members are the Secretary of State, Secretary of the Treasury, Attorney General, Postmaster General, Secretary of National Defense, Secretary of the Interior, Secretary of Public Works and Utilities, Secretary for Agriculture and Commerce, Secretary of Public Instruction, and a Director General of the National Public Health Service. All office holders are nominated by the President and subject to confirmation by the Senate.

The judicial branch of the government is headed by a Supreme Court consisting of a Chief Justice and four associate justices. Subordinate courts are established, as necessary, by acts of the legislature. All judges are appointed by the President.

For purposes of administration the country is divided into two main regions, designated the County Jurisdiction and the Hinterland Jurisdiction. The County Jurisdiction applies only to a strip of coast about 40 miles deep. Each of the five counties and the one "territory" in this belt are administered by a superintendent. "In the County Jurisdiction the constitutional and statutory laws of the Republic apply, together with the common law of America and England and current administrative regulations in the form of Executive Orders and Administrative Circulars issued from time to time by the President and approved by the legislature. The county officials [including the superintendent] are appointed by the President with the 'advice and consent' of the Liberian Senate, and hold office during good behavior."[17]

The Hinterland Jurisdiction is divided into three administrative provinces, which, in turn, are divided into eight districts. As in British territories, the provinces are administered by provincial commissoners, the districts by district commissioners. But, unlike their British counterparts, the Liberian commissioners owe their appointments to the head of the state, and can be relieved of them at his will. As Earle Anderson has observed, the President does not believe in leaving the creation of "effective and honest government in the Provinces to the unsupervised authority of subordinates, not even to subordinates of cabinet rank. Instead, he has time and again made extensive trips into the interior, has heard complaints, tried cases, acquainted himself on the spot with local conditions, [and] dispensed summary justice where, as happened in some instances, he found District Commissioners or other officials abusing their power."[18]

Ethiopia. Separated though he is from the Liberian President by more than mileage, the Emperor of Ethiopia shares his predilection for "personalized" administration. He, too, is credited with knowing everything of consequence that goes on; with seeing everyone who comes and goes; with requiring that even routine administrative decisions be referred to him; and with being the one person in the entire country who can get things moving once they have been stalled, as they readily are, by the entangling tape of his ministries.

This is not to say that the Emperor is content to have it so. On the contrary, he has consistently shown himself to be the country's leading advocate of greater administrative efficiency. To this end he has brought in American agricultural and State Department experts, British police instructors,

[17] R. Earle Anderson, *Liberia: America's African Friend,* University of North Carolina Press, Chapel Hill, 1952, p. 213.
[18] *Ibid.,* p. 220.

French railway engineers, Canadian educationists, Swedish public health, mining, business and defense service specialists. But the national diversity of his hired help is generally taken to be an expression of the Emperor's intention to maintain the age-old dynastic tradition of not letting the left hand know what the right hand is doing, and of not letting either hand have too much free play. Certainly there is little or no evidence that the administrative reforms under way are headed in the direction of greater departmental and ministerial autonomy, let alone greater provincial autonomy. It is still laid down that all departments and ministers of the government shall carry out their duties under the direction of the Prime Minister. The Prime Minister's duties are still restricted pretty much to those of administrative aide-de-camp to the Emperor, being defined as responsibility for the good administration of the ministries, the harmonizing of their duties and the transmission of the Emperor's orders. And the good administration of the ministries still requires that their ministers spend much of their time at the Gibbi, the imperial palace, waiting to see the Emperor. Even in so small a matter as the residential qualifications of a candidate for parliamentary election, good administration requires that all disagreements arising therefrom be referred to the Emperor for settlement.

The twelve provincial governments are likewise kept on a tight administrative rein. The Governor-General of each province is supplied with a director and secretary appointed, as he himself is, by the Emperor. These directors are "capable and dedicated to the Emperor's policy of centralization and modernization. Their task is to watch quietly and check the governor-general, to supervise expenditure of funds, and to forward all accounts to the central Ministry of Finance."[19]

The law of the land is administered through district, provincial and high courts, the Supreme Imperial Court and a political court, "a purely Ethiopian institution for the trial of

[19] Simon D. Messing, "Changing Ethiopia," *Middle East Journal,* Vol. 9 (1955), No. 4, p. 426.

political offences."[20] Any person accused in one of the lower courts has the right to have his case transferred to the high court, provided he asks for this before any evidence has been taken in the court of first instance.

In recent years the legal code of the country has been reformed. Slavery and slave trading have been abolished, polygamy, except for Moslems, forbidden, and banditry outlawed. The administration of the law has been greatly humanized. Thieves no longer have their hands cut off. Executions are no longer public (but gallows may still be seen in some public places, their deterrent value being said to be substantial). Guarantors of loans can no longer be seized bodily by creditors; and the inhabitants of a region in which there is an unsolved crime can no longer be incarcerated en masse and for an undisclosed period. Even so, the judicial power of the Emperor remains considerable. Thus, every Ethiopian continues to have the right to appeal a grievance directly to the Emperor. However, in these times of transportation by Rolls-Royce, the appellant is less likely to exercise it by throwing himself in the royal path than by taking his complaint to the court of cassation provided for the purpose.

Sudan. In the seventy-odd years of the condominium, the British developed an administrative service (called the Sudan Political Service) which they came to look upon as the elite of all their overseas administrations. The Sudanese frequently had other words for it—expensive, exclusive, exploitative— but they were ready to concede that it was efficient, uncorrupted and seemingly incorruptible. Upon becoming independent in 1956 they paid the British the compliment of leaving its machinery intact. Their country, consequently, continues to be administered by provinces and districts. The provinces, of which there are nine, are each under a Governor, who is assisted by an advisory provincial council[21] and a

[20] *The Statesman's Year-Book, 1959*, Macmillan & Co., Ltd., London, 1959, p. 963.

[21] Except Khartoum Province, which is under a Commissioner and has no provincial council.

team of specialists in such fields as agriculture, health and co-operatives. The districts, of which there are approximately 70, are each under a District Commissioner or subordinate officer.

The administrative (as also the legislative) headquarters, with their associated ministries and departments, are located in Khartoum.

While the machinery is intact, the working of it has, under-standably, given some trouble. As the new rulers are finding, it is one thing to "Sudanize" an administration, but another thing to get the unenfranchised peoples of the south to accept rule by the Moslems of the north. "Southernization" would, it seems, be rather more to their liking.

Local Government

To govern any one of the large tropical African territories is to govern a multiplicity of groups occupying discrete parts of that territory. The basis of effective government in such territories is therefore effective local government.

From the first, the "partition" powers realized that if they were ever to win their wards over, they had to throw a wide-mesh net over the whole of the area for which they were responsible and make whatever use was possible of local talent. The first was necessary as much for the purpose of "showing the flag" as of keeping the peace. The second was necessary partly because it was physically and financially im-possible for them to do all the work themselves and partly because they could do little to upgrade the quality of African life until the Africans were competent to do a few things for themselves.

Belgian territories. The Belgians have never been a people to copy, and have seldom been greatly concerned about what their colonizing neighbors were doing. All the same, their work in local government bears resemblances to that of their British and French colleagues. It could hardly be otherwise. In the Congo basin they found themselves dealing with people cast in much the same ethnic mold as those in the surrounding territories and living in an environment that, like most other tropical African environments, put a premium on inertia. They also found, as did the British and French, that it is not only the Africans who suffer from inertia in such environments.

Like the British in west Africa, the Belgians were not long in coming to see that they could not govern without the active participation of the traditional rulers of the country. They had neither the manpower nor, at first, the financial means to do the job themselves. Their attempts in the early, unhappy days of the Congo Free State to rule by dividing had led only to disaffection and hatred, and would, had they been continued much longer, almost certainly have resulted in the paralysis of all government. In 1906, as a result of the findings of the Commission of Inquiry appointed in 1904, the first of a series of decrees dealing with local government matters was put into effect. What it did was to reinstate the institution of chieftainship as understood by the indigenous people and make it the instrument of indirect rule, which it has continued to be in most parts of the Belgian Congo and Ruanda-Urundi.

In the Belgian Congo proper, the role allotted to the chief was, to begin with, of very small consequence. In their solicitude not to overlook anybody with chiefly pretensions, the Belgians rounded up virtually all those who claimed to have a following, if only a hundred or so adults. By the end of World War I more than 6,000 *chefferies* had been recognized —enough to defeat the purpose they were intended to serve, namely, the re-establishment of tribal authority. To forestall this possibility, and to increase the effectiveness of African participation in local government, the Belgians began, in the early 1920s, to put the *chefferie* system on a more manageable footing. Where the *chefferies* were large and more or less coincident with ethnic boundaries, they were left undisturbed. Where they were very small, several of them were grouped together in a *secteur*.

Each administration unit, whether *chefferie* or *secteur*, had a council that operated along the lines of the French "council of notables." In the case of the *chefferie*, the council was composed of the traditional leaders, such as the heads of kinship groups; in the case of the *secteur*, it was composed of the chiefs of the constituent units, along with members of native tribunals and other persons nominated by the district officer (*commissaire de district*), who was himself a member of the council and entitled to preside over its meetings.

In Ruanda-Urundi, the Belgians found a ready-made—and well-made—framework of local government, one that lent itself to their designs. While also a land of chiefs and subordinate chiefs, Ruanda-Urundi was a land of two kingdoms, whose hereditary rulers (Bami; singular, Mwami) commanded the feudal-like fealty of their chiefs and followers.

Although the Belgians, like the Germans before them, clipped the wings of their absolutism, the Bami of Ruanda and Urundi continue to exercise wide authority over their nearly 5 million subjects, a circumstance that has enormously facilitated the work of the Belgian-appointed residents who act as advisers to the Bami and see that the wishes of the central government are carried out. They retain the right to receive tribute (now in cash); to appoint chiefs, subordinate chiefs and the members of their administrative staff; and, with the consent of their council (*conseil du pays*), to make rules and issue orders that have the force of law, including the right to raise labor levies for works in the public interest. At the same time, the central government has injected some of its own ideas into the administration by introducing an elected element into the *chefferies* and higher agencies, and seeing that among the men in such agencies there are those who have an understanding of the social and economic problems of the territory.

Useful as such agencies unquestionably were in helping the administration with "all the minor duties connected with justice, census, taxation, and so on,"[22] it may be contended that they were something of an anachronism in these fast-

[22] A. F. G. Marzorati, "The Political Organisation and the Evolution of African Society in the Belgian Congo," *African Affairs* (London), April 1954, p. 104.

moving times. Essentially, they were tribally oriented agencies. Yet since 1920 a yearly increasing percentage of Congolese Africans have been living outside tribal borders and tribal control. This *population extra-coutumière* had reached the figure of 8 per cent of the total even before World War II; by the late 1950s it had passed the 25 per cent mark, or more than one third of the adult male population. Essentially, too, they were African-run agencies. Yet the Belgians had great difficulty all along in finding Africans capable of working in them satisfactorily; and the Africans who were capable came increasingly to resent the restricted scope of the work assigned to them and the subordinate nature of their position. They were, moreover, essentially agencies for the maintenance of a colonial relationship between ruler and ruled—a relationship that has lost its savor for most Africans in the neighboring British and French territories and has been losing it for increasing numbers of Congolese Africans.

To deal with the needs of its growing "extra-customary" population, the Belgian government set up in 1931 a new local government agency known as the *centre extra-coutumier*. Each such center consisted of a council (up to 12 persons), composed of representatives of the local tribunal and other local residents in good standing with the community in general and the *commissaire de district* in particular. The "chief" of the council was chosen from the councilors and served for a limited period only. The council was responsible for the maintenance of order, the making of by-laws considered to be in the public interest, and the raising of taxes (on plots of land, shops, the making and sale of palm wine, etc.) for local purposes. But, as in the "customary" *secteurs* and *chef-feries,* the council had very little real power. It may have worn the mantle of authority, but the mantle was a straitjacket. Down to 1959 all councils were subject to the will of a "watch committee" (*comité protecteur*) nominated by the Governor-General and consisting largely, if not always wholly, of Europeans. This committee was responsible for seeing that the good name, moral and social, of the *centres* was upheld. All council meetings were attended by, and frequently presided over by, the (European) *agent territorial;* and all actions taken at such meetings had to meet with his approval.

Progress in setting up *centres extra-coutumiers* did not keep pace with the urbanization of the country and the growth in size of its extra-tribal population. At the end of 1952, after more than twenty years of effort, there were only 35 such centers; these served the needs of less than one fourth of the extra-tribal population. The Belgians readily admit that this scheme, too, fell short of their hopes—and for much the same reason, namely, their inability to find enough Africans to play the "indirect" roles allotted to them. As for the cause of this inability, opinion is divided. Some continue to put it down to African incapacity; others, more realistically, to the inadequacy of training facilities and incentives.

Frustrated in their attempts to make indirect rule work, the Belgians made an effort during the last years of their administration to use more direct methods at the local level. For the most part, this effort was concentrated on the large African settlements that have grown up in the suburbs of such cities as Léopoldville, Elisabethville and Stanleyville. And not without reason, for a *cité indigène* the size of Léopoldville's (now well past the quarter-million mark) is no place for administrative inefficiency, whether revealed by poor sanitation, inadequate housing, lawlessness or corruption. Each such city was put under the control of a European administrator, who was assisted in his work by an advisory council, a number of African aides, an African tribunal (the members of which were selected by the district officer from the tribal groups most strongly represented in the population), and by a number of "chiefs." Until 1957 all of these positions, along with those occupied by Europeans in the administration of their own cities, were filled by nomination. But in December of that year the government allowed the people of Léopoldville to have a say, for the first time, in the ordering of the affairs of the eleven districts (*communes*) into which the city, including both European and African sectors, had been divided for administrative convenience. In the election held during that month, qualified European and African adult males were able to vote for the European and African councilors of their choice. However, down to 1959 the elected councilors had no more real authority than the nominated ones. The government continued in possession of all its long-standing prerogatives, including the right to reject the advice of its councilors, and to choose whomever among them it pleased to be chief of the council, that is, mayor of the *commune*.

After the troubles of late 1958 and early 1959 the mood of the administration changed. As a Belgian government publication put it, "A certain type of paternalism officially came to an end in the Congo on January 13, 1959."[23] In its place was put "the policy of emancipation." At the local government level this policy was implemented by bills confirming "the right of public meeting and freedom of association" for all such political bodies as did not "trouble public order," by holding "elections by direct suffrage" and by doing away with "the last traces of racial discrimination." At the same time, the government made it clear that it intended to preserve much of what was deemed good in the existing order. As King Baudouin put it in his proclamation of January 13, 1959, "far from imposing completely European methods on these peoples, we intend to promote original adaptations in accordance with their fundamental character and the traditions which they hold so dear." Among other things this meant that the government intended to take care "that the future election borough systems shall be reconciled with the maintenance of local customs in all their sane, respectable aspects by means of original rules adapted to our times and to the birth of a rural democracy. Furthermore, [that] the chieftains will be represented in all public bodies . . . without relying on election by universal suffrage." And it was hoped that by "playing the new part assigned to them, they [would] render the Congo a service equivalent to that which they rendered in the past when they agreed to place their wholehearted confidence in

[23] *Belgian Congo Monthly Information Bulletin* (Belgian Congo and Ruanda-Urundi Information and Public Relations Office, Brussels), July-August 1959, p. 1.

and cooperate with the work of civilization undertaken by Belgium."[24]

The willingness of the chiefs to play their assigned part can scarcely be doubted. What is in doubt is their ability (in view of their inadequate preparation) to play it, and the readiness of the "new men"—so soon to have the run of the country—to let them do it.

Commonwealth territories. With their regard for tradition and their age-long habit of building a day at a time, it is hardly surprising that the British should seek to take such indigenous institutions as they could find and adapt them to their administrative needs. Wherever feasible the existing framework of native government was used. "For example, the Muhammadan emirates of Northern Nigeria already had a well-developed system of administration, taxation, and courts of law which could easily be modified to meet the new circumstances. Therefore they were recognized as local agents of the central government, their authority and duties were defined, and they were placed under the supervision of white officials (Residents) whose duty it was to see that the orders of the central government were carried out. . . . It meant that new policy was enforced in familiar ways, and that it was more readily accepted for that reason."[25]

Wherever feasible, too, the existing authorities were invited to play new roles and serve new ends. They were seldom regarded merely as useful agencies for helping with the minutiae of local administration. Almost from the start, they were valued as the basis on which a new order of society, better adapted to modern conditions than the old, could be built. Among the tasks commonly assigned to these authorities were the maintenance of local hospitals, dispensaries, schools, markets, roads and ferries, the improvement of water supplies, the provision of agricultural and veterinary services, and the establishment of local treasuries for the financing of such work

[24] Part of a statement made by M. van Hemelrijck, then Minister of the Belgian Congo, on June 24, 1959.
[25] Batten, *op. cit.*, Part II, pp. 116–17.

and the payment of the salaries of those charged with doing it. Frequently the native authorities had a big share in maintaining law and order. Some of the large Nigerian administrations were given complete jurisdiction over all the Africans in their area, except for treason, sedition, corruption of government servants, and similar offenses. Commonly, also, they were given jurisdiction over such matters as school attendance, the manufacture and consumption of liquor, the carrying of weapons, the safeguarding of water supplies, and the control of tsetse fly and erosion.

These native administrations varied in size and capacity from the great, well-organized emirates of northern Nigeria, with large budgets even in the early years of the colonial era, to small groups of a few thousand, hardly recognizing the existence of a single political authority at all and with an annual revenue of no more than a few hundred dollars.

But there were large parts of British Africa where it was not practicable to use the existing authorities. This was especially true of British East Africa, where tribal units are, with some notable exceptions, very small, and where even the rudiments of a "central" local authority might be absent.

Sometimes it was hard to find any person or group of persons who were unmistakably in authority over the rest. In other cases, where a suitable form of government existed, its authority had been weakened in the process of Partition, or the chiefs were not considered reliable enough to be used as agents of the central government. For such conditions a more direct form of government was established, and headmen or "warrant" chiefs were appointed. Many of them were selected from chiefly families, but as government headmen they were in no sense exercising traditional powers through native institutions. They were chosen purely and simply as suitable individuals to be entrusted with limited powers as government agents . . .[26]

[26] *Ibid.*, p. 117.

Originally the duties of the warrant chiefs were to keep order, arrest criminals and repair roads. Later they were given additional responsibilities, such as the provision and maintenance of clean water supplies, the control of liquor and infectious disease, and the collection of local taxes. With the passage of time they came also to have wide judicial powers, and since the middle 1920s they have been assisted in their work by local councils, the members of which were, to a large extent, also government-nominated, and served under the chairmanship of the central government's representative, the district officer. These councils also had treasuries, but unlike the native administrations, received no share of the territorial poll tax, and so had to levy their own small local rates. To carry out the work for which they voted funds, they had to depend almost entirely on departments of the central government. Nevertheless, many of them can point to a record of achievement in the agricultural, veterinary and forestry services, education and public health and welfare that compares favorably with that of the best native administrations. Like the latter, too, the local (native) councils have frequently been able to get the ear of the central government on matters of general concern—though for this most of the credit should probably go to the district officer for allowing free expression of opinion.

Valuable as both of these institutions have been as instruments of local government and as training grounds for administrators, they have drawn the fire of increasingly large numbers of people, both African and European.

The native administration system, many African nationalists seem to feel, was an imperialistic device for keeping subject peoples docile. Others have argued, to use Ntieyong U. Akpan's words, that the system "could not possibly be for the progress of the territories concerned, since it merely favoured, sheltered and strengthened illiterate, conservative, unprogressive and sometimes autocratic chiefs at the expense of younger educated elements who, admitted into the Native Administration Councils, would be better able to understand and follow what was going on in the councils as well as be able to take bold initiative in matters with which the councils might be concerned."[27] Others, including Dr. Nnamdi Azikiwe of Nigeria, have seen the system as a rather clever piece of theater, in which the British officers of the central government were given the role of producer-director and the African players were taught to "think British" while continuing to "act African." Still others feel that it taught them to do no thinking at all. They believe that the primary aim of "indirect rule" was to leave the African alone to his own separate and unequal devices; that it led to a quasi-*apartheid* policy where Europeans "lived apart from the natives, had separate clubs, separate hospitals, in some places even separate churches, to which no African, no matter what his social standing, could be admitted . . . , where all senior posts in the civil or other services were clearly designated *European posts*."[28]

In some quarters, rule by warrant chief and nominated council came to be disliked no less strongly. The warrant chiefs "owed their position not to tradition . . . but to an external authority. . . . The new 'chiefs' were therefore not only free from traditional inhibitions but adequately strengthened and protected and could do anything that suited them, no matter how offensive and objectionable it was to custom and tradition, provided it did not offend, or come to the notice of, the authority to whom they owed their positions."[29]

[27] *Epitaph to Indirect Rule: A Discourse on Local Government in Africa*, Cassell & Co., Ltd., London, 1956, p. 28.

[28] *Ibid.*, p. 29. In a written comment, J. G. Liebenow makes the further point that "apart from the fact that it was sometimes misapplied (i.e., the wrong individuals were chosen to be rulers, or a portion of the indigenous system—the chieftainship—was mistaken for the whole), indirect rule was often built upon sand. By superimposing a layer of European officiality, it ignored the fact that the chiefs had the power they had in the pre-European period because there was no one (other than ancestors) who could be regarded as superior to them in their respective areas. Under colonial rule, not only administrators but also missionaries, settlers, merchants and other non-Africans could reside in a chief's area, but not be subject to his jurisdiction."

[29] *Ibid.*, p. 35.

Frequently the things that suited these chiefs did not suit their people, with results (such as the Women's Riots of 1929 in the Eastern Region of Nigeria) that were saddening and discreditable to all concerned.

However, even its most vehement critics concede that the system of indirect rule had its points, and that, in Lord Hailey's words, it has "unquestionably made a great contribution to the maintenance of order and the administration of justice; [that] in some of the more progressive areas it has made a useful contribution to the provision of local services; [that] to numerous communities it has provided an education, not easy to secure by other means, in the practice of managing their own affairs . . . [and that to] this extent it has materially assisted in preparing them to take part in the working of the new Local Government institutions indicated by the changed political outlook at the present day."[30]

But it was only natural that as more and more "commoners" became educated in the British democratic tradition, there should be a rising demand for a more democratically based local government system. It was no less natural, of course, that the intrusion of commoners into a field theretofore confined to born rulers or those who had ruling powers thrust upon them, should be resented by both classes. The change from either a hereditary or a nominated system to one more representative of the common people, largely if not wholly elected, has been going on for many years. Everywhere slow at first, the process has picked up speed since the end of World War II. This is especially true of west Africa, in parts of which the change is virtually complete.

Ghana may be taken as an example. Here the native authority system was slow in coming, largely because the British took the view that they were dealing with states, such as Ashanti, to which they were bound to allow a high degree of discretion in the handling of domestic matters. And it was fast in going, because it was incompatible with the stand

[30] *Op. cit.*, p. 541.

taken by the Convention People's Party, which was as opposed to sharing political power with the traditional authorities as it was to being subservient to the Colonial Office. It was not introduced into the territory until the 1930s, and by 1950 it was already being written off as obsolescent. In its place the government decided, under an ordinance of 1951, to set up a system of local government bodies, and to confine the chiefs and other traditional authorities to the exercise of their customary, tribal functions. In 1952, local government elections—the first of their kind in the history of the territory —were held for the purpose of bringing into being the 280 new councils which, it was estimated, would be necessary to make the scheme workable. Of these, 229 were designated as local, 14 as urban and 37 as district councils. All but 20 of the 280 had been set up before the end of 1954.

While the new system represented a major step toward the democratization of local government, it was still some way from being as democratic as its British prototype. One third of the membership was reserved for the nominees of state or "chiefly" bodies; and some of the normally elected remainder might in fact be nominated members, serving special interests such as mining. Further, it was agreed that every local authority should have a chief as its president, and that in the case of the Northern Region, the position should carry more than mere ceremonial significance. In general the functions and powers of these councils are not very different from those of their British counterparts, or those exercised by the more advanced native administrations. Whether they will work as well as their prototypes and predecessors has still to be seen. If history is any guide, nominated or hereditary administrators and elected administrators make poor bedfellows; each side is inclined to believe it would do better if it had the bed to itself. The local administrators of Ghana are further handicapped by their inexperience in the art of accommodation. As Lord Hailey has pointed out, "the Ministers who now regulate [the course of the new institutions] have themselves little direct experience of the working of such institutions, and . . . they can hope for little aid from a population which has itself had no knowledge of them."[31]

The British have been concerned also with bringing the native judiciary into line with the changing facts of African life. In pre-partition times there was seldom a clear divide between the judicial and the executive responsibilities of a chief and his council of elders. In many tribal areas there was no divide at all, the members of the local court being closely associated with the executive authority and responsible to it. Throughout British West Africa, for instance, there was no codified law, except in the predominantly Moslem communities, and there was always the possibility that judgments handed down by the courts would be overruled by the executive authority. Though objectionable in theory, these arrangements worked well enough at a time when disputes were confined to domestic problems devoid of any great complexity. It was not until African societies ceased to be traditional and became "acculturated"—infected with European social, economic and political ideas—that the intermingling of the executive and judicial functions of the native councils became unacceptable. Notwithstanding, the separation of the two has been slow to come about, even in the go-ahead territories of British West Africa, largely because of the difficulty of finding suitable replacements for the chiefs, and the still strong attraction to customary law and justice felt by the ordinary African.

It is in the towns, as a general rule, that the process of separation has gone furthest. For the towns are not only multitribal in their ethnic composition, they are also, to use the Belgian word, "extra-customary." The Africans who live there do not—cannot—live under tribal conditions, let alone under tribal control. Then, too, the towns are, with very few exceptions, European in origin, function, management and way of living, including way of dealing with offenders. If they are to serve the ramifying needs of their peoples and the territories about them, the towns can scarcely avoid re-

[31] *Ibid.*, p. 529.

taining their European complexion, any more than they can avoid conceding to the African (upon whom they are coming to rely increasingly for their manpower needs) the right of resort to his own courts, at least in those areas of his customary life which are held to be not offensive or hurtful to public order.

To try to meet the judicial needs of its urbanized Africans, the British have used different methods. In Kenya they have established, at Nairobi, Mombasa and other large centers, mixed courts, the membership of which consists largely of Africans selected by the British from lists prepared by the tribal associations of the towns in question. In some other territories, Tanganyika for instance, the British have favored the establishment of courts presided over by African magistrates. Such courts are expected to enforce local rules and by-laws, try tax cases, and deal with most civil and minor criminal cases. Out of them is gradually evolving a type of "natural" law that covers the more common needs of men of different tribal backgrounds. The judicial needs of the multi-tribal population of the Northern Rhodesian Copperbelt towns have been met in much this way since the late 1930s. Here the membership of the mixed urban (native) courts consists largely of representatives of the native authorities in the areas which contribute the bulk of the mine labor supply. It is generally agreed that these courts have been of great value both in codifying customary law and in adapting it to the very different conditions of the mining compound and town.

But because most of the towns are depositories of British institutions, rights and ideas, it follows that many of the offenses committed by the urbanized African are offenses against British-made laws relating to property, person, taxes, licenses and so on. Indeed, during most of his waking hours and almost all of his working hours, the urbanized African lives in a British judicial setting.

It is hardly surprising, therefore, that British ideas of law and order are permeating more and more the thinking of the African and influencing the reforms that are taking place in his customary law. In parts of Commonwealth West Africa, for instance,

> Side by side with the existence of traditional courts there has been created a parallel organization, based on the formalities of the English legal system. This system was originally introduced to deal with cases of major importance, but has now been extended to deal with a wide range of legal problems which result from the complexities of a modern society.
>
> The English system has therefore come to exercise a considerable influence on the community as a whole, who nevertheless still rely upon the traditional judiciary for the solution of many of their problems. Where the systems are at variance on common problems, difficulty may well arise. The final outcome has yet to be resolved. There are, however, indications that a process of integration will, at least for the immediate future, meet this situation.[32]

The French Community. The approach of the French to the problem of local government has been consistently different from that of the British. While the British administrator has, almost at all times, been willing to build on African foundations, the French administrator has always had difficulty, as Lord Hailey says, in conceiving "of any better destiny for the African people than that they should absorb the culture and adopt the institutions of France, which had for him not a comparative but a positive value."[33] He has, accordingly, always tended to show a preference for those methods of local rule which seemed most likely to hasten the fulfillment of this "destiny."

Since French government was, and still is, predicated on strength at the center, it was only natural that those trained in its ways should have sought to follow them in Africa. With one or two exceptions, they followed them pretty much to

[32] I. D. Cameron and B. K. Cooper, *The West African Councillor,* Oxford University Press, London, 1954, p. 27.
[33] *Op. cit.,* p. 543.

the letter. This can be seen in the role allotted by the French to the institution of chieftainship. At best, the chief has been an understudy. When he spoke or acted, he did so in the name of the *commandant de cercle* and with his foreknowledge and approval. Commonly, he was little more than a bit player, who did the unwanted village chores. Robert Delavignette, formerly High Commissioner for the French Cameroons, has described the kind of chores performed, all too often, by the *canton* chief of his territory in the 1940s: "We demand from him too many trivial tasks and we set too much store by the way in which he performs them. Instead of entrusting to him certain important tasks—a tax, a main road, a new crop—and judging his achievement on the spot in our tours, we make his authority a travesty by using him as an intermediary in small affairs—provisioning a camp, receiving a vaccinator, collecting witnesses for a petty court case, providing a supply of chickens."[34] When the chief wasn't doing this sort of thing, he was frequently required to perform duties scarcely less trivial, if more prestigious. For example, he would attend receptions on national holidays, visit exhibitions in tribal costume, and serve as gentleman-in-waiting to the local French authorities.

Over the years, many administrators sought to exploit more fully the potential of chieftainship. Delavignette argued that what was needed was "not to re-establish [the chiefs], but to establish them. Not to re-establish them in a social structure that is dying, but to establish them in a modern Africa that is being born." When he was Governor-General of French Equatorial Africa, Félix Eboué never tired of insisting that the success of the French *mission civilisatrice* was bound up with the ability of its agents to make more effective use of African institutions in general, and of chieftainship in particular.

Cogent as their arguments would seem to be, these men were singularly unable to move the policy makers in Paris. The policy makers showed a constant reluctance to do any-

[34] *Freedom and Authority in French West Africa*, Oxford University Press, London, 1950, p. 81.

thing that might seem to infringe upon the executive supremacy of the administration and its officers. To those who criticized it for its stand, the administration was usually able to point out that neither the chiefs nor their partisans among educated Africans appeared to be greatly interested in being anything but consultants to the administration and guardians of their tribal custom. From 1953 onward their legal status was that of "auxiliaries of the administration," scarcely distinguishable, at many points, from that of civil servants.

Even if the chiefs and their partisans had been greatly interested in playing a larger, more executive role, it is highly doubtful whether they would have been able to do so. The trend over the past generation has been toward the democratizing of local government, and the supression of indigenous systems, where they existed, by systems of French parentage. Thus, the "councils of notables" (*conseils de notables*) which came into existence in many areas of French Africa as early as 1919, and which for long consisted, as their name suggests, of the local aristocracy, had generally lost favor with both people and government in the last years of the Fourth Republic. In Togo, for instance, the "councils of notables" were replaced by "circumscription councils" (*conseils de circonscription*) by a local decree of 1951. This decree provided that these councils, elected indirectly by universal suffrage, could acquire legal status as soon as the economic development of the region enabled them to provide sufficient resources for their own budgets. There are well over 100 of these councils in Togo, covering the *cercles* or *régions* not served by the *communes mixtes*. The same system was extended to the more out-of-the-way parts of French West and French Equatorial Africa before they gained their autonomy.

In the more economically and socially advanced parts of the French Community, local government has been undergoing a remodeling process for more than a generation. The main instruments used for the purpose have been the *commune de plein exercice,* the *commune de moyen exercice* and the *commune rurale*. Each operates on a township (*commune*) basis, and each represents an attempt to accommodate the demands of government to the economic, social and political circumstances of those to be governed.

The *commune de plein exercice* is modeled on the metropolitan municipal commune: it is run by a democratically elected body, headed by a democratically elected mayor, who is its chief executive. Even in the large "European" cities, the mayor is frequently an African, and the majority of the councilors are also African. Although this type of *commune* has existed for nearly a hundred years (the first two were established in Senegal, at St. Louis and Gorée, in the 1870s), conditions favorable to its spread were hard to create until quite recent years. Even as late as August 1954 there were only 44 municipalities in the whole of French sub-Saharan Africa to which the French National Assembly was willing to grant the "full exercise" of municipal powers.

The *commune de moyen exercice,* or *commune mixte,* may be run by either an elected or a nominated council, headed by an officially nominated mayor. It may be set up in any locality, rural or urban, which, on the recommendation of the chief executive of the territory and by vote of the territorial assembly, is judged to be sufficiently advanced to provide itself with adequate revenues. Such *communes* may be advanced to the rank of *communes de plein exercice* by the same procedure after a period of five years.

The *commune rurale,* the newest and most experimental of the three, represents an attempt to cultivate French democracy at the bush-roots of African society. The working of it is seen to advantage in the French Cameroons, where it is helping to infuse new life into a countryside that was in danger of social atrophy. The councils are elected by universal suffrage and the areas served by them are much larger than those which make up the African's customary world.

Each type of *commune* derives its revenues from licenses and fees, particularly market fees; and each is empowered to levy a local rate. Each type also receives from the territorial government a part of all direct taxes levied in the area.

The system of local government in the Malagasy Republic differs somewhat from that in other parts of the French Community. Here the French succeeded in modernizing an indigenous institution, known as the *fokonolona*. This community-based rural system has since 1944 been extended to the whole island. It provides for a large measure of local autonomy in the raising and disbursing of funds, and in all matters relating to the community's welfare. The system also forms the base of the central government pyramid. Those who serve the *fokonolona* well may graduate to higher service in the island's district or regional councils.

The belief that what is good for Frenchmen should be good for Africans in process of being gallicized has also found abundant expression in the realm of justice. As far back as 1848, all Africans living in Gorée and St. Louis, the capital of Senegal, were accorded the rights and privileges of the Code Napoléon. Down the years these rights have been extended to more and more Africans. Until 1946, however, not many Africans found themselves close enough to the machinery of French justice to be able to use it when needed, with the result that *justice indigène*, cleansed of some of its more gruesome excesses, continued in force over most of the French domain. Nor did the 1946 constitution change the position overnight. It could decree that French justice in penal matters was immediately applicable to all of the millions of Africans it enfranchised, but it could not conjure into being the "perfected, but oh! so complicated apparatus of republican justice"[35] needed to give effect to the decree. Where the apparatus did exist, few courts, lawyers and judges knew enough about French law to be able to work it. As William Moreland notes in his working paper, "even most of the *administrateurs* had had no instruction or training in European French law . . . , [yet] the majority of the provincial administrators suddenly found themselves French judges and their offices courtrooms for the dispensing of French penal law." They also found themselves having to rustle up additional jail space, "as incarceration took the place of more colorful forms of punishment."

---

[35] From *Côte d'Ivoire* (Abidjan), January 15, 1954.

While the administrators and their aides rose to the occasion and succeeded, in a remarkably short space of time, in retooling the machinery of justice, the results of the operation were, as Moreland points out, frequently somewhat different from those intended. In many parts of French Africa, as elsewhere, customary law provided that theft, committed under certain conditions, was punishable by amputation: one hand for a first offense, the other hand for a second offense, and a leg or the head for a third offense. Repetitive theft was uncommon. "After April 30, 1946, the penalty for theft could only be some days in prison. Stealing became very popular. Many committed theft merely for the purpose of being able to spend a few days in prison, food and lodging free, out of touch with their hungry relations and relieved of the necessity to work."

The inapplicability of trying to adhere to the letter of the Napoleonic Code quickly became apparent; and, as quickly, steps were taken, at the local level at least, to make it inapplicable. Thus it is true to say that, the constitution of 1946 notwithstanding, the form of justice practiced in French Africa south of the Sahara remained "a careful blend of the French code, indigenous custom and, where it applies, Koranic law." In the civil realm it is probably no less true to say that of the three, the French code was the least important. For, although the African had the right to be judged by French law before the local administrator or a justice of the peace in matters relating to marriage and divorce, tribal property rights and so on, he was more than likely to prefer to be judged by his Moslem or pagan peers. It is possible that he always will.

Portuguese territories. The approach of the Portuguese to both local and central government is based on a very simple conviction, namely, that the end of all such government is assimilation. To the Portuguese, there are, accordingly, only two kinds of Africans: the man who is assimilated and the man who is not. (That cultural assimilation is often a matter of degree has been only lately, and not yet widely, recognized.) The first is called a Portuguese citizen; the second, a Portuguese native. The first is treated as a Portuguese and subject to the same rights, responsibilities and laws as an immigrant from Portugal. The second is treated somewhat as a minor who is allowed to follow his fancy so long as it is compatible with adult concepts of humanity and public order, but who is quickly and painfully recalled from following it once it ceases to please his seniors and betters. Since most of the indigenous inhabitants of the Portuguese overseas provinces still rank as minors, it follows that most of them still come under the jurisdiction of the native authorities.

For administrative purposes, each *concelho* and *circunscrição* is divided into *áreas* administered by a *chefe do posto*, roughly equivalent to the British district officer or French *commandant de cercle*. The *áreas* are divided into *regedorias*, each of which is normally headed by a hereditary chief (*regedor*) recognized as such by the administration.

The key men at the local level are the *chefe do posto* and the *regedor*. The duties of the *chefe do posto* are imposing. Afonso H. I. F. de Freitas, for some years the administrator of the Lourenço Marques *concelho*, has enumerated[36] no fewer than 20, among them the following:

To police his area and see that it is kept in a state of tranquillity.

To maintain the prohibition on the manufacture of alcoholic liquors in his area.

To "fiscalize" the use of guns (for hunting game).

To make frequent inspections of his whole area "to find out the population's needs and everything regarding their welfare [and propose] what may seem convenient in order to improve [their] moral, intellectual and material conditions."

[36] "Native Administration in Angola and Mozambique" in *Record of Proceedings of the Fourth Annual Conference,* held at Umtali, September 20–23, 1955, of the Institute of Administrators of Non-European Affairs (South Africa), pp. 68–69.

To transmit to the *regedors* and their subordinates "all orders they must accomplish . . . giving them all necessary explanations," and see that they are executed.

To encourage the people of his district to farm their land more productively and grow the kind of crops deemed most advisable.

To register all native weddings, births and deaths.

And, by no means least, to see that the poll tax is collected according to the law.

The responsibilities of the *regedors* and their subordinates (who commonly work in council) are no less clearly defined. They are also comprehensive, as the following sample (likewise taken from de Freitas) indicates:

To furnish men for defense or police when legitimately required; to disclose to the district officer, or the administrator, the presence of criminals or suspects and, where possible, to arrest them.

To oppose the practice of witchcraft.

To see that every native in his area is accounted for, and carries the *caderneta*, or identity book, required of him.

To encourage his people to learn Portuguese, to dress decently and cultivate their land as advised by the administration.

Among the many things they are not allowed to do are the following: to collect taxes for their own benefit; to levy fines; to act in the name of the administration without express authority; to leave the area of their circumscription without permission from the administration; or to refuse to carry out the orders of their Portuguese superiors. In short, their job is "to obey the Portuguese administrative authorities, promptly and faithfully and see that the Natives under their jurisdiction also obey them."

It is clear from this that the administration attaches much importance to the role of the native leaders in maintaining order and tranquillity in their areas. Frequently their work to this end is allowed to go far beyond the legal limits. Thus, officially there are no native courts, and officially the Portuguese administration takes no cognizance of customary law in dealing with offenders. However, in cases concerning Africans only, the shrewd *chefe do posto* (and to carry out the kinds of duties listed above the *chefe* has to be shrewd!) will almost always consult with the local *regedor* and his councilors before handing down judgment. Sometimes he does not even consult them, preferring to let them settle the issue in their own customary way. According to Cecil Scott, one of the contributors to this study, "there is no doubt that a great number of disputes involving criminal offenses never come before the *chefe do posto* but are settled in accordance with traditional usage by the unofficial courts of the village elders and tribal chiefs, as they have operated for generations past."

Liberia. During the first hundred years or so of its existence as an independent republic, Liberia was too much concerned about surviving to worry greatly about governing. For all practical purposes, the authority of the Americo-Liberians was confined to a narrow coastal strip. Such official relationships as these people had with the "natives" (as they called them) were, for the most part, nominal in amount, colonial in kind, and racist in mood. If they were productive of anything, it was a strong preference in each of the two groups for its own way of life. Accordingly, the government of the great bulk of the territory remained in the hands of the tribal peoples.

Although some things have changed during the past generation, the indigenous system of government has not been greatly changed. True, the Monrovia government has divided the whole territory into districts, each of which is administered by a presidentially appointed commissioner. But it has had some difficulty in finding Americo-Liberians who were at once competent to do the work of a district officer and willing to live in the roadless bush out of reach of the gaiety and distractions of the capital—and to do it for the benefit of those they ruled rather than for their own. It has also had some difficulty in commending the idea of government by edict, and by "aliens," to people unaccustomed to either. The central government's difficulties have been compounded by the ethnic and linguistic complexity of almost all of the districts. Frequently it has found that intertribal suspicion in a district is equaled only by the suspicion with which each of the tribal groups views the activities of its commissioner and his staff. The insistence of the Americo-Liberians on using English as their *lingua franca* in dealing with the indigenous people has done nothing to increase their favor, or further their ends.

It is largely for such reasons that, over most of the Liberian countryside, the pattern of government remains pretty close to the traditional design—closer to it perhaps than in any other "colonial" area of tropical Africa. Government in the tribal areas—the Hinterland Jurisdiction—is by clan and paramount chiefs under the direct supervision of district and provincial commissioners. In theory these chiefs owe their authority to the Monrovia government; but the real basis of it is usually their status, derived either by inheritance or by election, in the tribal group. Any departure from the established tribal customs in the selection of chiefs is apt to cause trouble, as the government has discovered in various instances.

The responsibilities of the chiefs, their courts and their councils are considerable. In addition to covering the traditional field of administration of customary law (or such parts of it as are acceptable to the Monrovia government), they include the provision of hospitality and entertainment for visiting representatives of the Monrovia government, the keeping in repair of roads and trails, the modernizing of huts and villages, the repair and maintenance of markets, the collection of taxes, and the requisitioning of labor for government work.

Ethiopia. In no tropical African country is local government of so little consequence as in Ethiopia. Far-reaching as many of the "Restoration" period changes in the government have been, they have scarcely reached—or if reached, scarcely affected—the lot of the ordinary countryman. Some would argue that they have scarcely affected the lot of the ordinary town dweller, even in a place like Addis Ababa. For the long tradition of centralized government shows few signs of being ended. What an educated Ethiopian recently said to Leo Silberman is also, it would appear, the sentiment of the illiterate Coptic priest in Debra Damo and the lettered policeman in Diredawa: "In the past there has been one man who ruled this country, and that was His Majesty. For my own part I should be appalled if in the future things were arranged differently."[37]

It is not difficult to see why such an arrangement should appeal to an Ethiopian. As practiced down the centuries, it has given him certain rights which, while they may seldom have had great utility, have been the source of great satisfaction, as, for instance, the right to carry a grievance directly to the Emperor. It has also relieved him of the often painful and always irksome duty of making up his own mind on important matters about which he knew nothing anyway, and of personal responsibility for the evils of his time. Sometimes it has saved him from being the plaything of greater tyrannies —those that arise when there is no central authority.

Nor is it difficult to see why such an arrangement should appeal to the Emperor. It enables him to know what is going on everywhere and what his people are thinking. It befits his status as "King of Kings," "Conquering Lion of the Tribe of Judah," "The Instrument and Power of the Trinity" (the meaning of "Haile Selassie"), and the associated belief, enshrined in the 1955 constitution, that the "person of the Emperor is sacred, His dignity is inviolable and His powers indisputable." Furthermore, in a land as inhospitable as Ethiopia to road builders and police patrols and as friendly

[37] "Ethiopia Elects," *The Listener*, November 14, 1957, p. 774.

to insurrectionists and guerrillas, the investment of supreme power in one person decreases the risk of anarchy.

In so far as the legislation of the post-Italian, or "Restoration," period has made any difference to the ordinary citizen, it has probably meant less rather than more autonomy for him. As Margery Perham observes in her study of *The Government of Ethiopia*, the Imperial Decree of 1942 contains, with one solitary exception, no "trace of the principles generally described as indirect rule, or even of any local self-government . . . [It] appears to aim at immediate bureaucratic concentration and at a complete uniformity which ignores the wide differences between the provinces and the peoples."[38] It is true that the decree dealt only with the higher levels of administration and that silence concerning the traditional *shum* (kindred group) and the *chiqa-shum* (locally elected or selected chief or council) implied continuing consent to their activities. At the same time, as Miss Perham goes on to say, it is difficult to see how the decree could ever become effective of its purpose without sapping initiative and responsibility from local institutions and leaders, for its whole tenor is "rapid centralization and uniformity." Much has happened in Ethiopia since Miss Perham made her study, but very little that would require her to revise this judgment.

Only in the municipal sector does the 1942 decree and subsequent legislation recognize the uses of decentralization, and even here the central government's grip on the reins of power remains firm and nobody can afford to be deaf to the crack of its whip. All the officers on a municipal council are under the jurisdiction of the provincial Governor-General, who is appointed by the Emperor. The mayor (*kantiba*) of the council is chosen, not by his peers, but by the central government, and most of his peers are nominated representatives of the ministries of the central government. All regulations drawn up by a council are subject to the approval of the Ministry of the Interior. The powers of a council normally

[38] *The Government of Ethiopia*, Faber & Faber, London, 1948, pp. 349–50.

extend only to registration (property, births, deaths, etc.), maintenance of roads, water supply and lighting, traffic regulations, licensing, and such other duties—mostly minor—as do not come under the aegis of the central ministries.

THE AFRICANIZING PROCESS

As Lord Hailey has reminded us,

So far as the mass of the population is concerned, the reality of constitutional advance towards self-rule is judged not so much by an alteration in the composition of a Legislature as by evidence that the indigenous people are being admitted to posts of executive responsibility. That observation is equally relevant to those types of Colonial Government in which the objective of policy does not envisage self-rule but the political integration of the dependency with the metropolitan Power. The dispatch of representatives to a metropolitan Parliament may appeal strongly to the *élite* or to the limited class of the *évolués* in a Colony, but for the great mass of people the reality of the objective only begins to be appreciated when they see a substantial representation of their own community in posts of administrative or executive responsibility.[39]

It is a readily understandable point of view. The world over, most people would rather do their own machine-minding, no matter how poorly, than have others do it for them, no matter how efficiently. If the machine breaks down, they can always blame its manufacturer for poor workmanship or design; if it continues to function, they can always use the fact as proof of their ability to mind something more complicated. It is also a point of view with which most of the colonial powers have some sympathy.

On the whole, it is the British who have shown the greatest willingness, and have done most, to further the Africanizing process.

[39] *Op. cit.*, p. 359.

Commonwealth territories. Although the Colonial Office had begun to give thought to the Africanizing process as far back as the 1920s, little was actually done about it until the end of World War II. Since then the policy of the Colonial Office has been, to quote from L. Gray Cowan's paper prepared for this study, "to train enough Africans to fill the top posts of responsibility in the government service in order that when the areas concerned become fully independent they will need to rely as little as possible on expatriates (whether British or any other nationality) to carry on the functions of government. Self-government in the British view means not only legislative control by the Africans but dependence, in so far as possible, upon indigenous personnel for the executive arm of government."

To this end, numerous schemes were put into operation, most of them in British West Africa, where the need was considered to be most urgent. These included in-service training and overseas scholarships for almost every branch of the civil service. These schemes have met with varying degrees of success. For general administrative posts they have, on the whole, done the job they were intended to do; for the services requiring a highly technical knowledge, particularly engineering, they have been less than adequate. By way of extenuation, it needs to be remembered that in 1946 hardly anyone, in or out of the Colonial Office, foresaw the rapid constitutional changes which have necessitated, especially in the new regional structure in Nigeria, a proliferation of administrative posts far beyond the normal needs of a single central government. For that matter, few people foresaw the equally rapid expansion of colonial economies, and the parallel demand for technologically trained help. To cope with these expanded needs in territories like the Gold Coast and Nigeria, the British had, for a while, to make so much use of expatriate skills that many Africans were heard to complain that it took an inordinate number of Europeans to Africanize a country! The number of expatriates in the civil service of the Gold Coast continued to rise until shortly before the time of independence. To this day, it has continued to rise in some other British territories. However, most of the responsible African leaders have realized all along the impossibility of doing without expatriate help, if their country is not to backslide into chaos when the administering authority goes. "Only rarely," says Cowan, "does one get the impression in official circles that Africanization is being pursued at the expense of high standards of efficiency within the civil service." But, as he goes on to say, no official circles can long remain closed to public opinion; if they were to do so, they would soon find themselves unofficial and outcircled. And public opinion, among those Africans who think about such things, is generally on the side of Africanization, even if it means loss of efficiency.

That there has been a falling off of the standards as a result of too hasty Africanization is widely conceded. That this is the lesser of two evils—the greater being mounting opposition by the African to the continued domination of government services by Europeans—is likewise widely conceded. Once the decision to grant self-government is made, it is difficult to see what feasible alternative there is to immediate Africanization, even though the personnel available is inadequate in number, training and experience. At the same time, as Cowan points out, sooner or later "the cost to the territory in reduced efficiency of government and in the resulting heavier burden on the taxpayer from too hasty Africanization becomes a problem which must be met, either by the administering authority or the independent government."

In the Gold Coast and the Anglo-Egyptian Sudan the pressure for Africanization came so soon and developed so strongly —from the postwar Labor government in Britain almost as much as from the politicians in the territories themselves— that the administering authorities had scarcely begun to think about the cost factor before their administering days were done. The problem in these territories is therefore one that must be met by the independent power. On the face of it, the problem should be the easier to solve because of this. What the Sudanese and Gold Coast leaders objected to most strongly was not the presence of Europeans in the senior grades of the civil service but the fact that they had no control over them. Now that they are masters in their own house, they are willing enough to have Europeans do jobs for which they themselves lack the skill, the time or the addiction. Though they may say they see no reason for upholding the European's standards of efficiency, the experiences of their first few years of office have made them well aware of the uses of efficiency both in making friends at home and in influencing people abroad. In June 1959 there were still more than 900 expatriates in the Ghanaian civil service (or only about 150 fewer than there were in the Gold Coast civil service in 1949); in addition, "several hundred" expatriates were employed as engineers, architects and technologists of all kinds in "development posts."

In Nigeria, which is being groomed for independence in 1960, the Africanization (there called "Nigerianization") of the civil service is likewise well along. In June 1958 there were 31,777 Nigerian and other west African officers on the payroll of the federal government, and only 1,514 European ("overseas") officers. The same is true of Uganda. Elsewhere in British Africa progress has been much slower. This, we may take it, is partly because the demand for Africanization has been weaker, and partly because the British—seafarers that they are—believe a convoy can safely proceed only at the speed of the slowest unit, and in such territories as British Somaliland, Bechuanaland, Tanganyika, the Rhodesias and Nyasaland some of the units are barely under way. But not many African leaders are greatly interested in safety; they wouldn't be leaders for long if they were.

The other administering powers have tended to take the view that the cost of too hasty Africanization in inefficiency, inequity and increased taxation is one that no colonial territory should be called on to bear; that their job, first and last, is to run a "tight ship." To them, this has meant manning it with the best-qualified people, irrespective of race.

The French Community. Over the years the prevailing French viewpoint has been that the African should not be given heavy administrative and executive responsibilities until, in Cowan's words, "he has absorbed enough French culture to be capable of administering a territory which is essentially an integral part of the mother country." Before any job was "Africanized," the applicant had to demonstrate his ability to operate an administrative department or post "in the same way, according to the same principles and with the same degree of competence, as a French officer . . . To assume an important position the African had to know not just the principles of taxation, public accounting or regulation of the public service, but *French* methods and forms in all these fields." At the same time, since the extension, in the early postwar years, of citizenship to the inhabitants of the entire French Union, it has become the policy of the government to permit all citizens, regardless of origin, to be employed in the public service, at all levels of administration, "on the basis of equality."

Most of the Africanizing done by the French has been in the lower civil service grades; and here the process was well-nigh complete by the end of 1958. In what was then French West Africa, for instance, the *cadres locaux* (consisting of messengers, typists, clerks, etc.) had been 100 per cent Africanized and the *cadres supérieurs* (chief clerks, bookkeepers, secretaries, etc.) three-quarters Africanized for several years. On the other hand, the *cadres généraux* (administrative assistants, heads of departments, professional and technical personnel, etc.) were no more than one-quarter Africanized; and only a handful of Africans in these *cadres* occupied posts of real responsibility where policy decisions were made. One reason for this, as Cowan points out, is that in the postwar period Africans capable of taking responsibility frequently found themselves chosen by the electorate to sit as deputies in Paris or Dakar. "They were thought to be better fitted as deputies because of their knowledge of the operation of government. But on election they were forced to relinquish their public service appointments."

In the other French territories the *cadres locaux* were likewise fully Africanized by the last years of the Fourth Republic, but the *cadres supérieurs* and *cadres généraux* continued to rely heavily on European personnel. In French Equatorial Africa, for instance, the corresponding figures for the three main categories, as of about 1955, were 100 per cent for the *cadres locaux,* approximately 33 per cent for the *cadres supérieurs,* and only 6 per cent for the *cadres généraux.* What is more, while the number of Africans employed in the civil service of these territories had been increasing steadily for many years, the number of Europeans had also been increasing—in some cases more rapidly.

Other territories. Until recently the Belgian viewpoint on Africanization was rather like that of the French. Africanization was thought of more as an incidental product than as the purposeful goal of colonial development.

The Belgians were of the opinion that it was pointless to talk about developing a responsible democratic form of government without first developing an educated bourgeoisie which had a vested interest in the stability and efficiency of government. In their opinion it was only when the African had learned how to operate the basic economy of the country and to see the value of the rational utilization of its resources that he would be ready to safeguard them against exploitation by a demagogue. Consequently, in the Belgian Congo Africanization was primarily a matter of fitting the African to run and maintain machinery, look after office equipment, do bookkeeping and so on. Cowan reports that

in the service of the central administration of the Congo, as of January 1954, there were 5,515 Europeans and 6,009 Africans in permanent posts, . . . the corresponding numbers in 1952 being 6,066 and 4,815 respectively. No information is available on the particular positions held by African personnel, but it is safe to assume that none was of a policy-making nature . . . In the territorial service (which serves the region outside the capital) none of the 1,222 officers were African, but the vast majority of the routine work is done by African clerks. The staffs of the administrative and judicial services of the *circonscriptions indigènes* are completely Africanized.

After the troubles of late 1958 and early 1959 the Belgian viewpoint changed radically. The government's intention thenceforth was "to integrate the maximum number of Congolese in the executive and legal system at all levels"[40] as quickly as possible. As an earnest of this intention, 459 Africans had already been promoted to a higher grade by the end of January 1959.

To inquire about Africanization statistics in Portuguese Africa is to waste time, since the problem does not arise officially. The natives of Angola, Mozambique and Portuguese Guinea can be considered capable of controlling their own destiny only when they have become, to all intents and purposes, Europeans. And by that time there will not, from the Portuguese viewpoint, be any question of Africanization; it will merely be a question of which Europeans are in the governing positions.

So also in Spanish Africa. The paternalistic administration of the Spanish government is not susceptible of being Africanized, because there is no expectation that at some future date Africans will have to take it over. Spanish officials with whom Cowan spoke "pointed out—what was obviously true—that the natives [in their territories] are in no position to govern themselves and that no effort is being made to prepare them for such an eventuality." They also pointed out that the territories administered by them are so small that they could never hope to stand as an independent nation, and that, for this reason alone, talk about Africanization was irrelevant. There are African clerks in administrative offices and in the police force of Fernando Po, but even these are frequently Nigerians who have settled permanently in Spanish territory.

But it is not only some of the administering powers that have reservations about the Africanizing process. Some of the

[40] See *Belgian Congo Monthly Information Bulletin*, June 1959, p. 8.

administered groups find the idea no more attractive. This is true not only of most "settler" groups, European and Asian, but also of those indigenous groups, mostly Moslem, who have been slow to imitate the ways and accept the schooling of their colonizers and who, because of this, now find themselves lagging behind their less conservative neighbors in technical and professional skills. In northern Nigeria, to quote again from Cowan's report (written in 1955),

almost all the clerks in government offices and in the trading houses are either Ibos or Yorubas; even in the Native Administration establishments in the provinces, southerners are to be found. The northerners are far from pleased at this kind of Africanization, yet they know they can do nothing about it until their own people are trained to take over the posts. They are fearful that the southerners will remain in control of the civil service and business after complete independence is achieved. In consequence they are not eager to see the British administrative officer replaced by an African, since the latter represents a greater threat to their tradition than the European ever did. The same picture is to be found in the northern [French] Cameroons, where the government employees are chiefly from the area south of Yaoundé. In French West Africa the role of the southern Nigerian is played by the ever-present Senegalese. Everywhere one gets the same reaction—dislike and fear of these outsiders, Africans though they may be. The northerners are more anxious for "northernization" then for Africanization in the sense that the southerners understand the term.

In Sudan, as was noted earlier, it is the southerners who most dislike and fear the Africanizing process; to them, this stands for "northernization."

Important as the issue of Africanization is, it is easy to overemphasize it. Like nationalism—with which it has come to be associated in the minds of many of its advocates—it is a "minority movement." To the great majority of indigenous Africans it means almost nothing, if indeed the word is known to them. What Cowan has written of the ordinary rural Nigerian and Ghanaian is true also of the ordinary rural Sudanese, Angolan, Rhodesian and Congolese African: "the thing that concerns him most is whether or not the administrator who collects his taxes is fair and just, not whether he is African or European." In so far as he has a preference, Cowan believes (as do many other well-informed observers) that it is probably for the European. Furthermore, even for the "minority," Africanization is not an all-or-nothing movement. Thus, no African government has so far thought it necessary to Africanize its leprosy services.

At the same time it would be foolish to underestimate the momentum of the Africanizing process. As with nationalism, it is growing; and it is certain that the ordinary African, of east, central and west Africa alike, will find more and more of his affairs administered by Africans. Whether he can be made to prefer the African to the European administrator will depend largely on the intellectual qualities and the moral probity of the young men now coming into public office. "If they can prove themselves," Cowan contends, "they will gain the place of respect which the European officer has occupied." If not, they risk being swept away by the enemies—domestic and foreign—of political progress. For what, in the last resort, matters most to the government of a country is not the quality of its machinery but the ability of its mechanics to keep the machinery running. And this is as much a matter of integrity as of endurance, of conscience as of carefulness.

CHAPTER 7

THE NEW ELITE

One of the more durable customs of colonial life is the courtesy call, the periodic paying of one's respects to the leading members of the community. In the old days, the calling circle was quite small and not many Africans were part of it. In bush communities it was composed of the local European representatives of the government; the European planters or farmers, if any; the European or North American missionary, if any; and the local African headman or chief. In the larger centers, it might also have included the more prominent businessmen, European or Asian, and any Africans who had been abroad.

Today, in most places, the circle is wider and rather differently composed. It may or may not include the headman: much will depend on his standing and outlook. It may still include the missionary, but more likely it will include his progeny, the indigenous church leader and schoolmaster. It will still include the local representatives of the central government, if they can be found—which is not always the case in this "do good and be expendable" age. It will certainly include those who have been abroad, for, in British and French Africa and territories formerly British and French, they are likely to be occupying positions of responsibility in business and government. Indeed, in many of these territories they will be "running the show," including, as has been pointed out, the political associations, the trade unions, the cooperatives and other community enterprises, and the newspapers.

To become acquainted with the leading Africans in any large center of the more advanced territories is, however, no longer just a matter of courtesy. It is a matter of inescapable necessity. For these are the mediators of the new covenant of equal rights for all civilized men and equal opportunity for all men to be civilized, the high priests of the new order of freedom to "go it alone," the apostles of the manifold graces of nationalism. These are the men with the keys of the kingdom, the chosen people: the new elite. To know them may not be to know everything about today's Africa; but not to know them is most assuredly not to know the makers of tomorrow's Africa.

Who are the new elite? What is their background? Where and how were they trained? What are their professional ambitions? Their views and interests?

THEIR BACKGROUND

From almost every point of view the new elite are an extremely mixed group. Some of their number are scions of royal and "chiefly" families of venerable antiquity; others are people of lowly birth and no wealth. Some have come from bush country only recently opened to commerce, while others have come from bazaars and marts that have had dealings with the outside world for hundreds of years. Some grew up in cattle-keeping country, and some in crop-raising country. Some came from Christian, and some from Moslem and pagan homes.

In an inquiry into the background of 90 west Africans (Nigerians and Ghanaians) studying in the United States during the 1954–1955 session, which he has summarized for this study, Alvin Zalinger found that approximately 40 per cent of them were country-born, the rest town-born; that nearly 40 per cent of them came from families where neither father nor mother had been to school, and that only three fathers and no mothers had been to college or university; that six of the ninety came from chiefly families, the rest mainly from petty trading, small farming and white-collar families; that about 75 per cent reported themselves as having a Christian father or mother or both; that 45 per cent reported themselves as coming from polygamous households; and that 24 per cent of the fathers and 28 per cent of the mothers reported as being Christian were also reported as being polygamous.

This much, at all events, can be said of all the new elite: they are products of the white man's schools, either mission-run or state-run. In most cases they have managed to get both primary and secondary schooling; an increasing number of the younger ones have also been to college or university.

It is not difficult to see why the schools (more especially the secondary schools) and the colleges should have served as the novitiate of the new elite. In the first place, it is there that the African has become enfranchised intellectually. True, a man does not need to go to school or college to graduate in the culture of his tribe. But this culture does not normally enable him to communicate with either his governors or his neighbors, and without the ability to do this, he cannot communicate where communication is most often wanted—in the advocacy of political rights, social equality and economic opportunity. For this he must learn the language of his government.

Second, it is in the schools, most of which are residential, that he has been able to learn the price of intellectual progress, in self-discipline, perseverance, courage and loyalty transcending family, tribe and even faith. Of course, not all schools, in Africa or elsewhere, are interested in inculcating such virtues, or adept at doing so, but the percentage that are is high—much higher, very likely, than in America; for, whatever criticisms may be leveled at mission teachers, lack of discipline, loyalty, perseverance and courage is certainly not among them. Those who visited the Alliance High School, near Nairobi, Kenya, during the Mau Mau emergency are not likely to forget the experience. Although the school grounds were in Mau Mau country and 90 per cent of the students were Kikuyu, no students defected, in spite of repeated threats to them and their parents; no teacher asked for home leave; and no activity, curricular or otherwise, was curtailed. What is more, the performance of the graduating classes during the emergency period was unsurpassed.

Third, it is in the secondary schools and colleges that the African has a chance to acquire facility in the techniques of intellectual progress, such as public speaking, the running of

magazines, committees and other group activities, the preparing of reports, appeals and petitions, and the raising of
funds.

Fourth, it is there that he has been exposed to the contagion
of other men's thought—his European or North American
teachers', his fellow Africans' (the Alliance High School has
representatives of some 20 tribes; Makerere College at Kampala, Uganda, of at least 80 tribes), and that of the great
minds of other times and places. Not many African students
may yet be able to talk with authority on social adjustment,
group dynamics, the conquest of complexes, the development
of personality and leadership potential, but many of them can
talk on Aristotelian politics, Christian ethics, Thomas Paine's
The Rights of Man and dialectical materialism. This may not
make them the easiest of people to get along with, but it
certainly makes them redoubtable opponents of injustice and
so most attractive to their less articulate fellows.

Fifth, it is in the schools and colleges that the African
learns skills that can later be converted into cash, and the
cash into property, stocks and bonds, business partnerships
and so on. Without such skills, the task of making ends meet
is, for most Africans, unremitting and well-nigh unsupportable.
Where this is so, there is clearly no time for other "ends." Yet
it is these other ends, whether cultural, political or spiritual,
that give the elite their identity.

All this is not to say that the man with the best education is
necessarily the man most esteemed by the new elite. There
are different conceptions and orders of eliteness, and some
of them have less to do with a man's educational achievements
than with his political or economic ones. In tropical Africa,
as elsewhere, the best-educated people do not always make
the best politicians and businessmen. They may not even be
interested in being politicians and businessmen; if they are,
they are unlikely to be adept at demagoguery, self-deception
and the daily cut-and-thrust of the forum and the market place.
At the same time, the chances of the poorly educated African
coming to a position of influence and maintaining it, in any
field, are quite small and getting smaller. The kinds of skill

and ability most needed by the African called upon to wear the mantle of the departing European are those that come by way of the classroom and seminar, the laboratory and the field station. This nobody realizes better than the African who has already had some schooling.

THEIR PROFESSIONAL AMBITIONS

What educated Africans hold to be the most necessary skills and abilities, or those best befitting their newly enfranchised status, is not always easy to say. Much depends upon the amount and the quality of the education they have had, but much also depends on the attitude of their rulers and the range of openings made available to them. And, needless to say, much depends on the Africans in question.

Several sample surveys have been made in recent years of the prestige rating of occupations. Of these, the survey made by J. Clyde Mitchell and A. L. Epstein is undoubtedly one of the more significant, partly because of the size of the sample (653 students with at least a secondary school education were questioned), and partly because the country in which it was carried out—Northern Rhodesia—is one where the African is being encouraged to raise his sights, in some fields as high as his ability and aptitude incline him. The students were asked to rate 31 occupations on a five-category prestige scale. When their ratings were converted into a simple mean rank (by apportioning a weight to each of the categories), it was found that professional work, in education, religion, welfare and so on, was placed first; that this was followed by white-collar work in hospitals, mines, government and trade unions; this, by skilled manual work (such as carpentry, bricklaying and motor maintenance) and "boss-boy" work in mines and on construction jobs; and this, finally, by unskilled work, such as gardening, wood cutting, and household and hotel service. "Response to an open-ended question made it quite clear that occupations which were normally those of Europeans, but which some Africans followed, were accorded high prestige and that, in general, those occupations which required the highest educational qualifications were ranked the highest. This held true even for a group of students who were training to be artisans."[1]

Although Mitchell does not claim that the results of this survey provide a basis for generalization, he believes, as do some other students of the African social scene, that to live like the European elite in their midst is the dearest ambition of most educated Africans; that the "civilized way of life . . . provides a scale along which the prestige of Africans in urban areas (and to an increasing extent in rural areas) may be measured." At the same time the Mitchell-Epstein survey makes it clear that there are those for whom admission to the ranks of the elite, conferred by a secondary schooling, does virtually nothing. They have been exposed to the "civilized way of life," but they have not been induced to want any part of it that they could not have had without going to school. Among the 653 there were 47 who gave the highest prestige ranking to the occupation of messenger, 26 who gave it to either domestic or hotel service, and 5 to scavenging. For these, it would seem, the quality of eliteness—if any—consisted in having been to a secondary school or other institution of higher learning, not in the profit derived from the experience. Anthony Wilmot notes in his report prepared for this study that in some parts of British Africa, indeed, the "been-to"—the man who has been somewhere—is a man above his fellows.

We could wish that surveys of this kind told more about the motives of the respondents; that we could know, for instance, what precisely it is about the "civilized way of life" that most attracts the aspiring African. Is it the desire to be somebody, if only a "been-to"? Is it the chance to trade ignorance for understanding, superstition for reason? Is it the opportunity to acquire money and the things that money can buy? Or even of helping others to be "civilized"? Doubtless

[1] J. Clyde Mitchell, "The Kalela Dance: Aspects of Social Relationships among Urban Africans in Northern Rhodesia," Rhodes-Livingstone Papers, No. 27, Manchester University Press, Manchester, 1956, p. 14.

all this, and more, enters into the aspirant's reckoning, since here, as in many another matter, he tends to take his cue from his "civilized" tutors, in whom all these wellsprings of action can be found. But to judge from appearances (which in the circumstances is almost unavoidable), either the tutors do not always seem to have taught as well as they knew or else the tutored do not always seem to have practiced what they were taught.

Observations such as the following, from Wilmot's report, are made too often, and by people too warmly disposed toward the educated African, to be dismissed as of no consequence:

> Students freely admit that their main interest is to secure the employment which is at once the most lucrative and the least arduous or uncomfortable . . . Where materialistic considerations are dominant . . . ambitions toward any particular vocation show little rigidity. When the time to seek employment comes, the cash return and other material aspects of the jobs available will often be prime factors regulating the final choice, irrespective of previously expressed ambitions.

> In west Africa there is often some contempt for the illiterate peasant and no marked enthusiasm for rural occupations which would throw the educated man among such people . . . There is little acknowledgment that the illiterate to whom education has been denied may include amongst their number some who are endowed with an intellectual potential at least equal to that of many university students. There is no widespread pity or sympathy for the illiterate.

> In many cases it has been necessary to effect a process of education in man-management designed to wean students away from the habit of lording it over college servants. The example of some Europeans, who have tended to be brusque in their handling of African labor, may be partially responsible for this display of snobbery.

It would be wrong to suggest that there is no ambition to serve the community. As everywhere, "there are those whose sense of vocation is stronger than the climate of materialistic opinion." In a survey of the occupational preferences of third- and fourth-year secondary students in Stanleyville, Nelly Xydias found[2] that 30 per cent gave as the reason for their preference the desire to be useful to the mother country, or to the tribe, or to God; that only one fourth were primarily concerned about what other people thought of them; that less than one fourth were mainly interested in the monetary yield of the occupation, and only one per cent in considerations of easiness and security. And it is probable, as Wilmot observes, that the desire to serve is frequently stronger than young people, in their student days, are willing to admit; that it merely needs cultivating, as do all the choicest flowers of the spirit. From his long observation of the west African scene, Wilmot is firmly of the opinion that the best soil for the purpose is the faith and philosophy enshrined in the teachings of the New Testament. Unfortunately, these teachings seem to get little more than lip service from the great majority of the intelligentsia. In this, too, the tutored would appear to be merely following the cue of their European tutors, for most of whom these teachings are "hard sayings."

THEIR EUROPEANIZATION

If there is one thing more than another that identifies the new elite, it is their general acceptance of the things taught them and the examples shown them by the European. Paradoxically, as was seen in the preceding chapter, it has become the custom to speak of the process by which the educated African takes over the customary European roles of administrator, teacher, healer, preacher and so on as "Africanization." Ethnically the term is apt enough; but from almost any other

[2] *Social Implications of Industrialization and Urbanization in Africa South of the Sahara* (prepared under the auspices of UNESCO by the International African Institute, London), UNESCO, Tensions and Technology Series, Paris, 1956, p. 353 ff.

point of view it could hardly be more inept, since what has qualified the African for these roles is not the color of his skin or his cultural inheritance but his schooling and apprenticeship in the ways of his tutors—his "Europeanization," in fact.

The extent of this Europeanization naturally varies from place to place and with the individual. It is less conspicuous in Moslem territories than in Christian ones. It is less in evidence on the rubber plantation of a Liberian administrator than in his town house; and often less in evidence in the kitchen of his town house than in his living quarters. It is generally less apparent in the man who has lived all his life in his own territory than in the man who has been abroad. But it is always there, even when concealed from view. Thus, while the Moslem administrator of Kano is likely to keep his wife (or wives) behind doors, pray toward Mecca and be a total abstainer, in the approved Mohammedan manner, he is as likely to read the London *Times,* speak English with an Oxford accent, and be partial to flashy European or American cars. While the Liberian plantation may not look very different from the surrounding countryside, the chances are that its owner keeps a well-stocked larder of American canned goods and liquors. And while the "boss-boys" on the Copperbelt are seldom able to resist their tribal rhythms, they are probably as adept at ballroom dancing.

With many of the new elite the Europeanizing process has gone further, covering not only dress, speech, food, drink and recreation, but etiquette, sentiment and intellectual tastes. An African dinner host is likely to be as punctilious in his regard for the comfort of the ladies as any American; and his table is almost as likely to be set in the approved *Ladies' Home Journal* manner. Africans who have returned to Nigeria or Kenya after living in Europe or North America for extended periods are almost as much given to nostalgia, and genuine affection, for the persons and places they came to know while abroad as any G. I. in foreign parts is for his homeland. There are many Africans in the former French West Africa whose knowledge and esteem of French culture would do credit to the metropolitan Frenchmen domiciled in their midst; some

speak of "our French culture" as though it was. The same is
true of some of the more highly educated Africans of British
and once-British West Africa. For these Dr. Kofi Busia, a
former Leader of the Opposition in Ghana's Legislative Assembly, spoke when he said, at the time of Ghana's independence (March 1957): "We have also benefited from
British administration and law, to which we owe our concepts
of nationhood, democracy and individual freedom; and European education introduced to us under British rule has made
us heirs of the literature and accumulated wisdom of the ages
preserved in books for succeeding generations. The English
language has not only enabled us to communicate with our
fellow countrymen of different tongues and tribes, but has also
prepared us for effective membership in the wider community
of nations to which we now come as adults and no longer as
wards . . ."[3]

But extent is one dimension; depth is another, and it is
here that opinion about the Europeanizing process begins to
be divided.

On the one side there are those who contend that the highly
educated African is as much a European as the highly educated American negro is an American; that long-continued
exposure to European minds and modes of thought has given
him a European mind; and that it could hardly be otherwise
since, intelligent man that he is, he is bound to embrace the
highest when he sees it. Those who are of this persuasion
point to the Kwame Nkrumahs, the Houphouet-Boignys, the
Kabakas who are as much at home in New York, Paris and
London as in Accra, Abidjan and Kampala; who write as
Europeans do; who have the cultured European's sophistication, poise and wit; and who, not infrequently, take a European for a wife. They also point to those "expatriate" Africans
who at the end of a long professional training in Europe feel

[3] Within two years or so of expressing these generous sentiments,
Dr. Busia became a political refugee. In his judgment, Ghana
ceased to adhere to the "concepts of . . . democracy and individual freedom" almost as soon as it had gained its own freedom.

themselves to be more European than African and make Europe their home.

On the other side there are those who contend that the mind of the African works differently from that of the European; that no matter how steeped it may be in European ideas and ideologies, it has a hard core that is impervious to all foreign tinctures and retentive of all indigenous traditions and usages; that Europeanization is but a thin overlay. Those who follow this line of argument have no difficulty in supporting it. They point, for instance, to the many "Europeanized" Africans who have gone back to the bush, there to lose their European habits and religion, and even the skills they had acquired under their European tutors. According to the former Governor of one territory, this "rebushing" comes as easily to those educated in Europe as it does to those educated in Africa. The followers of this line of thought can also point to such atavistic manifestations as Mau Mau, the progenitors of which—as far as they are known—were men of as much education as any of the Africans who opposed them. While Jomo Kenyatta may never have been Mau Mau's leader, he was surely one of its inspirers, and one of the most Europeanized Africans of his generation. For seventeen years he lived in Europe as a student, at the London School of Economics and Moscow University, and as a writer of articles, pamphlets and a monograph on the Kikuyu which Malinowski described in his introduction to it as "a pioneering achievement of outstanding merit." Anybody who had the chance of talking to "hard-core" Mau Mau prisoners knows that it was not only the Kenyattas that were Europeanized.

Whatever the truth is regarding the Europeanizing process, it is probably less complimentary to the European than to the African. For what matters as much as a man's inherent capabilities in a process of this kind is the social climate in which the process is set. In tropical Africa the social climate has seldom been easy on the evolving African.

THEIR SOCIAL STATUS

Many things go into the making of a climate, whether atmospheric or social: among them environment, energy and the relationship between its physical components. In the making of a social climate, the last of these is almost certainly the most important. In tropical Africa the relationship between the components of almost any given social group is one capable of generating friction. Youth and age, tenant and owner, progressive and conservative can rub each other the wrong way as readily in Ghana as in Georgia. To these traditional zones of conflict have been added over the years those between black and white, indigenous and expatriate, unschooled and schooled. These, needless to say, have done nothing to simplify the business of acclimatization for the new elite, or, to change the figure, to give them an assured place in the sun. In other words, the new elite are having status troubles.

The most conspicuous of these troubles is that arising from the presence of the European, and the less-than-total acceptance of the elite by the European. The educated African has always been extremely sensitive to racial prejudice, and he has not had to go very far to find it. If he was not raised amid it, he has sooner or later been exposed to it. A little exposure to it goes a long way; as a professional man said to Gray Cowan, "You have only to be called a damn nigger once!" Most educated Africans have had more than a little such exposure. They have had it in the college classroom, the company office, the train, the ship, the shop, the club, the hotel and the church. They have had it in places where it was not supposed to exist (as in the colonial Gold Coast and Nigeria) as well as in places like Southern Rhodesia, where it has been condoned by custom and the courts. If they have not met it at home, they have met it abroad, in the streets of Philadelphia, the lodginghouses of London and the restaurants of Paris.

It is true that "legalized" prejudice is disappearing from the scene, and that "legalized" discrimination against the elite has

been removed from the field of government and private employment in most territories. But what is as irksome to many
Africans is the unwillingness, or outright refusal, of their European peers to accept them socially and intellectually. This
non-acceptance is expressed in several ways. In one place it
is expressed by the failure of the European to invite his African government colleagues into his home, or the failure of his
wife to pay courtesy calls on the wives of his colleagues. In
another place it is expressed by the habitual impatience of a
European lecturer with his allegedly idle and incompetent
African students. Elsewhere it is expressed in the inability of
an African to catch the eye of a hotel waiter or a shop clerk,
in the silence that descends on a club meeting when a leading African is put up for membership, and in the arguments
advanced for not promoting an African to a position theretofore held only by Europeans.

In some territories, the most grievous expression of this non-
acceptance of the educated African is the failure of the Europeans to supply him with the physical facilities necessary for
leading an educated life. What, asks Enoch Dumbutshena in
a recent article,[4] is there for the educated Africans of Southern Rhodesia to do in their leisure hours?

> The overcrowded African townships offer them nothing
> that can be regarded as recreationary . . . The type of film
> shown in African townships does not appeal to them . . .
> [and no] African can attend a cinema show in [Salisbury].
> The laws and traditions of the land prohibit the mixing of
> Africans and Europeans at film shows . . . [Nor can he]
> listen to distinguished men of learning who visit the Federa-
> tion from time to time, except if they happen to address
> meetings of the Southern Rhodesia National Affairs As-
> sociation or those organized by inter-racial associations.
> [And if we] take the environment in which such an African
> spends [his non-working] life, . . . the prospects of him
> enjoying the quietness of his home are very remote . . .

[4] "Africans Are Starved of Culture," *Central African Examiner*
(Salisbury, Southern Rhodesia), February 15, 1958.

Since most of the residents do not read and some spend their week-ends drinking, the week-ends are spent in a den of singing and shouting. Quiet, an element necessary to reading, is thus impossible to obtain . . . Because there are no decent libraries in these townships, it is difficult for a man to find a place where he can read undisturbed.

True, this is not the full story, for, as Dumbutshena points out, the Salisbury City Council has recently built the Africans a recreation hall with a library and reading room, and there is in Salisbury a social and cultural club that endeavors to care for the leisure needs of the African. But, as he implies farther on, it can never be anything but a rather sad story until there are much greater opportunities for the educated African to meet Europeans, Indians and others of his own standing. Such opportunities are not yet in sight, either in Salisbury or in any one of a score of other cities in central and east Africa.

In the circumstances, what is remarkable is not that the educated African bears so much resentment against his European peers, but so little. Many of the most highly educated Africans bear none at all, and those who do seem able to "particularize" it. Wilmot believes this to be especially true of west Africans, who, "themselves individualists, tend to judge each European on his own merits." In this connection, he tells us that "when an essay was set to a class of students at a west African college of technology on the subject of 'The person I admire most,' half of the students wrote on the African prime minister of their country, one quarter on other Africans (none of whom, incidentally, was on the college staff), while the rest wrote on a variety of Europeans, some of whom were their own college lecturers." At the same time Wilmot suggests that it is quite possible for the student who professes to judge individuals on their merits to depart from this principle when things go wrong: "For instance, failure in an examination will readily be blamed on the racial prejudice of the European examiner, and in this and a host of similar ways a suspicion of Europeans is frequently displayed."

Not the least of the educated African's difficulties, as this attitude hints, is to maintain status with his fellow African, both elite and non-elite. In some instances, indeed, this would appear to be a bigger difficulty than maintaining status with the Europeans, who, after all, are not unaccustomed to failing examinations, to say nothing of losing jobs. This may explain why most educated Africans will work harder not to fail examinations and lose jobs than most Europeans.

It is perhaps this desire to "arrive," and to be thought of as having arrived, that causes many of the elite to conduct themselves in a manner more appropriate to the music hall than to mid-century Main Street. We have already spoken of the hauteur, not to say outright bad manners, which many students affect in their day-to-day dealings with menials, and of the similar frictions in child-parent relationships. No less apparent is the liking of many educated Africans for flamboyance in writing, speech and gesture, dress and daily habits. Editorials in the African press are characteristically heavy with metaphor and latinity. Public speeches frequently appear to have been penned in purple ink, and are delivered in a style reminiscent of Gladstonian oratory. Taste in clothes not infrequently runs to the bizarre.

This liking for flamboyance is shown in other ways. It is shown in the "conspicuous consumption" of prestige goods, such as bicycles and shoes among those of modest means, and liquor, jewelry, clothes, phonographs, radios and motor cars among those more affluent. It is shown, too, in the cult of the grandiose, of which some of the more striking manifestations have recently come from Ghana: the erection in Accra of a 10-foot statue of Kwame Nkrumah; the conversion, at a cost of more than £100,000, of Christiansborg Castle, the former residence of the Governor, into the Prime Minister's official residence; and the pretensions of the government to pan-African leadership.

It should not be supposed, however, that the gain in status resulting from this kind of showmanship is necessarily commensurate with the effort put into it. A good showman, it is true, can always find a following, whether on the soccer field, on the floor of the Senate, or in the college classroom; and certainly Africa has its share of those who are impressed by showmanship. But it also has many who are not. In every tribal community there are those, such as the more elderly chiefs and headmen—the elite of earlier days—who have little but contempt for the posturings, as they may hold them to be, of the new elite. Among the Teita, for instance, there is still a strong disposition on the part of the older people to equate "shoe wearer" and "reader," and even "Christian" with "custom breaker" and "ruiner of the country."

What is more, in every group of shoe-wearing and reading Africans there will be those who, whether from delicacy of feeling, innate refinement or sheer disinclination, want no part of the "show." These people seemingly care very little if at all about status—theirs or their neighbor's, African or European. For them nobility's true badge is "the cause above renown" and the high idea humbly lived. These people are not necessarily the best educated or the most affluent. They can be found in a bush schoolroom as readily as in a cabinet office; in a machine shop as on a college faculty; they may be running a clinic, a newspaper or an art school. Whatever they are and do, they are the true elite.

THEIR VIEWS

What do these new men believe in? What do they think of the traditional cultures of their homelands? The current economic and political developments? What are their ideological commitments and loyalties?

Needless to say, it is easier to put these questions than to answer them satisfactorily. Africans are not alone in their reluctance to be "quizzed" for the benefit of people they do not know, and for undisclosed purposes, or in their ability to answer questions according to the circumstances. Like people everywhere, many Africans answer questions according to the dictates of fashion and not of conscience; their expressed opinions are an intellectual affectation, not the distillation of their own beliefs and experience. Further, as Alvin Zalinger says in his working paper, "the reasons for an opinion, the way it has been arrived at, the 'sacredness' or rationality with which it is held may be of far greater significance than the opinion itself."

In the endeavor to get at the real thinking of the "new men," Zalinger conducted "semi-structured, intensive interviews" with the 90 students whose background and attitudes he was investigating. While he does not claim to have penetrated into the inner keep of their minds, or to be able to extrapolate his findings to other parts of Africa and to other elite categories, he does claim that "in respect of characteristics which might conceivably affect opinions and attitudes," his respondents came close to being a representative sample of the Nigerian and Ghanaian students in the United States at the time of the study (1954–1955). Since in every tropical African land it is the student, past or present, who forms the intellectual spearhead of the new elite, it is probable that many of the opinions and attitudes expressed by the ninety have a wider significance than Zalinger, with his scientific caution, is willing to concede.

Traditional culture. The chief aspects of their culture on which the respondents were invited to express opinions were the institution of chieftaincy, the family (including family obligations, the parental role in marriage, and polygamy), indigenous religion and arts, and their feelings about the older generation.

Concerning chieftaincy, Zalinger found that all his respondents were opposed to it in its traditional form. Nearly half the students wanted to abolish it completely. Of these, most were in agreement with the Nigerian who said: "You just can't abolish it all of a sudden . . . The chiefs must be deprived of political power and influence gradually and without antagonizing people who believe in them. They are more than symbols to those who still believe in them." But there was also considerable support for the rather more "positivist" viewpoint expressed by another student: "The chiefs have no place in these modern political and administrative developments. They are not versed in government and don't understand contemporary problems . . . We should pension them off, but give them no authority."

Even those respondents who belonged to tribal groups in which chieftaincy has conferred great power and wealth were generally opposed to continuing the institution. As one Ashanti student put it, "Although I am in line to become a chief, I do not believe there is much place for chiefs in the Gold Coast . . . In my opinion, they should not have any political power, but be kept like art objects as a symbol of our traditions."

This feeling that the institution should be preserved, rather like the British Crown, for its symbolic value, was expressed in one way or another by about 40 per cent of the students. The farthest any respondent was willing to go was to say that "Chieftaincy has worked very well for the masses of the people—and for many it still does . . . Obviously, the chiefs cannot cope with the problems of political administration in a city like Accra . . . but in small villages . . . chiefs can still serve many administrative functions. You can't replace them all at once without serious consequences . . . Wherever they are capable of handling affairs . . . they should, at least for a while, be given as much power as they can handle, and as much as would be expected and desired by their people."

Concerning family institutions, by far the great majority of the respondents took an ambivalent view of the changes that had taken place or were likely to take place in the near future. Says Zalinger: "They display a high degree of effective involvement in the norms and customs of the traditional family, and express considerable approval for the cohesion, mutual aid, respect for elders, and other personal relationships which characterize the traditional family. At the same time they expect that Western socio-economic developments are bound to result in a breakup of the extended family systems, and a development in the direction of the more isolated conjugal-type family of the West."

Many of them would undoubtedly have endorsed the following statement made by a Nigerian respondent: "I feel sorry to see the old way go. The bond of [family] love has weakened. The family is getting further apart. But I know that we cannot have both this and progress." There were some, however, who felt no such sorrow. Said one Nigerian student: "If the price of industrialization and Westernization is the breakup of the traditional family, it is a good price to pay . . . We cannot let the family system stand in the way of these developments." Or, to quote another Nigerian: "Our family obligations place too much of a strain on successful individuals. My father had to cater to so many people that he was not able to do much for himself . . . It isn't the close ties that I object to, but the dependency . . . There are a lot of people in Ibadan who don't work because they know they can go and live with relatives. This is why you can't amass wealth. Let them call me bad names. I will not help such people." But in this he did not speak for all. No less than 45 per cent of the students believed that the fulfillment of one's family obligations was still "the proper thing"; only 5 per cent claimed that they would have absolutely nothing to do with such obligations.

Weakening of the old family ties is revealed in other ways, too. Thus, of the 68 students with whom the parental role in marriage was discussed, only 9 stated that they would ask and abide by their parents' wishes. Nearly half of the 68 maintained that they would ask their parents' advice out of respect, while reserving the right not to follow it. Forty per cent said that they would do their own deciding in the matter. Almost as many, it seems, were less worried about what their parents would say than what the person of their choice would say—a worry not unknown in American society! And the respondents had a pretty clear idea, it seems, of the kind of person they would like. "Virtually all students say that they would want to marry a college-educated mate, regardless of tribal affiliation, nationality or color."

As for polygamy, only two students fully endorsed the institution, but only one was for outlawing it. All the rest, while opposing it, insisted that polygamy was a matter that should be left to the individual. The main reasons for their opposition to it were "not moralistic, but pragmatic . . . [that]

polygamy is too expensive, and that under modern conditions it is no longer functional economically." But it was obviously not a matter on which the great majority of them felt deeply. The following point of view, expressed by a Nigerian coming from a polygamous family, is, according to Zalinger, representative: "I think that if people want polygamy, they should have the right to practice it. There is nothing wrong with this system except that today it is probably too expensive and too much trouble. Even though the church thinks it is wrong, I do not oppose it. People should not judge others by their own biases."

One of the most interesting facts to emerge from this part of Zalinger's inquiry is the extent to which the respondents' views on family affairs had been influenced by their residence in America. "Forty-three per cent of the respondents stated that their American experience—and, more particularly, their contact with both negro and white families—had resulted in changes of attitude . . . Although most of the respondents tend to be critical of the extreme form of family individualism alleged to exist in the United States and the lack of family feeling and of respect for parents and elders, there is much in the American feeling that they both admire and endorse with enthusiasm. [In particular] they admire the relative independence of young people, and husband-wife team work and equality." The prevailing opinion was summed up by the social work graduate student from Nigeria who said: "I think our changes will be in the 'American' direction. People will be more independent and will have fewer responsibilities to the family . . . If we want all the things of the modern world, the family must change . . . Now that I have been in this country, I can see how close family relationships prevent progress. People cannot be independent and accomplish things for themselves if they are restricted by the family."

Like polygamy and other aspects of the old family system, indigenous or traditional religion was treated by the majority of the respondents as a matter to be left to the forces of erosion. These, they recognized, were slowly removing the superstitious overlay. This was good. What was not so good, in their view, was the possibility that the same forces might also remove the bedrock of wholesome belief and practice. The case for preserving the ancient good was put by one student as follows: "Our religion and juju have been referred to as superstition, but there are many aspects of our religion which could be retained along with Christianity. In fact, today many people believe in both types of religion. It should be left to the people to decide which parts of each they want to keep." By another it was put thus: "I don't believe in all the ordeals, tortures and cutting [of juju], but many of the medicines of our native doctors are okay. I know of many cases where the Western doctor failed and our own doctors with native herbs succeeded. [The Western doctors] could do much good if they would conduct research with our herbs."

Only one in four of the respondents held that the old beliefs should be destroyed at once and, if need be, by government action. As to how such beliefs might be destroyed "at once," none did say.

There was considerable divergence of opinion regarding the preservation of the old artistic values. Only 16 per cent of the respondents were interested in preserving much of the traditional ceremonial; and only 27 per cent had very much use for native dress, even as occasional wear. However, 72 per cent favored the retention of indigenous music, dance and plastic art forms, but here, also, there was a strong disposition to believe that they could only be retained by being changed. A graduate art student put the case for change as follows: "What I want to preserve are the basic themes in these art forms, but I believe strongly that they should be modernized. Art is always changing and is international." Another student pointed out that "Music is not just Mexican, American or African music. When the ear is trained, all music is appreciated by everybody. If we produce music in Nigeria it will be modern. It will be the same with our art. [Our arts] should be studied for the meanings they have and interpreted to the world . . . Of course, there are some things—such as our songs—which will have an African flavor. But our objective should be to modernize them, not to keep them as they are."

On the subject of relationships between the generations, four out of every five respondents admitted that things were difficult, especially in the home circle. But most of them were convinced that they need not be as difficult as they were, since "it is the work of an intelligent man to be able to adjust to both groups." Many felt that their education "was only accidental" and that "a lot of people would be as smart if they had the education"; accordingly, they maintained that "we must be patient." But, as Zalinger remarks, it does not follow that back at home the respondents would be able to maintain "this level of compassion and understanding."

Political development. The topics covered by Zalinger under the heading of political development included self-government, forms of government, parties and their leaders, and the degree of the respondents' interest in political affairs.

Naturally enough, all the respondents were happy at the promise of self-government. Nevertheless, they were not all sure that the announced time of its arrival would, or could, be kept. Four out of five conceded the possibility of a postponement. Of these, 95 per cent agreed that, if there was a postponement, it would be the result, not of British foot-dragging, but of internal dissension. The things most likely to produce dissension, it was agreed, were tribalism, regionalism, and the self-interest and petty jealousies of their political leaders.

Slightly more than 90 per cent of the respondents considered that the current tribal or regional differences were the Number One obstacle to immediate self-government; 22 per cent tended to minimize these differences, maintaining that tribalism had been grossly exaggerated; 48 per cent insisted that tribalism is a serious problem only among the uneducated; while 30 per cent maintained that, in many cases, it is still a serious problem among educated people as well. Virtually all Ghanaian students pointed out that it was most serious in Ashanti and in the Northern Region, with the Nigerian students maintaining the same for their Northern Region. . . . Nearly all of the students expressed their own disapproval of ethnocentrism and most of them appeared to consider the fight against tribal and regional thinking to be extremely important . . . [However,] two out of every three maintained that current political tensions and attempts to unify groups under the banners of political parties have intensified some of the older tribal feelings and self-centeredness . . .

Although most students attributed some degree of responsibility for tribalism to British rule and the creation of regions, only 2 per cent claimed that current tribal difficulties were primarily the fault of the British; and only 7 per cent maintained that the United Kingdom was currently exploiting these differences. On the other hand, 67 per cent maintained that home-country politicians and traditional rulers were primarily responsible for exploiting and intensifying tribal tensions.

A Ghanaian student phrased this majority opinion thus: "Ethnic differences are still very important for the majority of people. It is only among the intelligentsia that any sort of national consciousness has developed . . . It is not very realistic to blame the British for these tribal feelings. They have always existed . . . If one wants to blame somebody, it would be more honest and accurate to blame the African . . . Of course, the British have had their hand in the pot, helping to stir."

Opinion concerning the reason for granting self-government likewise reflected a desire to think well of one's rulers. Nine per cent of the respondents believed that the British were simply interested in doing the right thing and living up to official declarations. Thirty-nine per cent believed that the motives of the British were compounded of equal parts of good faith and "enlightened self-interest." However, all but two students saw it as being equally a matter of self-interest —economic, political and military—to stay within the Commonwealth after independence had been won.

At the same time there were matters on which many students found it difficult to give more than a passing mark, if that, to their tutors. As one Nigerian put it, "I do not think that the willingness to grant self-government indicates a genuine change of heart on the part of the British. Rather, they see the direction in which history is moving and are adjusting to it . . . Of course, it would be unfair to say that the United Kingdom has done nothing for Nigeria. But whatever they have done has been much too slow and many of the good things were not really intended. They were mainly interested in exploiting the country and making a profit. Yet we cannot say they were there only to tap the well."

With self-government assured, how did the respondents view the problem of developing a government system at once viable and stable?

Opinion concerning the respective merits of unitary and federal forms of government was divided. Forty-four per cent were "unalterably opposed" to federalism in any form. Another 39 per cent held no brief for federalism but thought it would probably serve as a "temporary compromise." Only 10 per cent actually favored federalism. "The majority of those who were opposed to any type of regional federalism failed to specify what they would prefer in the way of a unitary system. However, 25 per cent stated that they would prefer the division of their countries into a number of smaller states with very little autonomy. The major reason for this was that such an arrangement would break the hold of the major tribal groups in the present regional structure . . . All those specifying a unitary system based on many states were Nigerian." The division of student opinion by territory was as follows (per cent):

	Ghanaian Students	Nigerian Students	Total
For federal form	14	9	10
For unitary form	73	35	44
For federal form as temporary compromise	9	49	39
No opinion	4	7	6

Opinion concerning the respective merits of the various political parties and leaders was also divided, but on the whole unenthusiastic. Whereas 14 per cent of the Ghanaians and 6 per cent of the Nigerians were "very satisfied" with the current (1954–1955) political situation at home, 40 per cent of the Ghanaians and 19 per cent of the Nigerians were "extremely dissatisfied and critical" of the situation, the rest being only moderately pleased with the way things were going. All told, 92 per cent of the respondents were "somewhat less than highly satisfied with the political parties and leaders in their home countries." Most of them had misgivings about the adequacy of the party programs and of their leaders. Thus, none of the Ghanaian respondents who claimed allegiance—as most of them did—to the Convention People's Party was "completely uncritical of either the party or Kwame Nkrumah." Almost all of those who were not members of the party expressed doubt about the competence of the current government leaders and their ability to build a truly democratic system. Some doubted even their willingness to build such a system.

The degree of the students' dissatisfaction with home-country politics appeared to be closely related to the length of their sojourn in the United States. Whereas only 10 per cent of those who had been in the United States less than four years were "highly critical" of the situation at home, 43 per cent of those who had been in the United States more than four years were reported as being highly critical.

Of course, not all students, African or otherwise, are equally interested in politics. In Zalinger's group not more than half were found to be "highly interested," and of the rest little more than half were even "moderately interested." The reasons for the rather surprising lukewarmness of so many (notably Nigerian) students were not always articulated, but in several cases they appear to have been related to the subjects they were studying. By no means all African students who come to this country major in political science; many are far more interested in economics, and in finding their future in the field of business, industry or technology.

Economic development. While none of the respondents held self-government to be an automatic solution to the economic problems with which their countries were faced, none saw any reason why these problems should be aggravated by self-government. "They argued that partnership in the Commonwealth would mean greater advantages for both west Africa and the United Kingdom, and that the tempo of change and development would increase under self-government." But, except for a few advanced social science students, most of the respondents had only a vague idea of what these advantages were likely to be, and how they could be secured. "At the same time, all students recognized the need for as rapid an industrialization program as was feasible. All recognized the need for modern agricultural methods and techniques. Although the great majority of students were for large industrial developments like the Volta River project, they were much more concerned about medium-sized industries. The majority also recognized the need for greatly accelerated training programs to provide necessary technical and administrative specialists."

The question of how developments of this kind could be brought about was one to which many students had obviously given a great deal of thought, and for which many of them had a ready answer. Most of the capital for such undertakings, it was generally accepted, would have to come from abroad. The use of foreign capital admittedly involved risks, such as the control of business by expatriate firms and the overseas flight of profits, but more than four out of five believed that their government should take the risks. Most of the rest seemed to feel, in the words of one Ghanaian student, that "We should avoid trying to get too much help from outsiders . . . When someone has interests in a country, he inevitably gets control of it . . . My personal belief is that foreign capital should not be invited."

If not from abroad, where then should the capital come from? Probably the clearest answers to this question were those given by the Nigerian student who believed that "after self-government much heavier taxation should be imposed on the big trading companies in order to keep the profits in the country" and by the Ghanaian student who "much preferred to see some sort of portfolio investment of funds raised by bond sales."

It was also recognized that such developments would call for a good deal of cooperation; that nothing was to be gained by "going it alone"; that there would have to be more cooperative relationships, not only between companies and governments, but between one government department and another, and between one company and another. It was realized that there would long continue to be a need for such "foreign" skills as business management and planning, banking, investment and insurance, and that without the close cooperation of expatriate and national in these fields, there could be no economic development worthy of the name. Not least, it was recognized that development of almost any kind would take time. As one student put it, "To be frank, the Gold Coast hasn't enough capital to develop rapidly, but we could go gradually without too much outside help. This might mean slower progress, but I think, in the long run, it would be the better policy."

Ideological issues. In the realm of ideas, most of Zalinger's respondents showed themselves to be close kin to the newly enfranchised of all lands. They had more questions than answers; such answers as they did have were not always very convincing, either to others or to themselves.

Take the matter of religious belief, for instance. While three in every four respondents claimed affiliation with one of the Christian denominations, one in two appeared to regard this affiliation as merely nominal. One in every five called himself either a free-thinker or an agnostic.

Or take the matter of political belief. While only a little over half of the respondents maintained that they were socialists, four out of five wanted government ownership of large industries and public services, with private ownership of smaller businesses and farms. Yet only one in four explicitly favored "a mixture of socialism and free enterprise." Not infrequently, respondents who started from identical premises finished with diametrically opposed conclusions. As a case in point, consider the following two statements by Nigerian students:

Actually [the following of a modified socialism] is not a matter of choice. We don't have that kind of opportunity in Nigeria which is available to richer nations. Nigeria is a frontier nation and we have to start from scratch. There are no large holdings and no really wealthy businessmen. Therefore, almost all types of economic activity will have to be sponsored by government loans and a welfare state. Socialized medicine is a necessity as are other social security measures.

I am opposed to socialism in any form. It doesn't work out, and our country is much too poor for this kind of system. The best system for Nigeria would be free enterprise, providing there are certain restrictions and a good guard against malpractices and fraudulent competition.

But even among those who think of themselves as avowed socialists or free-enterprisers, there is little familiarity with the basic principles of their creed, or commitment to it. Zalinger points out that "Their thinking is governed much more by what they consider to be the practical needs of their home countries than by any set of abstract principles of political theory, socialist or otherwise. Although some 73 per cent of the respondents took the British Labor Party as a model for their political ideas, the content of this model is not the philosophy of the party, but the specific welfare state policies associated with its period of office."

The one creed on which almost all the respondents spoke in unison and with conviction was communism. Of the approximately four out of five students who discussed it, none appeared to be even moderately attracted to either the communist ideology or the Soviet Union.[5] None of them believed that it held the answer to their home-country problems, or that it would make a strong appeal to the people of their home country. Their people, so three out of every four respondents contended, wanted to develop in their own way and were not interested in copying other people's systems, or in changing one set of masters for another, as they certainly would if they went communist. Many of the respondents also contended that, being a totalitarian and anti-democratic society, the Soviet Union was not adapted to their people's traditional values or their present political orientation toward the Western democracies. At the same time many thought that communism might have some appeal in those African territories in which there were "acute racial tensions, little hope for self-government, widespread hunger, severe economic exploitation, and a class of frustrated and discontented intellectuals. With respect to such areas, the respondents thought that the appeal of communism would lie in Russia's opposition to Western colonialism, its alleged idealism, whether true or not, and its symbol as a land of revolution and widespread economic reform."

Opposed to communism though they were, they were generally ready to defend the right of a man to be a Communist, and to be given legal recognition of the fact, whether in the United States or in west Africa. Thus, 64 of the 66 respondents discussing the issue held that the People's Republic of China should be admitted to the United Nations, largely, it would seem, because China was a non-white, underdeveloped and long-exploited country. And 70 per cent of those questioned maintained the right of Communists to form parties in their home countries and to enjoy "complete freedom" of activity. To deny them this right was, in their view, as inconsistent with democratic principles as McCarthyism—an ideology that, almost to a man, they found distasteful.

The majority view on communism was put by one student as follows:

[5] Six per cent of the students maintained that they had never heard of communism before coming to the United States.

I don't think communism will have much effect in Africa. I never believed in the doctrine that communism appeals to illiterates. The average Chinese, even the average Russian, is not a Communist . . . Eliminate the causes of discontent in a country, and you won't have to worry about communist influences . . . Africa is not prone to violence. If there is violence, it is usually because people have been pushed too far. People at home have no preoccupation with communism. They don't know about it and they don't care. Our affiliation with Britain has made us conservative in our outlook. We tend to be like the British, realists and moderates. If any Communists exist at home, I would favor the British attitude of free speech and the right to organize as a party. I do not favor the American way, McCarthyism and all; I think it is anti-democratic.

Nor did many of the students favor the United Nations' way of dealing with ideological issues. There was strong support for the principles of the United Nations as enshrined in its charter, but it was held that these principles got no more than lip service from most of its member countries. "Chickens cannot win a case in a court of oxen" was the proverbial way in which one student expressed his feelings in the matter. Another put it as follows: "The U. N. in general is not a United Nations. It is a compromise between struggling powers and their allies. It functions not on principles, but on power politics and self-interests. As long as it is dominated by the big powers, there will be a division of the world into two worlds. What is needed is more autonomy and more power for the smaller countries."

Of all their disillusionments none was greater than the failure of the United Nations to deal with "colonialism" and the failure of the United States to give the U. N. a lead in such matters. A Nigerian student expressed what was virtually a unanimous opinion when he said: "American foreign policy has been a great disappointment to me. How can the government behave the way it does? It votes with the big powers, and at the same time poses as the champion of freedom and the world's democratic leader." Yet the disillusionment had produced little bitterness or hostility. Even the most critical respondents thought of themselves, "not as uncompromising foes, but as disappointed friends." And there had been no defections to the communist camp.

Two other subjects on which many members of the new elite are no less forthcoming are Africanization and ethical conduct.

Africanization. It goes without saying that, as a class, educated Africans assume that they have the capacity to take over their own affairs. Are they not intelligent men? Have they not been trained according to the highest traditions of their rulers, often in the very same schools and colleges? Do they not know the people of their lands far better than their rulers? It also goes without saying that many of them have demonstrated that they have the capacity. In almost every territory there are those—from file clerks to lawyers and politicians—who can turn in as satisfactory a performance as their European colleagues. According to Wilmot, "If the student bodies of west African universities and technical colleges were asked the direct question: 'Are the majority of Africans in higher posts justifying their appointments?' the answer would be a resounding affirmative." In Wilmot's view it would be a well-earned judgment, too.

In these days, however, a good many educated Africans who applaud the principle of Africanization are increasingly disturbed about the practice of it. Some of them are disturbed about its pace, some about the kind being practiced, some about the consequences of it. There are those, of course, for whom the pace cannot be too rapid. In their opinion, the more rapid the pace, the sooner the goal of dominion will be reached, and the greater the power and the glory redounding to them. But there are those who see rapid Africanization as a horse without a rider. The goal may be dominion, but what, they wonder, is dominion without internal order and outside respect and confidence? In Nigeria this fear of going too fast too soon has been expressed in a number of ways. In recent years more than one small party has been founded on a "Go slow" policy, and in one federal election a seat was won on the slogan "Delay Self-Government," which, to the popular mind, was virtually the same as "Delay Africanization." In Wilmot's opinion, the sounding of this note of caution in Nigeria is "not a reflection on the course of events in Ghana or in any other territory which has moved toward self-government in recent years, but rather a symptom of the mistrust in which Nigerian politicians are held by some Nigerians and of the fear of increasing corruption."

The elite have reservations about the ability of some Africans to do jobs formerly held by Europeans. While such reservations rarely imply that it would be better to let Europeans go on doing these jobs, they do frequently imply that the wrong African has been selected. To judge by the rising volume of criticism, the number of "wrong Africans" is considerable. Nor, in Wilmot's opinion, is it difficult to see why. There are not enough educated Africans in any country to give the selectors much scope for their abilities. The output of the schools and colleges is insufficient to furnish the kind of competition to which all aspirants for higher-level service appointments in all democratic countries are accustomed. Many educated Africans, moreover, "greatly overvalue paper qualifications to the virtual exclusion oftentimes of qualities of character, personality, judgment and man-management."

These reservations notwithstanding, the general view among students is that Africanization must be pressed ahead, even if it takes a lot of Europeans to do the "Africanizing." The process, they freely admit, will be painful, as all learning processes are; it will also be attended by inefficiency and inconvenience. Whether, as some fear, it will be attended by demoralization has yet to be seen. Much will depend on the ethical conduct of those caught up in the process.

Ethical conduct. To speak of conduct is to speak of values. And to speak of values is to speak not only of conviction and truth but also of convention and tradition. Frequently, in the company of the educated African, it is to speak more of the latter than the former. For years now the West has come selling new wine in new bottles. While the African has taken a fancy to many of the bottles, he has not yet developed a palate for many of the wines. On the whole, the old suit him better, or so he seems to think.

Take, for instance, the matter of property. In the context of the extended family, in which most of the new elite were raised, goods and chattels are not regarded as possessively as in most Western societies. They tend to be thought of in much the same way as the family name: as a perquisite of birth or marriage. By extension, the material successes of one member of the family tend to be regarded as the property of all, to be shared according to need or fancy. But since, not infrequently, the expectations aroused by a success are out of all proportion to the actual magnitude of the success, the winner of it is constrained to look around for ways of increasing its magnitude. According to Wilmot, two of the commonest ways of doing so among students are the use of scholarship money intended for the purchase of textbooks or other educational needs, and the borrowing of funds from a society in which they hold office.

This is understandable, if not very commendable. What is neither understandable nor commendable by Western standards is the habit of rationalizing behavior of this kind. At a gathering of African students, Wilmot reports, it was agreed that "the disappearance and misappropriation of society funds and property is more to be regarded as carelessness than dishonesty, though a measure of the latter was admitted. The same students added that the failure to complete a satisfactory handover when a secretary or treasurer leaves college was quite as much the fault of the society as of the individual, and perhaps more so. . . . One student, with the obvious approval of others present, went as far as to dismiss the whole subject with the words 'It doesn't much matter anyway.'" However, in view of "the constant burden of obligation to the family," what Wilmot finds most surprising is not the existence of attitudes of this kind, but the comparative infrequency with which they are encountered.

The prevailing sexual attitudes of today's elite can also be related, in part at least, to their traditional culture. "A representative body of African students, when questioned on this subject, stated that the majority of students, if they could be encouraged to be frank (as indeed they can be), would vote in favor of premarital intercourse, and that many practiced it." In their opinion, such conduct was in keeping with the pre-missionary custom of most of their peoples and, for that matter, the post-missionary custom. While, as Wilmot points out, not all the evidence is on their side, enough of it is to make them look for modern justifications of the custom. These they have found, allegedly, both in biology and in the Bible; with the result that even many professed Christian students "regard promiscuity as normal and right," and feel remorse, if at all, when caught rather than when sinning. Those eschewing promiscuity "are certain that their number is few." In one university college, "a male student declared with finality that only one of the female students was uncorrupted and incorruptible," an opinion which Wilmot was disposed to accept on the ground that "Africans usually have a remarkably detailed knowledge about each other's private affairs." Those who do eschew promiscuity are, almost without exception in Wilmot's experience, those for whom Christianity is vital, as distinct from nominal. Such students, he asserts, set "an example of selfless service, faithfulness and integrity which few non-Africans can emulate." They may sometimes talk as though comfort and greed ruled their lives, "but their actions reveal that better motives insistently assert themselves."

THEIR ARTISTIC INTERESTS

In the popular mind, the elite are distinguishable from the non-elite mainly by their interest in the world of art and letters. Among educated Africans this interest derives its inspiration from several sources. One of the most productive of these

has its headwaters in Western Europe. As Thomas Hodgkin
has recently reminded us:

> The African *élite* has been taught in schools organised on
> the model of British public schools or French *lycées*. It has
> sat for its Senior Cambridge [school-leaving examination] or
> its *Baccalauréat* . . . It has been taught to reason in the
> style of Hume and Ayer, or Descartes and Gilson . . .
> When it succeeds in winning a measure of self-govern-
> ment, its institutions take the form of a Parliament on the
> British model (complete with Speaker and mace), or a ter-
> ritorial assembly derived from the French *Conseil-Général*.
> When this *élite* wants to write poetry, or do scientific re-
> search, or run a business, or make political speeches, or
> philosophise, it is obliged as a rule to use a European lan-
> guage. Friendship, family relationships, love-making, can
> be handled in the vernacular, but little else.[6]

Other external sources of inspiration, as suggested earlier,
are Eastern Europe (including Russia), America, Palestine,
Arabia and India.

More powerful than any of these, however, is the African's
own artistic tradition. Without doubt one reason for the
strength of this inspiration is reaction against the "cultural
colonization" he has undergone at the hands of his rulers.
This reaction is especially noticeable in the former French
West Africa, where the educated man has been exposed to
"assimilation in its most uncompromising form." Not surpris-
ingly, therefore, it is among the intellectuals of that region
that we meet the most uncompromising opposition to a con-
tinuance of the "colonizing" process. In Commonwealth West
Africa the reaction among the intellectuals has been nothing
like as strong, possibly because, as Davidson Nicol, a bio-
chemist and writer from Sierra Leone, recently put it, "the
distressing but stimulating convenience of a setting of Afro-

---

[6] "The African Renaissance," *The Listener,* August 15, 1957.

European conflict [has been] fortunately or unfortunately denied them."[7]

There is also a more radical reason for the strength of this
source of inspiration, namely, the growing conviction of
Africa's most influential intellectuals that the African's artistic
traditions and abilities are as worthy of respect and emulation
as those of any non-African people. True, Africa may not have
produced a Shakespeare or a Descartes, a Macaulay or a
Dumas (though, if it had, in the bookless, non-individualistic
world of pre-European Africa, would anybody know about it
in the mid-twentieth century?). But does that prove anything
about the intellectual parity of African and non-African, or the
lack of it? According to Léopold-Sédar Senghor, himself a
distinguished poet and professor of African languages at the
Sorbonne, it proves nothing. For in his view, by Hodgkin's
account,

the Negro-African genius is essentially different from the
European, and has produced different sorts of fruits. (Only
Europeans, with their itch to act as the world's schoolmas-
ters, or the world's examiners, would attempt the absurdity
of judging between fruits—giving an "alpha" to Shakespeare
and a "beta double plus" to the Benin bronzes.) African
culture is what it is because Africans are what they are—
rational, but in a different way from Europeans, understanding through insight and sympathy rather than through dis-
cursive thought. . . . African culture is the complex of activities, symbols, rhythms, through which African man expresses his understanding of the world and society and
sense of unity with them. African art is essentially a collective art, done for everyone with the participation of everyone. It is a practical art: Senghor quotes as an example an
episode from Camara Laye's novel, *The Dark Child*, in
which the forging of the golden jewel, the recitation of a
poem about the jewel, the dance to celebrate the comple-

[7] In an address at the First International Congress of Negro
Writers and Artists, held at the Sorbonne in Paris, September 1956,
under the auspices of *Présence Africaine*.

tion of the jewel, are all parts of a single process. It is a committed art; the artist mirrors his people, his times, his history, but he mirrors them from a definite personal point of view. And it is an art which virtually goes on all the time.[8]

So, on the one side, stand the "traditionalists"—those who want African scholars and artists to drink deep at their own Pierian springs, where, in Hodgkin's words, they can find "as rich a variety of myth and story, poetry and drama, sculpture and decoration, as any man could desire—based on a kind of grasp of man's essential nature that Europe has lost." On the other side stand the "Westernizers"—those who wonder whether there is any future to a backward-looking art, or, for that matter, whether it has any relevance to the present. Or, to put it somewhat differently, on the one side there are those who say, "We are very old, and all our future achievement depends upon grasping and using this ancient African inheritance"; and on the other those who say, "We are very young; and while we can admire this ancient culture, we must recognise that, where it survives, it is the reflection of a moribund medieval metaphysic: the ideas which we can use are secular, scientific, western."

Naturally, not all see the issue so simply. In the view of many the intellectual wellsprings of Africa have been poisoned beyond recovery by colonization or, as some would have it, by "coca-colonization." As these see it, wherever the colonizer has gone he has created "a new barbarism—islands of bogus traditionalism, occasional human 'zoos' to divert the tourist or interest the anthropologist, among a waste of pseudo-westernised men . . . living in a 'cultural undergrowth' that has grown up among the ruins of the old civilisation."[9] Others say that the African—man of two worlds that he is—can survive as an autonomous being only if he draws selectively upon both his inherited ideas and attitudes and his acquired Western values.

[8] Hodgkin, loc. cit.
[9] Ibid.

Wherever the truth may lie, this can be said: The art of the contemporary African intellectual, whether written or acted, whether done in wood, clay, stone or metal, with music or dance, provides an illuminating commentary on his times, their confusion and tensions, their pride and passions.

The works of indigenous writers, though marked by great diversity of style and form and varying greatly in quality of craftsmanship, have in common a capacity to stir the spirit of their African readers. The themes that occupy them are *their* themes: the mirth of children, the wisdom of the aged; the deeds of the fathers and forefathers of their people; the symbolism of all things, living and dead. They are themes, moreover, that are calculated to lay the ghost of barbarism, which, over the years, had come to worry Africans almost as much as Europeans. In this quickening of interest in indigenous Africa (as the interest had never died, it cannot truly be called a renaissance, in the fashion of the hour), many writers have played a part. To name but a few of the vanguard: J. M. Sarbah, who published an important work on Fanti customary law around the turn of the century; Apolo Kagwa, who was writing on the Kabakaship of Buganda about the same time; the Reverend Samuel Johnson, who wrote a history of the Yoruba people of Nigeria (published in 1921); J. B. Danquah, the Ghanaian lawyer who, over the last thirty years or so, has published several monographs on the Akan people of his country; the Abbé Alexis Kagamé, who has made a long study of the "dynastic poetry" of the Ruanda people of Ruanda-Urundi; Keita Fodeba, whose Théâtre Africain in the former French West Africa is an eloquent expression of the search for new artistic forms to fit old indigenous themes; Amos Tutuola, the Yoruba writer of fantasies; and Léopold-Sédar Senghor and David Diop, whose poetry at once evokes the past and elucidates the present.

Some of the writing does more. It "changes" the past and thereby challenges the present. Considerable effort is being made nowadays, by Senghor and other writers, to strengthen the rather tenuous cultural link between the Nile valley and sub-Saharan Africa. While the movement gathers little evidence, it yearly gathers momentum. In 1956 at the Sorbonne conference, Senghor went so far as to suggest that "the historical relationship between ancient Egypt and the peoples of Africa might well justify substituting ancient Egyptian for Latin and Greek as a classical language."[10] There has been a somewhat similar effort on the part of a number of west African writers to establish a close cultural link between the medieval Kingdom of Ghana and the country now going by that name. Here, too, the momentum of the movement has proved too much for the evidence.

Nor is this all. As with every reawakening of the spirit of a people, there is a growing interest in the use of vernaculars for both literary and scientific purposes. Recently Cheikh Anta Diop has done translations into Wolof of works by Racine, Marx and Einstein, which have demonstrated, so it is said, the ability of that language to cope with the virtuosity of Western thought. In more than one west African territory the campaign for a national vernacular is being waged with eloquence and zeal. In Ghana there is now considerable support for the adoption of one of the five main vernaculars as the official language of the country. In Liberia there are many who feel that Vai, one of the very few languages of tropical Africa to be reduced to writing before the time of the "partition," should be used for the same purpose. In his introduction to Senghor's La Nouvelle Poésie Nègre et Malgache, Jean-Paul Sartre speaks for many of Africa's most influential minds when he says: "Like the scholars of the sixteenth century who understood each other only in Latin, the Blacks rediscover themselves only on the terrain full of traps which White men have set for them . . . This syntax and this vocabulary, forged in another time . . . to answer to other needs and to designate other objects, are inadequate to provide [the Negro] with the means to speak of himself, of his cares or of his hopes."[11]

The world of music has begun to come under the influence

[10] See ibid.

[11] Translation by Thomas Hodgkin (pp. 176–77 of Nationalism in Colonial Africa, Frederick Muller, London, 1956).

of the same invigorating winds. Not that it has yet been transformed by them, for over much of Africa music is still, to use Hugh Tracey's word, in decay. "Sympathetic magic has played a large part in bringing about the decay of indigenous musical forms wherever contact with foreigners has been most effective. Imitation of the foreigner and all his ways has been considered, not without justification, to be the highroad to an easier and more prosperous life. The consequent spurning of indigenous music and emulation of foreign styles produced results pathetic by any standard." Among these Tracey numbers American-style jive, crooning of songs that amount to little more than "commercialized eroticism," and much of the hymnody of "a militant evangelism." At the same time, there is, as Tracey says in his working paper, "a clearly discernible tendency among many Bantu musicians to make their music more effective by expressing themselves in forms which more closely approximate to the original patterns." While this tendency is not confined to educated Africans (there are "genuine country musicians who are returning to those instruments and styles of song that best express their talents"), it is they who have become "sufficiently emancipated from the social pressure of their time to view indigenous music objectively and exercise their critical faculties in a constructive manner without a false sense of shame. Indeed, in the more talented individuals, a mounting enthusiasm for the genuine artistry of African musical styles with proper adherence to the rules of tone and stress has already found expression in new compositions of considerable complexity in which the virtue of continuity with the past has been rediscovered. Musicians of every country have reverted to the folk music of their own people to renew the vigor of musical composition, and Bantu musicians are now showing signs of doing so deliberately and intelligently."

Outstanding exponents of this school—who are not afraid to combine the resources of traditional African music with those of the Western world—are Ephraim Amu of Ghana, T. K. E. Phillips and Fela Sowande of Nigeria, and Joseph Kiwele of the Belgian Congo.

The problem of escaping from what Sartre calls "the prison house" of alien cultures is, however, not as easily resolved for the composer as it is for the writer. For the associative, and hence evocative, power of a rhythm, an instrument, a tune and a key is much greater, even for most literate people, than that of the spoken word. And most Africans who listen to music or dance to it are not yet literate. When words are married to rhythms, instruments, tunes and keys, the associative power is greatly increased; so much so that in the part-Christianized, part-Westernized, part-"Grundyized" Africa of today, there are some areas of life in which the use of the "vernacular" in music is virtually out of bounds.

As a case in point, Tracey cites the following story told by Canon E. E. Lury of the Diocese of Zanzibar:

> [On one occasion] a very beautiful setting of the *Te Deum* based on a native African melody was sung in Kampala Cathedral, Uganda. One of the members of the Universities' Missions to Central Africa was present and remarked afterward to the Bishop of Uganda how much he admired it. Shortly thereafter at luncheon a very keen and educated African Christian leaned across and said: "Bishop, you must never allow that *Te Deum* to be sung again in the Cathedral; it has too many wrong associations for us."
>
> There, in a nutshell, is shown the general attitude of Africans to their own music in church. The deplorable consequence is that there is no possibility of building an African music in African churches.

While Tracey believes that the story puts the outlook for African church music in an unwarrantably dim light, he does not for one minute belittle the difficulty which the educated African is having in emancipating himself "from a viewpoint dictated by sympathetic magic where associations of ideas entail identity of motive."

In the world of fine art similar difficulties, but rather different trends, may be discovered. The life of the pre-European African touched mystery at every point, and where there is mystery, there is fear; where fear, a search for security. For most Africans the greatest security, or greatest defense against insecurity, lay in giving "a local habitation and a name" to their fears: in fashioning symbols of the animal, ancestor, deity, or whatever else was the object of their fear. Consequently almost all works of art traditionally had a religious—a functional—inspiration. Further, almost all of them were done by honored men for the members of their own highly integrated community. As the exorcisers of their community's fear and the servants of its hope, they were as indispensable to it as it was to them. The community was proud of their skill, and grateful for every newly created expression of it.

But all this has changed. Though the artist and his clients may still stand in fear of the unknown, they have been told that their grounds for it are baseless and their security symbols as unavailing as a rabbit's foot; that if the artist's work is symbolic of anything, it is of the credulity of his clients and their gross ignorance of the laws of nature. At best it has "curio" value. But curios are the work of craftsmen rather than artists. Gone, then, is the need for the consuming love and patience that formerly went into the work of the sculptor's hands. Gone, too, the sense of awe, without which no artist can long withstand the seduction of his own success.

Because the traditional art of the African is no longer functional and there is no hope whatever of the old half-religious, half-magical function being restored in a world that has learned to exorcise its fears on Christian altars, and with the help of police forces, prophylactics and sewers, it is pointless to look to the past—as many African writers and composers are doing—for a new artistic synthesis. Where shall it be sought? Certainly not in the mass production of bookends, paper knives, "elephantine" lampstands, coffee tables and other "useful objects" to be found on show outside almost every hotel in Africa and at almost every airport. Nor yet in the equally sterile copying and "hybridization" of Western art forms encouraged by many so-called teachers of "art." Where else, then? An unsigned article in *Les Beaux-Arts* would seem to point the way: "Today the individual must find within himself the need for artistic creation, and must work out his own means of expression, for he can no longer rely on tradition and collective inspiration. Standing alone before his forests, his animals, his vanishing gods, and the new life of his people in factories, mines and cities, the native artist must seek new roots in his own conscience."[12]

And many are seeking new roots within themselves. With what success it is perhaps still too early to say; there must be root before fruit, and in Africa both are slow to form. But one thing is certain: the African's artistic conscience has not died. On the contrary, it is extraordinarily alive to suggestion and fertile in invention. Much of the new art, perhaps, is the work of suggestion and little else, and much has nothing to commend it except its inventions. Even so, there is a not inconsiderable residue that has all the authenticity and power of the older African art, and as much craftsmanship. To find it, we need only go to any one of the art schools, ateliers and museums opened in tropical Africa in the past generation. For whether they are in Achimota (one of the oldest in the region), Brazzaville, Dakar, Elisabethville, Ibadan, Kampala (Makerere) or Léopoldville, they clearly bespeak the resilience of the African's artistic conscience and his ability to "be himself," no matter what intellectual company he is keeping.

It is true that in some of the schools, notably the Saint-Luc schools in the Belgian Congo, the student has been obliged to study art systematically along European lines, and that, in so doing, his art sometimes has become more European than African in its provenance. But even this need not make him any less an artist. And further, it is arguable that, if, as many people believe, the future of the Congolese African lies in his adoption of European culture, he should be given every opportunity of acquiring it, in art schools and elsewhere.

On the other hand, there are those who believe that the African art student should be given a maximum of encouragement and a minimum of direction. Of those who have

[12] *The Belgian Congo: From Wilderness to Civilization,* special issue of *Les Beaux-Arts,* Brussels, 1955, p. 36.

taken this viewpoint none has been more convinced of the rightness of it than the late Pierre Romain Desfossés, a French amateur painter who, in 1946 at the age of sixty, went to live in Elisabethville. His story is briefly told in the *Beaux-Arts* article already referred to:

> One day, when he was away, his colored chauffeur took his palette and made a crude painting. This gave him the idea to start a studio where any native, regardless of his background or economic situation, could come and work as he pleased, free from any preconceived ideas or formal instruction. Desfossés left his pupils entirely alone to think up their own subjects and to execute them as they wished. He picked the boys and girls he thought had promise, and then gave them brushes, paints, and encouragement. The chauffeur, who started the whole thing, became known as Pili-Pili. His paintings of animals are reminiscent of Persian miniatures illustrating fables. Others followed. [Among these was Mwenze Kibwanga. Mwenze] came from the Saint-Luc art school [in Elisabethville], and he drew like a European child who had been taught in the traditional way. Desfossés did not want him; he thought that he had been spoiled for any original creation. But Mwenze begged to be allowed to stay on, and was finally accepted as the workshop's errand boy. One day Desfossés found him doing a painting in delicate strokes of alternate colours [and in a completely personal technique] . . . From then on Desfossés encouraged him, and soon he became one of the school's leading artists.[13]

Though Desfossés has been dead several years (he died in 1954), his atelier still opens its doors to all who show promise of being able to do original work in any of the fine arts. And the promise is certainly abundant. What is not so certain is the ability of the promising artist to live by his art in a society that has renounced its belief in the validity of the old art and has not yet acquired either the means or the desire to pa-

[13] *Ibid.*, p. 37.

tronize the new art. It is an uncertainty that bothers both teacher and student, and one that is unlikely to be quickly removed, in any town or territory. All the same, the number of domestic outlets for the artist's work is growing and will undoubtedly go on doing so as the economic and educational standards of his people are raised. Already there are artists, in the Makerere school and elsewhere, who are making a name for themselves as designers of textiles for the African market. Others are turning their skill to profit by designing and carving church altars and crucifixes, panels for pulpits, and statuary, or by designing and making decorative objects for the home. The work of some, notably the sculptor Ben Enwonwa of Nigeria, the painter Vincent Kofi of Ghana and the wood carver Job Kekana of Southern Rhodesia, finds as ready a market abroad as in their own country.

But frail and uncertain prospects are nothing new to the man of art; nor have they ever been the foe of inspiration. Indeed, much of the world's great art has been done in the presence of poverty and anxiety. What African art needs more than security for its reinstatement as the living oracle of African society is a new self-assurance, or, to use Léopold-Sédar Senghor's word, a new *sagesse*. This is something that cannot be bought with money, or conferred by self-government, but may be found by faith.

It has yet to be shown whether the things which exercise the minds of the African elite are big enough and durable enough to capture their allegiance, and keep it.

CHAPTER 8

THE PRICE OF GROWTH

To describe a growing thing is usually much easier than to explain its growth. Evidences of growth can be named and numbered; its sources, however, are frequently hidden and intangible, and the subject, therefore, of doubt. In tropical Africa the evidences of cultural growth are now so numerous and frequently so beguiling that there is danger not only of our forgetting whence they came but also of supposing that the only reason there aren't still more of them is bad husbandry. While it would be foolish to contend that tropical Africa has not had its share of bad husbandmen over the past fifty to a hundred years, it would be equally foolish to contend that growth is solely a matter of husbandry, and that there is nothing wrong with the economy, society and polity of the region that a supply of good husbandmen could not put right.

In the realm of culture, no less than in that of crops, growth is a compound of many ingredients. Genes are as much a part of it as growers; breeding no less than tillage. Time and effort, stamina, fitness and versatility are all involved. Without proper nurture the strongest nation languishes and dies. And not even the easiest environment in the world can compensate for constitutional deficiencies.

As has often been pointed out in this study, tropical Africa is not the easiest of environments, and many of its appearances of constitutional strength are deceptive. It is in most respects a difficult environment—as difficult for man as it is for animals and plants. What strength it has, whether of physical resource, social cohesion or political stability, is more readily impaired than improved, and has often been undermined by the exertions of invader, enterpriser and agitator.

Because it is a difficult environment, it is costly to work

with. To do virtually anything with it takes money; and among people still short of almost every kind of service, still largely untutored in the obligations of stewardship, still inexpert in the art of maintenance and ignorant of most labor-saving skills, money does not go very far. The company, agency or administration interested in developing this part of the world will find no tables "spread in the wilderness," no soft options or quick returns. There has hardly been an announced goal yet that did not take a little longer—and cost much more—to reach than anybody foresaw. When reached, some of the goals have taken a lot of defending. Some have never been reached.

Because tropical Africa is a costly environment to work with, it has had trouble in finding the things needed to make it less difficult and more rewarding. The needed things—investment capital, long-term loans, welfare and development funds, research organizations and the highly qualified personnel that goes with them—are also needed in many other places. Though the world has never lacked men or agencies willing to use their resources where most needed, philanthropy remains a minority movement. The places to get most attention from investors of money and skills have always been those offering the best prospects of steady yields, high market prices, security, congenial working and living conditions, and so on. On these scores, most parts of tropical Africa trail well behind Western and Central Europe, North America and, indeed, most other parts of the free world.

In the circumstances, it is surprising that tropical Africa has fared so well. Its showing, whether in the realm of capital formation, research, development or planning, is impressive.

CAPITAL FORMATION

The sources of tropical African investment capital are private and public, domestic and overseas. Reliable estimates of the capital derived from each of these sources are hard to come by. In addition to the uncertainties arising from the use of different national criteria of what is private and public in-

Table 5

PUBLIC AND PRIVATE CAPITAL ENTERING
SELECTED TERRITORIES BETWEEN 1870 AND 1936

TERRITORY	TOTAL		PUBLIC		PRIVATE[a]	
	(Millions)		(Millions)	(Per Cent)	(Millions)	(Per Cent)
British West Africa	£ 116.7		£ 50.9	44	£ 65.8	56
British East Africa	98.0		62.9	64	35.1	36
French territories	70.3		43.0	61	27.3	39
Belgian Congo (inc. Ruanda-Urundi)	143.3		35.8	25	107.5	75
Portuguese Africa	62.0		19.0	31	43.0	69

Source: S. H. Frankel, *Capital Investment in Africa: Its Course and Effects*, Oxford University Press, London, 1938.

[a] Includes all "non-listed capital."

vestment, there are those arising from the inadequacy of the published data, domestic and overseas.

For the pre-World War II period, the best estimates are undoubtedly those published, in 1938, by S. H. Frankel in his *Capital Investment in Africa*. These are given, for the major territorial divisions, in Table 5. It will be seen that while private capital—almost all of which came from overseas sources—contributed well over half of the total traceable investment, its relative importance was much greater in some territories (notably the Belgian Congo and Portuguese Africa) than in others (notably the French territories and British East Africa).

For the postwar period, no equivalent study exists, and what published material there is on the subject continues to be of uneven coverage and reliability. Several attempts have been made to estimate the postwar rate of capital formation. One of the most recent of these—by analysts of the United Africa Company—is given in Table 6. Total fixed capital in-

Table 6

ESTIMATED GROSS FIXED CAPITAL FORMATION, SELECTED TERRITORIES, 1956

	GROSS DOMESTIC PRODUCT	EXPENDITURE ON GROSS FIXED CAPITAL FORMATION		
TERRITORY		TOTAL	PER CENT OF GROSS DOMESTIC PRODUCT	PER CAPITA
	(*Millions*)	(*Millions*)		
British West Africa	$1,960	$364	19	$ 9.2
British East Africa	1,120	308	27	15.1
Belgian Congo (exc. Ruanda-Urundi)	1,176	328	28	25.5
French territories	n.a.	(616[a])	n.a.	(22[a])

Sources: The Colonial Territories, 1956–57, H.M.S.O., London, 1957; *Bulletin de la Banque Centrale du Congo Belge et Ruanda-Urundi* (Conseil de Direction des Fonds de Développement Economique et Social, Brussels), October 1957.

[a] Average 1954–1955.   n.a.: not available

vestment in 1956 in the territories there listed (they are the
territories in which the United Africa Company operates)
was over $1.6 billion. The average for the past few years is
thought to be somewhat less, about $1.4 billion. But even
this figure is a high one both in absolute terms and in relation
to the incomes in the territories. In relation to the gross domestic product, it is higher than the figure for the industrialized
countries of Western Europe, which have recently been putting about one sixth of their national income into domestic
fixed investment.

A detailed analysis of the contributions of private and public, domestic and overseas capital to this investment must
await the publication of better statistics than are now available for most territories. But at least three things are already
apparent. First, in the territories for which there are data
the ratios of private to public investment have not changed
radically since the war and the implementation of the various
development plans. "As far as we know," says Gaston Leduc
in his working paper, "private investment remains much
larger than public investment in the Belgian Congo, and probably also in the Portuguese territories and those of British
West Africa." The same would also seem to be true of the
two Rhodesias and Nyasaland. In the territories of the French
Community, however, the ratio of private to public investment
has undoubtedly fallen, largely because public financing,
within and outside the various territorial development plans,
has been at an unprecedentedly high rate (about 125 billion
francs C.F.A.[1] in French West Africa alone for the period
1947 through 1954). Second, although the contribution of
domestic capital to the total internal investment is growing,
it is still quite small. Third, in so far as any long-term trend
is discernible, it is in the direction of a lower ratio of private
to public investment. Among the reasons for this Leduc names
the following: "the risks and difficulties inherent in any large
tropical enterprise, the high costs, the long delays before
such an enterprise becomes self-supporting, political instabil-
ity and the cautiousness of prospective investors."

[1] Since 1948 the franc C.F.A. (*colonies françaises d'Afrique*)
has been equivalent to two metropolitan francs.

Leduc emphasizes, however, that the role of the private investor is in no danger of being eliminated except as a consequence of political upheavals.

PRIVATE INVESTMENT

In these days of growing government activity in the investment field, it is well to recall that private enterprise was the principal agency by which tropical Africa was brought into contact with the Western world. Private enterprise was behind virtually every economic and commercial development (other than railroad construction, much of which was publicly financed), and so in large measure responsible for the development of external trade, which is still the mainspring of Africa's prosperity. It has also contributed to the fund of material wealth upon which advancement in the spheres of politics, education and health largely rests.

While the relative importance of private capital has decreased in the postwar years, the actual amount of private investment has increased steadily and in some territories spectacularly. In most territories it shows little sign of leveling off, let alone of declining.

Domestic

The domestic supply of private investment money is small for several reasons. Among the lesser ones, as Leduc reminds us, are the African's understandable disinclination to save for an uncertain tomorrow what he has no difficulty in spending and enjoying today, and the expatriate European's equally understandable disinclination to invest his savings in enterprises that are characteristically slow-growing and in territories whose political future is clouded.

The chief reason, no doubt, is the lowness of the average income levels. Misleading as comparisons of per capita income can be, especially when they refer to territories with differing felt needs and at differing stages of cultural sophistication, they are probably worth making, if only to show the order of

magnitude of the domestic savings possible in tropical Africa.
Figures for some of the territories are given in Table 7.

Table 7

AVERAGE PER CAPITA INCOME, SELECTED TERRITORIES, 1956–1957

TERRITORY	APPROXIMATE AMOUNT
France	$1,000
United Kingdom	980
Belgium	980
Ghana (Gold Coast)[a]	194
Fr. West Africa[b]	133
Rhodesia & Nyasaland	132
Malagasy Rep. (Madagascar)[b]	119
Kenya[c]	78
Belgian Congo	76
Sierra Leone[b]	70
Gambia[b]	56–70
Nigeria	69
Uganda[c]	57
Tanganyika[d]	48
Ethiopia	30

Source: United Nations, *Economic Survey of Africa Since 1950*,
New York, 1959.

[a] Gross national product at factor cost.
[b] Gross domestic product at market prices.
[c] Net domestic product at factor cost.
[d] Gross domestic product at factor cost.

Higher though they are than they were even five or ten years
ago, these incomes can by no sleight of mind be described
as anything but low. Nor, in every case, can they be said to
be a measure of the African's purchase-*cum*-saving power, as
part of the national (or domestic) product that provides the
basis of calculation of these incomes is generated in the non-
African sector of the economy. In the case of Nigeria this
part is very small (less than 5 per cent), but in the case of
the Belgian Congo it is about half (46 per cent in 1956),
and in the case of Kenya, about three quarters.

Such incomes make it virtually impossible for the average African worker to be a systematic saver. In so far as he manages to save anything, he saves it for such short-range needs as shoes, suits, a bicycle and bride wealth. More often than not, however, he spends all he gets, and does so within a few hours of getting it. It is only the well-above-average African—the "boss-boy," the teacher, the cocoa farmer, the *infirmier*, the lawyer and the politician—who is able to think of accumulating savings for investment. While there are Africans who have saved and invested modest fortunes, the general run of African savings is small, and by any Western yardstick the aggregate of such savings is small. In the African context it is by no means negligible. According to Leduc, savings bank deposits in French West Africa and Togo at the end of 1954 totaled 697 million francs C.F.A., or approximately $3.5 million. At the end of 1957 the figure was slightly less, 674 million francs. Of this amount, not less than 80 per cent, Leduc estimates, belonged to African depositors. In the Belgian Congo in 1950 African savings contributed $14 million to the financing of the government's internal investment, and in 1956, more than $11 million. In most territories, African savers are also making increasing use of the commercial banks.

But many Africans are still shy of banks, commercial or otherwise. In some areas—not only the more backward bush areas—the chief depository of a man's savings continues to be the floor, or roof, of his hut, often to his neighbor's gain more than his own. In other areas—not only the more advanced ones, either—steadily growing amounts of savings are being put into term insurance, mutual loan associations, small businesses (cycle repair, tailoring, trucking, general trading), farm cooperatives (for the purchase and rental of equipment, etc.) and real estate.

Small, too, as is the amount of non-African savings invested domestically, it is likewise far from negligible in the African context. According to Leduc, in French West Africa non-African deposits in savings banks amounted to 140 million francs C.F.A. at the end of 1954; those in commercial banks amounted to 95 per cent of the total. In French Equatorial Africa, according to the same authority, 70 per cent of the deposits in savings banks and 99 per cent of the deposits in commercial banks at the end of the same year were owned by non-Africans. Here again, as Leduc points out, it is practically impossible to give meaningful figures for "non-African" savings or to specify precisely the uses to which they are put. "Permanent residents may invest a significant part of their savings locally, especially in real estate, but temporary residents probably send all their savings to the mother country. For many Frenchmen, the goal of a prolonged stay in tropical Africa is the ability to build or purchase a home somewhere between Marseille and Nice." Much the same tendency to send savings to the homeland is true of nationals of other countries. At any rate, the south of England is full of former overseas service administrators living, servantless, in the drafty, damp red-brick cottages they dreamed about when they were stationed in the African bush. Nor would it be difficult to point to Asians and Levantines who have been more active, and successful, in the buying and selling of property in Africa than any resident Europeans. In many of the large cities —Nairobi among them—the ground whereon the European stands is often Asian ground and the house in which he lives Asian-built and Asian-owned.

It would be an oversimplification to suppose that all the temporary European residents are in the habit of exporting their savings or that the primary investment interest of all the permanent European residents is real estate. From the number of British and continental insurance firms that have opened African offices since the end of World War II, notably in Kenya, the Federation of Rhodesia and Nyasaland, and the Belgian Congo, and from the size of their staff, it is quite apparent that many resident Europeans and Asians must be putting a large part of their savings in local pension and superannuation schemes and in life insurance. It is equally apparent, from even a cursory glance around the "settler" countrysides, that many European farmers have been using a large part of their postwar earnings for development. They have invested in everything from piped water supplies, anti-erosion measures and stock improvement to the modernization of their homes and the rehousing of their African employees.

Overseas

The chief source of private investment money has always been the incorporated company. As with individual capital movements, comprehensive data on the capital entering and leaving the territories through the medium of such companies do not exist. "Private business secrets," Leduc observes, "are as well kept south of the Sahara as anywhere else." To judge from the accusations leveled against them, some of the commercial companies have had good reason for their secrecy. "They have repeatedly been accused of failing to see their mission other than in a strictly commercial light, and of having endeavored, with evident success, to reap the maximum profits in the minimum time. These profits, one hears, were not distributed to local shareholders or reinvested locally, but regularly sent back to the mother countries as sizable shares and dividends, or to form more or less hidden reserves; with the inevitable result that the local economies suffered a loss of substance and a continual draining of their available investment financing."

As Leduc goes on to say, it is difficult to get to the bottom of such assertions, since the dealings of the incriminated companies are not open to public scrutiny. But not all of the companies are incriminated, and some of the incriminated ones have had little trouble in clearing their names. In the French territories Leduc has been able to show that "after World War II a notable amount of corporate savings was reinvested locally." He estimates that from 1947 through 1953 "an average of 31 per cent of capital investment came from accumulated reserves—7.2 billion francs C.F.A. out of 23.2 billion. Inquiries among 44 corporations doing business in black French Africa, including Madagascar, show that the average profits plowed back into business before constitution of reserves were as large as capital increases financed by other means than the drawing on reserves, that is, for the period 1947 through 1953, about $23 - 7 = 16$ billion francs C.F.A. Total corporate savings immediately reinvested or placed in reserves would thus total at least 23 billion francs C.F.A." Even though this figure cannot be compared with other accounting items in the "national" economy of the territories concerned, because the data are lacking, none can call it insignificant.

In the Belgian Congo in 1950 corporate savings contributed nearly $157 million to the territory's internal investment, and in 1956 nearly $200 million—more than half of the total internal investment. It is not improbable that an inquiry into the capital movements of private corporations doing business in some other areas would disclose similar results.

The United Africa Company, which for years has operated on a very big scale in many parts of tropical Africa, and on that account has been the object of frequent "incriminations," has recently released some figures which, while they may not silence its enemies, go far to explain how it has come to have so many friends. Since its formation in 1929 the Group forming the United Africa Company[2] has reinvested locally $180.6 million of its profits, or more than $6 million a year. Bearing in mind the postwar decline in the value of money, it is probable, as the company contends, that this figure considerably understates the real worth of the investments made in the prewar period. The company also contends that it has helped to increase the domestic supply of investment capital by systematically seeking to complement rather than to supplant indigenous enterprise. To quote from the March 1958 issue of its *Statistical and Economic Review:* "By means of supplies, advice and financial support, the Group has assisted many thousands of African traders to build up successful businesses. In Commonwealth West Africa[3] alone it has on its books some 6,000 Africans with credit accounts, [selling]

---

[2] Excluding three palm oil companies once part of the company but now independent.

[3] The company's term for Ghana (including Togoland), Sierra Leone, Gambia and Nigeria (including British Cameroons).

about £25 million [$70 million] worth of goods annually. The net amount on trust with African customers at any one time may exceed £2 million [$5.6 million]."

The company has been promoting African business interests in other ways, too. Thus, in west Africa it has handed over to Africans most of its trade in such commodities as cocoa, palm oil, peanuts and rubber. In the same region it has helped to bring into being a number of industrial schemes that otherwise would have remained beyond the African's grasp. In some instances it has done this by providing the necessary capital; in others, by providing the merchandising experience and managerial skills; in still others, by providing both. A singlet factory in eastern Nigeria offers a good illustration of the company's "foster-parent" role. It was built by the company with Nigerian money. It is entirely owned by Nigerians, and managed by a company-trained Nigerian staff. It uses a company-supplied fabric and finds a guaranteed market for its finished product in the company's many merchandising outlets.

It is in ways such as these, so the United Africa Company believes, that the interests of its shareholders can best be served, for are they not best served by what best serves the African people?

Other large private companies with a fine reinvestment and "service" record are the Union Minière du Haut-Katanga, the Copperbelt companies (the Anglo American Corporation and the Rhodesian Selection Trust), the Office d'Exploitation des Transports Coloniaux (Otraco), and Firestone Plantations Company in Liberia.

In the absence of detailed statistics of company capital entering and leaving the region, it is probable that local company registrations provide as useful a measure as any of financial growth. For most of the companies registered in tropical Africa are floated, in part if not in whole, by overseas funds, and all of them add to the investment strength of the territories in which they do business.

In British East Africa the nominal capital of new local companies, which was only a little more than $4 million in 1938 and less than $10 million in 1945, rose to nearly $43 million in 1956. In 1956, 98 new companies were incorporated in Nigeria (this figure includes 38 companies which were incorporated overseas and registered in Nigeria). Between them these companies had a nominal capital of over $11 million. In the Belgian Congo new companies have been formed at an average annual rate in recent years of approximately 300. This represents a nominal capital inflow of between $24 million and $28 million a year. During the same period the capital of existing companies in the Belgian Congo has been expanding by upward of $30 million a year.

PUBLIC INVESTMENT

In tropical Africa the bulk of public investment capital is derived from two sources: (1) domestic savings effected through ordinary government budgeting and through profits, after amortization, etc., of public agencies; and (2) development funds, financed for the most part by metropolitan governments and other interested overseas powers.

Domestic

The low average level of incomes places limits on the amount of public saving that can be done. The budgetary revenues in 1956 of a selected number of territories are given in Table 8. These, too, by contemporary Western standards, can only be termed modest.

There are those who argue that these revenues, derived as they are very largely from indirect taxation, are more modest than they need be; that the yield of direct taxes on individuals and corporations could be greatly increased without significantly affecting the yield of import and export duties. But, as an article in the aforementioned issue of the United Africa Company's *Statistical and Economic Review* points out, "Equitable imposition and cheap collection of direct taxes is hard to achieve in tropical Africa . . . The Governments of Ghana and Eastern Nigeria have confirmed experience elsewhere that taxation of a large number of comparatively modest incomes is expensive in relation to the revenue yield." Further, incomes are difficult to ascertain and evasion is easy, except for the employees of government and large firms, who have the tax deducted at source.

There are others who argue that the yield of import and export duties is lower than it need be in some territories. But, as the same article goes on to say, there are strict limits to the rates of indirect taxation which it is feasible to impose. "Territorial boundaries in Africa are long and the number of

Table 8

BUDGETARY REVENUE, SELECTED TERRITORIES, 1956

TERRITORY	TOTAL	PER CAPITA
	(Millions)	
Ghana (inc. Togoland) (Gold Coast)[a]	$138.0[b,c]	$29.4
Kenya[a]	98.6[b,c]	16.0
Fr. West Africa	290.6[b,d]	15.7
(Fr.) Cameroons	47.9[d]	14.8
Gambia	4.2[b]	14.0
Belgian Congo (inc. Ruanda-Urundi)	227.9[e]	13.4
Sierra Leone	25.8[b]	12.9
Somalia (Ital. Somaliland)	14.3[f]	11.0
Fr. Equatorial Africa	50.1[d]	10.4
Uganda[a]	50.7[b,c]	10.0
Nigeria (inc. Brit. Cameroons)[h]	261.2[b,c]	9.0
Tanganyika[a]	60.2[b,c]	7.8
(Fr.) Togo	7.0[i]	6.7
Liberia[g]	12.8	6.4

Sources: The Colonial Territories, 1956–57, H.M.S.O., London, 1957; Bulletin Mensuel de Statistique d'Outre-Mer (Paris), passim; Bulletin de la Banque Centrale du Congo Belge et Ruanda-Urundi (Brussels), 1957.

[a] July 1956–June 1957.
[b] Includes Colonial Development and Welfare funds, and grants-in-aid.
[c] Original estimates. [d] Principal receipts only.
[e] Ordinary and extraordinary revenue.
[f] Including contribution (amounting to more than 50 per cent of total revenue) of Italian government.
[g] 1955. [h] April 1956–March 1957. [i] Custom receipts only.

customs officials limited. As the Marketing Boards in Ghana, the Gambia and Eastern Nigeria have found, evasion is hard to check." Furthermore, "prices and rates of duty cannot be markedly out of line with those that are in operation in neighbouring territories." If they are, the cost of putting the illicit frontier-runners out of business is quite likely to exceed the gains accruing from the higher imposts.

Confronted with such an array of hard fiscal facts, some governments have taken, with unconcealed satisfaction, to "raiding" the reserves of their produce-marketing boards. And, as was shown earlier, most of the boards have been able to accumulate substantial reserves, by keeping the level of prices paid to growers providently low. While research and other activities aimed at directly benefiting producers have usually been the first to profit from such raids, several development projects have done handsomely out of them. Thus, the Ghana Cocoa Marketing Board made available to its government for the 1951–1957 development plan loans in excess of $47 million, representing 14 per cent of the total cost of the plan. Since its setting up in 1948, it has also made substantial grants to the University College (approximately $8.1 million) and to health and welfare (including education) projects (approximately $6.2 million). In Nigeria, loans made by the regional marketing boards to the federal government up to 1958 exceeded $31 million; and in the Western Region more than $52 million (18 per cent) of the total expenditure of $293 million envisaged under the 1955–1960 development program was scheduled to come from the Regional Marketing Board in the form of loans or grants.

Overseas

Contrary to the widely held belief, most of the metropolitan governments have been sinking money into their African territories ever since they assumed administrative responsibility for them. By present standards, the amount invested was not large, but even at £211.6 million (S. H. Frankel's figure for public investment in Belgian, British, French and

Portuguese tropical Africa during 1870–1936), it is considerably larger than the amount which found its way back to Europe in the form of salaries, transfers to reserves, interest payments on national debt, pensions of personnel, etc. As the administering authorities soon discovered, the pumps of Africa prime slowly.

As late as the 1930s public debt charges formed a substantial element of the budget in almost every territory. In 1934 they amounted to nearly half of the public expenditure in the Belgian Congo, and in the four years 1934–1937 the Belgian government granted a total of 640 million francs to cover deficits in the Belgian Congo budget. In 1937 French West Africa received a subvention of 79 million francs—a sum almost equal to the entire debt charge of the territory in that year. From 1929 onward British government aid to its African colonies included development grants and interest-free loans as well as grants and loans to meet budget deficits in particular territories. Only in the Portuguese territories of Mozambique and Angola and in Liberia, in none of which had very much basic development been undertaken, did debt charges form a relatively inconsiderable item of the annual budget. But let it be said to the credit of the early primers, smallness of yield seldom discouraged them from pursuing the search for likely pump sites and the supply of priming fluid. It is probably not too much to say that the objective of government priming has been social as much as financial, the benefiting of the governed as much as the governors.

Since about 1945, the search for good development projects and the supply of funds with which to get them started have both been stepped up. In the early postwar years specific programs of development were prepared by each of the colonial powers in consultation with their respective dependencies. Although there were degrees of consultation (on the whole the territorial governments of British and Belgian areas were allowed more of a say in such matters than those of Portuguese and French areas), the aims of the plans varied little from territory to territory. In essence, according to the *Statistical and Economic Review*, they were designed to "increase the

Table 9

GOVERNMENT EXPENDITURE UNDER
DEVELOPMENT PLANS, SELECTED TERRITORIES

(Per Cent)

| MAIN CATEGORIES | BRITISH WEST AFRICA | | BRITISH EAST AFRICA | | | | FRENCH TERRITORIES 1947–56 | BELGIAN CONGO 1950–56 |
	GHANA 1951–57[a]	NIGERIA 1955–60[b]	KENYA 1954–57	UGANDA 1955–60	TANGANYIKA 1955–60			
Total development expenditure	100	100	100	100	100		100	100
Transport and communications	31	25	13	14	29		45	46
Agriculture, forestry and fishing	7	9	26	4	19		15	6
Electricity and water	9	7	16	29	17		4	11
Education	15	21	10	6	15		4	6
Housing (inc. surveys and town planning)	6	3	7	12	8		1	4
Health	6	9	4	5	5		5	5
Commerce and industry	3	5	1	11	1		3	2
Miscellaneous[c]	23	21	23	19	6		23	20

Source: Statistical and Economic Review (United Africa Company Limited, London), March 1958, p. 22.

[a] Excluding development of new town and harbor at Tema.
[b] Federal and regional.
[c] Mainly public works.

knowledge of the natural resources of the country concerned and exploit those resources more effectively; provide the groundwork for future development in the shape of public utilities and communications; and improve the health, education and living conditions of their population."

Table 9, prepared by the United Africa Company, shows the way in which the development funds of selected territories were allocated to these various objectives. Because of variations in the way governments classify expenditures, the table does not warrant our reading significance into small percentage differences. It leaves no doubt, though, about which types of programs have been given the highest priority in each region. It also shows that the priorities have differed from region to region—sometimes between adjacent regions. Thus, whereas in Kenya agriculture, forestry and fishing have had over one fourth of the government's development funds, in Uganda they have had only one twenty-fifth. While the sectors of economic and social life getting most of the funds are those which the governments concerned believe to be the most in need of them, it does not follow that the sectors getting very little have been neglected. In some cases, for instance education in Uganda, they are sectors in which past expenditure has been heavy. In others, for instance agriculture in Ghana and Uganda, they are sectors which have been largely left to private enterprise. In still other cases, for instance housing in French territories, they are sectors which, in the view of the administering authorities, do not warrant heavy expenditures until the people have shown themselves able—or willing —to earn enough to take care of the upkeep.

Viewing the table as a whole, two things stand out clearly. The first is the emphasis on the provision of basic services such as transport and communications. This emphasis has been most marked in the French and Belgian territories, which are large and on the whole sparsely peopled, and where, on that account, almost any new road or telephone system has to be a long one to serve a useful purpose. The second is the large provision being made for public utilities, such as electricity and piped water, which hitherto have been numbered among the luxuries of tropical African life. What the table does not show, but what is quite as important, is the recently increased emphasis on productive projects, such as agriculture, fisheries and cooperatives. These, it is hoped, will be able to contribute to the maintenance of the *infrastructure* and, in time, to pay for extensions to it.

These development funds have come from various sources —not all of them, as we have seen, external. Indeed, in the case of one or two territories by far the larger portion of them has been raised domestically.

Commonwealth territories. A first approximation of the relative importance of external and internal sources of development funds to the Commonwealth territories is contained in the issue of the United Africa Company's *Review* which we have already referred to. According to these figures, the east African territories have recently been relying on external sources (such as Colonial Development and Welfare grants and loans) for no more than 60 per cent of their development funds and the west African territories have been getting only one third of their funds in this way. As the authors of the analysis point out, the Commonwealth territories "have been encouraged to make maximum use of their local reserves for financing the current Development Plans. To this end the United Kingdom Government suggested that colonial Post Office Savings Banks and the Currency Boards should employ in local investments some proportion of the funds which they had raised. It has also prompted some of the territories to find at least part of their requirements by running down their sterling balances rather than by borrowing on the London market."

These sterling assets date back, for the most part, to World War II, when about all the United Kingdom could offer the Commonwealth territories in exchange for their much needed foodstuffs and raw materials were some sterling-filled safe deposits in the Bank of England. Since the war the sterling balances held by most of those territories have continued to rise, thanks largely to such prudent housekeeping devices as the produce-marketing boards. By paying farmers prices lower than those prevailing in the open world market, the same authors add, these boards, have "dampened import demand and permitted the accumulation of sterling holdings which could be used to meet less favourable circumstances which may arise in the future and to finance future development."

While most of these balances may properly be regarded as domestic funds, a part of them represents assets held in London by banks operating in tropical Africa and consists of deposits originating from undertakings either owned or controlled by United Kingdom residents. Such deposits cannot be regarded as in any sense domestic. Nor, of course, can all of them be regarded as a "nest egg" for the developer, for part of them belongs to governmental and quasi-governmental agencies for whom a sterling balance represents a financial reserve, and part to the various territorial currency boards as backing for the local currency. And, as has been noted, part of the funds accruing to the various marketing boards is earmarked for things other than development.

To supplement the domestic sources, the United Kingdom government has since 1940 made available substantial amounts of development money, most of it through the following media: the Colonial Development and Welfare funds, the Colonial Development Corporation and the Commonwealth Development Finance Company, Ltd.

The Colonial Development and Welfare Act passed in 1940 made available up to £5 million a year for ten years for "schemes for any purpose likely to promote the development of the resources of any colony [not merely African] or the welfare of its people," together with a further £500,000 a year for research. In 1945 the government passed a further Colonial Development and Welfare Act authorizing the spending of a total of £120 million on such schemes. In 1950 this amount was increased to £140 million. In 1955 an additional £80 million was voted for development work to be carried out in the period 1955–1960. Issues from C. D. and W. funds during the eleven years ended March 31, 1957 totaled nearly

£ 137 million. Of this amount, over £ 34 million went into British East African projects, over £ 56 million into British West African projects, and over £ 6 million into British Central African (Northern Rhodesia and Nyasaland) projects. In relation to the cost of the development plans of any one territory, the amounts made available by the C. D. and W. acts are generally small. In 1956 the current development plans for African dependencies of the United Kingdom provided for a total expenditure of over £ 560 million. Of this, only 7 per cent (£ 40.5 million) was being met from grants made under the C. D. and W. acts; the rest came from local revenues (about one third) and loans (about three fifths) secured on these revenues. It is also true that some of the things into which C. D. and W. money was put did very little for either the territory concerned or the welfare of its people and that, as Lord Hailey has observed, "most of the early drafts of the Development Plans were little more than a series of departmental estimates inflated above their normal level by anticipation of the receipt of extra-territorial aid."[4]

At the same time, there is not a British dependency in Africa that cannot point to some major piece of economic or social development made possible by C. D. and W. funds. Among such undertakings were the building of the University College, Ibadan, Nigeria, and the Royal Technical College at Nairobi; the drainage and reclamation of the formerly rather unhealthy area around Bathurst, the capital of Gambia; the maintenance of the Desert Locust Control Organisation in east Africa; the construction of rural water supplies in the Northern Region of Nigeria; and the improvement of African agriculture in Kenya. Hardly less important, these funds have been a spur to the imagination of the administrator—long stunted by the rigors of a budget that allowed few schemes and no dreams—and to the appetite of the administered for better living. Without C. D. and W. funds there would still have been development plans in most of the African dependencies, but the chances are they would

[4] *An African Survey: Revised 1956*, Oxford University Press, London, 1957, p. 1336.

have been less closely related to the needs and desires of the people being "developed," and much more costly.

The Colonial Development Corporation came into existence in 1948. The Overseas Resources Development Act of that year authorized the setting up of two separate public corporations, the Colonial Development Corporation (CDC) and the Overseas Food Corporation (OFC). The CDC was given power to borrow up to £100 million (since increased to £150 million) for long-term and £10 million for short-term schemes of economic development in colonial territories. It was the intention of the Labor government which sponsored the act that the corporation should supplement private investment rather than replace it, by assisting in schemes which, although offering reasonable long-term prospects, might prove unattractive to private capital working alone.

It was considered that there was a shortage of risk capital in the United Kingdom relative to the colonies' needs. Furthermore, the cost of floating a moderate issue (say, under £500,000) on the London market was such as to deter many private concerns from undertaking projects unless they had sufficient profits to re-invest.

A final argument put forward in favour of a Government corporation was that the financial attractiveness of an investment might not be a true reflection of its value to the community.[5]

It was also the intention of the government that the corporation should pay its way. This it began to do in 1955, notwithstanding the restrictions on its borrowing power (all loan money has so far come from the United Kingdom Treasury) and on the repayment terms it can impose upon those who borrow from it. On long-term loans, interest payments are postponed for the first seven years; loans and interest are repayable by 33 annuities starting in the eighth year.

By the end of 1958 the total capital approved for African projects amounted to more than £54 million. The corpora-

[5] *Statistical and Economic Review*, September 1957, pp. 21–22.

tion's range of interest is wide. It has put money in hotels (Kenya), housing (Kenya, Nyasaland, Southern Rhodesia, Nigeria), mining (Kenya, Tanganyika, Uganda), manufacturing (Kenya, Tanganyika, Northern Rhodesia, Nigeria), power (Kenya, the Federation of Rhodesia and Nyasaland), ranching and meat processing (Bechuanaland), forestry (Tanganyika, Nyasaland) and airlines (Central African Airways Corporation). As with all pioneer work of this kind, the maturing period tends to be long (often longer than the seven-year interest-free period), the yield uncertain and, in some instances, unpalatable. More than one African project has had to be written off. At the present time most CDC investments fall into four categories: directly operated projects and investigations; shares in associated companies; debentures and loans; and mortgages. The corporation notes in a recent annual report that it is also willing to make grants "for investigations and research which may or may not lead to anything productive [and] for special sociological purposes connected with projects."

The Overseas Food Corporation, which came out of the same 1948 act, was designed to develop new sources of food supply for Great Britain. As far as British Africa is concerned, its main job in the early years was to salvage what it could of the remaining assets of the Tanganyika Groundnut Scheme and turn them to account in experimental work. This work has sought to establish the value of mechanized agriculture in certain types of tropical environment and to test the potentialities of peasant farming.[6] In March 1955 the corporation turned over its responsibilities to the Tanganyika Agricultural Corporation.

The object of the Commonwealth Development Finance Company, Ltd., incorporated in 1953, is "to provide or procure financial facilities of all kinds for the development of the natural and other resources of any part of the Commonwealth." Although more of its authorized share capital of £15 million is subscribed by private than public agencies, the Bank

[6] See *Land and Livelihood*, Chapter 5.

of England—a government institution—is its largest single shareholder (with 45 per cent). The policy of the company is to make loans to private schemes only after their promoters have exhausted the normal money market channels and have shown that they can furnish expert management. Other things being equal, it favors schemes which promise to give an early return, such as electricity supply, sugar estates and cement manufacturing. Down to the end of 1959 the company had not done very much for the Commonwealth territories of tropical Africa.

The French Community. There have been two main agencies through which metropolitan France has dispensed aid to her overseas territories. These are FIDES (Fonds d'Investissement pour le Développement Economique et Social) and CCFOM (Caisse Centrale de la France d'Outre-Mer), now (since 1959) called the Caisse Centrale de Coopération Economique. Crédit Nationale, one of France's state banks, has also granted medium- and long-term loans to private companies in the overseas territories. The French government has made large investments out of its own budget over the years in the services, such as air navigation, post office and telecommunications, which it has administered directly from France.

The administrative and financial machinery of the postwar "General Plan for Modernization and Development of the French Overseas Territories" was set in motion by the law of April 30, 1946. This law created FIDES, which had as its object the financing of public development plans in all French overseas territories. These plans were of two kinds, general and overseas. Plans in the general category were aimed at benefiting all the territories; those in the overseas category were confined to individual territories or groups of territories. The cost of the "general" plans has been borne by the metropolitan treasury; that of the "overseas" plans, partly by subventions from the metropolitan treasury and partly by contributions from the territories concerned. To raise their contribution, the overseas territories have generally relied on subventions from CCFOM.

At the start, the metropolitan contribution to the "overseas" plans was 55 per cent, the territories being obliged to find the balance. However, despite the low rate of interest charged, the amortization payments on the CCFOM loans proved too heavy a burden for the limited budgets of the overseas territories. In 1953 the metropolitan contribution, which was derived from annual parliamentary votes, was increased to 75 per cent; in 1956 it was still further increased, to 90 per cent. Expenditures authorized by FIDES in the first twelve years (1947–1958) of its existence amounted to $2,-140 million. Of these appropriations, 58 per cent were grants in both the "general" ($305 million) and "overseas" ($940 million) categories, and the rest ($895 million) were loans which were almost evenly divided between the "overseas" classification and CCFOM loan funds.

Unlike the British C. D. and W. grants, those made by FIDES have covered virtually the whole cost of a given overseas development plan; and they have been made to state-controlled and mixed companies as well as to the territorial governments.

The designers of the ten-year "General Plan" of 1946 had two main objectives. The first was to provide the *infrastructure*, particularly transportation, needed for subsequent economic and social development. More than half of all development expenditure during the period 1946–1952 went into ports, railways, roads and airfields. Most of the rest went into hospitals and schools, mining and industrial installations (especially hydroelectricity), agriculture and research. The second objective was to promote enough revenue-earning schemes to meet, in time, the heavy operating and maintenance costs of this *infrastructure*. Although the constitutional relationship of the overseas territories to metropolitan France has changed greatly since 1946, this objective is still being energetically pursued.

The Caisse Centrale de la France d'Outre-Mer has been the central financial organization responsible for managing the accounts of FIDES. Its capital has come from an initial grant of approximately $8.4 million and from annual advances from the French Treasury via FIDES. The amount of these advances has varied considerably; in 1954, for instance, it was approximately $56 million; in 1956, only $14 million. As a rule these variations have been more a reflection of the ability of CCFOM to find suitable projects than of the willingness of the Treasury to find funds.

CCFOM has been able to advance money, on loans of short, medium or long term, to the territorial governments (usually at one per cent interest plus one per cent service charge) to enable them to make their own contribution to FIDES, and to state-controlled, mixed or private companies. It has also taken shares in certain kinds of undertakings. Private enterprises being assisted by CCFOM in 1957 included the Société Alucam, which is producing aluminum in the French Cameroons, and the Société Fria, which is developing bauxite deposits in the Republic of Guinea. Not the least of CCFOM's functions has been to provide for minor as well as major capital works by creating within the overseas territories subsidiary credit societies for the purpose of financing the needs of small-scale business enterprises.

Belgian Africa. In contrast to the British territories and those of the French Community, those of Belgium have had to raise, and pay for, almost all of their development funds. For instance, the Belgian Congo's Ten Year (1950–1959) Plan was financed through its own special budgets, the money for which was derived from loans—by far the larger part floated in Belgium and the Congo—and, after 1954, from surpluses in the territory's ordinary budgets.

Exact details are not published but the greater part of the rise in the National Debt of the Congo,[7] from around £60 million[$168 million] to over £230 million [approximately $650 million] at the end of 1956, is clearly attributable to execution of the Plan. In round figures 79 percent

[7] Excluding the "indirect" debt which consists of state guarantees of repayment of capital or of interest by public utilities. This amounted to approximately $154 million at the end of 1956.

of this sum originated in loans from Belgium or floated within the Congo; 11 percent represents loans from the International Bank for Reconstruction and Development; 8 percent, loans floated in Switzerland; and 2 percent, miscellaneous dollar loans.[8]

The amount raised by ordinary budget surpluses between 1954 and 1957 was approximately $75 million. The cost of the plan was originally estimated to be approximately $500 million. In the ten years since its inception, however, both actual costs and estimates have doubled. It is almost certain that more than $1 billion will have been spent on the plan by the time all the accounts have been settled.

It is only in the Trust Territory of Ruanda-Urundi that development funds have been supplied directly from Belgium. Virtually the entire cost—about $90 million—of the territory's own Ten Year (1950–1959) Plan was underwritten by non-interest-bearing loans from the metropolitan government.

In aim and content both plans were quite similar to the development programs of British and French areas, for, in Lord Hailey's words, "their objective is to create an environment in which private enterprise can develop to the greatest advantage of the community."[9] To this end, about half of the total development expenditure was earmarked for the *infrastructure*, especially railways, roads and inland waterways. Most of the rest was put into public utilities (e.g., water supply, electricity), health services, research of the widest possible scope, and resettlement schemes (especially in the congested parts of Ruanda-Urundi). While some parts of this comprehensive program were carried out through the ordinary departmental agencies, others were put in charge of quasi-governmental, semi-autonomous institutions. Among the more important of these were the Fonds du Bien-Être Indigène (FBEI), which was set up after World War II in recognition of the war services of the Congolese, and the Institut pour la Recherche Scientifique en Afrique Centrale (IRSAC), estab-

[8] *Statistical and Economic Review*, March 1958, p. 27.
[9] *Op. cit.*, p. 1340.

lished in 1947 to coordinate, promote and prosecute scientific work, both physical and social, in the Belgian Congo and Ruanda-Urundi. In addition to the government funds received by it, the FBEI also has received annually a share of the profits of the colonial lottery run in Belgium; and in addition to what it has received from the government, IRSAC also has received annual grants and subsidies from various corporate bodies.

Portuguese Africa. Although their methods and results may not always have been the same as their neighbors', the Portuguese yield to none of them in their enthusiasm for planned development. They have been operating development plans since the setting up of the Colonial Development Fund in 1938. These plans have been financed with the help of loans from the metropolitan government, local surpluses, and the proceeds of special taxes on imports and exports. The first plan coincided with the war years and could not be realized for lack of capital equipment. Even so, over $7.5 million was spent on such major developments as the construction of a new port and high school at Luanda and the extension of the Malanje and Moçâmedes railways in Angola. The second plan, covering the period 1946–1950, encompassed a much wider field, including public health, education, hydroelectricity, agriculture and forests, and cost approximately $15 million. In 1952 the government announced its National Development Plan (*Plano de Fomento Nacional*) costing $500 million, of which approximately $200 million was to be spent in the African provinces, mainly on transport, hydroelectricity, irrigation and land settlement by Portuguese and Africans alike, mining and industry, and geological survey. This six-year plan came into operation in 1953 and was so energetically pursued that its main objectives had been realized by the end of 1958. A second six-year plan was initiated in 1959. More than half of the approximately $360 million allocated to it is to be used for colonization schemes and the further development of roads and railways.

United States government agencies. The United States government makes available development funds through its International Cooperation Administration and its Export-Import Bank.

The ICA, like its alphabetical forerunners ECA, MSA and FOA, exists to provide capital equipment or basic raw materials whose cost cannot be met by local and foreign private capital, or by loans from the World Bank and similar organizations; and to carry out programs of teaching, training and exchange of information. Assistance of these kinds began in 1948 as part of America's contribution to the European recovery program. Until 1954 most of the aid to the non-self-governing territories took the form of loans and dollar credits to their administering powers for developmental projects in such fields as transportation and power. Since then, the emphasis has shifted to technical assistance with varying degrees of cooperation, financial and otherwise, from the metropolitan countries. Among the recipients of such types of aid are the railways of the now independent Ghana, the mining industry of Nigeria, the anti-locust campaign of east Africa, and the African small businessmen of Uganda and Tanganyika. From April 1948 through March 1956 the Commonwealth territories of Africa received U. S. aid in currency and kind valued at approximately $67 million. The corresponding figures for French and Belgian territories were $365.5 million[10] and $18.8 million.

Similar types of assistance have been made available to the independent territories of tropical Africa. Thus, both Liberia and Ethiopia have had large "Point Four" programs (as the people of the two countries still prefer to call them) since the early 1950s. The "techniques" covered by these programs include agriculture, animal husbandry, education, hydrology and hydroelectricity, commerce and industry, mapping and trades training.

The operations of the U. S. Export-Import Bank in tropical Africa have not been very large so far. The chief territories

[10] Including a grant of $297.6 million made to metropolitan France for overseas development.

to be directly involved in them are Liberia, Ethiopia and Mozambique, to each of which loans have been made.

United Nations agencies. The agencies of the United Nations chiefly concerned with the financing of development are the International Bank for Reconstruction and Development (commonly called the World Bank), the International Monetary Fund, the International Finance Corporation and the United Nations Technical Assistance Board.

The World Bank's main purpose is "to assist in the reconstruction and development of its member countries by facilitating the investment of capital for productive purposes, and thereby to promote the long-range growth of international trade and the improvement of standards of living." The chief way in which it seeks to achieve this purpose is by making fixed-interest loans carrying the guarantee of the member government concerned. This guarantee is required whether the loan is made to the member government itself, or to a government authority or agency, or to a private enterprise in the member country. The project for which the loan is required must be of sufficient importance to warrant the incurring of a foreign exchange liability to finance it. Before making a loan the bank usually sends a mission of experts to ascertain whether the project is sound and likely to fulfill its sponsor's expectations. The bank is also empowered to authorize private persons and organizations to make investments in projects which it has passed upon. When invited, it will advise member countries, and their dependencies, on the planning and execution of programs of economic development. In 1954, for instance, it did this for Nigeria in a highly comprehensive fashion.

The bank's funds, which at the beginning of 1959 totaled almost $10 billion, are obtained from the contributions of its member countries (68 as of the same time), the sale of its own bonds, and the sale of securities obtained from borrowers in return for earlier loans which it financed.

The fields in which the bank has done most of its comparatively small tropical African business are transport (examples are the purchase of equipment by the East African Railways and Harbours, railroad modernization in certain west African territories of the French Community, road construction in the Belgian Congo, port and road construction in Uganda, port and railroad improvements in Sudan), and electrical power (in June 1956 it made a loan of $80 million to the Federation of Rhodesia and Nyasaland toward the financing of the Kariba hydroelectric scheme).

In 1955 the bank established in Washington, with the financial help of two American foundations, an Economic Development Institute for the purpose of training government personnel from the less developed member countries in the handling of development problems. Among those attending the first courses were officials from the Belgian Congo, Nigeria and Uganda.

The much smaller International Finance Corporation (its authorized capital is only $100 million) was brought into being in July 1956, with the purpose of fostering productive private enterprise and the movement of private capital, particularly in those member countries which still rank as underdeveloped. This purpose it hopes to fulfill by investing in projects in association with private investors, and by serving "as a clearinghouse which will bring together investment opportunities, private capital and experience in management."[11]

Down to early 1959 the International Finance Corporation had not entered into any tropical African commitments. It was still looking for medium-sized projects, preferably industrial, that were in need of capital and technical and managerial skills, and that promised to become self-supporting at a comparatively early date. While it did not have to look far for evidences of such need, evidences of such promise were hard to come by.[12]

[11] *Statistical and Economic Review*, September 1957, p. 7.
[12] Recently, the United Nations has established another agency, headed by Paul G. Hoffman, called the Special United Nations Fund for the Economic Development of Underdeveloped Countries (SUNFED). The purpose of this agency, which is pressing for a working capital of not less than $250 million, is to make large grants-in-aid and long-term loans at low rates of interest to countries

Unlike that of the World Bank, the contribution of the International Monetary Fund to the development of its member countries is made indirectly. Its resources (down to April 1959 the Fund had made available about $4.2 billion) are used to supplement exchange reserves rather than to finance specific development programs. Its aim in so doing is to eliminate foreign exchange restrictions which hamper the growth of world trade, and to promote stability and, ultimately, full convertibility of the currencies which it is supporting. Much of its work may be likened to that of a field casualty station: it consists in administering first aid and giving shots in the arm to ailing economies, leaving to others the removal of any deep-seated troubles which may beset those economies.

The United Kingdom, France and Belgium—three of the largest subscribers to the fund—have each made considerable use of its resources to supplement their reserves of gold or foreign currencies, and so to alleviate balance-of-payments difficulties into which their African dependencies had run.

Although the United Nations Technical Assistance Board (TAB) is principally concerned with the supplying of skilled personnel to carry out specific development tasks, it does dispense a certain amount of financial aid. The program is financed by the voluntary, and often rather reluctantly given, contributions of the members of the United Nations. In recent years these contributions have averaged about $30 million annually. In addition to providing technicians for field assignments, TAB awards fellowships and scholarships, runs training programs and finances the supplies and equipment necessary to make these programs effective. In 1956 the Economic and Social Council of the United Nations recommended that to these activities there be added a program designed to ac-

---

that have so far failed to attract the private investor and such existing agencies as the World Bank. Unhappily, it takes more than sunshine to sustain development projects; but as of late 1959 other sources of sustenance were still proving rather elusive. Projects involving the modest sum of $23.7 million had been authorized by the year's end; even so, the "United Nations [did] not have the funds to carry out the projects at once." (*New York Times*, December 7, 1959.)

celerate the rate of industrialization of the underdeveloped countries with which the TAB deals. Wherever possible, the TAB works through the existing specialized "technical" agencies of the United Nations, such as the Food and Agriculture Organization, UNESCO and the World Health Organization. However, many projects are carried out under its aegis.

From the inauguration of the "expanded program" in 1950 down to 1959, United Nations expenditure on technical assistance in tropical Africa amounted to approximately $10 million. The total cost of the programs in which the TAB has assisted would probably be nearer $100 million, for the TAB has always taken the view that its role is to help only those who are willing to help themselves. Among the tasks which it has tackled in Africa are the training of meteorological observers and the preparing and packing of coffee for export in Ethiopia, the organizing of science teaching in the University of Liberia, the preparation of a five-year education plan in Somalia, the eradication of the desert locust in British East Africa, and the raising of housing standards in Ghana.

RESEARCH AND DEVELOPMENT

If money may be said to be the soil of growth, research is its fertilizer. Adequate supplies of both are indispensable to the success of any development program. Without adequate money it is impossible even to talk of development. Without adequate research it is impossible to tell whether any such program is desirable, let alone able to achieve its announced goal. Money may talk, but it has a habit of talking nonsense when it is undisciplined by the knowledge that is born of research.

In an environment like that of tropical Africa, fertilizer is an even scarcer commodity than soil. For research costs money—money that is wanted for a hundred and one immediate, self-evident needs, and research, by its very nature, deals with matters that are neither self-evident nor in the habit of disclosing their secrets to the first questioner. Further, in many fields the feeling still lingers that the work dignified by the name of research is often little more than a euphemism for the reducing of mountains of questionable data to molehills of academic inference, and that much of the rest succeeds only in making obscure what every well-informed government and company official had always supposed was perfectly clear. That the feeling has more than a fleck of substance to it any reader of technical journals dealing with tropical Africa can testify.

Even so, in recent years increasingly large amounts of money have been found by governments, educational institutions and corporations for tropical African research. While some of this money appears to have fallen on barren ground, much of it is certainly performing its intended function. The amount of research work being done is impressive. The *Directory of Scientific Institutes, Organizations and Services in Africa South of the Sahara* published in 1954 by the Scientific Council for Africa South of the Sahara lists 286 public and quasi-public institutions engaged in research in the area covered by this study.[13] A few of these are research institutions only by courtesy of the council, since they do little more than maintain an office and serve as a repository for unwanted bric-a-brac. But many are large, handsomely equipped, expertly staffed, and highly productive on a budget that would seem ample to most American graduate schools. More impressive than their number is the scope of their interests. The *Directory* has 15 entries under the heading of "social sciences," 42 under "physical sciences," 43 under "medical sciences," 161 under "natural sciences," in addition to 25 under a general heading.

Some of the institutes are highly specialized, dealing with a single field of inquiry. Typical of these are the Institut National pour l'Etude Agronomique du Congo Belge (INEAC), the West African Cacao Research Institute, the Institut de

---

[13] The number, which has since increased to over 300, takes no account of the considerable research work being done by large business and industrial corporations. Nor does it include research institutions in the independent territories of Liberia, Ethiopia, etc.

Recherches du Coton et des Textiles Exotiques, the East African Trypanosomiasis Research Organization and the Desert Locust Survey. Others have been given much broader terms of reference, and undertake research work in two or more of the four categories listed in the *Directory*. Outstanding among these are IRSAC, which operates in the Belgian Congo and Ruanda-Urundi, and the Institut Français d'Afrique Noire, which operates in the former French West Africa (including Togo).

Scarcely less striking than the scope of the research being done is its broad territorial distribution. Thirty-four separate research organizations are listed under the Belgian Congo (including Ruanda-Urundi); 65 under French West Africa; 16 under French Equatorial Africa; 17 under French Cameroons; 11 under Madagascar; 34 in the Federation of Rhodesia and Nyasaland; 29 in British West Africa (including the then Gold Coast); 59 in British East Africa. Even Portuguese Africa, which has long had the name of being the least progressive of the non-self-governing territories, is represented by 20 entries, 7 under Angola and 13 under Mozambique.

Belgian territories. The range and caliber of the research work done in the Belgian Congo and Ruanda-Urundi have been second to none. First-class facilities now exist for basic and *ad hoc* research in almost every field. Indeed, the facilities —residential, recreational and scientific alike—available at such places as Yangambi (near Stanleyville), the territorial headquarters of INEAC, and Lwiro (near Bukavu), the headquarters of IRSAC, are probably not surpassed by any similar institutions in the world.

Of the many public research institutions in the territory, INEAC is undoubtedly the largest. In the opinion of many it is also the one that has done most to strengthen the territory's economy. In 1958 the "general services" section alone employed approximately 5,000 people (representing a family population of more than 16,000), and the number of European specialists exceeded 400. The scope of INEAC's interests is suggested by the fact that its research center comprises the following divisions: botany, plant physiology, forest economy, plant pathology, agricultural entomology, agrology, agricultural chemistry, climatology, genetics, biometry, agricultural technology, rural husbandry, agricultural economy and agricultural sociology. There are, additionally, divisions that deal with the application of the facts disclosed by research to the Congo's major cash crops, notably palm oil, rubber, coffee, cocoa and indigenous foodstuffs, and to animal husbandry and fisheries. There isn't a farmer, African or European, in the Congo who is not the richer for having used some technique or some strain of seed first tried out in INEAC's field stations.

Although a comparative late-comer (it was established by *arrêté royal* in 1947), IRSAC has lost no time in making its presence felt. The headquarters plant, consisting of laboratories, library, museum and residences, is at once a thing of splendor and a tool of the greatest utility. Under its roof, Belgian and foreign scientists have been working, since the early 1950s, on fundamental problems in such diverse fields as geophysics, nutrition, mammalogy, medical zoology, neuropathology and ornithology. Besides Lwiro, IRSAC has other centers at Astrida (mainly for sociological and demographic research) and Uvira (mainly for hydrobiology, entomology, zoology and botany) in Ruanda-Urundi; at Elisabethville (for medical biology) and Mabali (for plant biology) near Coquilhatville.

Most of the other outstanding research organizations in the Belgian Congo fall into the following categories: physical (including mining), medical and veterinary, sociological. In the first category come the Institut Géographique du Congo Belge, the Centre de Recherches Minières du Congo Belge (Bukavu), Comité Spécial du Katanga (Elisabethville), Comité National du Kivu (Bukavu), Mission Anti-Erosive (Bukavu), Service Géologique du Congo Belge et du Ruanda-Urundi (Léopoldville) and Service des Mines du Congo Belge (Léopoldville). In the second category come Fonds Reine Elisabeth pour l'Assistance Médicale aux Indigènes (Léopoldville), Institut de Médecine Tropicale Princesse Astrid (Léopoldville), and the various centers of the Service Médical

Provincial and the Service Vétérinaire Provincial. In the third category comes the Centre d'Etude des Problèmes Sociaux Indigènes (Elisabethville).

Almost all of these organizations have so far derived their financial support in large part, or entirely, from public funds raised either in Belgium or locally.

Commonwealth territories. The interest of the British in African research goes back a long way. A fund for research into tropical diseases had been set up at the end of the nineteenth century, and almost from the start of the African occupation small research units were attached to many territorial departments. But down to the late 1930s the total funds available for research were pitifully small, with the result that the work done was patchy, and short-term rather than long-term. Many times the findings were simply filed, for lack of funds to apply them. It was not until the passing of the 1940 Colonial Development and Welfare Act that very much attention was given to the logistics of colonial research and to the organization of a research strategy.

To ensure the wise employment of the quite large sums which this act and its successors have made available for research, the United Kingdom government relies heavily on the judgment of its Colonial Research Council and such affiliated technical bodies as the Colonial Products Research Council, the Colonial Geological Surveys, the Anti-Locust Research Centre, the Colonial Social Science Research Council, the Colonial Medical Research Committee, the Committee for Colonial Agricultural, Animal Health and Forestry Research, and the Colonial Economic Research Committee. Of the funds disbursed on the advice of the Colonial Research Council, the major part has consisted of grants to territorial governments for use by specific departments. In most territories C. D. and W. grants have been supplemented generously by territorial funds, derived either from the ordinary budget or from the surpluses of produce-marketing boards, etc. In the case of Southern Rhodesia, which by virtue of its self-governing status has been ineligible for C. D. and W. grants, almost all the money for research has had to be raised domestically. Here and there government research workers have found valuable allies in the large public corporations, such as the United Africa Company and the Rhodesian Selection Trust; in such bodies as the Tanganyika Sisal Growers Association; and, increasingly of late years, in the larger centers of higher education.

Today, the work being done by the dozens of research agencies scattered all over Commonwealth tropical Africa is substantial in amount, comprehensive in coverage, and increasingly well coordinated interterritorially. Many of these agencies have already "paid for their keep," and now yield dividends of improved health and efficiency, greater productivity and security that could not have been otherwise obtained. Deserving a high place on any listing of such agencies are the following:

1. In the physical and agricultural fields—the West African Cacao Research Institute at Tafo in Ghana; the East African Agriculture and Forestry Research Organisation at Kikuyu, Kenya; the Empire Cotton Growing Corporation's Cotton Research Station at Namulonge, near Kampala, Uganda; the Tea Research Institute of East Africa at Kericho, Kenya; the Tanganyika Sisal Growers Association's Experimental Station at Mlingano, Ngomeni; the West African Institute for Oil Palm Research near Benin City in Nigeria; the Tobacco Research Board of Southern Rhodesia at Salisbury, Southern Rhodesia; the meteorological services of British West Africa, British East Africa and the Federation of Rhodesia and Nyasaland

2. In the medical and veterinary fields—the East African Trypanosomiasis Research Organisation at Nairobi, Kenya; the East African Veterinary Research Organisation at Kikuyu, Kenya; the Makerere College Medical School at Kampala, Uganda; the Medical Research Council Laboratories at Bathurst in Gambia and Kampala in Uganda

3. In the social and economic fields—the West African Institute of Social and Economic Research at Ibadan, Nigeria; the East African Institute of Social Research at Kampala, Uganda; the Rhodes-Livingstone Institute at Lusaka, Northern Rhodesia.

Less publicized, but in the aggregate no less productive of good, are the generally small research units attached to many territorial departments of agriculture, forestry, game, fisheries, geological survey, and medical and veterinary services. Indeed, as far as most of the local inhabitants are concerned, the work done by these departments is the only kind that matters, since it is research done, so to speak, on the spot, patently for their benefit.

The French Community. In keeping with their general approach to the business of developing overseas territories, the French have sought to centralize their research effort. For long possessed of the widest domains of any European state in Africa, but of only modest resources of money and manpower, they took the view that a few large and well-equipped agencies were likely to serve the needs of a given territory or group of territories better than a great number of small, understaffed and widely scattered agencies. They also preferred to let their Paris administrators settle the strategy, if not the tactics, of all major research enterprises. "In the earlier days research in their African territories was carried out by *missions* from the *Institut Pasteur* in Paris," Lord Hailey reports, "and the first local research organizations were the branches of this institute, established at St. Louis in 1896 and Brazzaville in 1910."[14]

At the present time the central direction of overseas research is vested in the Office de la Recherche Scientifique et Technique d'Outre-Mer (ORSTOM) and the Conseil Supérieur de la Recherche Scientifique et Technique d'Outre-Mer. The latter body, constituted first as a division of the Ministry of Overseas France, but now as part of the General Secretariat of the French Community, "publishes the results achieved

[14] *Op. cit.*, p. 1604.

and keeps all organizations concerned with overseas research informed of what is being accomplished in each territory."[15]

One of ORSTOM's tasks has been to train a corps of research workers capable of furnishing assistance to all of the member states of the French Community. Candidates for these posts (selected from graduates of such centers of higher learning as the Ecole Polytechnique and the Institut Agronomique) are given a two-year training course. The first year is spent at Bondy near Paris. Here basic instruction is given in a wide range of topics that includes ethnology, entomology, geology, pedology, plant physiology, plant breeding, plant diseases and oceanography. The second year is spent "on location," either at one of ORSTOM's institutes, such as the Institut d'Enseignement et de Recherches Tropicales at Adiopodoumé (near Abidjan) in the Ivory Coast, or in a field station. Here the students are trained in research techniques under environmental conditions that resemble those they will later have to deal with.

The capital cost of the administrative and training centers set up by ORSTOM has been met from FIDES; the current costs have come out of ORSTOM's own funds and those of the territory concerned. Since there were a number of research institutions in French West Africa before 1943, ORSTOM has concentrated most of its African interest on the other territories. The most important research centers sponsored by ORSTOM are the Centre de Pédologie in Dakar-Hann (Senegal), the Centre de Géophysique in M'Bour (Senegal), the Institut de Recherches du Togo in Lomé (this specializes in pedology, geophysics, nutrition and sociology), the Institut de Recherches du Cameroun in Yaoundé (specializing in entomology, pedology, hydrology, nutrition and geography), the Institut d'Etudes Centrafricaines (specializing in entomology, geography, botany, sociology and hydrology) in

[15] "Scientific Research: A Basis for Economic and Social Progress in Africa," *African Affairs* (French Embassy, Service de Presse et d'Information, New York), April 1953, p. 1. Before 1955, ORSTOM was known as ORSOM, the "Technique" being added to its responsibilities only in that year.

Brazzaville, Bangui and Pointe Noire; and the Institut de Recherche Scientifique de Madagascar (specializing in pedology, entomology, oceanography and hydrology) in Tananarive.

Most of the agronomic, forestry and animal husbandry research has been done under the auspices of the Services de l'Agriculture, de l'Elevage et des Forêts of the onetime Ministry of Overseas France. Most of the research work in the field of health (including nutrition, hygiene, sleeping sickness, leprosy and preventive medicine) has likewise been done under the auspices of the Ministry of Overseas France.

Outstanding among the institutions supported by the metropolitan government, but not coming under the jurisdiction of ORSTOM, are the Institut Pasteur and the Institut Français d'Afrique Noire. The Institut Pasteur, from its Paris headquarters and field stations in Africa, has, for over half a century, been carrying out research designed to relieve suffering and improve living conditions. To it belongs much of the credit for the control of sleeping sickness, malaria, rabies, smallpox and plague in French tropical Africa. Besides its Dakar headquarters, the Institut Français d'Afrique Noire (IFAN) maintains a network of "local centers," "associated centers" and "substations" throughout the region formerly known as French West Africa. The interests of its large scientific staff range over the whole field of the natural and social sciences, including geography.

Understandably, in view of the magnitude of its task and the modesty of its resources, the French government has consistently encouraged the establishment of privately supported research centers. Among the most enterprising and productive of these are the following:

1. The Institut des Fruits et Agrumes Coloniaux, founded in 1941 to promote the growing of better-yielding citrus and other tropical fruits. It maintains four research stations in tropical Africa.
2. The Institut de Recherches pour les Huiles de Palme et les Oléagineux, founded in 1942 for a like purpose. It

maintains oil palm research centers in four territories and peanut and *karité* centers in three.

3. The Institut de Recherches du Coton et des Textiles Exotiques, founded in 1946. It maintains vegetable textile research stations in seven territories and an experimental station in one (the Malagasy Republic).

4. The Compagnie Générale des Oléagineux Tropicaux, which for some years now has been carrying out highly productive research in peanut culture on its large holdings in Casamance (Senegal) and Niari (Republic of the Congo).

Portuguese and Spanish territories. For various reasons, that include lack of manpower and money, and perhaps also lack of interest, both Portugal and Spain were late in getting into the field of systematic colonial research. Although their learned societies include in their number some of the most ancient and honored in the world, they did very little until recently to promote the better knowledge of their African possessions.

In Portugal, the Junta das Missões Geográficas e de Investigações Coloniais (later, do Ultramar), established in 1935, was the first publicly expressed recognition of the need for a colonial research organization; but even this council was not empowered at first to do much more than advise the Colonial Ministry. However, it has since come to be supported by annual grants from both the metropolitan and provincial (i.e, colonial) budgets, which have enabled it, among other things, to conduct a number of wide-ranging research expeditions and to compile an atlas of the overseas areas.

Today, there are also Portuguese research organizations in the fields of medicine (notably the postgraduate school of the Institute of Tropical Medicine, which has been doing good work since the turn of the century, and the Trypanosomiasis Combat Mission in Lourenço Marques), the social sciences, including ethnography and languages (the Institute for Overseas Studies in Lisbon, the Society for Mozambique Studies in Lourenço Marques and the Centre for Portuguese Guinea Studies in Bissau), agronomy and plant breeding (notably the

Center for the Scientific Study of Cotton in Lourenço Marques and in Catete, Angola), and the physical sciences (the meteorological services and the geological and mining services of Angola and Mozambique).

In Spain the recognition of the need for systematic colonial research came even later. The first Spanish institute for African studies was set up in Madrid in 1945. This institute, which now operates under the auspices of the Dirección General de Marruecos y Colonias, is mainly concerned with research in physical and cultural geography. Research in hygiene, tropical diseases, etc., is undertaken in Spain and Spanish Africa by agencies of the same ministry.

Other territories. Except for Sudan and Guinea, the other territories had next to no research work done within their borders until quite recently. Nor is it difficult to see why this should be so. These territories, consisting of Liberia, Somalia and Ethiopia, are poor in developed skills and other resources; and some of their leaders have been slow to perceive the gains that would accrue to them and their people from research done—as it had perforce to be done—by outsiders. But the postwar years have seen noteworthy changes of circumstance in all three territories. Their governments have had at their disposal much larger budgets (if still very small by contemporary standards); they have been able to send some of their best young men abroad for training in research techniques; and, indirectly or directly, they have received a great deal of outside technical help, especially from the United States and the United Nations. Today, as a result, all three territories can point with some pride to work being done by research agencies in their midst.

In Liberia, the Booker Washington Institute at Kakata (now attached to the University of Liberia) is carrying on research in a number of fields, including agronomy and animal husbandry. The Firestone Plantations Company at Harbel operates a research laboratory in which experimental work is being done not only on rubber but also on tropical fruits and livestock.

The Liberian Institute of the American Foundation for Tropical Medicine, also located at Harbel, is carrying out investigations into the occurrence and control of malaria, filariasis, river-blindness, bilharziasis and malnutrition. The World Health Organization also has a number of research projects on hand, mainly in malaria, yaws and sleeping sickness. And some of the work undertaken by the Joint Liberian–United States Commission for Economic Development in geology, aerial photography and mapping, agriculture, public health and other fields is in the nature of research.

In Somalia, government-supported research work is being done in agriculture (in dry-land farming and the cultivation of cotton, banana and the castor oil plant); medicine and public health (in the control of bilharziasis, etc.); and linguistics (in the problem of using Somali as a written language). Almost the only privately supported research is that being done by the Sinclair Somal Corporation and Mineraria Somala. Their explorations have called for the geophysical and geological mapping of very large sections of the territory, much of it hitherto almost unknown to the outside world.

The United States International Cooperation Administration mission in Somalia has conducted a number of surveys that, in the intellectual context of the country, may be said to rank as major pieces of research. Among other matters, these surveys have dealt with forest and range management, livestock, mineral deposits, hydrology and fisheries. Somalia also has a number of U. N.-sponsored research projects. The most important of these have to do with malaria and tuberculosis control (WHO) and fundamental education (UNESCO).

The story is much the same in Ethiopia, where the government is struggling to add inches to the lowly economic and social stature of its people by "force-feeding" techniques. And, thanks in large measure to the encouragement and direct aid of the United States ICA program and the specialized agencies of the United Nations, it is succeeding.

Among the fields of inquiry covered by "Point Four" agreements between the U. S. and Ethiopian governments are the following: mapping and survey (including geology, soil, water resources); soil conservation; insect (including locust) control; cattle breeding; pasture management; seed selection and breeding (notably coffee); public health (including disease control); and the educational system of the country. Among those covered by agreements between the specialized agencies of the United Nations and the government are health training, control of epidemics, and fundamental education.

The chief agencies in the country engaged in research are the Imperial Ethiopian Mapping and Geography Institute (at Addis Ababa), the Imperial Ethiopian College of Agricultural and Mechanical Arts (near Lake Haramaia), the Central Agricultural Experiment Station (at Bishoftu), the Public Health College and Training Center (at Gondar) and the University College of Addis Ababa.

Largely because of its long association with the British Commonwealth, Sudan has fared better than the foregoing territories. From 1899 down to the time of its independence (1956), the country received its share of the services made available to all the non-self-governing territories of British Africa. In the matter of research and development it undoubtedly received more than most of the other territories, for in none of the others was there done such a mighty agricultural work as that administered by the Sudan Gezira Board, and in none of the others was the medical record of the Sudan surpassed, if indeed equaled. Were it not for the exertions of hydrologist, irrigation engineer, agronomist, plant geneticist, pathologist and the whole Research Division of the Ministry of Agriculture, there could have been no Gezira—and no independence, as cotton is the country's "currency." Without the work of the Stack Medical Research Laboratories, the Wellcome Chemical Laboratories, the Kitchener School of Medicine and the School of Hygiene, and the medical services generally, there could have been no well-being—and no growth. Nobody knows these things better than the Sudanese leaders. Not the least of their concerns since 1956 has been to maintain the efficiency and, wherever possible, expand the scope of the research activities of their various government departments.

Besides the above-named agencies, the following also have important research interests: the Equatoria Projects Board, which has successfully introduced cotton cultivation among the Azande people of the south and is now experimenting with coffee and other cash crops; the University of Khartoum, whose numerous faculties—arts, science, agriculture, engineering, veterinary science, medicine and law—are a measure of its research interests; and the Philosophical Society of the Sudan, which, its name notwithstanding, has been as much interested in how the people of the country eat as in how they think.

Guinea, like Sudan and for a similar reason, has had a good deal of research work done within its borders. For years prior to its independence, it played host to the Centre d'Etudes des Pêches (Conakry), the Centre de Recherches Rizicoles (Koba), the Institut Français d'Afrique Noire (Conakry), the Institut des Fruits et Agrumes Coloniaux (Kindia), the Institut Pasteur (Kindia), and the Section de Recherche sur le Quinquina et les Cultures de Montagne (Seredou). It profited no less from the developmental work—mostly unpublicized and invariably undermanned—done in the field by various government and private agencies.

International organizations. There is much to be said for organizing research internationally, particularly in an underdeveloped area like tropical Africa. It saves duplication of effort where all effort tends to be difficult and where sustained research effort is frequently made impossible by administrative or climatic circumstances. It saves money where money for research tends to be as scarce as wadi water and just about as quick to evaporate. It saves time where time is no longer on the researcher's side, as it seldom is in these days when a disease can be carried from Sudan to the Zambezi overnight and an idea can travel even faster. It is, in fact, the only rational approach to those problems that are the product of social change, for social change is not halted by a territorial border. The problems of urbanization are basically the same whether they are encountered in Salisbury, Stanleyville or Asmara, and the ingredients of nationalism are basically the same whether the compound bear a British, Belgian, French, Portuguese, Spanish or Italian label.

To give them their due, the colonial powers of tropical Africa have long recognized the desirability of intercolonial and international cooperation in the scientific field. During the interwar years they held several consultations on problems of agriculture, animal husbandry and public health. During the dark years of World War II they found time to organize an inter-African forestry conference at Abidjan and to develop the scheme of locust control first suggested by the French in 1938. In the early postwar years they held interterritorial conferences on such subjects as nutrition, forestry, transportation and communications, rinderpest and trypanosomiasis.

It was not until 1950, however, that the colonial powers put their cooperation on a formal, statutory basis by the creation of the Commission for Technical Co-operation in Africa South of the Sahara (Commission de Coopération Technique en Afrique au Sud du Sahara, or CCTA), an executive body; and the Scientific Council for Africa South of the Sahara (Conseil Scientifique pour l'Afrique au Sud du Sahara, or CSA), which is primarily an advisory body.

Since its creation CCTA, which now consists of representatives of the governments of Belgium, the Federation of Rhodesia and Nyasaland, France, Ghana, Guinea, Liberia, Portugal, the Union of South Africa and the United Kingdom, has been instrumental in setting up more than two dozen technical bureaus and committees. These include the Inter-African Bureau for Soils and Rural Economy, in Paris; the Tsetse Fly and Trypanosomiasis Permanent Inter-African Bureau, in Léopoldville; the Inter-African Bureau for Epizootic Diseases, at Muguga near Nairobi; the Inter-African Labour Institute, at Brazzaville, Republic of the Congo; the Inter-African Pedological Service, at Yangambi, Belgian Congo; and the Inter-African Committees on Statistics, Social Sciences, Housing and the Mechanisation of Agriculture. It has also set up a Foundation for Mutual Assistance in Africa South of the Sahara and an Inter-African Research Fund. The former of

these is designed "to collect and disseminate information on
offers of and requests for technical assistance in the region,
promote the provision of technical assistance by facilitating
bilateral arrangements between donors and recipients . . .
and maintain co-operative relations with the various organisa-
tions operating technical assistance programmes for the benefit
of Africa South of the Sahara." The Research Fund has been
set up "to promote joint scientific research and technical projects, in the following categories: Broad surveys, including
information and liaison work; Research on problems which involve uniform study by small highly specialized staffs operating over wide areas; Research on problems which affect many
countries but which should be investigated initially in one
limited area." Among the first projects sponsored by the fund
were the compilation of a climatological atlas of Africa and a
study of the role of science in the development of Africa south
of the Sahara.

The members of the Scientific Council for Africa South of
the Sahara are eminent scientists, "chosen [by CCTA] in such
a manner that the main scientific disciplines important at the
present stage of the development of Africa shall be represented." The council's main function is to recommend to
CCTA subjects appropriate for discussion by conferences, or
for investigation by technical bureaus and committees. A joint
Secretariat, with two seats—one in London and the other in
Bukavu, Belgian Congo—serves the needs of both bodies.

Other international organizations engaged in investigating
tropical African problems are the International Red Locust
Control Organization and the International Organization for
Control of the African Migratory Locust; the World Council
of Churches, which has been making a special study of "areas
of rapid social change"; such specialized agencies of the
United Nations as WHO, FAO and UNESCO, whose Advisory Committee on Arid Zone Research sponsors studies in
climate, soil erosion, the water requirements of plants, human
physiology and cognate fields; and the International African
Institute, which, since 1926, has been energetically promoting

the study of African anthropology, ethnography, linguistics and sociology.[16]

Philanthropic agencies. For many years now a number of philanthropic institutions, for the most part American, have interested themselves in problems of African economic and social growth. Since the early 1920s the Phelps-Stokes Fund has made grants to various educational institutions (among them the Booker Washington Institute at Kakata in Liberia), and its survey of African educational needs published in 1922 probably did more than any other single document to arouse the interest of American educators in tropical Africa. The Rockefeller Foundation and the Carnegie Corporation of New York have maintained a steady interest in African social problems and have financed numerous studies in ethnography, sociology and education. The Rockefeller Foundation also undertook much of the yellow fever research done in west Africa in the interwar years. More recently the Ford Foundation has made a number of grants to African institutions of higher learning, and to American scholars and universities (notably Northwestern University and Boston University) to further their African interests. Other money-granting agencies to do the same include the Fulbright Program, the Social Science Research Council, the Wenner-Gren Foundation for Anthropological Research, the Guggenheim Foundation—all of the United States; and the Horniman, Leverhulme and Nuffield Trusts of the United Kingdom.

HUSBANDRY

There is, needless to say, more to growth than soil and fertilizer. Vital though these are for the nurture of a land and its people, husbandry is a no less indispensable ingredient. Without it the best soil in the world can grow nothing but

[16] The "Select Annotated Bibliography of Tropical Africa," published by the Twentieth Century Fund in 1956, was compiled by this institute under the supervision of Professor Daryll Forde, its Director.

weeds and all that fertilizer can do is to make the weeds grow faster.

Husbandry, whether of an economic, social or political sort, calls for effort, and in tropical Africa effort is irksome and expensive, psychologically if not always physically. It calls for skills of hand and eye, of timing and judgment, planning and persuasion—skills which are still foreign to most Africans and which many non-Africans lose when they live too long in the land. It also calls for experience, which comes only after the skills have been learned; for faith, which is slow to take root in any environment and in tropical Africa is frequently regarded as a rather poor substitute for fatalism; and for integrity, that hardest of all qualities to nourish and soonest to wither under the brazen skies of selfishness. Which, perhaps, is merely another way of saying that good husbandry is fundamentally a matter of good husbandmen.

So far most of the means of growth—the capital, the research and the development plans—have been manipulated by Europeans and other non-African groups. While there have never been enough means, and some of the manipulators of them have behaved ineptly or worse, the fact remains that it is the non-Africans who are primarily responsible for what has been done with these means and so for the general direction and overseeing of the growth process. To look at any manifestation of growth—from a bridge to a ballot box, from a coal mine to a church—is to look at the result of non-African husbandry. Increasingly, however, it is the African who is putting himself, or is being put, in charge of the husbandry; who is building the bridges, using the ballot boxes, controlling the coal mine labor (and thus the coal mine) and carrying out the ministries of the church. With the exception of the white supremacists, this right of the African to do his own husbandry and be his own husbandman—to be "lord of the harvest," in fact—is readily conceded.

What is not so readily conceded is the ability of the African husbandman to take over without damage to the growth process. It is difficult to talk with any European who has worked closely with African executives without being made aware of his doubts of their readiness for responsibility and his fears for their ability to resist the seduction of the ever greater responsibilities they are facing. Granted, some of these doubts and fears may have their roots in regret at the passing of the controls from his own hands, while others may spring from remorse at not having made better use of his hands. But, on the whole, those most plagued by doubts and fears are those who have worked hardest to prepare the African for such responsibilities—the district officer who has been striving to get his African assistants to put equity before self-interest; the business manager who has struggled to develop in his African subordinates the gift of foresight and efficiency; the educator who has been seeking to raise the sights of his students above the tables of the market place; the missionary who has labored to furnish his converts with inner resources for their moral warfare.

It is not that anybody who knows the educated African questions his ability to grow things—to grow anything, for that matter—but rather that, at the present point of his intellectual development, he lacks the patience to stay with slow-growing stock, and the conviction that the things he has been taught to grow are necessarily better than the things he sees growing in other men's fields. In other words, so the argument runs, he is still a man of little faith, and husbandry is no job for those of little faith.

Africans themselves have these doubts and fears. Many African leaders-to-be, especially those who have lived abroad, express them publicly, and many existing leaders express them privately. Comments such as the following, culled in the course of a recent tour of tropical Africa, are made too often, and by people too well informed, to be dismissed as the sought-after echoes of European opinion:

I do not see a rosy future for our country—especially with our present leadership. Many of our leaders have no real qualifications. But most of us don't care enough about the future to worry about leadership. Life is easy, our people say; why should we worry?

Everybody wants to become a "conspicuous consumer." Very few people would be willing to curb their desire for furniture, fancy foodstuffs and clothes in favor of higher taxes for schools and hospitals. Very few of our newly qualified doctors are interested in becoming general practitioners in the bush where they are most sorely needed. They nearly all want to become high-priced specialists.

I do not want to see our link with the Commonwealth severed. The British have done us good. Any complaints we have today are against our own people, especially our politicians.

Western democracy needs to be modified to meet African needs. What we probably need most is a strong man who will tell us what to do and see that we do it. We need him soon if we are to survive the birth pains of nationhood.

Independence sounded pretty good when we first heard about it. Now it is within our grasp, it has got us scared. We don't have enough of any skill to "go it alone."

It would look from these reflections as if the greenness of a pasture bears something of an inverse ratio to the distance at which the pasture is viewed.

The husbandry problems of tropical Africa will, we may take it, be resolved eventually. Whether or not the way in which they are resolved will flatter those who found the capital and did the research and development is another question—one that will be taken up in the concluding chapter.

CHAPTER 9

THE SHAPE OF THINGS

The present-day traveler to tropical Africa is likely to return home with a feeling of great frustration, especially if he went there for those new and newsworthy generalizations it is every traveler's joy and pain to bring to birth. Tropical Africa has always been an unaccommodating place for the generalizer; the number of things that apply to the whole of it has always been small, and in recent years their number has been getting smaller. It can no longer be characterized as dark—if indeed it was ever as dark as our ignorance of it. Its rivers have been explored, its peaks scaled and its contours traced, in enough detail at least to prevent any wide-awake traveler from getting lost. Its rocks and soils are slowly giving up their secrets and its peoples are the subject of a very considerable anthropological literature. It cannot all be called dangerous, for while parts unquestionably are uncongenial to both Africans and non-Africans, in plenty of others it is possible to live a lifetime without so much as seeing a poisonous snake or being bitten by a mosquito. It cannot all be called difficult, for whether we are thinking of the business of making a living, of keeping cool or warm, of getting about, or of getting on with one's neighbors, there are many localities where these things present no greater problem than they do in Connecticut or California.

Why tropical Africa is such an unaccommodating place for the generalizer is not hard to see. To begin with, it is not really a "place," except in the sense that it has definable limits. Rather is it a mosaic of places, the component pieces of which have so far eluded the generalizer's grasp. The political map may show 40 or so clean-cut pieces, but there is nothing all-of-a-piece about the lives lived by the people in any one of them. To talk of the Belgian Congo, or of Ethiopia or Ghana, as though its peoples shared a common heritage, life, outlook and goals is as unrealistic as to suppose that all those who live behind Soviet-controlled frontiers share anything besides the Iron Curtain.

The real "places," as distinguished from those that have been contrived for political purposes, are those compounded of earth, air and water, cattle and crops, language and tradition, feelings and beliefs. Within the bounds of every major political unit, there are enough variations in some or all of these "place" components to produce enough differentiations of land, life and livelihood to disconcert the most incorrigible generalizer. Around the slopes of the Ruwenzori Mountains there are as many kinds of climate as there are between Florida and Maine, and a correspondingly large number of kinds of vegetation. In Kenya there are no fewer than 70 different ethnic groups; in the four British East African territories of Kenya, Uganda, Tanganyika and Zanzibar, at least 200. The fact that the great majority of the people who live within the borders of tropical Africa have dark skins, crinkly hair and thick lips, and live primitively and, by American standards, inadequately in a pestilential environment has unfortunately made it hard for us to appreciate the order of magnitude of less palpable differences.

Tropical Africa being not one place but many, and the many all different, makes generalization difficult enough. What makes it more difficult is the differing rate of change to which these places are subject, as a result of which many of the differences between place and place are becoming sharper. Until the turn of the century, or thereabouts, the amplitude of economic, social and political differences was seldom great. There were wealthy ones and poor ones, but few very wealthy or very poor. There were rulers and ruled, masters and servants, but the divide between them was low and could often be crossed without much trouble. Now, however, large plantations and farmsteads adjoin minute *shambas* in many parts of the region. Stately homes—not all of them belonging to Europeans or Asians—rise from the ashes, so to speak, of mud-and-thatch hovels. Chain department stores with upward of 50 selling sections flourish where once stood the one-room *duka* and the one-man market stall. There are other differentiations, too: men with votes and men without them; men with Western learning and illiterate men; men of the tribe and detribalized men; men who can go anywhere and men who can go nowhere without a passbook.

There is a further obstacle—or so it frequently seems to be—in the path of the Western generalizer, namely, the difficulty of becoming immunized to the virus of suggestibility in an environment highly favorable to its growth. The "yonder cloud" of evidence that is shaped like a camel to one looks uncommonly like a weasel to another and a whale to a third, especially to those who are looking for weasels and whales. And it is always possible to find an African Polonius willing to concur in the opinions of an American or European Hamlet, because in many communities courtesy requires that a man be told what his informant thinks he would like to be told. For that matter, it is always possible to find an African Hamlet willing to persuade an American or European Polonius that he is seeing what the African would like him to see.

The shaping clouds. The truth is, of course, that in these days most African "clouds" bigger than a man's hand are continually changing their shape, thus compounding the difficulties of the generalizer's task. This is not to say that they are as incapable of classification as some people suppose, or that they are all without form and void. Even he who looks at them through the darkened glass of prejudice and ignorance cannot fail to see that certain things are taking shape.

First, and most fundamental, of these is the desire for a better life. By now most Africans know that it is not necessary for their children to be "damned into the world" with disease, or for themselves to be subject all their lives to its debilitating and incapacitating effects. They know, by looking at the Europeans and Asians about them, that there is no very good reason why they should go on forever being inadequately housed, clothed and fed. They see that some of their own kin have already done better for themselves; and there is no spur

like the spur of a kinsman's success. They know that there
are people in the outside world who share their desire and are
set on helping them realize it. This desire for betterment can
be sensed almost everywhere the traveler goes. He meets it in
the bush in the African's increasing interest in money-making
crops, cooperatives and all-weather roads; in the villages, in
his increasing support of literacy campaigns, clean water
supplies and community development generally; and in the
towns and mining compounds, in his increasing appreciation
of the uses of in-service training and recreational facilities of
all kinds.

But it is not only indigenous Africans—*les noirs*—who have
these rising expectations. Many Europeans and Asians who
live in tropical Africa have them also. They have them because as farmers they seek to prosper in the land of their
birth or adoption, as merchants they are interested in developing larger markets for their goods, as miners and industrialists
they see in tropical Africa one of the largest sources of natural
wealth in the world (wealth that can be turned to the African's account as to their own), and as administrators they
see a chance to do a new thing—to educate Africans in the
art of running schools, churches, businesses and governments.

Second, and related, is the determination of more and
more Africans to have a greater share not only in the "equity"
of their country but in its management, local and regional no
less than territorial. Without the latter, the former—in the
view of these Africans—cannot be obtained, or, if obtained,
preserved. Unless they have control of the legislative and
fiscal machinery of their country, what assurance can there
be that their increased share in the equity will not be spirited
away from them in taxes and duties, or that the export of
mining and manufacturing dividends will be kept within
bounds?

There are other arguments, too: that it is the divine right
of every people to run its affairs in its own way; that self-
government, no matter how bad, is more ennobling than
non-self-government, no matter how efficient; that "self-government with danger" is infinitely better, as one west Afri-

can newspaper used to put it, than "subservience with tranquillity"; and that there can be no peace in the world, and no prospect of any, so long as men arrogate to themselves the right to govern without the consent of the governed.

Third, and likewise related, is the disposition of more and more Africans to do their own thinking and deciding about the kind of world they want to live in. This is expressing itself in many ways. Frequently it takes the form of skepticism concerning the suitability of Western political forms in countries still largely illiterate. Some political leaders, notably in Ghana, Guinea and Sudan, have gone so far as to speak of the advantages of authoritarianism, and have begun to practice it, curbing, deporting and imprisoning those who do not stay close enough to heel. Where the leaders still lay claim to being democratic, they are, as a rule, speaking not of "negative" or parliamentary democracy but of "positive" democracy—a democracy in which the government represents the true will of the people, whether or not the people themselves consciously apprehend it. As Oliver Woods reminds us in a recent article, "Of such are the 'peoples' democracies,' and indeed the fascist states of the period between the wars. From the western viewpoint, such a democracy does not qualify for the name at all."[1]

Frequently, too, it takes the form of skepticism concerning the propriety of Western standards of efficiency and integrity in a cultural environment where traditionally the race has been to the canny rather than the swift, and the battle to the smart in action rather than the strong in character, and where corruption has had no meaning because every rendered service has had its reward. And almost everywhere there is skepticism concerning the value of being too closely identified with the West. "Neutralism" has its supporters in every independent territory, as also does the idea that it is impossible for a country to be really autonomous while its peoples cling to other peoples' morals, language and religion.

Nor is it just a matter of reluctance to go along with West-

[1] "Is Africa Going Too Far, Too Fast?" *Optima* (Anglo American Corporation, Johannesburg), September 1959, p. 115.

ern ways. It is also, for many, a matter of finding some non-Western ways better suited to the African mind and situation: of preferring Islam, with its greater concessions to human frailty and its colorblindness, to Christianity, with its call to discipline, its complex theology and confessional differences, to say nothing of its identification with the "ruling classes"; of being more at home, and healthier, in a loose-fitting mantle than in a business suit; of remaining convinced that there are values in the old social order—its family organization, initiation rites, its judicial procedures and its arts—that are not surpassed, if indeed they are matched, in the white man's world. And how drab the white man's world can look alongside the African's!

On this point Elspeth Huxley feels as strongly as many Africans. In comparing the Ashanti of the turn of the century with the Ashanti of the early 1950s, she has written: "How dull life has become, how monotonous, how anaemic, how inert! Impatience with British rule is due, I am sure, as much to this as to anything. It is called a revolt against imperialism, but in truth I think it is, in part at least, a revolt against *ennui*, and that when the British Empire finally crumbles we might write as its epitaph: 'We bored them to death.'"[2]

How far this revolt against the West will go none can say, but there are many who share Elspeth Huxley's point of view on this also. "A revulsion to more natural ways? Perhaps the end of British rule [she was writing only of the four British West African territories] will see not a tidy, democratic, bourgeois state run by an imitation parliament, full of things we so much enjoy—adult suffrage, housing committees, sewerage schemes, welfare clinics, reform schools and women's institutes—but reversion to an older, harsher, more haphazard and satyric order, expressing the passions of Saturday night rather than the intentions of Sunday morning."[3]

And, fourth, in keeping with this growing desire of Africans to run their own show in their own way, is the determination

[2] *The Four Guineas: A Journey Through West Africa*, Chatto & Windus, London, 1954, p. 127.
[3] *Ibid.*

to see that their less advanced neighbors get a chance to do the same. The wine of freedom is strong and quickly goes to the head. Most African leaders have developed a palate for it in recent years, and are commending its virtues to all and sundry. Some are doing more: they are giving away the recipe for it to anyone who asks. If there was one thing more than another that united the independent states of Africa at the Accra conference of 1958, it was the determination to render "all possible assistance" to the remaining dependent peoples of Africa in their struggle for independence. Judging from recent happenings in the Belgian Congo, Tanganyika, Angola, and .elsewhere, it would look as though the recipe were in considerable demand.

The haze. Important as is this shaping and reshaping process, its dimensions should not be exaggerated. Most Africans are still caught in the old tribal web and cherish its security too well to exchange it for the "labyrinthine ways" of the white man's mind. Most of them, too, still live in unawareness of the world of cause and effect; for these, a shower of rain is still the work of the rain maker, and disease the result of bewitchment. What is going on is more truly a ferment, than a revolution, of rising expectations—a ferment, moreover, that has barely begun in many areas. In some, such as the Turkana country of Kenya and the Karamojong country of Uganda, the traveler is tempted to wonder whether it has begun at all, the people show so little curiosity about what is happening around them or concern about what is *not* happening to them.

Where the ferment has begun, the expectations to which it has given rise are generally modest in scale and utilitarian in kind. Frequently they consist only of such things as a sewing machine, a bicycle, an umbrella, a second pair of trousers and a pocketful of cash. The ideological expectations produced by the ferment are usually still more modest. Some Africans appear to have none at all. A medical missionary in the Belgian Congo, speaking recently of his Lokele *infirmiers,* said: "There are very few of them, even the brightest, who have ideas about anything beyond their daily work. They never talk about their country, the administration, or the kind of world they want. They are apparently content with things as they are." An Ethiopian schoolmaster, questioned on the subject of expectations, spoke of being willing "to wait for the future."

Many Africans, in so far as they are waiting for anything, are waiting for the past, albeit refurbished and sanitized. They see more hope in traditionalism than in modernism; they find the consolations of sorcery, witch doctoring and juju greater than those of the social center, the mission church and the clinic. For them the highest and only loyalty is loyalty to family, kin and tribe. As the *Times* of London put it in an editorial (October 17, 1957), published on the occasion of the appearance of Lord Hailey's *An African Survey: Revised 1956,* "The tribe is still the strongest entity in Africa. It is stronger than the individual, it is stronger than the nation, it is stronger than the race. The only points at which it is yielding are where urbanization is taking over. It may even be that the tribe is getting stronger rather than weaker."

We of the West, sired by democracy out of industrial progress and raised on a diet of advertising in a climate of emulation, find it difficult to believe that all Africans are not as we are. But isn't it time to concede the possibility of our thoughts not always being their thoughts, or our desires their desires? It is a supportable possibility. Just because a European builds a better house for Africans than the one in common use, it does not follow they will beat a pathway to its door. Often they do, but in some places they are more likely to stay away from it until somebody thinks of putting a high fence around it, thereby insuring the privacy they appreciate more than plumbing. Because a government builds a beautiful school it does not follow that the African will send his children to it. Usually he does; but even after forty years of friendly pushing the Tanganyika government has difficulty in getting more than a few Masai to send their children to school. Because we are willing to work in factory, mine or marshalling yard day after day, week after week, year after year, it does not follow that the African is willing to do the same.

Lately, members of the African elite have affirmed that there are very real differences between their way of looking at the world and ours. Some have gone so far as to speak of a distinctive "African personality" or *négritude*, characterized by esteem for the natural vitality of man rather than for the appurtenances he acquires—for what he is spiritually rather than for what he can do materially.

Hurray for those who have never invented anything,
Hurray for those who have never explored anything,
Hurray for those who have never conquered anything,
But who, in awe, give themselves up to the essence of things.

Could "otherness" be proclaimed less equivocally? True, Aimé Cesaire, the writer of these lines, is not an African negro (he comes from Martinique), but his views on *négritude* are held in the highest regard by many of his African contemporaries, for the concept is, paradoxically, his invention.

It is also time to question whether all the peoples of tropical Africa are as we are in their comprehension of what it takes to become a free nation. No doubt it takes nationalism, of which there is no shortage in the emergent states. No doubt it takes political leadership, social resilience and the ability to make friends of other nations—of all of which there are signs. But it also takes the right of self-determination, as the United Nations is continually insisting. The opening words of an article debated by the Social Commission of the Economic and Social Council of the United Nations in the fall of 1955 read: "All peoples and all nations shall have the right of self-determination, namely, the right freely to determine their political, economic, social and cultural status." But if self-determination means anything in tropical Africa, it means freedom for each of the 600-odd groups to be autonomous. These groups have as much identity as the eighteenth-century Americans and the twentieth-century Jews, and as much right to the appellation of "peoples." Yet this fact is seldom recognized in the words, let alone the deeds, of any leader whose country has newly come to autonomy. Even before Ghana gained its independence, Dr. Nkrumah let it clearly be understood that the principle of self-determination must not be carried too far. On more than one recent occasion the leaders of Sudan have made it equally clear that attempts by the Negro peoples living in the pagan south to rid themselves of the hegemony of the non-Negro peoples living in the Moslem north would likewise meet with armed resistance—as, indeed, they have done. The still more recently instated champions of self-government in the Belgian Congo and elsewhere have spoken in much the same tenor. They promise freedom from external rule, but not freedom for all the peoples in their countries to determine how they shall govern themselves, or be governed. If the plans of the dominant political parties come to pass, some Congolese peoples will get a lot less freedom than others after June 30, 1960.

Just as it takes self-determinism to become a free nation, so it takes resources to remain one. Here, too, we could wish for a greater comprehension of what is involved. Nations need food as well as freedom; lumber and livestock no less than leaders; durable soils, water supplies and economic minerals more than spellbinders. Some of the newly independent states and those about to be independent, such as Nigeria, can make a good showing on most of these scores; some, like Somalia, cannot. While the former may come in time to support the full paraphernalia of power, the latter have next to no chance of doing so. An ordinary revenue of less than $18 million (most of it furnished, up to now, by the Italian and British administrations) is not enough to provide Somalia with an adequate school system, let alone with an army, air force, ambassadorial, consular and civil services, trade commissions and the like.

But no emergent country yet has enough revenues or, what amounts to the same thing, enough developed resources—whether mines or mills, commerce or capital, skilled labor or management—to be able to maintain itself in the estate to which its European founders were accustomed and which many of its leaders considered to be their charter right. The accolade of independence confers many precious gifts, but few of them can be traded for cash and used to erase poverty. If the experience of the younger Asian nations is any guide, even freedom, that most precious gift of all, sometimes means little more than the power to decide how you would cut your cake if you had one. For the discarded governments are seldom disposed to maintain the flow of funds and skills at pre-independence levels, and there are few investors in their lands, or elsewhere in the free world, who care to put money into countries whose leaders are unschooled in the handling of large enterprises, public or private, and who show a tendency to conduct their affairs in the manner of dictators.

It would look, therefore, as though most of the "peoples" of tropical Africa will have to settle for something less than self-rule and riches. If they don't there will be no peace for them, or for the rest of Africa. If they do, there may not be too much peace either, because it is always possible to change one master for a worse. Some people believe they have already done this; some, in Nigeria, the Cameroons, Somalia and elsewhere, fear they may be doing it in the not too distant future.

None of this should be taken to imply that the answer to the problems raised by the "shapelessness" of tropical Africa —its plethora of instances and dearth of generalities, its embarrassment of social riches and lack of economic and political experience, its wealth of peoples and its poverty of nations— lies in attempting to find a master mold, let alone in attempting to mold it in the image of Europe or North America. Nor should it be taken to imply that we should ignore the differences that divide African from African and African from Asian, and both from European, as though they were of no more concern than the differences between one shapeless cloud and the next. Rather the implication is that this quite fantastic diversity should be seen for what it is: at once an enrichment of the color, form and substance of African life, a hindrance to the early satisfaction of the demand for sovereignty, whether political or economic, and a challenge to statesmanship, understanding and humility.

With statesmanship—indigenous and alien—it should not prove impossible to bring into being cohesive, viable states capable of keeping their sanity and integrity in the face of flattery, browbeating and intrigue. With understanding, it ought to be possible to appreciate the desire, and the need, of the 600-odd peoples of tropical Africa to retain something of their individuality—their sense of being valued for what they are, and not merely for what they can do. With humility, it might even be possible for those who go to tropical Africa, whatever their purpose, and those who live there, whatever their status, to keep the right look in their eyes, without which all words, skills and benefactions are of little worth.

There is certainly nothing novel about this formula; indeed, it is as old as the prophet Micah. But has there ever been a truer touchstone, whether for men or for nations, than to do justly, love mercy and walk humbly with one's God?

EPILOGUE

The day for Africa is yet to come.

> David Livingstone, writing from Bambarre,
> near Lake Tanganyika, to his son Thomas
> in 1869

We live and learn, I trust, and the greatest of
all lessons in Africa is wisdom to adapt the
"how" to the "when."

> Daniel Crawford, writing from Lake Mweru
> in 1893

When minds are the same, that which is far off
will come.

> Swahili proverb

SELECTED TERRITORIAL DATA

SOURCES

United Nations publications, as follows: *Demographic Yearbook, 1959; Statistical Yearbook, 1960; International Financial Statistics,* July 1961; *Monthly Bulletin of Statistics,* July 1961; *Yearbook of International Trade Statistics, 1958; Economic Survey of Africa Since 1950* (1959); also *The Statesman's Year-Book,* 1960, 1961, Macmillan & Co., Ltd., London, 1961, and various territorial publications.

NOTES

Information here given is the latest obtainable in the summer of 1961; it is for the most part more recent than that given in the body of the book, which is based on sources available at the end of 1959 or early 1960. All figures are approximate. 1959 and 1960 figures are, in most cases, provisional. Dollars are U. S. dollars if not otherwise specified.

Exports: Figures are f.o.b.

Leading exports: Items are arranged alphabetically.

Imports: Figures are c.i.f. Because of their similarity from territory to territory, import lists have been omitted. As a rule, the leading imports fall into one or more of the following categories: beverages and foodstuffs, metalware and machinery, petroleum products, textiles and clothing, transport equipment.

S = special trade. (Special imports are the combined total of imports directly for domestic consumption and withdrawals from bonded warehouse, or free zone, for domestic consumption or transformation. Special exports comprise exports of national merchandise, i.e., goods wholly or partly produced or manufactured in the country, together with exports of "nationalized" goods, i.e., special imports which are later exported without transformation.)

G = general trade. (General imports are the combined total of imports directly for domestic consumption and imports into bonded warehouse or free zone. General exports are the combined total of national exports and re-exports, i.e., exports of nationalized goods plus goods which, after importation, move from bonded warehouse, or free zone, without having been transformed.)

Motor vehicles: Figures are for passenger and commercial vehicles in use.

Schools and enrollments: Figures include kindergarten, primary, secondary, teacher-training, and higher types of education.

ANGOLA

Political status	Overseas province of Portugal
Capital	Luanda
Area	481,000 square miles
Population	4.6 million (1960 estimate); non-African population: 150,000 (1959), of whom about 110,000 were Europeans
Per capita income	Under $100 (1955–1957 average)
External trade (S)	Exports: $124 million (1960)
	Imports: $128 million (1960)
	Leading exports: coffee, diamonds, fish (inc. meal), maize, sisal
Motor vehicles	37,700 (1959)
Currency unit	Escudo (= 100 centavos): 28.9 escudos = $1 U. S.
Revenue	2,470 million escudos (1958)
Expenditure	2,228 million escudos (1958)

Schools and enrollments   1,973; 100,152 (1958)
Official language   Portuguese

BECHUANALAND

Political status   British protectorate; preliminary internal self-government established in 1961
Capital   Lobatsi (provisional capital)
Area   275,000 square miles
Population   337,000 (1959 estimate)
Per capita income   Under $100 (1955–1957 average)
External trade (G)   Exports: $6.75 million (1957)
    Imports: $7.64 million (1957)
    Leading exports: asbestos, butter and butter fat, carcasses, cattle, sorghum
Motor vehicles   Not available
Currency unit   South African pound: par value same as British pound
Revenue   £1.24 million (1959–1960)
Expenditure   £1.89 million (1959–1960)
Schools and enrollments   190; 31,083 (1958)
Official language   English

BRITISH CAMEROONS

Political status   United Nations Trust Territory. In a U. N.-supervised plebiscite on February 11, 1961 the northern part voted to become part of Nigeria; the southern part voted to join the Republic of Cameroun,

	although it may become an independent state eventually.
Area	34,000 square miles
Population	1.6 million (1959 estimate)
Per capita income	Nigeria as a whole: $69 (1956)
External trade (G)	Exports: £6.92 million (1958)
	Imports: £2.96 million (1958)
	Leading exports: bananas, cocoa, palm kernels, rubber
Motor vehicles	Not available (included with Nigeria)
Currency unit	West African Currency Board pound: par value same as British pound
Revenue	£1.99 million (1959–1960)
Expenditure	£1.89 million (1959–1960)
Schools and enrollments	475; 57,000 (1957)
Official language	English

BRITISH SOMALILAND (SOMALILAND PROTECTORATE)

Political status	British protectorate until June 26, 1960, when it became independent; five days later it became part of the new Somali Republic.
Capital	Hargeisa
Area	68,000 square miles
Population	650,000 (1958); non-African population: approximately 1,000
Per capita income	Under $100 (1955–1957 average)
External trade (G)	Exports: $3.9 million (1957)
	Imports: $11.3 million (1957)
	Leading exports: hides and skins, livestock
Motor vehicles	700 (1958)
Currency unit	East African shilling: 20 shillings = £1 East African

Revenue	£1.17 million (1958–1959)
Expenditure	£1.64 million (1958–1959)
Schools and enrollments	54; 3,055 (1958)
Official languages	English and Arabic

CAMEROUN, REPUBLIC OF (formerly French Cameroons)

Political status	Independent republic since January 1, 1960. Formerly a United Nations Trust Territory.
Capital	Yaoundé
Area	167,000 square miles
Population	3.2 million (1959 estimate); non-African population: 16,000 (1956 estimate)
Per capita income	$142 (1956)
External trade (S)	Exports: $108 million (1959)
	Imports: $82 million (1959)
	Leading exports: bananas, cocoa, coffee, cotton, peanuts, rubber, wood
Motor vehicles	27,900 (1959)
Currency unit	Franc C.F.A.*
Budget	Balanced at 11,679 million francs C.F.A. (1957)
Schools and enrollments	2,600; 306,000 (1958)
Official language	French

CENTRAL AFRICAN REPUBLIC (formerly Ubangi-Shari)

Political status	Autonomous state in the French Community from December 1, 1958 until August 13, 1960, when it became an independent

* One franc C.F.A. (*colonies françaises d'Afrique*) = two metropolitan French francs.

state within the Community. Has joined with neighboring states in Union of Central African Republics. Ubangi-Shari was an overseas territory of France and part of French Equatorial Africa.

Capital	Bangui
Area	238,000 square miles
Population	1.2 million (1959–1960); non-African population: approximately 5,000 (mostly French)
Per capita income	Under $100 (1955–1957 average)
External trade (S)	Exports: $14.8 million (1958)
	Imports: $20.6 million (1958)
	Leading exports: coffee, cotton, diamonds, wood
Motor vehicles	Not available
Currency unit	Franc C.F.A.
Budget	1,792 million francs C.F.A. (1958)
Schools and enrollments	258; 46,818 (1957)
Official language	French

CHAD, REPUBLIC OF

Political status	Autonomous state within the French Community from November 26, 1958 until August 11, 1960, when it became an independent state within the Community. Has joined with neighboring states in Union of Central African Republics. Formerly it was an overseas territory of France and part of French Equatorial Africa.
Capital	Fort Lamy
Area	495,500 square miles

Population	2.6 million (1960); non-African population: approximately 5,000 (mostly French)
Per capita income	Under $100 (1955–1957 average)
External trade (S)	Exports: $26 million (1958)
	Imports: $34 million (1958)
	Leading exports: cotton, fish, livestock, peanuts
Motor vehicles	Not available
Currency unit	Franc C.F.A.
Budget	2,519 million francs C.F.A. (1958)
Schools and enrollments	157; 33,095 (1957)
Official language	French

COMMONWEALTH EAST AFRICA

Constituent territories   Kenya, Tanganyika, Uganda, Zanzibar (including Pemba), and, until it became part of the new Somali Republic in mid-1960, British Somaliland (Somaliland Protectorate). Services common to the first three are administered by the East Africa High Commission, but neither political federation nor fusion of the existing governments is involved.

COMMONWEALTH WEST AFRICA

Constituent territories   British Cameroons, Gambia, Ghana, Nigeria, Sierra Leone

2

COMORO ARCHIPELAGO

Political status	Overseas territory of France, and so part of the French Republic
Capital	Dzaoudzi
Area	838 square miles
Population	185,000 (1959 estimate)
Per capita income	$180 (1955–1957 average)
External trade (S)	Exports: 711 million francs C.F.A. (1958)
	Imports: 565 million francs C.F.A. (1958)
	Leading exports: cocoa, coffee, copra, perfume plants, sisal, vanilla
Motor vehicles	Not available
Currency unit	Franc C.F.A.
Budget	314 million francs C.F.A. (1958)
Schools and enrollments	39; 2,900 (1958)
Official language	French

CONGO, REPUBLIC OF THE (formerly Belgian Congo)

Political status	Belgian colony until June 30, 1960, when it became independent. Katanga Province declared its "total independence" from the Congo on July 11, 1960 but this has been disputed and on September 13, 1961 U. N. troops took over with the aim of re-uniting it with the Congo.
Capital	Léopoldville
Area	905,000 square miles
Population	14.2 million (1960 estimate); non-African population: 116,000

	(1958), of whom approximately 87,000 were Belgians
Per capita income	$76 (1957)
External trade (S) (*including Ruanda-Urundi*)	Exports: $489 million (1959) Imports: $308 million (1959) Leading exports: cobalt, coffee, copper, cotton, diamonds, palm kernels and palm oil, rubber
Motor vehicles	58,000 (1958)
Currency unit	Congolese franc, interchangeable with Belgian franc
Revenue	13,541 million francs (1960)
Expenditure	17,748 million francs (1960)
Schools and enrollments	30,520 (1957); 1,700,000 (1959)
Official languages	French and Flemish

CONGO, REPUBLIC OF THE (formerly Middle Congo)

Political status	Autonomous state in the French Community from November 28, 1958 until August 15, 1960, when it became an independent state within the Community. Has joined with neighboring states in Union of Central African Republics. Middle Congo was an overseas territory of France and part of French Equatorial Africa.
Capital	Brazzaville; in process of change to Pointe Noire
Area	132,000 square miles
Population	795,000 (1959); non-African population: approximately 10,000 (mostly French)
Per capita income	Under $100 (1955–1957 average)
External trade (S)	Exports: $15.6 million (1958)

	Imports: $44.0 million (1958)
	Leading exports: lead ore, palm kernels and palm oil, peanuts, tobacco, wood
Motor vehicles	Not available
Currency unit	Franc C.F.A.
Budget	2,397 million francs C.F.A. (1958)
Schools and enrollments	492; 80,937 (1957)
Official language	French

COUNCIL OF THE ENTENTE

| *Constituent territories* | Republics of Dahomey, Ivory Coast, Niger, Upper Volta. These states were at one time part of French West Africa. |

DAHOMEY, REPUBLIC OF

Political status	Autonomous state in the French Community from December 4, 1958 until August 1, 1960, when it became an independent state within the Community. Has joined with neighboring states in the Council of the Entente. Formerly it was an overseas territory of France and part of French West Africa.
Capital	Porto Novo
Area	44,500 square miles
Population	1.93 million (1960); non-African population: approximately 3,000 (mostly French)
Per capita income	Under $100 (1955–1957 average)
External trade (S)	Exports: $13.0 million (1958)

	Imports: $17.3 million (1958)
	Leading exports: palm kernels and palm oil, peanuts
Motor vehicles	Not available
Currency unit	Franc C.F.A.
Budget	3,534 million francs C.F.A. (1958)
Schools and enrollments	444; 77,663 (1957)
Official language	French

ETHIOPIA AND ERITREA, FEDERATION OF

Political status	Independent state. Eritrea became an autonomous unit within the Federation, under the Ethiopian Crown, in 1952.
Capital	Addis Ababa (Federation); Asmara (Eritrea)
Area	457,000 square miles (Ethiopia, 409,000 square miles; Eritrea, 48,000 square miles)
Population	Estimates vary from under 12 million to 21.8 million (U. N. estimate in 1959).
Per capita income	$30 (1957)
External trade (G)	Exports: $78 million (1960)
	Imports: $88 million (1960)
	Leading exports: coffee, hides and skins (sheep and goats), oilseeds, pulses
Motor vehicles	22,000 (1959)
Currency unit	Ethiopian dollar (divided into 100 cents): one Ethiopian dollar = approximately 40 cents U. S.
Revenue	$ Ethiopian 201.88 million (1958–1959)
Expenditure	$ Ethiopian 183.61 million (1958–1959)

Schools and enrollments	Excluding mission and Ethiopian Church schools and enrollments: 641; 164,365 (1958)
Official languages	Amharic and English

FRENCH EQUATORIAL AFRICA

Constituent territories   Four overseas territories of France which in 1958 became autonomous states, and in 1960 inpendent states, within the French Community. The four were: Chad, Gabon, Middle Congo (now Republic of the Congo), Ubangi-Shari (now Central African Republic). Three of these states have formed the Union of Central African Republics, to which the fourth, Gabon, is geographically and economically linked.

FRENCH SOMALILAND

Political status	Overseas territory of France, and so part of the French Republic
Capital	Djibouti
Area	8,500 square miles
Population	70,000 (1959); non-African population, excluding Arabs: approximately 4,000 (mostly French)
Per capita income	Under $100 (1955–1957 average)
External trade (S)	Exports: $10 million (1959)
	Imports: $20 million (1958)
	Leading exports: hides and salt. The territory also does an impor-

tant transit trade with Ethiopia, most of whose trade passes through the port of Djibouti.

Motor vehicles 2,100 (1959)

Currency unit Djibouti franc (= 2.3 metropolitan French francs)

Budget 1,123 million Djibouti francs (1959)

Schools and enrollments 23; 2,518 (1958)

Official language French

FRENCH WEST AFRICA

Constituent territories Eight overseas territories of France which in 1958, with one exception (French Guinea), became autonomous states, and in 1960 independent states, within the French Community; French Guinea opted for independence outside the Community. The eight were: Dahomey, French Guinea (now Republic of Guinea), French Sudan (now Republic of Mali), Ivory Coast, Mauritania, Niger, Senegal, Upper Volta. The four following have combined in the Council of the Entente: Republics of Dahomey, Ivory Coast, Niger, Upper Volta.

GABON REPUBLIC

Political status Autonomous state in the French Community from November 28,

	1958 until August 17, 1960, when it became an independent state within the Community. Formerly part of French Equatorial Africa.
Capital	Libreville
Area	103,000 square miles
Population	440,000 (1960); non-African population: approximately 4,000 (mostly French)
Per capita income	Under $100 (1955–1957 average)
External trade (S)	Exports: $33.6 million (1958)
	Imports: $31.0 million (1958)
	Leading exports: cocoa, gold, petroleum, wood
Motor vehicles	Not available
Currency unit	Franc C.F.A.
Budget	1,983 million francs C.F.A. (1958)
Schools and enrollments	319; 40,788 (1957)
Official language	French

GAMBIA

Political status	British colony and protectorate
Capital	Bathurst
Area	4,000 square miles
Population	301,000 (1959 estimate)
Per capita income	$56–$70 (1957)
External trade	Exports: $8 million (1959)
	Imports: $9 million (1959)
	Leading exports: palm kernels, peanuts
Motor vehicles	1,700 (1959)
Currency unit	West African Currency Board pound: par value same as British pound
Revenue	£1.56 million (1959)

Expenditure   £1.75 million (1959)
Schools and enrollments 59; 8,093 (1958–1959)
Official language   English

GHANA, REPUBLIC OF

Political status   Self-governing dominion of the British Commonwealth from March 6, 1957 until July 1, 1960, when it became a republic (while maintaining its Commonwealth tie). Ghana is composed of the territories formerly constituting the Gold Coast and Togoland under United Kingdom administration. Joined with Guinea and Mali in the Union of African States in 1961.

Capital   Accra
Area   92,100 square miles
Population   6.7 million (1960 census); non-African population: approximately 7,000 (mostly Europeans)
Per capita income $194 (1957)
External trade (G)   Exports: $294 million (1960)
                         Imports: $363 million (1960)
                         Leading exports: bauxite, cocoa, diamonds, gold, manganese, wood (logs, sawn timber)
Motor vehicles   34,000 (1959)
Currency unit   Ghana pound (issued since July 14, 1958). West African Currency Board pound remains legal tender. Both are interchangeable at par with British pound.
Revenue   £53.4 million (1959–1960)
Expenditure   £52.9 million (1959–1960)

Schools and enrollments	5,061; 631,858 (1958–1959)
Official language	English

GUINEA, REPUBLIC OF (formerly French Guinea)

Political status	Independent state since October 2, 1958. Joined with Ghana and Mali in the Union of African States in 1961. French Guinea was part of French West Africa.
Capital	Conakry
Area	95,000 square miles
Population	3.0 million (1960); non-African population: approximately 7,500, of whom 5,000 or so were French
Per capita income	Under $100 (1955–1957 average)
External trade (S)	Exports: $29.1 million (1956) Imports: $37.7 million (1956) Leading exports: bananas, bauxite (and alumina), coffee, diamonds, iron ore, palm kernels
Motor vehicles	Not available
Currency unit	Franc C.F.A. until early 1960; thereafter Guinea franc of same par value
Budget	6,328 million francs C.F.A. (1958)
Schools and enrollments	485; 83,936 (1959)
Official language	French

IVORY COAST, REPUBLIC OF THE

Political status	Autonomous state in the French Community from December 4, 1958 until August 7, 1960, when it became an independent

state within the Community. Has joined with neighboring states in the Council of the Entente. It was formerly part of French West Africa.

Capital	Abidjan
Area	124,500 square miles
Population	3.2 million (1960); non-African population: approximately 20,-000 (mostly French)
Per capita income	Under $100 (1955–1957 average)
External trade (S)	Exports: $125.8 million (1958)
	Imports: $91.2 million (1958)
	Leading exports: bananas, cocoa, coffee, wood
Motor vehicles	Not available
Currency unit	Franc C.F.A.
Budget	26,245 million francs C.F.A. (1959)
Schools and enrollments	1,023; 172,323 (1958)
Official language	French

KENYA

Political status	British colony and protectorate
Capital	Nairobi
Area	225,000 square miles
Population	6.55 million (1960); non-African population: approximately 279,-300, of whom 66,400 were Europeans, 169,900 Indians, Pakistanis and Goans, and 37,100 Arabs
Per capita income	$78 (1957)
External trade (G)	Exports: $112 million (1960)
	Imports: $252 million (1960)
	Leading exports: coffee, hides and

	skins, sisal, sodium carbonate, tea, wattle extract
Motor vehicles	68,400 (1959)
Currency unit	Shilling (East African Currency Board): 20 shillings = £1 sterling
Revenue	£42.91 million (1959–1960)
Expenditure	£41.90 million (1959–1960)
Schools and enrollments	4,820; 668,828 (1958)
Official language	English. (Swahili is widely employed in government and commerce.)

LIBERIA

Political status	"Free and Independent Republic" (since 1847)
Capital	Monrovia
Area	44,000 square miles
Population	1.25–2.5 million (current estimates); non-African population: approximately 6,000
Per capita income	Under $100 (1955–1957 average)
External trade (S)	Exports: $83 million (1960)
	Imports: $69 million (1960)
	Leading exports: diamonds, iron ore, palm kernels, rubber
Motor vehicles	Not available
Currency unit	U. S. dollar (since 1942). There is also a Liberian coinage (of various denominations from ½ cent to 50 cents) in silver and copper.
Revenue	$17.8 million (1959)
Expenditure	$18.1 million (1959)
Schools and enrollments	637; 48,402 (1958)
Official language	English

MALAGASY REPUBLIC (formerly Madagascar)

Political status	Autonomous state in the French Community from October 21, 1958 until March 27, 1960, when it became an independent state within the Community. Madagascar was an overseas territory of France.
Capital	Tananarive
Area	228,000 square miles
Population	5.3 million (1960); non-African population: approximately 68,000 Europeans, 17,000 Asians
Per capita income	$119 (1956)
External trade (S)	Exports: $75 million (1960)
	Imports: $112 million (1960)
	Leading exports: cloves, coffee, rice, sugar, tobacco, vanilla
Motor vehicles	34,600 (1958)
Currency unit	Franc C.F.A.
Budget	General: 13,758 million francs C.F.A. (1959)
	Provincial: 13,381 million francs C.F.A. (1959)
Schools and enrollments	2,833; 396,799 (1959)
Official language	French

MALI, REPUBLIC OF (formerly Sudanese Republic and earlier French Sudan)

Political status	Autonomous state (as the Sudanese Republic) in the French Community from November 24, 1958 until June 20, 1960, when the Mali Federation (in which

the Sudanese Republic had joined with the Republic of Senegal) became an independent state within the Community. The Federation was dissolved on September 22, 1960 and no further connection with Senegal exists. Mali joined with Ghana and Guinea in the Union of African States in 1961. French Sudan was part of French West Africa.

Capital	Bamako
Area	464,500 square miles
Population	4.1 million (1960); non-African population: approximately 8,000 (mostly French)
Per capita income	Under $100 (1955–1957 average)
External trade (S)	Exports: $115.2 million (1958)* Imports: $175.0 million (1958)* Leading exports: cotton, fish, gum arabic, *karité*, livestock (cattle, sheep and goats), rice, skins
Motor vehicles	Not available
Currency unit	Franc C.F.A.
Budget	5,818 million francs C.F.A. (1958)
Schools and enrollments	286; 43,630 (1957)
Official language	French

MAURITANIA, ISLAMIC REPUBLIC OF

Political status	Autonomous state within the French Community from November 28, 1958 until November 28, 1960, when it became

* These figures are for Mauritania, Mali and Senegal; since almost all of their external trade passes through the port of Dakar (Senegal), separate figures for the three republics are not available.

an independent state within the Community. It was formerly part of French West Africa.

Capital	Nouakchott
Area	419,000 square miles
Population	725,000 (1959); non-African population: approximately 1,600 (mostly French)
Per capita income	Under $100 (1955–1957 average)
External trade	Exports: see under Mali
	Imports: see under Mali
	Leading exports: fish, gum arabic, livestock (cattle, sheep), salt
Motor vehicles	Not available
Currency unit	Franc C.F.A.
Budget	1,627 million francs C.F.A. (1959)
Schools and enrollments	75; 5,783 (1956)
Official language	French. (National language: Arabic)

MOZAMBIQUE

Political status	Overseas province of Portugal
Capital	Lourenço Marques
Area	302,000 square miles
Population	6.3 million (1959); non-African population: approximately 118,000 (1955), of whom 66,000 were Europeans
Per capita income	Under $100 (1955–1957 average)
External trade (S)	Exports: $77 million (1960)
	Imports: $126 million (1960)
	Leading exports: cashew nuts, copra, cotton, sisal, sugar, tea
Motor vehicles	38,400 (1959)
Currency unit	Escudo (= 100 centavos); 1,000 escudos = 1 conto: 28.9 escudos = $1 U. S.

Budget	3.15 million contos (1959)
Schools and enrollments	3,022; 408,183 (1958)
Official language	Portuguese

NIGER, REPUBLIC OF THE

Political status	Autonomous state in the French Community from December 19, 1958 until August 3, 1960, when it became an independent state within the Community. Has joined with neighboring states in the Council of the Entente. It was formerly part of French West Africa.
Capital	Niamey
Area	459,000 square miles
Population	2.9 million (1960); non-African population: approximately 3,000 (mostly French)
Per capita income	Under $100 (1955–1957 average)
External trade	Exports: $15.2 million (1958)
	Imports: $8.8 million (1958)
	Leading exports: gum arabic, livestock, peanuts, skins and hides
Motor vehicles	Not available
Currency unit	Franc C.F.A.
Budget	3,613 million francs C.F.A. (1958)
Schools and enrollments	128; 12,328 (1957)
Official language	French

NIGERIA, FEDERATION OF

Political status	Independent country within the British Commonwealth since October 1, 1960. Formerly a British colony and protectorate.

Capital	Lagos
Area	339,000 square miles, excluding British Cameroons
Population	34.3 million (1960); non-African population: 10,000 (1956 estimate)
Per capita income	$69 (1956), including British Cameroons
External trade (G)	Exports: $462 million (1960), inc. British Cameroons
	Imports: $603 million (1960), inc. British Cameroons
	Leading exports: cocoa, palm kernels and palm oil, peanuts and peanut oil, tin, wood
Motor vehicles	53,000 (1959), including registrations in British Cameroons
Currency unit	West African Currency Board pound: par value same as British pound. Nigerian currency issued beginning July 1, 1959.
Revenue	£ 83.92 million (1959–1960)
Expenditure	£ 80.02 million (1959–1960)
Schools and enrollments	16,916; 2,720,724 (1958). This does not include British Cameroons.
Official language	English

NORTHERN RHODESIA

Political status	British protectorate, one of the three territories forming the Federation of Rhodesia and Nyasaland
Capital	Lusaka
Area	288,130 square miles
Population	2.4 million (1960); non-African

	population: approximately 80,-000, of whom 72,000 were Europeans
Per capita income	Federation as a whole: $135 (1958)
External trade	Since 1953 this has been computed on a Federation-wide basis, and no figures have been issued for the individual territories.
Motor vehicles	44,200 (1959)
Currency unit	Rhodesian pound, interchangeable at par with sterling
Revenue	£ 15.84 million (1959–1960)
Expenditure	£ 16.18 million (1959–1960)
Schools and enrollments	African only: 1,865; 248,905 (1958)
Official language	English

NYASALAND

Political status	British protectorate, one of the three territories forming the Federation of Rhodesia and Nyasaland
Capital	Zomba
Area	46,066 square miles
Population	2.8 million (1960); non-African population: approximately 20,-000, of whom 8,500 were Europeans
Per capita income	Probably less than $50; Federation as a whole: $135 (1958)
External trade	Since 1953 this has been computed on a Federation-wide basis, and no figures have been issued for the individual territories
Motor vehicles	10,200 (1959)

Currency unit	Rhodesian pound, interchangeable at par with sterling
Revenue	£ 5.45 million (1959–1960)
Expenditure	£ 9.11 million (1959–1960)
Schools and enrollments	African only: 3,146; 272,735 (1958)
Official language	English

PORTUGUESE GUINEA

Political status	Overseas province of Portugal
Capital	Bissau
Area	14,000 square miles
Population	570,000 (1960); non-African population: about 7,500 (1958), of whom about 2,500 were Europeans
Per capita income	Probably less than $50
External trade (S)	Exports: $7.0 million (1959) Imports: $8.0 million (1959) Leading exports: hides and skins, palm oil, rice, seeds
Motor vehicles	440 (1953)
Currency unit	Escudo (= 100 centavos): 28.9 escudos = $1 U. S.
Revenue	156.5 million escudos (1957)
Expenditure	150.1 million escudos (1957)
Schools and enrollments	184; 12,479 (1958)
Official language	Portuguese

RHODESIA AND NYASALAND, FEDERATION OF

Political status	The Federation, formed in 1953, consists of the self-governing colony of Southern Rhodesia and the protectorates of Northern

	Rhodesia and Nyasaland, all of which retain their pre-Federation constitutional status. The Federation is also known as the Central African Federation.
Capital	Salisbury
Area	486,722 square miles
Population	8.3 million (1960); non-African population: approximately 325,000 (1958), of whom 290,000 were Europeans
Per capita income	$135 (1958)
External trade (G)	Exports: $576 million (1960)
	Imports: $495 million (1960)
	Leading exports: chrome ore, clothing, cobalt, copper, gold, lead, maize, meat, tea, tin, tobacco
Motor vehicles	156,500 (1959)
Currency unit	Rhodesian pound, interchangeable at par with sterling
Revenue	£ 53.1 million (1959–1960)
Expenditure	£ 72.3 million, including £ 18.2 million from loan funds (1959–1960)
Schools and enrollments	7,611; 951,640 (1958)
Official language	English

RUANDA-URUNDI

Political status	Belgian-administered United Nations Trust Territory. Has had internal self-government since January 28, 1961; is expected to become independent in 1962.
Capital	Usumbura
Area	21,000 square miles

Population	4.8 million (1959 estimate); non-African population: 10,500 (1958), of whom more than 7,000 were Europeans
Per capita income	Under $100 (1955–1957 average)
External trade (S)	Exports: $48.29 million (1957) Imports: $50.72 million (1957) Leading exports: coffee, cotton, palm products, pyrethrum, tin
Motor vehicles	4,700 (1958)
Currency unit	Congolese franc, interchangeable with Belgian franc
Revenue	979 million francs (1958)
Expenditure	1,103 million francs (1958)
Schools and enrollments	2,900; 246,000 (1957)
Official languages	French and Flemish

SÃO TOMÉ AND PRÍNCIPE

Political status	Overseas province of Portugal
Capital	São Tomé
Area	372 square miles
Population	64,000 (1959 estimate); non-African population: approximately 5,500 (1958), of whom 1,200 were Europeans
Per capita income	Under $100 (1955–1957 average)
External trade (S)	Exports: $8.0 million (1959) Imports: $5.0 million (1959) Leading exports: cinchona, cocoa, coffee, copra, palm oil
Motor vehicles	700 (1958)
Currency unit	Escudo (= 100 centavos): 28.9 escudos = $1 U. S.
Revenue	83.6 million escudos (1958)
Expenditure	75.6 million escudos (1958)
Schools and enrollments	23; 2,429 (1958)
Official language	Portuguese

SENEGAL, REPUBLIC OF

Political status	Autonomous state in the French Community from November 25, 1958 until June 20, 1960, when the Mali Federation (in which the Republic of Senegal had joined with the Sudanese Republic) became an independent state within the Community. The Federation was dissolved on September 22, 1960 and no further connection with the Sudanese Republic (now the Republic of Mali) exists. Senegal was part of French West Africa.
Capital	Dakar
Area	76,000 square miles
Population	3.1 million (1960); non-African population: approximately 50,000 (mostly French) (1958)
Per capita income	Under $100 (1955–1957 average)
External trade (S)	Exports: see under Mali
	Imports: see under Mali
	Leading exports: peanuts and peanut oil, phosphates
Motor vehicles	Not available
Currency unit	Franc C.F.A.
Budget	14,944 million francs C.F.A. (1959)
Schools and enrollments	458; 87,644 (1957)
Official language	French

SIERRA LEONE

Political status	Independent state within the British Commonwealth since April

27, 1961. Formerly a British colony and protectorate.

Capital	Freetown
Area	28,000 square miles
Population	2.4 million (1959); non-African population: about 3,000
Per capita income	$70 (1957)
External trade (*G*)	Exports: $80.0 million (1960)
	Imports: $75.0 million (1960)
	Leading exports: chrome ore, cocoa, coffee, diamonds, iron ore, kola nuts, palm kernels, piassava
Motor vehicles	4,800 (1956)
Currency unit	West African Currency Board pound, interchangeable at par with sterling
Revenue	£10.43 million (1959–1960)
Expenditure	£11.85 million (1959–1960)
Schools and enrollments	556; 76,672 (1958)
Official language	English

SOMALI REPUBLIC (formerly Italian Somaliland)

Political status	Italian-administered United Nations Trust Territory until July 1, 1960, when it became the independent Somali Republic (also known as Republic of Somalia).
Capital	Mogadishu
Area	178,000 square miles
Population	1.99 million (1959); non-African population, excluding Arabs: approximately 5,000 (mostly Italian)
Per capita income	Under $100 (1955–1957 average)
External trade (*S*)	Exports: $13.4 million (1958)
	Imports: $14.2 million (1958)

	Leading exports: bananas, charcoal, cotton, fish, hides and skins
Motor vehicles	5,900 (1959)
Currency unit	Somalo, which has been linked with the Italian lira, but equated in value with the East African shilling: 7.2 somali = $1 U. S.
Budget	113.3 million somali (1958)
Schools and enrollments	342; 37,180 (1958–1959)
Official languages	Somali (spoken only) and Italian. Arabic is the language most generally used among the educated Somalis.

SOUTHERN RHODESIA

Political status	Self-governing British colony, one of the three territories forming the Federation of Rhodesia and Nyasaland. External (including intra-Federation) affairs are handled by the Federal Government.
Capital	Salisbury
Area	150,033 square miles
Population	3.0 million (1960); non-African population: approximately 230,200 (1959), of whom 215,000 were Europeans
Per capita income	Federation as a whole: $135 (1958)
External trade	Since 1953 this has been computed on a Federation-wide basis, and no figures have been issued for the individual territories.
Motor vehicles	102,100 (1959)

Currency unit	Rhodesian pound, interchangeable at par with sterling
Revenue	£ 19.52 million (1959–1960)
Expenditure	£ 22.23 million (1959–1960), including £ 6.26 million expenditure from loan funds
Schools and enrollments	African only (1959): 2,683; 467,567
Official language	English

SPANISH GUINEA

[Rio Muni, Fernando Po, Corisco, Elobey, Annobón]

Political status	Spanish colony
Capital	Santa Isabel (on the island of Fernando Po)
Area	11,000 square miles
Population	216,000 (1959); non-African population: approximately 5,000 (mostly Spanish)
Per capita income	Under $100 (1955–1957 average)
External trade	Exports: not available
	Imports: not available
	Leading exports: cocoa, coffee, vegetables and fruits, wood
Motor vehicles	Not available
Currency unit	Spanish peseta
Budget	Not available
Schools and enrollments	121; 17,797 (1958)
Official language	Spanish

SUDAN, REPUBLIC OF (formerly Anglo-Egyptian Sudan)

Political status	Independent state since January 1, 1956. Formerly administered by

	Great Britain and Egypt as a condominium.
Capital	Khartoum
Area	967,500 square miles
Population	11.8 million (1960); non-Sudanese population (mainly Arabs, Egyptians): 437,000 (1956)
Per capita income	Under $100 (1955–1957 average)
External trade (S)	Exports: $180.0 million (1960)
	Imports: $181.0 million (1960)
	Leading exports: cattle, cotton and cottonseed, dura (millet), gum arabic, peanuts, sesame
Motor vehicles	25,700 (1959)
Currency unit	Sudanese pound (= £ 1.025 U. K.)
Revenue	£ S.42.89 million (1959–1960)
Expenditure	£ S.42.78 million (1959–1960)
Schools and enrollments	2,546; 323,091 (1959–1960)
Official language	Arabic. (English is also used.)

TANGANYIKA

Political status	British-administered United Nations Trust Territory until April 26, 1960, when it attained preliminary internal self-government. Full internal self-government was attained on May 1, 1961 and complete independence (within British Commonwealth) will be granted on December 9, 1961.
Capital	Dar-es-Salaam
Area	361,500 square miles
Population	9.2 million (1960); non-African population: 127,000 (1958), of whom approximately 21,000

were Europeans and 77,000 Indians, Pakistanis and Goans

Per capita income $48 (1957)

External trade (S) Exports: $155.0 million (1960)

Imports: $83.0 million (1960)

Leading exports: cashew nuts, coffee, cotton, diamonds, hides and skins, lead ore, oilseeds (inc. nuts and kernels), sisal

Motor vehicles 32,000 (1959)

Currency unit Shilling (East African Currency Board): 20 shillings = £1 sterling

Revenue £24.01 million (1959–1960)

Expenditure £25.28 million (1959–1960)

Schools and enrollments 3,250; 438,000 (1958)

Official language English. (Swahili is widely employed in government and commerce.)

TOGO, REPUBLIC OF (formerly French Togoland)

Political status United Nations Trust Territory administered by France as an autonomous republic within the French Community until April 27, 1960, when it became the independent Republic of Togo.

Capital Lomé

Area 22,000 square miles

Population 1.4 million (1960 estimate); non-African population: 1,300 (1956)

Per capita income Under $100 (1955–1957 average)

External trade (S) Exports: $18.0 million (1959)

Imports: $15.0 million (1959)

Leading exports: cocoa, coffee,

	copra, cotton, manioc, palm kernels and palm oil, peanuts
Motor vehicles	2,900 (1957)
Currency unit	Franc C.F.A.
Revenue	2,125 million francs C.F.A. (1959)
Expenditure	2,550 million francs C.F.A. (1959)
Schools and enrollments	490; 81,136 (1959)
Official language	French

UGANDA

Political status	British protectorate
Capital	Entebbe (administrative); Kampala (commercial)
Area	94,000 square miles
Population	6.7 million (1960 estimate); non-African population: 67,600 (1958), of whom 9,000 were Europeans and 56,600 Indians and Goans
Per capita income	$57 (1957)
External trade (G)	Exports: $120.0 million (1960)
	Imports: $40.0 million (1960)
	Leading exports: coffee, copper, cotton, feeding stuffs, tea
Motor vehicles	29,400 (1959)
Currency unit	Shilling (East African Currency Board): 20 shillings = £1 sterling
Revenue	£19.84 million (1959–1960)
Expenditure	£20.50 million (1959–1960)
Schools and enrollments	5,712; 606,619 (1959)
Official language	English. (Luganda is widely employed in government and commerce.)

UNION OF AFRICAN STATES

Constituent territories   Republics of Ghana, Guinea, Mali. Formed July 1, 1961, for mutual defense and common orientation of diplomacy and economic and cultural policies. Conference of heads of states of the Union expected to meet quarterly.

UNION OF CENTRAL AFRICAN REPUBLICS

Constituent territories   Central African Republic, Republic of Chad, Republic of the Congo (the former Middle Congo). The Gabon Republic is geographically and economically linked to the Union. All of these states were at one time part of French Equatorial Africa.

UPPER VOLTA, REPUBLIC OF THE

Political status   Autonomous state (also known as Voltaic Republic) in the French Community from December 11, 1958 until August 5, 1960, when it became an independent state within the Community. Has joined with neighboring states in the Council of the Entente. Formerly it was part of French West Africa.

Capital	Ouagadougou
Area	106,000 square miles
Population	3.5 million (1959); non-African population: 3,700 (mostly French)
Per capita income	Under $100 (1955–1957 average)
External trade (S)	Exports: $4.4 million (1958)
	Imports: $7.2 million (1958)
	Leading exports: fish, *karité*, livestock, peanuts
Motor vehicles	Not available
Currency unit	Franc C.F.A.
Budget	4,081 million francs C.F.A. (1958)
Schools and enrollments	313; 43,549 (1959)
Official language	French

ZANZIBAR (including Pemba)

Political status	British-protected sultanate. The Sultan rules with the advice of the British Resident.
Capital	Zanzibar
Area	Island of Zanzibar, 640 square miles; island of Pemba, 380 square miles
Population	307,000 (1960)
Per capita income	$98–$126 (1957)
External trade (G)	Exports: $13.0 million (1959)
	Imports: $15.0 million (1959)
	Leading exports: cloves, coconut oil, copra
Motor vehicles	2,000 (1959)
Currency unit	Shilling (East African Currency Board): 20 shillings = £1 sterling
Revenue	£2.57 million (1959)

Expenditure	£ 2.80 million (1959)
Schools and enrollments	95; 18,834 (1958)
Official language	English. (Swahili is the language most generally spoken.)

INDEX